CIMA

STUDY TEXT

STRATEGIC

PAPER P10

TEST OF PROFESSIONAL COMPETENCE IN MANAGEMENT ACCOUNTING (TOPCIMA)

In this edition:

- A user-friendly format for easy navigation

- Exam-centred topic coverage, directly linked to CIMA's learning outcomes, syllabus content and assessment matrix

- Exam focus points showing you what the examiner will want you to do

- Analysis of past papers

- A methodical approach that offers step-by-step guidance with practical exercises covering all areas of the assessment matrix

FOR EXAMS IN SEPTEMBER AND NOVEMBER 2008 AND MARCH, MAY, SEPTEMBER AND NOVEMBER 2009

LEARNING MEDIA

First edition 2004
Fifth edition May 2008

ISBN 9780 7517 5293 9
(previous edition 9780 7517 4220 6)

British Library Cataloguing-in-Publication Data
A catalogue record for this book
is available from the British Library

Published by

BPP Learning Media Ltd
BPP House, Aldine Place
London W12 8AA

www.bpp.com/learningmedia

Printed in Great Britain by
WM Print
45-47 Frederick Street
Walsall
West Midlands
WS2 9NE

Your learning materials, published by BPP Learning
Media Ltd, are printed on paper sourced from
sustainable, managed forests.

We are grateful to the Chartered Institute of Management
Accountants for permission to reproduce past
examination questions. The suggested solutions in the
exam answer bank have been prepared by BPP Learning
Media Ltd.

Contents

How the BPP Learning Media Study Text can help you pass

This Study Text has been written for the TOPCIMA exam.

- It is written at the **right level.**

- It is targeted to the **exam**. We have taken note of past papers, questions put to the examiners, the assessment methodology, and the cases set to date under the previous syllabus.

You may be studying at home on your own until the date of the exam, or you may be attending a full-time course. BPP has material to suit both options. The key to the case is to **prepare** and to **practise.**

Work through this Study Text before CIMA issues the pre-seen data. Then use the BPP Learning Media TOPCIMA Toolkit. Written around the real pre-seen data, the Toolkit contains analyses and exercises to get you thinking, as well as a number of 'mock' unseens to prepare you for the real thing.

Recommended use

Six to two months before the exam	**This Study Text** This Study Text shows you a step by step approach to tackling the TOPCIMA exam and gives you the opportunity to practise on previous case studies with unseens and full answers.
Two months before the exam	**BPP Learning Media TOPCIMA Toolkit** **CIMA** posts the pre-seen part of the case on its website about six weeks before the exam. The BPP Learning Media TOPCIMA Toolkit is written by BPP Learning Media authors and tutors around the real pre-seen. It many exercises and practice exams to help you pass. Look on our website for details. **BPP Professional Education TOPCIMA discussion board** Joint this study discussion board by visiting www.bpp.com/topcimaforum. Here you can send TOPCIMA-related messages to other TOPCIMA students and to BPP Professional Education's excellent team of tutors and BPP Learning Media authors.

Suggested study approach

Throughout the BPP Learning Media series, we offer advice on how to study. The TOPCIMA exam is different from all other exams in that it does not require any specialist knowledge, more the ability to apply knowledge you have gained from other CIMA papers, particularly those at Strategic Level.

This is how we help you through your study for the case.

Key steps	Activity
Chapter 1	Describes the case in detail, with questions bringing some of the key issues into perspective.
Chapter 2	Describes the marking scheme in depth. It is **vital** that you understand this so that you can focus your efforts.
Chapter 3	Gives a brief overview of some important technical knowledge areas.
Chapters 4–5	**Suggests** a structured sequence of tasks to take you through the two months before the exam. (Throughout you are given the opportunity to practise your written communication skills.) These are **tools** to help you through. You do not have to use all of them.
Chapter 6	Gives you some hints and tips on report writing.
Chapter 7	Describes how you should approach exam day.
Chapter 8	Your first case to practise on: Zubinos set in March and May 2006.
Chapters 9–10	A step-by-step analysis through Zubinos, applying the approach outlined in Chapters 4–5.
Chapters 11–12	The unseen data from March and May 2006 with an answer for you to consider.
Chapters 13–24	Three further TOPCIMA case studies. It is important that you get an idea of the variety of approaches that could be taken. We have added some analysis to help you to work through these exams.

Syllabus: learning aims and outcomes

Learning aims

The aim of the Test of Professional Competence in Management Accounting (TOPCIMA) is to test the capabilities and competence of students, to ensure they:

A   Have a sound technical knowledge of the specific subjects within the curriculum

B   Can apply technical knowledge in an analytical and practical manner

C   Can extract, from various subjects, the knowledge required to solve many-sided or complex problems

D   Can solve a particular problem by distinguishing the relevant information from the irrelevant, in a given body of data

E   Can, in multi-problem situations, identify the problems and rank them in the order in which they need to be addressed

F   Appreciate that there can be alternative solutions and understand the role of judgement in dealing with them

G   Can integrate diverse areas of knowledge and skills

H   Can communicate effectively with users, by formulating realistic recommendations, in a concise and logical fashion

I   Can identify, advise on and/or resolve ethical dilemmas

The Test of Professional Competence in Management Accounting (TOPCIMA) comprises a case study that requires students to primarily apply strategic management accounting techniques to make and support decisions within a simulated business context.

Rationale

The TOPCIMA will provide an integrated test of syllabus content that is mainly included within the three Strategic level papers. However, it will also draw upon content covered within the six Managerial level papers.

The TOPCIMA will require the student to deal with material in less structured situations than that encountered in previous Strategic level papers, and to integrate a variety of tools in arriving at a recommended solution. It is unlikely that there will be a single right answer to a complex business problem and students will be expected to recognise the possible alternatives in dealing with a problem.

The emphasis will be on assessing candidates capabilities and competence in the practical use of appropriate, relevant knowledge, the ability to demonstrate the application of the higher level skills of synthesis, analysis and evaluation, and skill in effectively presenting and communicating information to users.

Learning outcomes

Students will be required to go through the following stages to prepare for, and to answer, the requirement of the case set within the TOPCIMA.

A – Preparatory to the TOPCIMA exam

- Analyse and identify the current position of the organisation
- Analyse and identify the relevant problems facing the organisation

Note: Activities undertaken using published 'pre-seen' case study materials.

B – TOPCIMA exam

- Appraise possible feasible courses of action available
- Evaluate and then choose specific proposals
- Identify and evaluate proprieties related to the proposals
- Recommend a course of action
- Prepare and present information in a format suitable for presentation to senior management

The exam

Obtaining the exam paper

The 'exam' paper effectively comes in two sections.

- At least six weeks before the exam CIMA will post the **pre-seen** data on its website. You are expected to become familiar with this.

- In the exam, you are given a fresh copy of the pre-seen, up to five pages of 'unseen' data that you have not seen before, with additional data, and the requirement.

The need for Internet access

CIMA will not distribute the pre-seen case study data by post. Instead, you will be told when the material is available on CIMA's website, and you will be able to download it. The material is likely to be in PDF format, readable by Adobe Acrobat software. This is free software and is available from CIMA's (and BPP's) website.

If you do **not** have Internet access, CIMA advises you to contact CIMA's local office or the Student Services Centre.

Taking TOPCIMA

There are two ways of taking TOPCIMA

1 **Computer-based capture**

In this approach you sit the exam on specially modified computers at an exam centre. You will use Word and Excel.

2 **Conventional paper based exam**

You will write your report on paper in the normal way at an exam centre.

The following has been extracted from CIMA's website.

'There will be a written TOPCIMA examination paper of **three hours with 20 minutes reading time before the exam**, with a limited number of questions (requirements). They will normally be answered using the form of a report and/or presentation, with supporting documents, to a variety of users. The questions will be based upon a case study which will be published on the CIMA website, at least six weeks in advance of the examination. This will provide sufficient time before the examination to allow the student to undertake preparatory analysis based upon the pre-seen material. Further information regarding the case will be added as part of the examination paper.

'As a guide to the volume of material within the case, it is likely to be between fifteen and twenty sides of A4, published in advance of the exam and up to six sides of A4 contained within the examination paper.'

'Questions will test the student's capabilities and competence in the application of appropriate knowledge and the processes undertaken in dealing with the problems identified in the examination, together with their ability to present and communicate information'.

Please note that CIMA gives candidates an additional 20 minutes reading time at the start – a total of 200 minutes of exam room time.

Requirement

There will essentially be one requirement but it could contain more than one element. You will be a asked to answer the requirement using a stated format such as

(a) A report
(b) Power point slides
(c) A memorandum

Past TOPCIMA exams so far have required a report format and this should follow a standard layout (see Chapter 6).

The May 2005 paper

The May 2005 paper concerned the recycling industry, and contained data for *two* firms within that industry. They were alike in some ways and different in others. Facing the same market forces, their respective management teams were seeking ways to grow their business.

The unseen data covered a third company, interested in the potential acquisition of a recycling company to strengthen its own recycling division. Candidates were required to place themselves in the shoes of the Business Development Director of this company, and present a report to the board on such an acquisition – its problems, benefits, and a recommendation on one of the two companies presented in the pre-seen data.

The September and November 2005 papers

These papers concerned the construction industry with data for Domusco, a listed company based in a fictitious country. Domusco had overseas subsidiary companies and undertook international construction work.

The unseen data in September depicted Domusco as going through a very successful phase with a significant cash surplus and a number of projects that it was considering.

Candidates were required to place themselves as a consultant required to produce a report that prioritised and advised on the main issues facing Domusco and made appropriate recommendations.

The unseen data in November had a cash forecast that showed a large deficit, with urgent action needed to manage the company through a difficult time. There was also a take-over that had been over-valued with a fall in share price for Domusco, low investor confidence, the resignation of the Finance Director, a bribery issue and some organisational problems.

The requirement was the same as for the September exam.

The March and May 2006 papers

These papers concerned a chain of branded coffee shops called Zubinos undergoing rapid growth, with ambitious further growth targets and associated control issues.

The unseen data in March contained a significant number of diverse issues to be evaluated and prioritised such as a takeover bid, bad publicity and investment opportunities.

Candidates were again required to place themselves in the role of a consultant writing a report that prioritised and discussed the issues facing Zubinos and made appropriate recommendations.

The unseen data in May again contained a significant number of diverse issues such as securing new sources of supply, a franchising proposal and the absence of the Managing Director.

The requirement was the same as for the March exam.

The September and November 2006 papers

These papers concerned a clothing manufacturing company called Kadgee set in the declining clothing manufacturing industry in Europe. The pre-seen material gave details on growing competition from China and a growing cash deficit.

The unseen data in September contained a significant number of diverse issues to be evaluated and prioritised including a factory fire, a cash flow crisis and a proposal to move some manufacturing to China.

In November, candidates were faced with fewer issues, with the central issue a need to turn around Kadgee by shifting operations, and much of the management, to China or other Asian countries. There was also a pending danger of the withdrawal of overdraft facilities.

The requirement in both papers was the same as in previous years.

The March and May 2007 papers

These papers concerned a medium sized, international airline called Flyqual Airlines. The pre-seen material gave details on pressure from investors to reduce costs and conflict with staff. It also looked at potential growth areas and aircraft replacement issues.

The unseen in March concerned issues such as negative publicity about poor maintenance, the loss of two senior managers and potential strike action.

In May the most important issues were the financing of the purchase of new aircraft and potential delays in bringing them into service.

The September and November 2007 papers

These papers concerned a luxury boat building company called Merbatty. The pre-seen material highlighted a developing industry with plans for expansion of Merbatty and the use of new technology.

The unseen in September concerned issues such as delay in the opening of a new boat building facility and technological problems.

In November candidates needed to discuss a hostile take-over bid and proposals to increase profits.

The March and May 2008 papers

These papers concerned a group of resort hotels called Solberri. The pre-seen material gave details of the competitive pressures facing Solberri and the need for a strategy to improve financial performance.

The unseen in March concerned issues such as reduced occupancy levels and operational problems.

At the time of publication, the unseen data for the May exam was not available.

Exam advice in overview

The following is a summary of relevant TOPCIMA exam advice taken from the examiners' comments on the exam sittings under the new syllabus.

General overview

The TOPCIMA exam is designed to test higher level skills. Candidates need to be able to apply their technical knowledge and understanding of the business setting in which the case is set. It is essential that this is applied to the new data supplied in the unseen material on the exam day. They will need to use their judgement to solve multi-faceted problems given in the pre-seen and unseen material and to 'think on their feet'.

Candidates need to research the business setting in which a case is set and have a good understanding and familiarity with the pre-seen material, but **must** discuss the unseen material on the exam day and answer the requirement that has been set. An open mind will be much more useful on exam day than pre-prepared answers.

Candidates should ensure that their answers cover all of the criteria of the TOPCIMA assessment matrix (see Chapter 2 for detailed guidance). They will need to clearly identify the key issues and discuss them in a priority order, justifying the choice of priority. Fully justified, well reasoned recommendations are required, covering all areas of the report, preferably at the end. It is suggested that 'check-lists' are used by candidates of issues to be discussed and the recommendations for each issue.

Key tasks to improve your performance

(a)   Thoroughly research the business setting for the case you will be sitting and be totally familiar with the pre-seen material.

(b)   Revise relevant business strategies and techniques and be able to apply them.

(c)   Identify the relevant key issues in the unseen material and ensure your report covers these issues.

(d)   Familiarise yourself with the TOPCIMA assessment matrix and ensure your answer covers all of the criteria.

Tackling the case study

The Test of Professional Competence in Management Accounting (TOPCIMA)

Introduction

TOPCIMA is the culmination of all the work you have put into your CIMA qualification so far. Although you have completed scenario questions in other Strategic level papers, TOPCIMA is a totally different type of exam.

Topic list
1 TOPCIMA paper: what it is and what it's for
2 The TOPCIMA paper and other exams
3 Getting hold of the case
4 How to use this Study Text
5 Other help from BPP

1 TOPCIMA paper: what it is and what it's for

1.1 What it is

The Test of Professional Competence in Management Accounting (TOPCIMA) is the culmination of your CIMA studies. It is unlike any other exam. Here are the main features in outline.

1.1.1 Before the exam

About **six weeks** before the exam you will access CIMA's website and download between 15 and 20 pages of **'pre-seen'** data (plus supplementary background information, possibly).

The pre-seen data:

- Contains a description of an organisation
- Identifies some issues about the organisation and its context
- Shows you what the examiner will be looking for

> You must use the two months before the exam to become **familiar** with the organisation in the pre-seen data. (This BPP Study Text will show you some techniques for becoming familiar with the organisation in the case.) Why?

Memory

You cannot take **anything** you have prepared into the exam room.

AND

Challenge

You will be given **more 'unseen' data in the exam** about the organisation and its environment.

1.1.2 The exam

You cannot take your analysis with you, and you will have to leave everything at the door.

In the exam room this is what you will be given.

Data	*Requirement*
• A clean copy of all the **pre-seen material**: this should be identical; if not you will be told where to find the differences.	There will be a requirement describing one or more **tasks** that you must complete in a given format (eg report format).
• New **unseen** material.	*Answer booklet or computer*
• Relevant mathematical tables.	You must write or type your answer here. In the computer based exam you will use Word and Excel.

> Effectively, you have **three long hours** to write in your **answer booklets or on your PC** the answer to a short, possibly unstructured, question.

1.1.3 After the exam

Your answer to the requirement will be reviewed against the **assessment matrix** you will have seen and the markers will be looking at how well you have performed against the matrix. (See Chapter 2.)

1.2 So what is the case for?

The case is specially designed to test what CIMA calls **higher level skills**. These skills do not comprise the ability to remember facts or formulae but relate directly to the type of business situation you might, having qualified though CIMA, encounter as a management accountant in practice at strategic level. These higher level skills are shown in the table below.

Synthesis	Analysis	Evaluation	Presenting and communication
Gathering together diverse items of data, getting the big picture	Manipulating data to find useful information	Making an informed judgement as to the information	Communication of information to an audience

Mainly during the exam

Mainly before the exam

The case study enables you to show that you have these skills. They are treated in more depth on the **assessment matrix** which we discuss in Chapter 2, but here is a brief example.

1.3 Example: higher level skills in miniature

This is a very simple exercise to show what we mean by higher level skills. You have the following data on your desk.

- A request from A Co's marketing staff to extend the credit period they offer to A Co's customers
- A Co's sales ledger (which has 100 customers)
- A letter from A Co to its customers saying that it has increased its prices by 20%
- Recent financial statements of B Co, a customer accounting for 10% of A Co's turnover
- An article from the *Financial Times* describing new competition in B Co's market

How might skills of synthesis, analysis, evaluation and communication be applied here?

Skill	What it is	A Co
Synthesis	Gathering together diverse items of data. Getting the big picture	B Co is facing competition and a huge increase in costs. If B Co goes under, A Co loses 10% of its turnover.
Analysis	Manipulating data to find useful information	You could use B Co's accounts to calculate profit margins and cash position, and hence whether it is a good credit risk.
Evaluation	Making an informed judgement	You might suggest that extending the credit period to B Co is risky for A Co.
Presenting and Communication	Communication of information to an audience	You might have to present a report to the Finance Director.

To test these skills, you may be required to carry out a number of tasks.

Synthesise	Analyse	Evaluate	Communicate

Task

In the case study:

- Analyse and identify the current position of an organisation
- Identify and analyse the relevant issues facing an organisation
- Evaluate possible feasible courses of action available
- Evaluate a range of specific proposals
- Make appropriate recommendations
- Produce information in a suitable format for presentation to management

↓

Your answer

↓

Assessment matrix (Ch 2)

↓

Exam success

2 The TOPCIMA paper and other exams

How is the TOPCIMA paper different from all the other CIMA exams?

There is no real **syllabus.**	BUT	You have to show **higher level** skills.
You do not have to learn anything new. It is not a test of knowledge.	BUT	You have to **use** your knowledge of all the strategic level syllabus and your CIMA studies.
There is no 'right' answer.	BUT	How you show you tackle the case (the process) is as important as the actual recommendations you make.
The business situation and data is unstructured.	BUT	You need to use a number of tools to make sense of it.
You will see a lot of the material in advance.	BUT	You will be presented with **new** data in the exam and you cannot take anything you have done into the exam.
You have plenty of time to prepare.	BUT	You cannot question-spot.
There is not a marking scheme.	BUT	You will be judged on an 'assessment matrix'.

3 Getting hold of the case

3.1 What is the pre-seen material?

About six weeks in advance of the sitting, you will obtain the case and the assessment matrix from CIMA's website *www.cimaglobal.com*. Should you not have Internet access, you should contact your local office or Student Services Centre.

CIMA has stated that the CIMA **pre-seen material** will consist of the following.

Feature	Description
A list of contents	
An introductory scenario	This sets the scene for the case study
A series of 'exhibits' (documents) relevant to the scenario	These could be: • Letter • Memorandum • Minutes of a meeting • Notes made by a colleague • Published accounts • Management accounts • Brochure • Press article • Academic or professional journal article • Report

4 How to use this Study Text

4.1 The design

This Study Text for the TOPCIMA has been designed to familiarise you with the case format and methodology. We suggest some useful tools to help you make sense of the data and offer a structured approach.

Clearly, if you are taught in a class, your lecturer may want to deal with it in a different way, with good reason. **Your lecturer knows best.** Each case is different, so our approach is non-prescriptive: we offer you tools, not instructions.

4.2 The assessment matrix: Chapter 2

Given that the TOPCIMA exam **is** so very different from other exams, the first thing you need to do is examine **how it will be marked**. This is the purpose of Chapter 2, where we show you the **assessment matrix** and test you with questions covering each element so you know what the **examiners are expecting:** knowledge is not enough.

4.3 Technical knowledge: Chapter 3

The examiner has stated that candidates should be familiar with techniques and theories learned in the strategic level subjects and should be able to use them to solve some of the business problems facing the organisation in the case.

Chapter 3 has a brief revision of a range of business and financial techniques that you should use and incorporate in your answers.

4.4 The BPP approach: Chapter 4

Chapter 4 describes our **suggested** approach to tackling the TOPCIMA.

(a)   We have broken the six weeks between receipt of the case and the exam into a **structured sequence of tasks**. This is not meant to be **completely prescriptive** – after all, every case is **different**. However preparing for the case is like doing a project. It is an axiom of **project management** that establishing a **work breakdown structure is vital for success.** This is what we do in Chapter 4.

(b)   The tasks are designed to focus on the **individual criteria** of the assessment matrix, as well as to stimulate your thought processes about the case, so that you become thoroughly familiar with the business situation. **They are a set of tools. You do not have to do all of them.**

(c)   When faced with the real case, you may **adapt** the BPP approach – indeed, **always follow your tutor's or lecturer's advice** on this, as each case situation is very different.

(d)   We feel that a structured sequence of tasks will reduce your **analytical work to manageable proportions**.

As in Chapter 2, most stages of the approach are accompanied by useful questions and examples to get you thinking and, as important, to give you practice in communication.

4.5 Part B: Teaching case: Zubinos

As well as suggesting an approach for you to take, we apply our approach in practice.

We apply **each tool** in the BPP approach to Zubinos with examples of 'good' and 'not so good' responses to the data. Then, to enable you to practise your skills on the unseen data, there is the material from the March 2006 exam. You will be able to mark your own efforts and compare them with ours.

4.6 Part C: Previous TOPCIMA cases

We reproduce three more cases, with BPP's analysis, the actual unseens and requirements, and suggested answers.

5 Other help from BPP

5.1 Further resources

The **BPP Learning Media TOPCIMA Toolkit** contains a detailed analysis of the pre-seen, many activities covering all areas of the assessment matrix and mock unseens with full answers. This is developed by BPP's authors and tutors and is available about three weeks after the pre-seen material is issued. Our website (www.bpp.com/CIMA) will contain details. CIMA also offers on-line case resources to students.

If you need to revise your **knowledge**, for example when sitting the case study six months after having sat the other strategic level subjects, then **BPP Learning Media Passcards** are the ideal solution.

How you will be marked: the assessment matrix

2

Introduction

This chapter covers the most important thing you need to know: the **criteria** by which you will be assessed.

We show you the TOPCIMA guidance on the mark breakdown that will apply to your exam.

We then go through each criterion of the matrix, with brief exercises to get you thinking.

1 Marking the case study

1.1 The assessment matrix

The case study is not like a normal exam, and nor is it marked like a normal exam. You know that the requirement may be relatively unstructured. You cannot expect to get 20 marks for Section (a) followed by another ten marks for (b) and so forth. If there is one requirement, you have to consider your performance in the examination as a whole.

A great deal of your success in the exam depends on the quality of the preparation that you do – and this preparation must be targeted at the key issues the examiners are looking for.

It is not easy for the examiners either. How do they assess the higher level skills of synthesis, analysis, evaluation and communication? These all seem quite subjective.

To deal with this problem CIMA has devised an **assessment matrix**, which will be used to judge your script. This is shown on the following page. Look at it carefully. (We will discuss how marks are allocated shortly.)

Exam focus point

> From the September and November 2008 sittings, the assessment matrix has been changed and new guidance issued. This chapter looks at the **new** assessment matrix.

1.2 Awarding the marks

In order to succeed in TOPCIMA, you, in your role as consultant to an organisation, need to:

1   Use analytical techniques to help you analyse the issues in the unseen with relevant reference to the pre-seen material and the industry setting as well as real life parallels of the issues; you will also need to apply your technical knowledge.

2   Prioritise the issues and discuss the impact these issues may have on the organisation; you will then need to suggest a range of alternative actions that the organisation could undertake to address the issues. You will need to discuss the impact these issues may have on the organisation. In doing this, you also need to recognise any relevant ethical implications of the issues.

3   Make recommendations to whoever has commissioned your report on your choice of action for each issue from the alternative actions discussed earlier.

Marks are awarded for fulfilling each of the three stages according to the criteria shown below.

Analysis of Issues		
Technical	Use relevant theoretical techniques and frameworks and perform relevant calculations to help you to analyse the case material and support your arguments.	5
Application	Use the techniques, frameworks and calculations you have produced to support your analysis of the issues and your choices of actions.	15
Diversity	Display knowledge of relevant real life situations within the same or a similar context as that in which the case is set. Additionally, display knowledge of real life commercial or organisational issues relevant to the situation in the case. These may occur in the industry or organisational setting in which the case is set or in different industries or settings.	5
		25

Strategic Choices		
Focus	Select the issues you feel to be the most important and make sure that you properly address these issues in the report you produce.	5
Prioritisation	Rank the key issues, stating clearly and concisely your rationale to justify your ranking. Issues should be given high priority primarily because of their impact on the organisation in the case. Their urgency may also be a factor. Also, state the issues that you feel deserve a lower priority ranking and give your reasons.	10
Judgement	Exercise commercial and professional judgement to discuss the key issues. Discuss the impact the priority issues have on the organisation. Discuss alternative courses of action, with reasons, that the organisation could take to resolve these issues. Your analysis should include relevant supporting financial analysis.	20
Ethics	Using your judgement, highlight and analyse the ethical issues in the case and state why you consider these issues to have ethical implications. Discuss alternative courses of action that the organisation could take to resolve the issues.	5
		40

Recommendations		
Logic	Make clear, well justified recommendations for each of the prioritised issues and ensure the reasoning for the recommended courses of action is clearly stated. The recommendations should follow on logically from the weight of the arguments and choices of actions given earlier in the report.	20
Ethics	Make clear, well justified recommendations for each of the ethical issues and ensure the reasoning for the recommended courses of action is clearly stated. The recommendations should follow on logically from the weight of the arguments you make in your report.	5
Integration	Produce a well-structured report in an appropriate format and linguistic style. (3) These marks are awarded holistically according to the overall quality and functionality of your report. (7)	10
		35
		100

2 The assessment matrix in detail

2.1 Technical

TOPCIMA directly rewards your technical knowledge and the examiner expects to see it displayed in the exam.

Key term

> **Technical** 'Use relevant theoretical techniques and frameworks and perform relevant calculations to help you to analyse the case material and support your arguments.' You have the relevant **detailed subject knowledge** from your earlier CIMA studies particularly at Strategic Level.

You may need to refresh your knowledge of the important technical areas and this is covered in Chapter 3.

Relevant theories from past TOPCIMA exams have included:

- SWOT analysis
- PEST analysis (Political, Economic, Social, Technological
- Ratio analysis
- Porter's generic strategies (Cost Leadership, Differentiation, Focus)
- Industry life cycle (Introductory Growth, Shakeout, Mature, Decline)
- Ansoff's growth vector matrix (Market Penetration, Product Development Market development, Diversification)
- BCG matrix
- The balanced scorecard (Financial, Customer, Business Process, Innovation and Learning
- Suitability, Acceptability and Feasibility model from strategic option evaluation.
- Project appraisal
- Make or buy decisions
- Cash flow forecasts

Marks are awarded for the breadth of technical theories you present. But writing out theory takes a long time for very few extra marks.

Exam focus point

> Ensure you:
>
> - Select technical theories that make a contribution to your reader's understanding of the situation of the firm
> - Limit yourself to two or three pieces of technical theory – because the mark allocation is too little to justify spending more time than this
> - Present technical theories as Appendices to your report, eg Appendix 1 – SWOT Analysis, Appendix 2 – Stakeholder analysis, Appendix 3 – Cash flow forecast
>
> The quality and inclusion of relevant calculations will gain additional marks under the application criteria.

2.2 Application

Key term

> **Application** 'Use the techniques, frameworks and calculations you have produced to support your analysis of the issues and your choices of actions.' You can demonstrate how to **use** technical knowledge.

This criterion overlaps the Technical Knowledge criterion. BPP's belief is that in practice they are assessed together.

The main skills rewarded are:

- Ability to conduct financial analysis of issues in the case
- Ability to apply the technical theory above to shed light on the case

Financial analysis usually involves:

- Calculation of NPV of projects, often with probabilities
- Updating a cash flow or profit forecast
- Preparing or commenting on a business valuation

Non-financial applications have included:

- Relating analysis of issues, options and recommendations to elements in the SWOT analysis
- Explaining falling profitability in terms of the intensification of the 5 Forces (Porter)
- Warning of the risks of an overseas venture by reference to PEST analysis
- Applying Balanced Scorecard to developing a performance related pay scheme

Numerical skills are an important part of the 'technical' criteria. The techniques required will all be techniques that you have learnt already, so the key issues here are these.

(a) Do calculations that are **relevant** to your analysis and conclusions, and that **add value** (eg by clarifying the position or evaluating solutions).

(b) Explain your calculations and present your workings clearly.

Exam focus point

> (a) Don't waste time doing detailed, unnecessary calculations at the expense of discussion. Make sensible assumptions to save time and cover any lack of knowledge of more complex techniques eg WACC is 10%.
>
> (b) The case study fundamentally tests higher level skills, not arithmetic. **So, can you afford to get your sums wrong?**
>
> **Yes and No.** If your numerical skills are very poor, this will **reflect badly** on your **overall ability to present sensible, well argued conclusions** – in other words you will not be fit to be let loose on unsuspecting businesses as an ACMA!
>
> As you have come this far in your exams, this is unlikely. Any errors of this nature are likely to be caused by panic.

As the case study draws on all strategic level papers, you may need to apply some knowledge of financial management.

In your **preparation** for the exam, and in your review of the 'pre-seen' material, you need to use your numerical skills to become properly acquainted with the company's situation. We will provide a checklist of the type of questions you should be asking in Chapter 5.

Exam focus point

> To make the point again. 'While numerical skills are important, being able to comment on the significance of the figures is even more important.' Remember also that it will not be necessary to try to study the entire syllabus again, as you will be able to identify any relevant knowledge areas from the pre-seen material.
>
> Ensure you:
>
> - Refer to your technical theory appendices in the main body of your report
> - Provide a formal numerical analysis of options, cash flow forecasts etc
> - Present your financial workings as separate appendices to your report
> - Refer in the main body of the report to the key figures and conclusions from your financial analysis
> - Remember that you are not permitted to conduct calculations during the 20 minutes reading time allowed

Question

Using numerical data

Iolinda Co is a biotechnology company about to be listed on a stock market. It has used genetic manipulation (GM) technology to generate a species of rose that is impervious to aphids. The company is very confident that the new rose will be a huge market success, but needs to conduct trials in plant nurseries. Of course, these trials may have unintended consequences. There is a risk that the trials may fail and/or that environmentalists will disrupt them. Iolinda does have some other valuable patents, in GM technology for farmers, but this is the first time it will market directly to consumers as opposed to other businesses. Consumers and the gardening public will, in effect, be propagating GM plants.

The venture capital firms which have financed Iolinda want to recover their investment by selling shares. Other biotechnology companies have no difficulties in raising equity. However, the share prices of biotechnology firms have been quite volatile in relation to the market as a whole, with some spectacular successes and failures. Iolinda intends to float whatever the outcome of the rose project.

Required

In this question, you are going to **adopt the role of the examiner**. What **numerical analysis** would you like to see done, if you gave the student the following information?

(1)   Historic data on likely success/failure of trials of GM products (ie failure rate pre-launch)
(2)   Cash flows required for the trials pre-launch
(3)   Proposed pricing strategy (eg penetration or skimming strategies) and sales forecast; distribution and marketing costs assuming launch is successful; comparative volumes in relation to other products
(4)   Projected EPS for the company as a whole, or similar information from the prospectus
(5)   Interest rates
(6)   Market values, dividend levels and yields, and betas of similar companies

Answer

The examiner might expect you to investigate the following.

The **historic success rate** for GM product trials might give an idea of **risk**. You may also need to consider the risk that the **political climate** opposed to GM products may significantly reduce the sales turnover. All this will be relevant to **investment appraisal**.

If significant cash flows are involved, you may be required to prepare **cash budgets.**

The proposed pricing strategy will give an idea of what cash flows might be expected and hence you could estimate the significance of the rose trial in the **overall product portfolio**.

With suitable information you might analyse the **risk** of the project, and use the **beta**, if it meets the relevant tests.

2.3 Diversity

Key term

> **Diversity**: 'Display knowledge of relevant real life situations within the same or a similar context as that in which the case is set. Additionally, display knowledge of real life commercial or organisational issues relevant to the situation in the case. These may occur in the industry or organisational setting in which the case is set or in different industries or settings'. A wide range of views and knowledge is reflected. Remember that the TOPCIMA is designed as a multi-disciplinary case study.

This criterion rewards bringing real-life examples into your final report and involves an understanding of the industry setting ie **business awareness.**

Real life examples can include:

- Knowledge of legislation or other factors affecting the industry featured in the Pre-seen
- Illustration of issues by reference to real-world firms in the same industry
- Discussion of general business issues by reference to other firms

To gain marks under this criterion you should:

- Mention the names of real-world firms in the same industry, their real-world customers and suppliers, and the laws and policies they face
- Establish the relevance to the issues in the exam of any real-world fact you bring in
- Avoid excessive reading around or name dropping just for the sake of it

There will probably be one mark available per comment so five marks for diversity will require five good comments.

Why is **business awareness** relevant to the case study?

(a) The case study is normally set in an **industry context**, such as manufacturing or services. Each business context poses different questions. Remember that most of the developed economies in the western world are heavily orientated round the **service sector**.

(b) Case studies will be **realistic and representative** of the industry sector under consideration. **They do not, however, have to be based on a real company.**

(c) The **case study may not be set in an identified country.** This decision is entirely CIMA's, so that students will not be prejudiced if they do not live in the country where the case is set. So, you are likely to encounter imaginary countries such as Veeland, Aland, etc. This does limit your ability to cite political or social factors – dismaying, perhaps, as the case is supposed to be externally-based and forward looking.

Recent case studies:

- In **ReuserR** (May 2005) the industry was recycling with data for two firms, one of which was a private company. The unseen introduced a glass manufacturing company looking to backwardly integrate.
- In **Domusco** (September and November 2005), an imaginary country was used and the industry setting was the construction industry with international construction work.
- In **Zubinos** (March and May 2006), the setting was service sector coffee shops in the UK – easy to understand and analyse.
- In **Kadgee** (September and November 2006), the setting was clothing manufacturing in a global economy.
- In **Flyqual** (March and May 2007), the industry was airline travel, again with plenty of topical issues to research.
- In **Merbatty** (September and November 2007)), the industry was luxury boat building with some similar and easy-to-research real-life companies.
- In **Solberri** (March and May 2008), the setting was the hotel industry, again easy to understand and analyse.

How do I attain business awareness?

(a) **In general**

- Read the business press, such as the *Economist*, the *Financial Times* or the business pages of papers such as the *Times*, the *Guardian*, the *Independent* or the *Daily Telegraph*.
- Read Financial Management
- Look at websites such as bbc.co.uk, timesonline.co.uk, www.bized.co.uk

(b) **For the TOPCIMA exam**

- Use the Internet to research the industry and similar organisations
- Take a look at any specialist trade journals
- Obtain a company report from a firm in the industry
- See Chapter 4 for more detail

Exploiting business awareness

(a) So what to do with all this knowledge? At the very least:

- Try to understand the main **cost** and **revenue drivers** of the industry
- Do a brief **five forces** analysis (Porter)
- Who are the main customers of the industry's products (consumers or organisations)?

(b) Be sensitive to the **size** of the business. A corner shop with two people is very different from a large supermarket.

(c) What **terminology** does the industry use? For example lawyers have 'clients'. From the case data, or from your research, you should be able to identify any generic terms.

(d) Remember that most business decisions are **uncertain**. You will only have limited information and, if a lack of information means decisions will be riskier, you should say so. However, you will always be given enough information on the key issues.

(e) Make sure your examples are relevant.

2.4 Focus

Key term

Focus: 'Select the issues you feel to be the most important and make sure that you properly address these issues in the report you produce'.

Remember that a lot of the pre-seen and unseen material will turn out to be irrelevant to the key issues. You need to identify the relevant key data and issues in the case material ie what really matters.

In the exam you will face ten or so problems from which you must select and focus on four or five. You should not waste time talking too much about the rest.

The issues to focus on break down into:

(a) One or more **short-term 'emergency' issues** that must be dealt with quickly, eg:

- Imminent strike action that will halt production and let down valuable clients
- Running out of a key supply that will leave shelves empty and lose customer goodwill
- Fire that destroys capacity, delivery stocks and financial records
- A public relations disaster that must be headed off quickly
- A hostile approach by a predator company
- Loss of a key member of management
- Loss of key contract that means firm must cut costs quickly
- Potential breaching of borrowing limits with the bank that may lead to foreclosure.

These are usually introduced in the Unseen material.

(b) **Investment or other strategic options** that must be evaluated in relation to deeper background issues affecting the ability of the firm to prosper in the future, eg intensifying competition destroying margins in the industry:

- Firm lacks the finance and management structure and skills to grow
- Inappropriate portfolio of businesses that need to be pared down to a core business

These background issues can often be seen in the Pre-seen material and the decisions presented in the Unseen are there to test your appreciation of them.

(c) Some **ethical issues** that management should be alerted to, eg:

- Discovery that managers have been bribing people to win contracts or get legal favours
- Mistreatment of staff over pay or of dismissals
- Misleading statements made to customers
- Unsafe or socially undesirable manufacturing processes
- Products issues of Corporate Social Responsibility (CSR) affecting the business

Question   Knowledge

Bovine Burgers (BB) is a chain of fast food restaurants with branches over the whole world. They are considering changing their burger-manufacturing system from **heating** the burgers on a flat hot plate to **flame grilling** them. This will mean a significant change to the way the firm prepares and sells burgers, and a change to the equipment in each shop. BB must purchase and distribute this equipment. BB denotes each shop as a profit centre.

Your boss has asked for your views as to the strategic management accounting implications of the switch in burger-making technology.

Required

Identify which of the following concepts are relevant to Bovine Burgers and why.

Technical	Application: Relevant? Yes/Perhaps?/No	Focus: Why is it relevant (or not)?
Transfer pricing		
ABC		
WACC		
Marketing mix		
DCF		
JIT		
5 Forces		
McFarlan		
SWOT		
ROI		
TQM		

Technical	Application: Relevant? Yes/Perhaps?/No	Focus: Why is it relevant (or not)?
Transfer pricing	Perhaps	Head office will be transferring equipment over the world to divisions.
ABC	Yes	New grilling method involves new cooking activities and possibly different cost drivers.
WACC	No	Unless you are asked to do a project appraisal and are given WACC as the discount rate, you can ignore this.
Marketing mix	Perhaps	The change to the new grill may require more marketing spend, hence a different focus.
DCF	Perhaps	You may use DCF for appraising the strategy.
JIT	No	Fast food is already just in time, and JIT is not really relevant to this context.
5 Forces	No	Not relevant to **what you have been asked to do** – no competitors are mentioned.
McFarlan	No	Nothing at all about the use of information systems.
SWOT	No	Too high a level for this question.
ROI	Yes	Each shop is a profit centre.
TQM	Perhaps	A brand such as Bovine Burgers needs to offer **consistent** product and service quality.

Refresh your knowledge of these concepts from Chapter 3 if you need to.

2.5 Prioritisation

Key term

> **Prioritisation** – 'Rank the key issues, stating clearly and concisely your rationale to justify your ranking. Issues should be given high priority primarily because of their impact on the organisation in the case. Their urgency may also be a factor. Also, state the issues that you feel deserve a lower priority ranking and give your reasons.'

In short, to prioritise is to put items in a **logical order of importance**, **based on a clear rationale**. For example, if you are washed up on a desert island from a shipwreck, the underlying **rationale** for anything you do, initially, will be survival. Assuming you have no injuries, your first priority will be to find clean drinking water, and then food: this is because human beings can go without food for longer than without drinking water.

Exam focus point

> Time and again, the examiner has said that students do not give reasons for recommendations. This reflects badly on your ability to prioritise. This is a difficult skill to master, and you should practise prioritisation of issues in as many case studies as possible.

In order to gain good marks your **answer** must be prioritised throughout.

At the beginning of your report

- Identify and state the **key issues** in priority order
- Explain **why** they are key issues and why you have put them in the order they appear

In the body of your report

- Discuss each issue in a separate section so that your answer demonstrates depth of analysis
- Save time and keep focus by not wasting time writing lots about issues that are not priorities
- Keep Ethics issues in a section of their own

At the end of your report

- Give recommendations on what to do about the most important issues
- State **why** you have made your recommendations. Do not just list them: **justify** them

2.5.1 Elements to consider

Timescale:	Short-term	Long-term
Scale of impact:	Significant	Not significant
Risk:	High	Low

Exam focus point

> Note that a short-term problem (running out of cash) can have a significant impact and be a high risk. Anything fundamental to the survival of the business is important.
>
> Remember **impact** and **urgency** are the key tests for prioritisation.

Question | *Prioritisation*

In 2000, BMW pulled out of car manufacturing in the UK. It sold most of its investment in Rover Cars to another firm, with the Land Rover division going to Ford.

Here are some of the factors underlying the decision.

- Rover lost £750m in 1999.
- £150m of aid from the UK government to BMW was under threat from the European commission, given its concern over state subsidies.
- The pound sterling is very high compared to the euro, making goods exported from the UK to Europe very expensive for European buyers.
- 10,000 jobs in Rover were at risk, as were 40,000 supplier jobs in the West Midlands. BMW spent a lot of time and money on 'the English patient' since buying it.
- BMW had invested in Rover to enable BMW to become a volume car manufacturer as opposed to a niche maker of executive cars.
- BMW is the 14th largest motor manufacturer in an industry that has been consolidating recently.
- It is uncertain if the UK will abandon the pound sterling and adopt the Euro as its currency.
- Rover lost market share in the UK from 13.5% to 6% over the 5 years up to 2000. Too few British buyers were buying Rover Cars.
- BMW could be vulnerable to a takeover.
- The main BMW brand was suffering at the time.

What might have been BMW's priorities in reaching the decision? Show a rationale.

Answer (1) Clear pass

Rationale

Survival of BMW. BMW's management wished to preserve BMW as a successful, independent company, and considered that future involvement with Rover would jeopardise this aim.

Key issues underlying the decision:

Priority – importance	Justification
1 Stem losses: no prospect of future profitability	**Future**. BMW had invested a lot in Rover, but what concerned them was the future – future incremental cash flows were negative. Rover had been losing market share in the UK. Exports had tailed off because of the high level of sterling. New products had not been successful.
2 Concentrate on BMW brand	**External**. Too much management attention had been focused on Rover. No evidence existed that this had hit BMW brand yet, but managers were concerned about this.
3 Compete elsewhere: consolidation of motor industry	**External**. Motor firms are merging into larger groups – the reason why BMW bought Rover.

The answer above has a clear rationale and the relative importance of each item is shown.

Answer (2) Clear fail

- Rover lost £750m in 1999.
- The exchange rate is not favourable and so cars are expensive.
- Rover has been losing market share recently.
- BMW want to concentrate on building the BMW brand.

This is a clear fail because you are not clearly specifying the **rationale** behind the decision, which is that Rover will be a **future** drain of cash for BMW, and that investing in Rover will prevent BMW from protecting its brand.

The first three bullet points are background information not priorities. Priorities involve taking action.

If you have difficulty, use the grid below as a guide to prioritisation (with some possible applications to the BMW example above).

	Important	Not important
Urgent (must be done now)	Top priority (stem cash losses)	Mid-priority (state aid?)
Not urgent	Mid-priority (eg protect BMW brand)	Bottom priority (eg UK not participating in Single Currency)

Exam focus point

In BPP's experience, most students are weak in the 'prioritisation' area. Examples of prioritisation include separating key problems from less important ones.

Prioritisation and recommendations are the make or break of a candidate. The key strategic issues should be clearly identified and discussed in a priority order, **justifying** your choice of priority.

2.6 Judgement

Key term

Judgment : 'Exercise commercial and professional judgement to discuss the key issues. Discuss the impact the priority issues have on the organisation. Discuss alternative courses of action, with reasons, that the organisation could take to resolve these issues. Your analysis should include relevant supporting financial analysis.'

Focus and prioritisation concern issues. You show judgement by coming up with **solutions** to the issues raised. You will be rewarded for **breadth** of discussion and a 'business sense' of what is being said.

Judgement can be seen as the link between the discussion of the issues and the recommendations.

(a) When identifying strategic options, you might

- Pick out clues from the case
- Use strategy models to develop ideas

(b) When it comes to evaluating and ranking choices, you could use these tests

- Suitability, feasibility and acceptability, incorporating
    - SWOT
    - cost-benefit analysis
    - stakeholder mapping

(c) You need to demonstrate a good commercial understanding of how the organisation in the case could enhance shareholder value.

Exam focus point

To display good judgement in your report you should:

- Evaluate options using the terms suitability, acceptability and feasibility explicitly
- Ensure each recommendation is justified by showing how it addresses the problems you explained in your analysis of the issues
- Justify your recommendations by reference to the experiences of real-world firms
- Write your report using a depth of explanation and language appropriate to the situation of the people it is addressed to.

2.7 Logic

Key term

Logic: 'Make clear, well justified recommendations for each of the prioritised issues and ensure the reasoning for the recommended courses of action is clearly stated. The recommendations should follow on logically from the weight of the arguments and choices of actions given earlier in the report.'

To get good marks under this criterion ensure:

- **Recommendations appear at the end of the report** not at the end of each sub-section 'because a recommendation cannot be made until all of the other issues are discussed and assessed, as many are competing for the same scarce resources – manpower and finance'
- **Recommendations include a justification**. The reason for recommending the course of action should be justified by reference back to the urgency of the issue and the analysis you have presented of it
- **Recommendations must deal with the priority issues** at least

2.8 Ethics

Key term

Ethics refer to notions of 'right' and 'wrong'. In a business context, the impact of a company's strategic decisions will have an ethical implication (eg child labour, pollution, wage rates, dealing openly and fairly with stakeholders, suppliers, customers etc). The concept of 'corporate social responsibility' (CSR) is particularly relevant.

CIMA has published its own Code of Ethics for Professional Accountants which applies to all CIMA members and students from 1st January 2006. It is available on the Cimaglobal website.

You will need to **identify** the ethical issues and then briefly justify **why** the issue has an ethical dimension. You should then offer **realistic advice** on how to resolve the ethical issues.

Ethical issues may include (but are not limited to) the following

- Corporate governance
- Treatment of customers
- Social responsibility
- Business practices
- Treatment of staff
- Environmental concerns

For example, Severn Trent plc, the environmental services company, takes CSR very seriously. Its business principles include concepts such as 'corporate citizenship', 'integrity', 'respect for local cultures', 'lawfulness' and 'shared values'. Take a moment to think about these; they provide a useful checklist of ethical terms.

Question

Ethics

The notion of 'corporate social responsibility' suggests that organisations should consider the good of the wider community (both global and local) within which they operate (ie not just the interests of customers and profitability). Why are consumers increasingly looking for businesses to demonstrate a wider ethical commitment to society?

Answer

Here are a few suggestions. Ethics in business has been described as a 'bandwagon' gaining momentum.

- Consumers are increasingly aware of the issues eg fair trade, child labour, advertising standards
- High profile ecological problems
- Consumers tend to be cynical of big business claims – ethical 'badges' need to be genuine
- Treatment of employees is a high-profile area
- Human resource management policies often embrace the application of ethical principles
- Word-of-mouth is becoming very important, especially in the Internet age: many people will recommend (or avoid) a company because of its ethically responsible (or otherwise) reputation
- Government pressure

Exam focus point

Five marks are available for **identifying** the ethical issues and five marks for **recommendations** on how to deal with them.

To gain good marks under this criterion you should:

- Identify the ethical issues along with other issues at the start of your report
- Do not include discussion of ethical issues amongst discussion of priority issues but rather cover them in a separate section of your report
- Ensure you state the issue (eg dismissal of a sick employee) and the ethical principle (eg 'fairness of treatment')
- Make recommendations on ethical matters as you go along rather than in the main recommendations section

2.9 Integration

Key term

Integration: 'Produce a well-structured report in an appropriate format and linguistic style. (3 marks) These marks are awarded holistically according to the overall quality and functionality of your report. (7 marks)

This means that you have considered the diverse issues seriously and critically, have elaborated on them and combined them into a sensible whole. It overlaps other criteria such as Technical, Application, Judgement and Logic.

Key data calculated or presented in appendices must be further discussed in the main body of the report. The report should flow well and be in a logical sequence. This allows markers to use their discretion based on the 'professional feel' of the overall report and its fitness for purpose.

2.9.1 Structuring business communications

Too often, you can be let down by poor communication. Throughout this Study Text, you will be given opportunities to practise your skills in this respect.

We will cover **report** format and structure in Chapter 6 but here are some things to keep in mind. The examiner has proposed the following structure for any business communication, whatever the format.

Introduction: be brief

Contents: identification of issues and evaluation of each issue from all relevant perspectives

Conclusions: cross reference these back to the appropriate section

Recommendations: This is the most important section making clear justified recommendations on all of the issues identified.

Question		Conclusions

You're the examiner!

Context

Bastable Co is a firm specialising in the manufacture of balloons for recreational use and advertising. The firm is now considering manufacturing airships, filled with helium, as an environmentally-friendly alternative to airplanes. Each airship will offer berths for forty people, competing with sea cruises. Airship manufacture will involve raising money from investors. Bastable is facing competition in its core markets, mainly from firms which exploit new materials to produce lighter balloons that are cheaper to operate.

Two conclusions to student scripts ended as follows.

Script 1

> **Conclusion**
>
> Choices available to Bastable
>
> 1   Manufacture airships alone
> 2   Go into a joint venture with another manufacturer to manufacture airships
>
> *Recommendation*
>
> Option 1 is chosen. It generates a positive NPV and opens up new markets and business opportunities, without the firm sacrificing these benefits to a joint venture partner.

Script 2

> Bastable should not manufacture airships. Even if a joint venture partner is chosen, the NPV of the project does not look attractive enough in relation to the other option which is to focus on balloons and on the competitive threats.

As the examiner, how would you mark them?

Answer

Neither of the scripts evidences a clear pass, for the micro-case situation we have described, but for different reasons.

Script 1 – does not judge all the alternatives – one of which is not to go ahead. The positive NPV is not compared with other uses of the funds. There is a problem with content and analysis. However, in terms of presentation, the options are clearly numbered, and the recommendation is clear, separately identified and justified.

Script 2 – actually does address the alternatives: manufacture or not manufacture airships, and shows evidence of greater judgement in comparing all the options. However it mixes up a conclusion and a recommendation and is not presented well.

Exam focus point

To gain marks under this criterion you should ensure:

- Anything you cite as an issue, an opportunity or a threat also appears in your SWOT analysis
- The recommendations section has a sub-section of several paragraphs dealing with each of the main issues in the Unseen and Pre-seen material
- Your detailed calculations and analysis in the appendices are referred to in the main body of the report

We will look at how to write a report in Chapter 6.

The BPP approach (1): approach and explore the case situation

Introduction

In Chapters 1 and 2, we covered what the case exam is for and how you can expect to be marked. To repeat, you will obtain from CIMA's website the 'pre-seen' material six to eight weeks before the exam. You must live and breathe the company in the case, as you will not be able to bring in any analysis notes or crib-sheets into the exam room.

A key objective of the pre-seen data is that you become familiar with the company – the big picture as well as the detail. How does this chapter help you?

- Your objective: become familiar with the company in the case situation.
- You have to consider 'all the angles'
- You have to remember your analysis in the exam

We break down this process into a **sequence of stages** to structure your time.

- Approach the case
- Explore the case situation
- Synthesise what you know

In each case there are tasks that can be done: think of these as a resource of techniques for that stage. (You will not need to do all of them.)

A note for students

Every case is different, and this **suggested** generic approach may need to be supplemented, adapted, or radically recast depending on the case situation.

- You will benefit from **sharing your ideas with other students**.
- **Your lecturer will know best**.

Topic list
1 The BPP approach in outline
2 Approach the case
3 Explore the case situation
4 Conclusion

1 The BPP approach in outline

1	Tools to approach the case: Chapter 4	Time	Criteria of the assessment matrix
1.1	Read the case quickly twice without taking notes	1 hour	
1.2	Quickly re-read the case after a day	30 mins	
1.3	Mark up the case slowly, taking notes	2 hours	
1.4	Summarise the data in précis	1 hour	Diversity, Logic, Judgement
1.5	Carry out an information audit	1 hour	Diversity, Integration, Prioritisation
1.6	Research the industry and company	–	Diversity
1.7	Identify relevant technical knowledge	30 mins	Technical, Application, Focus, Diversity

2	Tools to explore the case situation: Chapter 4		
2.1	Analyse the numbers	Depends	Technical, Application, Focus, Logic, Diversity
2.2	General environmental analysis (PEST) and trends	1 hour	Diversity, Technical, Application, Focus, Logic, Ethics
2.3	Analyse the business environment and competitive strategy	1.5 hours	Diversity, Technical, Application, Focus, Logic, Ethics
2.4	Audit the product/service portfolio	1 hour	Technical, Application, Focus, Logic, Ethics, Diversity
2.5	How does the business add value?	1 hour	Integration, Ethics
2.6	Identify information systems and processes	1 hour	Technical, Application, Focus, Diversity
2.7	Identify key issues in structure, culture and personnel including management and internal control	1 hour	Technical, Application, Focus, Prioritisation, Ethics, Diversity
2.8	Identify investor objectives, capital structure and other stakeholder objectives	1 hour	Technical, Application, Focus, Ethics, Diversity
2.9	Identify and analyse possible business projects	1 hour	Integration, Technical, Application, Focus, Ethics, Diversity

3	Tools to synthesise what you know: Chapter 5		
3.1	Summarise your findings in an interim position statement	1 hour	Prioritisation, Logic, Judgement, Technical, Application, Focus, Diversity
3.2	Draw up a mission statement for the current business from the pre-seen data	30 mins	Logic, Prioritisation
3.3	Relate the business's distinctive competences to the critical success factors for the industry	30 mins	Logic, Judgement, Prioritisation
3.4	Identify and analyse risks, internal and external	1 hour	Diversity, Technical, Application, Focus, Prioritisation, Ethics
3.5	Carry out a graded SWOT analysis	1 hour	Prioritisation
3.6	Identify key business issues	1 hour	Prioritisation, Integration, Diversity, Ethics
3.7	Draw up a balanced scorecard	1 hour	Integration, Logic, Judgement, Prioritisation
3.8	Prepare a one page business summary	1 hour	Logic, Judgement, Prioritisation, Diversity, Integration

4	Practise report writing before the exam: Chapter 6		
5	The exam – three hours: Chapter 7	Time	
5.1	The night before: review your business summary and the pre-seen		
5.2	• Review the unseen and requirement • Skim read the data • Read the requirement carefully, making a mental note of the recipient of the report, the required format and what you have to do	Reading time 20 mins	
5.3	Read the unseen data in depth. Be sure to identify what has changed. Make notes on the question paper identifying the key issues.		

5.4	Consider the big picture and plan your answer. Do the calculations	45 mins
5.5	Draw up the appendices, terms of reference and introduction	10 mins
5.6	Prioritise the issues	15 mins
5.7	Write the main body of the report	55 mins
	Write the ethics section	15 mins
5.8	Write up your recommendations	35 mins
5.9	Write the conclusion and review your work	5 mins

2 Approach the case

Objectives of stage 1: Approach the Case

- Absorb the case without getting bogged down in detail
- Provide a sound basis for further analysis
- Identify information needs and deficiencies

Step 1.1 Read the case study quickly twice without taking notes

CIMA will put the case on its **website.** (CIMA will tell you when.) Keep this date in your diary. To download the case, you will of course, need Internet access and Adobe Acrobat software (this is free software, and you can obtain it from CIMA's website or BPP's). You will also need any student login or registration details.

Don't panic when you first look at the case, but **don't ignore** it for weeks. You have to **get to know the case situation**, and the best way is to get started now. You do have around six weeks, however, and BPP can help you. Before you do anything, however, **TAKE A PHOTOCOPY**, in case you lose the case, spill tea over it, or whatever. We advise you to photocopy the case on to large A3 paper (this book is A4) so you will have plenty of space to write on it **when the time comes.**

(a) Book a **quiet, uninterrupted hour** into your diary, when you know you can read the case. (You might find that **gentle background music** makes your brain more receptive. Scientific tests have shown that for many people certain types of music – baroque classical, mainly – can relax the brain.)

(b) **Read the case twice, quickly, without taking notes**. Speed-reading twice can improve memory retention, and you do not want to get overwhelmed by the detail. So, do not take notes at this stage – sit in an armchair, rather than at your desk, if you need this discipline.

Step 1.2 Quickly re-read the case after a day

Briefly reviewing information on a regular basis can help you absorb and remember it – scientific fact. Don't take notes this time. This re-reading session is just to refresh your mind.

Step 1.3 Mark up the case slowly, taking notes

Read the case more slowly, highlighting key points, introducing numbered paragraphs or drawing a mind map. The purpose of this stage is still to help you get a broad overview, and the **result of this will be a précis**, summarising the data in the case to fix it in your mind.

(a) At your desk, lay out your A3 copy. This will give you a lot of space to mark up the material or make notes.

(b) Give each paragraph of the case a **separate paragraph reference – you will find it easy to refer to later.**

(c) With a **highlighter** pen, highlight key facts – **do not analyse them for the time being**. Alternatively, you can note down if a fact is important on the side of the paper.

(d) Another technique is to do a **spider diagram** or **mind map**. Starting from the centre of the page, you can link issues in steps. Mind maps are excellent for linking different items of data together or fixing them in your brain. You will find examples throughout this Workbook.

(e)   You may also consider what you should do with the separate **Exhibits or Appendices**. These will certainly contain useful information.

Financial data	This will be analysed
People involved	These indicate some issues relating to 'internal politics'
Links	Sometimes they take the story forward, and contain valuable information

Step 1.4 Summarise the data in a précis

What is a précis? A concise summary of essential facts. In other words it is short, comprehensive (it summarises), focused, relevant (essential) and based on facts. **It does not incorporate analysis or opinions**. So what's the point of writing out a summary of a case you have read several times, taken notes on, and by now you know fairly well? There are two reasons for doing a précis.

(a)   You will start testing your **written business communication skills** – as you have seen already these are a major part of how you will be assessed in this case.

(b)   It is a fact that putting things into your own words **can help you absorb and understand the data.**

(c)   You should also include key issues arising from the **Exhibits** or **Appendices** in the pre-seen.

Question	Summarise

Here is some data from a newspaper. Précis it into 100 words. Give yourself a time limit.

Financial Times	Précis
Halifax, the mortgage bank, yesterday agreed to pay £760m for a controlling stake in St James's Place Capital (SJPC), the holding company for J Rothschild Assurance, in a deal designed to pull the upmarket life assuror into the internet age.	
Halifax bought 17 per cent of the company from Prudential late on Tuesday at 300p a share, a premium of 70p to Tuesday's closing price. It will now extend the offer to up to 60 per cent of the shares, leaving SJPC with a separate listing.	
The bid is the latest move in Halifax's aggressive internet strategy, begun earlier this year when it poached Jim Spowart from Standard Life bank to set up Intelligent Finance (IF), an online bank due to launch this summer.	
It hopes to add £5bn of assets to IF by selling a St James's-branded private banking service, run by IF, through SJPC's 1,000-strong salesforce.	
'This is an absolutely cracking business,' said James Crosby, Halifax chief executive. 'It increases the scale of our distribution operation in long-term savings and will assist our drive for diversification (away from mortgages).'	
Sir Mark Weinberg, chairman of SJPC, said the company had decided last year to seek a strategic partner to help it use the internet to extend its product range, and began talks with Prudential, which then owned 29 per cent of the shares. 'It became clear that their vision and our vision were	

Financial Times	Précis
not parallel to the extent that there wasn't the opportunity for a value-creating partnership,' he said.	
Analysts said the deal, which is expected to be earnings-enhancing in the first year, would help IF as long as the product, still under wraps, is as exciting as the bank claims.	
The SJPC salesforce own about 8 per cent of the company and have options on another 8 per cent.	

Helping hand

Financial Times	Précis
Halifax, the mortgage bank, yesterday agreed to pay £760m for a controlling stake in St James's Place Capital, the holding company for J Rothschild Assurance, in a deal designed to pull the upmarket life assurer into the internet age.	Halifax, the mortgage bank, has spent £760m to control St James's Place Capital (SJPC), a life assurer with Internet potential.
Halifax bought 17 per cent of the company from Prudential late on Tuesday at 300p a share, a premium of 70p to Tuesday's closing price. It will now extend the offer to up to 60 per cent of the shares, leaving SJPC with a separate listing.	Halifax acquired the controlling stake from Prudential Insurance in two stages.
The bid is the latest move in Halifax's aggressive internet strategy, begun earlier this year when it poached Jim Spowart from Standard Life bank to set up Intelligent Finance (IF), an online bank due to launch this summer.	The bid forms part of Halifax's strategy to develop internet businesses, such as Intelligent Finance (IF) an online bank.
It hopes to add £5bn of assets to IF by selling a St James's-branded private banking service, run by IF, through SJPC's 1,000-strong salesforce.	In addition, there will be cross-selling opportunities.
'This is an absolutely cracking business,' said James Crosby, Halifax chief executive. 'It increases the scale of our distribution operation in long-term savings and will assist our drive for diversification (away from mortgages).'	There are economies of scale in distribution and opportunities for diversification.
Sir Mark Weinberg, chairman of SJPC, said the company had decided last year to seek a strategic partner to help it use the internet to extend its product range, and began talks with Prudential, which then owned 29 per cent of the shares. 'It became clear that their vision and our vision were not parallel to the extent that there wasn't the opportunity for a value-creating partnership,' he said.	SJPC had been looking for a partner to develop its Internet business for some time.
Analysts said the deal, which is expected to be earnings-enhancing in the first year, would help IF as long as the product, still under wraps, is as exciting as the bank claims.	The deal will help IF and it is expected to increase earnings.
The SJPC salesforce own about 8 per cent of the company and have options on another 8 per cent.	

Answer (1)

Here is a possible précis

Halifax, the mortgage bank, paid £760m (in two stages) to Prudential Insurance to control St James's Place Capital (SJPC) a life assurer with internet potential. The bid formed part of Halifax's strategy to develop internet businesses, such as Intelligent Finance, an on-line bank. The deal offered cross selling opportunities, economies of scale in distribution and opportunities for diversification. SJPC had been looking for a partner to develop its internet business for some time. The deal was intended to help IF as it was intended to increase earnings.

What do you think? Could it be improved? It appears a bit unstructured.

Answer (2)

1   Halifax paid £760m to Prudential to acquire St James's Place Capital.

2   Rationale

(a)   Halifax and SJPC both wanted to develop an internet business and felt they would make good partners.

(b)   Other benefits included cross selling opportunities, economies of scale in distribution, and diversification, and increased earnings

Debrief

Answer 2 is probably too concise. It misses out the fact that Halifax is to launch an on-line bank, a key area of its strategy. However, it is clearer in terms of structure, because it adopts report format and has a heading ('rationale').

Whatever your précis, you have summarised the initial case situation in your own words, and you will then be in a position to analyse it further.

Step 1.5   Carry out an information audit

Now that you have summarised the case, you have an idea of what information you **have** and the information you **do not have**. Look at the checklists starting on the page after next.

(a)   **Rationale**

(i)   Conceivably it could form part of the **unseen** element – but this is unlikely. You will be able to classify the data.

(ii)   You can **derive information by further** analysis – it will feed into Stage 2 Explore the Case Situation.

(iii)   You will become more familiar with the case.

(iv)   It will help your analysis if you can relate different types of information to each other.

(b)   **Process**

You almost certainly will need to do a further analysis but this will feed into Stage 2 Explore the Case Situation.

Tick: yes, we have the data ✓

P: we have some data   P

Cross: no, we don't have this data   X

Alternatively, it may help you to use **colour highlighting** pens to shade each box so you get a visual overview of where you are lacking data.

(c) Notes about the checklist

(i) It is organised **according to business function;** however, the data may not be presented in this way. We suggest you clarify it by identifying where your data lands on the grid below. (Many decisions need to be taken on the basis of **forecast events** or performance. You may be given forecast balance sheets and income statements, or only forecast market data.)

		Orientation	
		Historic	*Future*
Focus	Internal	Internal historic For example: past financial data, existing corporate culture, past decisions, sunk costs, operating constraints, existing customer contracts	Internal future For example: new products planned, new projects, projected future costs or investments, forecasts
	External	External historic For example: past trends, history of regulation	External future For example: market trends, likely economic outrun, potential competitors

(ii) We also suggest you add paragraph references as you go through, especially useful when making connections between different areas.

(d) You will be preparing one of these sheets for Zubinos. **We suggest you photocopy these sheets on to A3.**

(e) The checklist is a suggestion. Add to it if necessary.

Step 1.6 Research the industry and company

Researching the industry is a vital component of your **knowledge**. Very soon you should be able to get an idea of recent developments, key issues and so on.

Exam focus point

This varies from paper to paper. Coffee shops (*Zubinos*) are easy for most people in the developed world to identify with; harder, perhaps, to grasp are the issues involved for a recycling company (*ReuseR*) or an internal construction company (*Domusco*).

Research the industry

In addition to **trade** and **business magazines**, here are some pointers.

www.cimaglobal.com

CIMA students can access the students' page after logging in. It includes case study details, a message board, and discussion threads about the case.

www.ft.com

You may have to register for this, but it gives you a wealth of information about the industry (and other industries).

www.economist.com

Downloadable surveys and articles

www.business.com

An American website, with companies arranged by industry sector and subsector.

You can also try the websites of relevant trade associations. Sometimes, a websearch using an engine such as *Google* can produce good results.

Note down – or suggest – critical success factors for the industry. You may need them later.

	Focus Int/Ext		Orientation		Notes (eg links, implications, possible calculations)
	Int ref	Ext ref	Hist ref	Fut ref	
Date of case scenario					
Managing director					
Your boss					
Financial data					
Balance sheet					
Income statementt					
Cash flow statement					
Notes to accounts					
Further management accounting data					
Product/service costs					
Revenue details					
Contribution					
Performance measures					
Budget vs actual data					
How the firm appraises projects and investments (eg payback, DCF)					
Planning					
Mission and objectives					
Planning process					
Risk management					
Operations data					
Location					
Plant and equipment					
Capacity					
Outsourcing					
Organisation					
Structure					
Culture					
Power					
Key personnel					
Management assumptions					
Systems					
Management info systems					
Mgt reports - content and format					
IT deployment					
Internal controls					
Funding data					
Equity shares					
Long term debt, and repayment schedules					
Working capital					
Cost of capital					
Interest rates					

	Focus Int/Ext		Orientation		Notes (eg links, implications, possible calculations)
	Int ref	Ext ref	Hist ref	Fut ref	
Product service					
Range					
Features					
Competiror					
Quality					
Demand					
Marketing mix					
● Product					
● Price					
● Place (distribution)					
● Promotion					
● People					
● Processes					
● Physical evidence					
Performance measures					
Customers					
Market share					
Market size					
Key customers					
Market research					
Market strategy					
Environment					
Political					
Legal					
Economic					
Social					
Cultural					
Technological					
Ecological/ethical					
Stakeholders					
Competition					
Current					
Potential					
Suppliers					
Current					
Potential					

Step 1.7 Identify relevant technical knowledge

You should by now have refreshed your technical knowledge.

You have to **apply** your knowledge and a good way is to **jot down**, as you go through the case, any areas of knowledge that come to mind and **why** they might be relevant. Do **not** try to use everything you know in the case – it will not all be relevant and at least 80% of the marks on the matrix do not address specific technical knowledge but rather its **use**.

Conclusion

In this stage, we have covered a lot of ground. You've read the case without taking notes, you've read the case whilst taking notes, and you've marked up the case and written down the information – without doing any other work.

This preparation has been essential. There is a lot of data to absorb, and you cannot easily question spot. As stated earlier, the purpose of this stage is to get you familiar with the case data in outline. Then you can analyse it.

3 Explore the case situation

Objective of stage 2: Explore the Case Situation

You should have soundly assessed the fundamentals in Stage 1 *Approach the Case.*

Now you need to start to apply your knowledge, analytical techniques and lateral thinking skills to what you know, so as to tease out more information from the case.

We suggest a number of models you can consider to help you analyse the data. Again, you need to do this systematically.

REMEMBER:

(1) EVERY CASE SITUATION IS UNIQUE SO YOU MAY HAVE TO ADAPT THE TECHNIQUES SUGGESTED HERE.

(2) YOU HAVE THE ASSESSMENT MATRIX SO YOU CAN FOCUS YOUR EFFORTS ON TECHNIQUES MOST RELEVANT.

Step 2.1 Analyse the numbers

Why should you do this now?

(a) Unlike case studies offered by other professional bodies, CIMA's case aims to integrate what you have learned in a **management accounting** context. In your career, one of the skills you will have to offer to future employers is numerical literacy, and the ability to present, mark up and explain the implications and significance of financial data.

(b) The financial data in the case is only **part** of the story, although it is an important part. It will enable you to put other aspects of the case in context. For example, if you work out the cost of capital, you will be able to use it as a discount rate for project evaluation, perhaps.

(c) Remember that you have to say why your analysis is meaningful. What do the numbers mean?

(d) As an accountant, don't be tempted to solve everything by numbers, to the exclusion of other analyses – but numerical analysis should underpin your conclusions.

(e) If you have access to a spreadsheet programme such as Excel, you may do some **simple financial modelling**. How sensitive, for example, is profit to changes in assumptions as to inflation or to any new projects envisaged?

This is good practice if you are taking the exam on computer.

(f)   You may find numerical data in a number of contexts.

Step 1   Review your information audit for the numerical data you have.

Step 2   From **internal company data**, calculate key ratios if possible, and identify trends in past, current and forecast data.

Step 3   Apply numerical analysis to **external data** where available, eg market growth rate.

Step 4   Analyse your data for reasonableness. Are internal growth objectives realistic in the light of market and competitor conditions? What about the cost base needed to generate these revenues?

Step 5   Write a report on the financial position. You will write a report because you **need practice** and you need to tease out the **meaning of the data.**

Below is a possible checklist you could use. Only calculate relevant ratios, and **invent your own if they are meaningful.** If you do invent ratios, note down what you are calculating and what you are trying to prove. Whose viewpoint are you taking: The managers'? Shareholders'?

Analytical tool	Issues	Other areas
Actual vs forecast	Identify trends: will they continue?	Comparable companies Competitors
Revenue	Price, volume and mix of products Limiting factors	PEST, business environment Pricing Market share (eg output volume) Forecast market share
Cost of sales	Step costs Learning curve impact Operational gearing (fixed and variable costs)	Production capacity Labour rates Suppliers Money-saving opportunities
Gross profit percentage	Useful marker – given market conditions	Competitor costs for comparison
Expenses	Activity based costing	Can relate to advertising costs used to purchase market share
Net profit	Useful to help forecast cash flows Sensitivity to changes in revenue, and costs	Company valuation (eg discounted future profits) if a take-over target
Interest cover	Cost of borrowing Project appraisal	Bank, investors, PEST analysis
Dividend cover	Shareholders' expectations Policy	
ROE (Return on equity)	Gives the investor's viewpoint	
ROCE (Return on capital employed)	Accounting measures, easy to manipulate You may need to take a nuanced approach to 'capital' employed for a company financed in part by long-term debt; reviewing **operating** performance by reference only to equity shareholders may not be 'helpful'.	Other firms

Analytical tool	Issues	Other areas
Retained profit/assets employed	Future investment in the business	
Non-current assets (gross and net)	Age and valuation (eg at cost) Valuation (historic vs market)	Capacity utilisation
Revenue/non-current assets		Compare with other firms
Revenue periods • Inventory • Receivables • Payables	Establish operating cycle, as cash can be released from working capital if managed more tightly	
Working capital/assets employed	Liquidity? Financing costs?	
Current/quick ratio	Working capital cash flows and timing	
Gearing	Can be calculated in a number of different ways	
Debt/equity	Timing of cash flows	
Earnings per share	Shareholders	
Price/earnings ratio	Company valuation	
WACC	Project appraisal financing	
Trends in share price	Shareholder concerns. Raising money	

Question

Presenting financial data

In the case study, you will be required to present financial information, which may well be written for a non-financial manager. You will need to avoid jargon or making too many assumptions as to what the manager might know. You will also need to explain what it means and what implications it has. We reproduce here a question from an exam of a former CIMA syllabus.

In a number of cities, music societies, which are charitable organisations, provide classical music concerts by operating concert halls and supporting orchestras employing full-time musicians. Earned income arises mainly from giving concerts, with additional earned income from catering activities, ancillary sales programmes, CDs and cassettes, souvenirs, and hiring out the concert hall facilities. The earned income is much less than the cost of running the orchestras and concert halls, which are also supported by subsidies in the form of annual grants from local government authorities and the central government, and from business sponsorship, which is a form of corporate public relations expenditure.

The broad aims of the music societies are to provide the best possible standard of live performance of classical music in their home cities (supported by grants from their local government authority) and in other areas of the country (supported by grants from the central government), and to encourage new music and musicians.

As they are charities, music societies do not aim to make a profit. Any surpluses are invested in improvements to the concert halls and spent on additional musicians.

Costs are largely fixed and are broadly 75% orchestral and 25% concert hall and administration (mostly staff). Levels of remuneration, especially for musicians, are low, considering the skills and training required.

The scope for increases in income is very limited. Grants will not increase, and may decrease. The orchestras (allowing for rehearsal time) are fully occupied. Fees for engagements elsewhere in the country and abroad are falling due to the competition from orchestras from other countries.

The chairman of the manufacturing company for which you are a management accountant has recently become a non-executive director of the local music society (X Music), which owns the concert hall and employs the orchestra. His first impressions are that the music is probably excellent, though he is no expert, but that the data available on operations is very limited.

Some comparisons are available with another music society (Y Music) in a smaller city: these are given below.

Required

On the basis of the available data, prepare a report for the chairman, comparing the key features of the business and financial performance of X Music with that of Y Music.

Comparative data

	20X7		20X2 (5 years ago)		20W7 (10 years ago)	
Number of performances	X	Y	X	Y	X	Y
Concerts in home city	74	84	77	91	75	91
Other concerts in home country	63	26	88	38	81	52
Overseas concerts	8	8	15	–	11	–
TV/radio/recording	5	11	9	5	14	9
Total	150	129	189	134	181	152
Income						
Concerts in home city	698	1,043	540	717	410	459
Other concerts in home country	916	762	697	361	518	371
Overseas concerts	282	333	154	–	100	–
TV/radio/recording	70	210	72	128	53	118
Other earned income	466	133	76	41	56	22
Business sponsorship	397	607	141	135	56	44
Total earned income	2,829	3,088	1,680	1,382	1,193	1,014
Grant – central government	1,300	1,500	900	1,000	500	900
Grant – local government authority	655	950	150	750	400	500
Total income	4,784	5,538	2,730	3,132	2,093	2,414
Total costs	4,872	5,356	2,703	3,147	2,059	2,402
Surplus/(deficit)	(88)	182	27	(15)	34	12
Cumulative surplus/(deficit)	(686)	311	80	(26)	141	62

REPORT

To: The Chairman
From: Management Accountant   Date: 3 July 20X8
Subject: Comparison of the performances of X Music and Y Music

This report provides a comparison of the key features of the business and financial performance of X Music and Y Music.

1   EXECUTIVE SUMMARY

1.1   **X Music's** results for **20X7** show a **marked deterioration** in financial performance. The society reported a **deficit** of £88,000 in 20X7 (compared with surpluses of £27,000 and £34,000 in 20X2 and 20W7 respectively) and a worrying cumulative deficit of £686,000 (compared with cumulative surpluses of £80,000 in 20X2 and £141,000 in 20W7).

1.2   **Y Music**, on the other hand, was **more successful** and reported a **surplus** of £182,000 and a cumulative surplus of £311,000 in 20X7. A deficit of £15,000 in 20X2 and a surplus of £12,000 in 20W7, and a cumulative deficit in 20X2 (£26,000) and a cumulative surplus in 20W7 (£62,000) point to the possibility that the society's **results have been fluctuating widely** over the last decade, however.

1.3   An analysis of business and financial data for the two societies highlights a number of factors which may well have played their part in these results.

2   NUMBER OF PERFORMANCES

2.1   Since 20W7, the **number of performances** given by **X Music** has **dropped** by 17% (from 181 to 150), while the number given by **Y Music** has **dropped** by 15% (from 152 to 129). The similarity in these figures tends to suggest that both societies have been **affected to a similar degree by competition from foreign orchestras**. Despite this fall, however, Y Music has reported both a surplus and a cumulative surplus in 20X7.

2.2   The **number of performances of all types of concert** given by **X Music** in **20X7** have **dropped** from those in 20W7 and 20X2. The number of concerts in other areas of the country (not the home city) in particular has dropped by over 28% to 63 from the 88 reported in 20X2. The number of performances in the home city has remained fairly constant (75 in 20W7 and 74 in 20X7).

2.3   **Y Music** has seen a significant **fall in the number of concerts played elsewhere in the home country** (a drop of 50% from 52 in 20W7 to 26 in 20X7). From playing no concerts abroad in 20X2, Y Music played 8 in 20X7 (as did X Music), and made 11 TV/radio/recording appearances in 20X7, compared with only five in 20X2.

2.4   In 20X7, **Y Music** gave 84 **concerts in its home city**, 10 **more than** the number of performances by **X Music** in its home city. This is **surprising** given that Y Music is based in a smaller city with, one assumes, a smaller concert-going population. **Overall**, however, **X Music** gave 150 performances in 20X7, 21 **more than Y Music**, principally because it made 63 performances in other areas of the country. X Music's disappointing results cannot therefore be attributed to the number of concerts it performed.

3   INCOME

3.1   **Both societies** have reported a **significant increase** in total earned income over the ten-year period. X Music's earned income was 137% higher in 20X7 (£2,829,000) compared with that in 20W7 (£1,193,000). Y Music's was 205% higher (£3,088,000) compared with £1,014,000. It is, however, the **income per concert** that has **led to X Music's poor financial performance**, as illustrated by the following figures for 20X7.

	20X7	
	X Music	Y Music
Income per concert in home city	£9,432	£12,417
Income per concert in home country	£14,540	£29,308
Income per overseas concert	£35,250	£41,625
Income per TV/radio/recording event	£14,000	£19,091

3.2 X Music achieves a significantly lower income per performance for all types of performance than that achieved by Y Music. The difference is most marked when comparing **concerts in the home country**, with **Y Music's income per performance being over double that of X Music's**. This could be because audience sizes are smaller at X Music's performances or ticket prices may be lower, but on the basis of the data provided it is not possible to state definite causes. If you were able to provide me with attendance figures and information about ticket prices I could provide you with a more detailed analysis.

3.3 **X Music's other earned income** of £466,000 in 20X7 (16% of total earned income) is significantly **higher than that of Y Music** (£133,000, representing 4% of total earned income) and hence its catering and merchandising activities are probably considerably more effective than those of Y Music. X Music's figure also compares well with the £56,000 earned ten years previously.

3.4 On the other hand, **business sponsorship** appears to have been extremely **lucrative for Y Music** in 20X7, bringing in £607,000, almost the same income as that earned from concerts in other parts of the country. X Music's business sponsorship at £397,000 was only 65% of Y Music's, although both societies have shown significant increases from the levels in 20W7 (X Music £56,000; Y Music £44,000) and 20X2 (X Music £141,000; Y Music £135,000).

3.5 The **grants** from both central government and the local authority **awarded to Y Music** in 20W7, 20X2 and 20X7 were **higher than those awarded to X Music**. In 20X7, grants represented 44% of Y Music's total income, compared with 41% of X Music's, with Y Music receiving £2,450,000 in grants compared with £1,955,000 by X Music. **Y Music's committee** appear to be **far more effective** in **applying for grants** and X Music's committee should be encouraged to actively pursue this source of income.

4 COSTS

4.1 Despite the fact that X Music put on more performances than Y Music in 20W7, 20X2 and 20X7, **X Music's costs have always been lower**. In 20X7, X Music's costs per performance were £32,480 (£4,872,000/150) whereas Y Music's were £41,519 (£5,356,000/129). Given that one would expect overseas concerts to be the most expensive to put on, and both societies gave eight overseas concerts, this cost difference **may highlight particular cost control skills at X Music** (or alternatively, of course, particularly poor cost control at Y Music). On the other hand, because 75% of the costs are related to the orchestra, it **could point to lower quality performances by X Music** (which might explain X Music's lower income per performance) **or to different forms of performance** by the two societies, the two forms requiring different numbers of musicians.

5 RECOMMENDATION

5.1 Given that X Music's total costs were not covered by total income in 19X7, and that there is no guaranteed level of grant income, X Music should carry out a detailed review of expenditure.

Signed: Management Accountant

Comment on answer

This answer is a very thorough examination of the issues. In terms of format, some of the comparative data could have been put into tables, rather than being incorporated in the narrative.

Exam focus point

It is quite possible that the financial data you will receive in the pre-seen or unseen will be incomplete and you may need to make assumptions.

Step 2.2 General environmental analysis (PEST) and trends

PEST analysis and its variants should be familiar to you from the **Business Strategy** paper, and the key issue here is to ensure that you have covered and prioritised everything that you can. You have already identified the information you have. To help you prioritise, you might wish to grade your PEST into order of importance (High, Medium, Low) perhaps with justifications.

Para in case	Type of factor	Comment and significance	Likely importance H, M, L
	Political		
	Legal		
	Economic		
	Social		
	Cultural		
	Technological		
	Ecological		
	Stakeholders		

Question   PEST

Airbus has built the world's largest passenger plane, the A380 ('super-jumbo'), seating between 550 and 650 people, challenging the Boeing 747. In December 2004, Airbus' main shareholder EADS, which has an 80% stake, revealed that the project was £1.6 billion over budget, at more than £8.4 billion. The UK's BAE systems owns 20% of Airbus. The UK government offered launch aid of £530m to get it started. This is a large plane, to be marketed at the major airlines. Airbus promises a 15% to 20% fall in aircraft operating costs. The terms of the launch aid were secret. (However, many years ago, the EU and US agreed on a formula for assessing state aid to their relative industries. American aircraft makers enjoyed indirect support thanks to the demands of the arms industry. Boeing and the US government are concerned that the launch aid breaches this agreement.)

Boeing is developing a smaller plane, the Dreamliner. Airbus and Boeing differ on the respective markets for these aircraft. Airbus believes that there will be a market for large jets flying between central hubs, where people will change planes for onward journeys. Boeing believes that the market for smaller, point-to-point aircraft is larger.

Below are some PEST factors, taken at random.

(a)   Classify them as of High, Medium or Low importance to Airbus (for the purposes of this Workbook).

(b)   Write a report about what the issues are.

(c)   Comment on the suggested report prepared by BPP for (b) above.

Factor

1   Better video-conferencing, eg via the Internet
2   More working at home
3   Greater demand in rich countries for tailor-made holidays
4   Genetically modified food
5   EU-US disputes at the World Trade Organisation
6   Deregulation in air markets (in terms of destination served)
7   Ageing population in western world
8   Political instability in Asia (N Korea)
9   Air traffic is projected to rise 5% pa to 2030
10   Stricter asylum and immigration laws applied over Europe
11   Continued expansion of high speed train networks in Europe
12   Disruption to tourism as a result of the terrorist attack on September 11, 2001 and subsequent wars
13   Disruption to travel as a result of the SARS epidemic in 2003
14   Growth of 'low cost' airlines in Europe flying to obscure airports
15   Airports will have to change

Answer

(a)   Classification of importance

You may well disagree with these – but you need a rationale.

High

5. May well affect financing of the project and Airbus's status as a company.

6. Firms can compete on different routes. This may restrain demand for jumbo jets and build demand for the dreamliner: but this might be overridden by overall growth.

9. A huge increase. Airports cannot expand fast enough and there is only so much space: bigger aircraft are one solution.

11. High speed trains compete with aircraft for speed and are often more convenient; more relevant to short haul flights than long distance flights.

15. Airports need to be big enough to take the planes

Medium

1. May reduce demand for business travel.

3. Affects destinations people want to fly to, and the market for scheduled and chartered flights: perhaps people will prefer smaller planes.

8. May slow demand for air traffic, or increase economic problems in the region.

12 and 13. Many airlines suffered since 11/9/2001 and this might lead to a delay in orders. Whether the 'war on terrorism' will lead to a permanent fall or change in demand for air travel – especially in growth markets such as Asia – is hard to say. Similarly, the long term impact of the SARS epidemic is not known. In practical terms, **security issues** may become more significant in the design and operation of large aircraft. In June 2003, Emirates, a growing airline, announced a large order for A380s on the assumption that passenger volumes would continue to grow.

14. Low cost carriers like cheap planes; perhaps the A380 is too big.

Low

2. Affects other transport firms but not airlines, as this deals with normal domestic commuting more than international business trips.

4. Nothing to do with Airbus at all!

7. Demand can come from elsewhere; population is getting wealthier in Asia.

10. Affects airline operations but not overall demand.

(b)   REPORT

To: A manager
From: Consultant
Date:

Re: Environmental influences on Airbus

1   Introduction

1.1   Airbus is one of the world's largest manufacturers of aircraft. It received £530m from the British government in launch aid for the new A380 super-jumbo jet, to compete directly with the Boeing 747.

2   Political factors

2.1   Airbus has always been a controversial feature of the political landscape, owing to its funding arrangements. The US government believes the funding is anti-competitive and potentially damaging to Boeing. Airbus counters that US companies benefit from huge defence contracts and state grants, which act as hidden subsidies.

2.2   The EU and USA are in dispute over other trade issues, and so there may be some further political fallout as a result of the proposed funding arrangements.

2.3   Political factors may also affect the stability of the Asian market, one of the world's growth areas. North Korea has a nuclear capability. There are concerns that China will invade Taiwan if Taiwan declares independence.

2.4   Aircraft have been used as weapons in the terrorist attack on September 11, 2001. The ramifications of this for the market for large aircraft has yet to be determined. Aviation is also affected by the price of oil, again affected by political instability.

3   Economic factors

3.1   Airbus's proposal for the A380 was based on predictions of increased demand for air travel, fuelled by overall prosperity and economic growth.

3.2   Much of this travel is discretionary, such as business or holiday travel.

3.3   Governments may have limited money to spend on increasing airport size. Super-jumbos, by carrying more people, can reduce the need for extra flights.

3.4   The effect of deregulation may be to undermine the business model on which Airbus depends.

4   Social and cultural factors

4.1   Air travel is scheduled to grow; however, evidence seems to suggest that holidaymakers prefer individual holidays to particular destinations rather than general packages. This might reduce demand for mass travel between hubs.

4.2   SARS may affect popular perceptions of the riskiness of overseas travel.

5   Technological factors

5.1   Airbus might be interested in other technologies, but technology can influence underlying customer demand. Will video and internet conferencing reduce the underlying demand for business travel? Will supersonic travel be preferred?

6   Conclusion

6.1   Airbus is investing a lot of money, taking a calculated risk that economic and market conditions will justify airplanes of this size.

6.2   The launch aid financing is also at risk owing to political factors.

(c) *Comment on the report*

1   Some **relevant** items are mentioned which did not appear on the list – this shows **business awareness.**

2   Rightly, the report does not cover the items which we classified as '**low**' on the list. They are just not relevant.

3   The factors are classified in logical order. However, more could be done to draw out the interrelationships between them.

4   There is a useful conclusion summarising the environmental factors affecting the product **concept** and the **launch aid.**

Step 2.3 Analyse the business environment and competitive strategy

The technical **knowledge** required should be familiar to you from the **Business Strategy** paper, but the tools employed are relevant to structuring your analysis of the case study. You will be using these tools to obtain a deeper understanding of the case and the context.

(a)   The key issues are: customers, suppliers, and competitors, and how they impact on the business – the important issue is to identify or bring to light key issues hinted at or stated directly in the case data.

(b)   What is the industry's stage of development? Is it an **emergent industry,** a **mature industry** or a **declining industry?**

(c)   You may have to deal with a **conglomerate** or a firm operating on a number of different industry sectors (eg Virgin: planes, trains, personal finance, recorded music, soft drinks). Each sector might have different characteristics.

(d)   We also suggest you carry out a **five forces analysis.** Classify each force as High, Medium or Low (H, M, L) in impact.

(e)   What is the firm's competitive strategy?

Five forces and industry analysis

(a)   **Identify the type of industry(s)**

	What industries does the company operate in?	Classify as emergent, mature, or declining
1		
2		
3		

(b)   **Threat of new entrants. (Add others if you wish.)**

	Item	Comment
1	High capital costs to enter?	
2	Is there a strong brand?	
3	Is the industry attractive?	
4	Does the case suggest new entrants?	
5	Ease of exit (if declining sector)	
	Threat of new entrants: high, medium or low (H, M, L)?	

(c) **Substitute products**

	Item	Comment
1	Can other industries provide the same benefit?	
2	Does the case evidence any threats?	
3	Other considerations	
	Threat from substitute products: high, medium, low (H, M, L)?	

(d) **Customer bargaining power and marketing issues**

	Item		Comment
1	Consumer or business to business? If B-to-B, any issues in customers' own markets?		
2	Total turnover		
3	Market size		Current and new markets
4	Market share		Compared to major competitors
5	Does the organisation really understand its customers and their needs?		
6	Can key segments be identified in the data? If yes, what are they and what percentage of turnover do they represent?		
	Segment 1 2 3 4 5 6	Percentage turnover	Do they have different needs?
7	Trends in turnover and other sales performance indicators		
8	Does the case identify any Key Customers who account for a significant proportion of turnover? • If Yes, note details • Is it possible to do a customer profitability analysis? • Are there some customers who are not profitable?		Are they profitable, loyal, happy?
9	Are current customers loyal or beginning to defect?		
10	Are customers price sensitive?		
11	Does the case identify customers and markets not served?		
12	Can customers obtain the same benefits easily elsewhere?		
13	Does the organisation have a coherent marketing strategy based on the 7Ps? Product – Price – Promotion – Place – People – Process – Physical evidence		
14	Does the organisation consider building long-term customer relationships?		
15	What is the branding policy?		
	Customer bargaining power: high, medium, low (H, M, L)?		

Suppliers and resources

	Item	Comment
1	Supplier industries – what resources does the business consume?	
2	Does the case detail suppliers?	
3	Trends in input costs – and volatility	
4	Are key suppliers identified? If so, whom? How close is the relationship?	
5	Ease of sourcing supplies from other/new suppliers	
6	Can firm easily pass on increases in input prices to customers?	
7	Is the supply chain managed strategically?	
	Supplier bargaining power: high, medium, low (H, M, L)?	

(f) **Competitors**

	Item	Comment
1	Does the case identify **particular** current competitors? If yes: • What are the competitors? • What are the competitors' competitive strategy?	
2	Does the case suggest potential new competitors in the current industry? Substitute products?	
	Competitive rivalry: high, medium, low (H, M, L)?	

(g) **Identify the current competitive strategy**

Cost leadership indicators	Differentiation indicators
• Price competitive • Production efficiencies	• Evidence of special products/ services • Higher prices • R&D department
Cost focus indicators	**Differentiation focus indicators**
• Segmentation • Cheapest for segment • Conscious decision to restrict customer base	• Conscious decision to restrict customer base • Needs of segments consciously identified and incorporated in decision making

Summarise the business environment by combining your '5 forces' analysis and PEST in a report or mind map.

To prepare yourself for **this** case study exam, we recommend you use a variety of techniques to stimulate your thinking. So far, we've given checklists and asked you to write reports. However because all the elements of the business environment are interconnected, we suggest you draw a simple **mindmap** or **spider diagram**.

- Start at the centre of the page
- Work outwards linking ideas with lines

More about Airbus. Review your PEST analysis of Airbus, and consider the data below.

There are relatively few aircraft makers in the world. Airbus's main competitor is Boeing. Airbus is giving up its status as a consortium in which each participant (Aerospatiale of France, BAe of the UK, DA of Germany and Casa of Spain) had the right to make part of the plane. It is turning into a more normal company. Governments have a great interest in the aerospace manufacturing industry for defence reasons, and Aerospatiale is part owned by the French government. Aircraft engines are supplied by Rolls Royce, Pratt and Whitney and GE. Furthermore, whilst Airbus is going ahead with a super-jumbo, Boeing has indicated it will not compete. Instead Boeing is seeking orders for a new supersonic plane.

The business model underpinning A380 assumes that people will fly from hub airport to hub airport and change on to connecting flights.

Boeing is developing a fast, supersonic plane, the Dreamliner, holding fewer passengers than the Airbus A380. It will, however, fly from 'point' to 'point'.

Required

Draw a mindmap of the general and competitive environment.

Answer

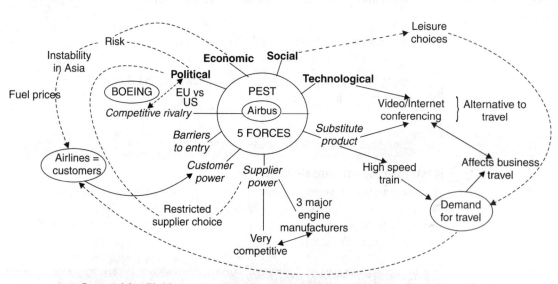

Demand for flights

The mind map technique, as you will see, enables you to make connections and see things as a whole. Note the environmental influences on Airbus's customers, who have significant power. You will also note the interconnection between technological factors and substitute products. Doubtless you could develop this further.

In practice, we have moved to the synthesis stage.

Step 2.4   **Audit the product/service portfolio**

Again, drawing on **Business Strategy**, you need clearly to define what is it the business does. As you are analysing the case study, you need to think a bit more deeply than just 'widgets' or products, but to try to link it with the customer analysis you have done earlier.

Step 1   Define the product in terms of customer needs satisfied.

- Customers buy a benefit: this can have a physical and a service component.
- Are customers' needs being satisfied in terms of the features offered by the product?

The purpose of doing this is that it can help enrich your understanding of substitute products that satisfy the same needs.

Step 2 Identify product and service elements.

Step 3 Use the Boston matrix to identify how the product or service is positioned.

Step 4 Use your numerical skills to identify and analyse product costs and profitability.

Fireclown Software produces and sells computer software that deals with timesheets and project management. The firm makes versions for a Microsoft Access database and also an SQL server database. Charges start at £2,400 per user on a declining scale, so with 10 users (the maximum recommended for the ACCESS version), the fee per user works out at £1,600, or £16,000 in total. The firm will charge extra for installation, and will offer either a standard shell, or tailor solutions to clients' individual needs. The firm charges 20% of the initial purchase costs per year for on-line support, and offers free upgrades. The typical Fireclown client is a firm that uses job production, that requires people in different departments to work together effectively, and that bills costs to clients, hence the importance of the timesheet software. The average 'age' of Fireclown's clients is ten years, and the average number of users per client is five.

Required

Audit the product/service portfolio.

Step 1 What is Fireclown offering?

Customers need to co-ordinate, plan and monitor complex projects and to bill their clients. Fireclown Software offers a **solution** to these needs.

Step 2 Product and service elements

The 'product' is the software, and the 'services' are the after-sales support, the installation, and so on.

Step 3 Fireclown's product portfolio

In the case, you may apply like models such as the **Boston matrix**. Here, there is not enough information for you to do so. What data would you need for this?

- Old and new products identified
- Old and new markets identified
- Cash flow, profit and growth data

Step 4 Identify product costs and/or customer profitability, if possible.

In Fireclown's case, if a customer stays for more than five years, the annual service fee of 20% of initial installation cost will be worth more to Fireclown than the initial software cost.

For example, take a customer with **five** users and **ten** years' service.

1 user £2,400 ⎤
10 users – cost per user £1,600 ⎦ 5 users, say £2,000 per user
Initial fee 5 users @ £2,000 = £10,000 initial revenue
Service contract = £10,000 @ 20% over 10 years = £20,000

From this, we can hazard a guess that 2/3rds of Fireclown's revenue is from **service** income **if the average customer 'age' is ten years**.

Step 5 Competitive strategy – see next question.

Step 2.5 How does the business add value?

Here, you can apply your knowledge of **value chain analysis**, say, and other techniques such as **functional cost analysis** to identify what is special about the business.

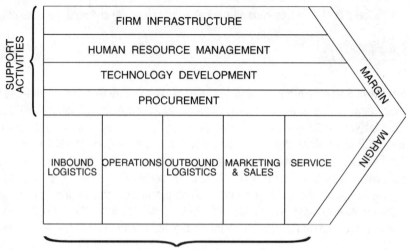

You can then comment on each area of the value chain.

Question

Value adding

Fireclown continued

How does Fireclown add value and what is its competitive strategy?

Answer

Inputs are minimal as Fireclown is in the business of creating, selling and servicing intellectual property. **Technology development** is perhaps the most significant aspect of its operations. **Outbound logistics** are likely to be relatively minimal but, as we have seen, **after-sales service** is a critical element of its revenue.

As for **competitors**, you might like to jot down what you consider its current competitive strategy to be. Fireclown, arguably, is pursuing a strategy of focus (based on size of user base) and differentiation.

Step 2.6 Identify information systems management controls and processes

Here you will need to draw on your knowledge of **Risk and Control Strategy**, as this could form an aspect of the case study requirement. This deals with the information and control systems available to the organisation in the case study. Here is a checklist.

	Issue	Comment
1	**Information technology**	
1.1	What are the structural arrangements for IT? (eg IT department, delegated to users, information, outsourced)	
1.2	Who looks after IT strategy and security?	

	Issue	Comment
1.3	What is the role of IT in the development of the company? (McFarlan's grid) • Factory • Support • Turnround • Strategic	
1.4	Is IT use considered within the business strategy and is its implementation harmonised with it?	
1.5	Is e-commerce relevant and does the firm have a stance towards this development?	
1.6	Main systems • Operational reporting • Corporate reporting	
2	**Knowledge and information**	
2.1	What internal communication systems are in use – eg paper, email, intranet? Is this advisable?	
2.2	Do managers receive good information in terms of the performance of the business (ACCURATE mnemonic)?	
2.3	Knowledge management – is information shared or hoarded?	
3	**Risk**	
3.1	Does current IT set up expose the firm to risk?	
4	**Management and internal control systems**	
4.1	How are activities and resources controlled in the organisation?	
4.2	Is the management accounting system well designed and managed?	
4.3	Who sets performance targets, and are they effective?	
4.4	What is the extent of centralisation versus divisionalisation?	
4.5	Is reporting timely?	
4.6	Are management accounting and information systems regularly audited?	
4.7	Generally, are principles of good corporate governance followed?	
4.8	Is the business susceptible to fraud (computer-based or otherwise)?	

EF Co is a long-established company which manufactures a large range of computers, from mainframe to portable, on a single site. Its turnover is about £500 million per annum. The company has recently undergone a major information systems change involving the following.

(a)   Capital expenditure of £50 million over three years (the NPV will be £7 million)

(b)   Workforce cut from 10,000 to 7,000 employees

(c)   Radical changes to work practices, both in the manufacturing systems (use of CAD/CAM) and reorganisation of managerial and administrative functions

The new Managing Director needs to identify and understand some indicators which can be used to evaluate the success or otherwise of this change.

Required

Recommend to the Managing Director up to five key indicators that he can use and explain why each is relevant to his requirements.

Answer

REPORT

To: The Managing Director, EF Co
From: Accountant
Date: 23 November 20X5
Subject: Recommendations for key indicators

In evaluating the effect of the recent changes within EF Co the following indicators can be recommended.

(a)   **Added value per employee** is useful as a possible measure of **productivity.** This could, for example, be defined as sales income less bought in services (including finance charges) and material, divided by the number of employees.

The company has proceeded down the route of replacing personnel with capital equipment. The productivity of the remaining workforce should therefore be significantly greater than before.

The **information** for this indicator is readily available from the **usual management accounting sources.** Knowing the cost of capital, the savings in payroll costs, and the budgeted throughput, a target added value per employee can be calculated that represents breakeven on the financial effect of the changes.

A **weakness** with this indicator is that certain elements are susceptible to **changes in economic conditions** as well as to internal changes.

Any business process re-engineering of this nature should bring about significant gains in productivity by **eliminating inefficient and outdated processes** altogether. New procedures should reflect **best practice** in the industry, and, for this reason, some use of **benchmarking against competitors** in the industry is also recommended.

(b)   **Responsiveness** to customers and the marketplace is vital.

The purpose of the changes is not simply to save money, but to enable the company to **react speedily to consumer needs.** The information technology industry is becoming a prime example of 'relationship marketing', wherein the supplier is attempting to become closer to each customer. This is a means of seeking competitive advantage. Thus the organisation will be trying to behave as if it were 'lean and mean' and provide fast response to each customer, not simply manufacturing 'boxes'. Hence the introduction of CAD/CAM.

An **important indicator** therefore, as an example of speed of reaction, is the **speed at which bespoke customer needs are met.** To make this indicator consistent, project times from agreement of customer specification to delivery need to be measured.

A **problem** with this is that the size of the project will affect the speed of delivery. Perhaps project times could be divided by the sales margin for comparability and consistency. The lower the ratio the better. A company target figure should be established as a yardstick.

(c) **Financial** indicators, such as **management accounting ratios** (credit risk, receivables days, WIP turnround etc) should also be used. Although **care** is needed in **interpretation**, because of distortions caused by accounting policies and the need for consistency from period to period, the **traditional measures** of working capital efficiency (summarised perhaps as 'working capital days', namely receivables days plus inventory days less supplier days) are **as relevant as ever** to modern industry.

The improvement in the **manufacturing systems** will have included measures designed to improve **inventory management** and **financial control**, probably one of the variants of JIT (just-in-time) and perhaps ABM (activity based management) or other relevant costing/management systems. The effect on cash flow should be dramatic once the new systems are in place.

These cost savings can be set against the capital costs incurred in developing new systems. Standard **investment appraisal** techniques can be used here: current thinking suggests that a balanced measure, incorporating NPV, payback and IRR gives the most rounded view. In addition **project management measures** relating to budget, timetables and quality (availability, response etc) can be used.

(d) **Strategic direction** is extremely difficult to assess as it involves such long-term factors. Major systems change of the type undertaken is certainly part of a strategic process and its success can only be seen by reference to the **overall market position** of the company and its **reputation**. The value of the **brand name** may be measured, but such measures are **subjective**. Better is a **long-term tracking of share price** and **market share**.

Although **strategic planning is long-term**, IT can sit awkwardly with this, as so much **technology is short-term** in nature, with manufacturers reducing product life cycles in their quest for competitive advantage. This means that IT-based decisions may need to be changed within the life of a particular strategy. This problem can to some extent be addressed by a formal **Information Systems Planning** exercise, which creates a framework for development, providing guidelines over a period of time to ensure that activities fit into strategic criteria.

(e) **Critical success factors** can be used. Each CSF will already have been ascribed one or more performance indicators. CSFs are fundamental to the strategic direction of the company. Here, the changes to be evaluated are more than just small improvements to individual parts of the company, they are a fundamental change to the very nature and shape of the organisation.

The ultimate measure of their effectiveness could be said to be in the **bottom line results** of EF Ltd; however, other factors will also be relevant, for example, **reliability indicators**. This might take the form of warranty claims/sales, or claims/number of products supplied, or may be based on customer surveys measuring the elusive characteristic of 'customer satisfaction'. The reputation of the company, and thus its potential to generate future cash flows – the definition of the value of the enterprise – depends on the quality of its service. It is important to know that the reduction in personnel numbers, and the introduction of automation have not compromised quality.

The above should be read in the light of the assumption that **systems development** is undertaken in general to **meet business needs** and **fulfil organisational objectives**. These might be categorised as:

- Reductions in cost base
- Investment in IT infrastructure
- Responding to, or anticipating, changing market conditions
- Ensuring that IT supports strategic plans

It is only by setting **appropriate performance indicators**, such as the above, that the success of systems development can be **measured**.

In conclusion, the measurement of the key components of the strategy of the company are vital to the **control and updating** of that strategy as it links **'hard'** cost/benefit analysis with **'softer'** areas which are difficult to quantify and often subjective.

Signed: Accountant

Step 2.7 Identify key issues in structure, culture and personnel

Structure and culture can be either a strength or a weakness, especially as senior management sets the tone. Although you only have so much information to go on, it is useful to have a reasoned opinion in your own mind. This may only be an opinion, but it will give you an underlying rationale for any changes.

(a) **Structure**

Issue	Comment
Step 1 Draw an organisation chart, if the case has not already provided you with one.	
Step 1.1 What sort of departmentation approach is used (eg functional, matrix)?	
Step 2 Does the case data indicate any problems with the current organisation structure, such as reporting/communication, co-ordination, corporate governance, focus on the business?	
Step 3 Does the case data offer opportunities for you to benchmark the performance of different departments with other firms? If so, how does the firm compare?	
Step 4 Identify any outsourcing arrangements currently in force, and arrive at a reasoned judgement as to how effective they are in terms of operations, risk and financial security.	
Step 5 Identify any possible opportunities for outsourcing and note feasibility.	
Step 6 In your opinion, is the structure a strength or a weakness in the light of the situation facing the business and why?	
Step 7 Recommend improvements: what structure (in brief) would you consider better?	

(b) **Culture**

Issue	Comment
Step 1 What does the case tell you about the culture of the organisation and its management? Classify it, if you can, according to a framework used in your earlier studies.	
Step 2 Is it a strength or a weakness?	

(c)   **Personnel and human resources management (HRM)**

Issue	Comment
Step 1 Who are the key people?	
Step 2 Do they have objectives which can affect the performance of the firm?	
Step 3 What influence do they have: • Internally? • Externally?	
Step 4 Does the firm have a succession plan?	
Step 5 Is there any evidence of poor industrial relations?	
Step 6 Is there a strategy for HRM and is it aligned with the business strategy?	
Step 7 What are its employment policies (contracts, rewords, performance appraisal)?	
Step 8 Does the firm invest in training?	
Step 9 Is there evidence of high staff turnover?	
Step 10 Does the firm have skills and competences base needed for the future?	
Step 11 What is the quality of the management team, given the challenges facing the business?	
Step 12 Do managers have a shared vision?	
Step 13 Do they understand their rules and responsibilities under corporate governance regulations (eg Turnbull)?	

Step 2.8 Identify investor objectives, capital structure and other stakeholder objectives

	Investors	Comment
Step 1	Identify share owning structure: • Privately owned? • Publicly traded?	
Step 2	Note information as to the return shareholders and investors are expecting from the company – use comparative information.	
Step 3	Note trends in the share price, if this information is given.	
Step 4	If you have a P/E ratio and a market value, calculate a **possible value for the business**.	
Step 5	Do you have information to calculate the WACC? If yes, do so.	
Step 6	Note comparative information about other companies for a benchmark as to shareholder expectations.	
Step 7	Note data as to the risk of the company (eg the beta).	

	Investors	Comment
Step 8	Review gearing ratios.	
Step 9	Would you invest in this company?	
Step 10	**Managers** Objectives Remuneration Performance	
Step 11	**Employees** Objectives	
Step 12	Lenders Exposure Relationship	
Step 13	Government (central and local) Relationship Power to influence	
Step 14	Customers and suppliers See '5 forces' analysis	
Step 15	Community Pressure groups etc	

The purpose

of this is to indicate to you the possible objectives of the actors in the case.

Exam focus point

> The issues of Betas, WACC and so on may come up, and it is conceivable the company valuation will also be something you have to do. The March 2005 case, Zubinos, required a valuation in connection with a takeover bid.

 Question   **Market values**

PMS is a private limited company with intentions of obtaining a stock market listing in the near future. The company is wholly equity financed at present, but the directors are considering a new capital structure prior to it becoming a listed company.

PMS operates in an industry where the average asset beta is 1.2. The company's business risk is estimated to be similar to that of the industry as a whole. The current level of earnings before interest and taxes is £400,000. This earnings level is expected to be maintained for the foreseeable future.

The rate of return on riskless assets is at present 10% and the return on the market portfolio is 15%. These rates are post-tax and are expected to remain constant for the foreseeable future.

PMS is considering introducing debt into its capital structure by one of the following methods.

(a) £500,000   10% Debentures at par, secured on land and buildings of the company
(b) £1,000,000 12% Unsecured loan stock at par

The rate of corporation tax is expected to remain at 33% and interest on debt is tax deductible.

Required

Calculate, for *each* of the *two* options:

(a) Values of equity *and* total market values
(b) Debt/equity ratios
(c) Cost of equity

The first step is to calculate the present cost of equity using the **capital asset pricing model** (CAPM):

$$K_e = R_f + [R_m - R_f]\beta$$

where
K_e	=	cost of equity (expected % return)
R_f	=	risk free rate of return (10%)
β	=	beta value (1.2)
R_m	=	market rate of return (15%)

In this case: K_e = 10% + (15 – 10)% × 1.2
= 16%

This cost of equity can now be applied in the **dividend valuation model** to find the **total market value of the firm**. It is assumed that all earnings are distributed as dividend; earnings and therefore dividends do not grow.

$$p_0 = d_0/K_e$$

where
p_0	=	market value
d_0	=	current level of dividends (post tax)
K_e	=	cost of equity
p_0	=	£0.4m × 0.67/0.16
	=	£1.675m

(a) The situation under the different scenarios can be summarised as follows.

	Current £'000	Scen 1 £'000	Scen 2 £'000
Profit before interest and tax	400.0	400.0	400.0
Less interest	(0.0)	(50.0)	(120.0)
	400.0	350.0	280.0
Less tax at 33%	(132.0)	(115.5)	(92.4)
Distributable profits	268.0	234.5	187.6

According to the basic theory of capital structure developed by **Modigliani and Miller**, the market value of a firm is independent of capital structure. When tax is introduced into the calculations, the market value of the firm will increase as debt is added to the capital mix because of the present value of the **tax shield** on interest payments. This can be expressed as:

$$V_g = V_u + DT_c$$

where
V_g	=	market value of the geared company
V_u	=	market value of the ungeared company
D	=	market value of debt
T_c	=	rate of corporation tax

In this case:

	Current £'000	Scen 1 £'000	Scen 2 £'000
V_u	1,675	1,675	1,675
D	0	500	1,000
T_c	33%	33%	33%
$D \times T_c$	0	165	330
Total market value (V_g)	1,675	1,840	2,005

The value of the equity can now be found:

$$E = V_g - D$$

Scenario 1: £1.84m – £0.5m = £1.34m
Scenario 2: £2.005m – £1.0m = £1.005m

(b)   The ratio of **debt to equity** is given by D/E:

Scenario 1: 500/1,340   = 37.3%
Scenario 2: 1,000/1,005 = 99.5%

(c)   Assuming that all distributable profits are paid as dividends, the **cost of equity** can be found using:

$K_e = d_0/p_0$

where K_e = cost of equity
        d_0 = dividend (distributable profit above)
        p_0 = market value of equity

Scenario 1: 234.5/1,340 = 17.5%
Scenario 2: 187.6/1,005 = 18.7%

Step 2.9   Identify and analyse possible business projects

The case data may provide you with information about business projects.

(a)   By this, we mean, for example, **new product development**, a proposed **acquisition**, new **information systems**. There could be projects currently in progress or being proposed. You may be given numerical data to evaluate the project. **Remember decision-making** (eg theory about sunk costs, money already spent). Your **technical skills** could be beneficial here.

(b)   A project could on the other hand be an **opportunity** in the market, or something crying out from the data. (It could be a project suggested by a deficiency in current operations, for example, which could be dealt with by improving the information system.) This is an examination of your ability to think critically.

(c)   We suggest you note down possible business projects in a schedule, with a rationale.

No	Project – rationale	Main para refs in case
1		
2		

 Question   Projects

Clothes Rus a UK retail chain, is facing difficulties, for a variety of reasons, and a programme of change has been put in place. This has included the appointment of a new chief executive and chairman, and the appointment of top staff from other retailers. The company faces a takeover. One cause is that Clothes Rus is alleged to have failed to respond appropriately to customer needs. At one time the inventory for each store were determined centrally. Every store was supposed to stock goods in pre-determined quantities, on the basis of **store size alone** (not patterns of actual consumer purchases). If a particular store ran out, in the past people would have driven to the next nearest Clothes Rus store, perhaps in another town. In recent years, however, they have just gone to another retailer, such as Next.

Can you identify any 'business projects' from the data above?

This is based on a real life example, the key issues being inventory and purchase information. From the data, the information system is at fault in that inventory decisions are taken **centrally** and not related to the individual buying patterns of each store. With data mining software, Clothes Rus would be able to identify store buying patterns and be able to respond more quickly.

In the schedule proposed, you could have analysed this as follows. If you had been provided with financial data, then you could have identified some of the cashflows.

No.	Project – rationale	Main para refs in case
1	Data mining • Protect/increase turnover by retaining customers • Provide information to ensure no stock-outs	x.1

It is quite possible that the case will provide you with details of current projects. You may be able to do a DCF analysis on these.

4 Conclusion

Keep in mind the following issues.

1	Who are the key players in each company and who is the most important?
2	What do you think is the key strategic problem facing each company?
3	What is the main element of each company's plans for the future?
4	What is the biggest immediate problem facing each company?
5	What are the main features of the companies' balance sheets at the most recent year end?
6	What are the main SWOT points for each company?
7	What information have you been given in the pre-seen (in overall terms); what information might you be given in the unseen and why?
8	Write down your approach for the exam, step by step, from start to finish.
9	Write down the nine areas in the assessment matrix and what you have to do to get marks for each area.
10	Compare your approach to the exam with the nine areas, and make sure that you include ways in your technique of doing what CIMA requires of you.

We have now done most of the analysis we want to do. You may feel awash with data and ideas. In the next chapter, we help you pull together all you have done, so you have a clear understanding of the business – in other words, so that it makes sense to you. You will then have a solid foundation to deal with what the examiner might throw at you in the exam.

The BPP approach (2): synthesise what you know

Introduction

In the last chapter, analysis was relatively easy. All you had to do was to apply what you already know. In **this chapter**, we **give you tools to help you** to synthesise this data into a coherent structure. In other words, we want to get you to understand the sinews of the business and the issues facing it.

- You will then find it easier to deal with the unexpected in the unseen.

- Remember, you are explicitly advised not to question spot. There are unlikely to be questions lurking away in the data.

- It will help you a great deal to talk over the issues with someone else doing the paper, to see what perspectives their analysis has brought to the situation. And remember, too, that your **lecturer can offer vital guidance** - each case is different, and your **lecturer will know best**.

Topic list
1 Synthesise what you know

1	Tools to approach the case: Chapter 4	Time	Criteria of the assessment matrix
1.1	Read the case quickly twice without taking notes	1 hour	
1.2	Quickly re-read the case after a day	30 mins	
1.3	Mark up the case slowly taking notes	2 hours	
1.4	Summarise the data in précis	1 hour	Diversity, Logic, Judgement
1.5	Carry out an information audit	1 hour	Diversity, Integration, Prioritisation
1.6	Research the industry and company	-	Diversity
1.7	Identify relevant knowledge	30 mins	Technical, Application, Focus

2	Tools to explore the case situation: Chapter 4		Technical, Application, Focus, Logic
2.1	Analyse the numbers	Depends	Diversity, Technical, Application, Focus, Logic, Ethics
2.2	General environmental analysis (PEST) and trends	1 hour	Diversity, Technical, Application, Focus, Logic, Ethics
2.3	Analyse the business environment and competitive strategy	1.5 hours	Technical, Application, Focus, Logic, Ethics
2.4	Audit the product/service portfolio	1 hour	
2.5	How does the business add value?	1 hour	Integration, Ethics
2.6	Identify **information systems** and processes	1 hour	Technical, Application, Focus
2.7	Identify key issues in structure, culture and personnel	1 hour	Technical, Application, Focus, Prioritisation, Ethics
2.8	Identify investor objectives, capital structure and other stakeholder objectives	1 hour	Technical, Application, Focus, Ethics
2.9	Identify and analyse possible business projects	1 hour	Integration, Technical, Application, Focus, Ethics

3	Tools to synthesise what you know: Chapter 5		
3.1	Summarise your findings in an interim position statement	1 hour	Prioritisation, Logic, Judgement, Technical, Application, Focus
3.2	Draw up a mission statement for the current business from the pre-seen data	30 mins	Logic, Prioritisation
3.3	Relate the business's distinctive competences to the critical success factors for the industry	30 mins	Logic, Judgement, Prioritisation
3.4	Identify and analyse risks, internal and external	1 hour	Diversity, Technical, Application, Focus, Prioritisation, Ethics
3.5	Carry out a graded SWOT analysis	1 hour	Prioritisation
3.6	Identify key business issues	1 hour	Prioritisation, Integration, Diversity, Ethics
3.7	Draw up a balanced scorecard	1 hour	Integration, Logic, Judgement, Prioritisation
3.8	Prepare a one page business summary	1 hour	Logic, Judgement, Prioritisation, Diversity, Integration

4	Practise report writing before the exam: Chapter 6		

5	The exam – three hours: Chapter 7	Time
5.1	The night before: review your business summary and the pre-seen	
5.2	• Review the unseen and requirement • Skim read the data • Read the requirement carefully, making a mental note of the recipient of the report, the required format and what you have to do	Reading time 20 mins
5.3	Read the unseen data in depth. Be sure to identify what has changed. Make notes on the question paper identifying the key issues.	
5.4	Consider the big picture and plan your answer. Do the calculations	45 mins
5.5	Draw up the appendices, terms of reference and introduction	10 mins

5.6	Prioritise the issues	15 mins
5.7	Write the main body of the report	55 mins
	Write the ethics section	15 mins
5.8	Write up your recommendations	35 mins
5.9	Write the conclusion and review your work	5 mins

1 Synthesise what you know

Objective of stage 3: Synthesise what you know

In Stages 1 and 2, you were becoming familiar with the broad outline of the case and you were exploring some of the issues, and teasing out some of the relationships between different items of data. The purpose of Stage 3 is to describe a number of techniques to bring all this thinking together into a coherent framework. All the tools in this stage try to help you integrate your knowledge into a few key issues.

Step 3.1 **Summarise your findings in an interim position statement**

Yet more summaries – you started off by doing a précis, and after that you did a lot of analysis to tease out key issues in the case study. Some issues may still be uncertain, of course, but you have come quite far. **You should now be able to reach genuine conclusions as a result of your analysis**. Whereas, with the initial précis, you were supposed just to review the data, this **position statement** should incorporate some of the results of your analysis.

(a) Ideally, your statement should be a page long.

(b) This is meant to help you draw your breath, so to speak.

(c) You could use your précis as a basis for this statement and re-write it or add to it with the results of your analysis.

(d) Try to build connections between the data you have identified in the case. **Here's a tip:** if you are unsure how to **link items,** use the **value chain** model.

Question	Synthesis

Here are some facts about Obsidian plc.

- Founded 1879, Sheffield UK
- Business: generalist stainless steel cutlery manufacture (80% turnover, 60% gross profit) plus luxury cutlery (20% sales, 40% gross profit)
- Net profit margin: 15% after overheads (no further analysis by department)
- Return on assets: 10% (the bare minimum needed, according to the chairman)
- Warranties and refunds: 1% of sales
- Competitors: low cost producers from China have captured two key accounts for mass produced cutlery
- Customers: UK supermarkets and department stores
- New product development: luxury silver cutlery, handcrafted for the US market, Obsidian plc's first attempt at exporting
- Factory workforce: 500 (of which 250 work in the speciality cutlery section)
- Capacity utilisation: 85%
- The website established 2 years ago receives 100 hits a month in 20X0 rising to 1000 a month in 20X1, showing some customer interest in the luxury cutlery
- Number of accounts: mass production, 100; speciality, 200

Required

Summarise this business situation. Do not be afraid to come to some initial conclusions.

1   **Introduction**

Obsidian plc is a long-established manufacturer of specialist and mass market cutlery, based in the UK, dealing mainly with UK customers.

2   **Customers and markets**

2.1   Obsidian has been losing business to competitors from China, perhaps due to a combination of price and quality problems. Obsidian spends 1% of turnover on warranties, and has recently lost two accounts.

2.2   Obsidian's luxury business has fared better, successfully exporting to the US. Most interest expressed from website contacts has been for the luxury manufactured cutlery. In two years, website hits have gone up by a factor of ten.

3   **Products and production**

3.1   There are two types of cutlery; products for the mass market and those produced for the luxury market.

3.2   The mass produced cutlery account for 80% of turnover but only 60% of gross profit suggesting thin margins. The specialist cutlery accounts for 20% of turnover but 40% of gross profit.

3.3   The specialist craft workforce is about 50% of the total, and there are many more accounts that need to be serviced in smaller quantities. (Perhaps activity based costing should be used to see how overheads are incurred.) The firm combines, possibly, mass production with job production.

3.4   The financial position will suffer – the firm has lost two major accounts (2% of its mass-production customer base, probably worth more by value).

4   **Financial position**

4.1   ROCE is 10%, and net profit is 15% of turnover.

Comment

This answer is a lot longer than a bald list of facts – and it does summarise **relationships** between them and draws out a narrative. For example, it **links** the **loss** of two accounts with **overseas competition** (your business awareness should tell you that China is a low-cost manufacturing centre) and with possible quality problems.

You could have organised this very differently, of course.

Step 3.2   Draw up a mission statement for the current business

In practice, **mission statements** can often be so much hot air, promising everything to everybody, and easily mocked.

(a)   However, the reason why your are doing this **now** is to ensure that you have a clear idea of the current business – it is a device simply to integrate your **thinking and understanding of the case**.

(b)   The unseen data in the case may suggest a quite **different mission** or data inconsistent with the mission.

(c)   Try to keep it to a **few lines.**

(d)   **Do not get tied up making objectives** – unless, say, it is clearly stated in the data that shareholders want a return. This is **just to help you grasp** the business's current position.

 Question   **Mission**

Draw up a mission statement for Obsidian plc (see Question 1).

Obsidian plc seeks to satisfy shareholders by making and selling cutlery, in hand crafted and mass produced format, in the UK and overseas.

Comment

Note that we have put in 'shareholders' first of all before getting carried away by what the business does. Some firms might quantify these objectives.

Step 3.3 Relate the firm's distinctive competences to the critical success factors for the industry

(a) A **distinctive competence** is what a firm does uniquely or better than other firms do. Of course, some firms do not have a distinctive competence as such, although they might have unique features.

(b) A **critical success factor** is what you have to achieve to be successful in the long term. It can be applied to an industry or a project.

Here is quite a tricky example.

Question

Competences

The *Virgin Group* (*Economist* April 8th 2000) runs diverse activities, often in partnership with other businesses: two airlines (Virgin Atlantic, shortly with Singapore Airlines, and Virgin Express a low cost airline, part floated); a music store (Virgin Our Price); a music label, V2 music (with McCarthy Corp), a drinks business (Virgin Cola), clothing and cosmetics (Victory Corporation); Virgin Rail (a train company, with Stagecoach); financial services (such as pensions and mortgages); telecommunications (Virgin mobile). Most of the Virgin group is private.

(a) What do you think is the **distinctive competence** of the Virgin Group?
(b) Identify relevant **critical success factors**.

Answer

(a) According to *The Economist* (April 8th 2000), Sir Richard Branson has described himself as a 'branded venture capitalist' investing in a variety of businesses. Perhaps Virgin has a genuinely distinctive competence in **branding**.

(b) **Critical success factors** for the Virgin group **as a whole** are hard to identify – there are separate factors for success For example, music retailing is not the same as rail transport. Arguably a CSF for the Virgin Group is that **its brand is easily recognisable and held in high esteem** and that it has a profitable image in each business (eg retailing, transportation, financial services).

Below are possible critical success factors for Virgin's **airline** business.

Success factors might be:

(1) Ability to attract **profitable** customers
(2) Ability to fill seating **capacity**
(3) **Safety and conformance** with regulatory requirements
(4) **Delivery** of services promised

Safety, factor (3), is **necessary** to be in the industry **at all**, so it is not critical to **success** in commercial terms. For **success** in the industry, factors such as profitable customers and seating capacity, supported by the delivery on the service promised, are more important.

Step 3.4 Identify and analyse and quantity risks, internal and external, to the business and its stakeholders

The purpose of doing a risk assessment **now** is that it forces you to integrate different areas of the business, the environment and stakeholders. (You could just as easily do this as part of your analysis work, but it does synthesise some issues.)

(a) For the purposes of the case study, we can say that **a risk** is any event that is uncertain and that could have significant consequences for the business, its performance operations or its stakeholders.

(b) This might have consequences for the **long-term survival** of the business or aspects of it. We have already analysed the **external** environment as a source of risks, but **internally,** risks could be caused by factors such as:

- Strike action
- Breakdown
- **Information systems** crashing (especially if operationally important)
- Customer response

(c) Risk can be **quantified** or be given a **value.** Boards need to consider any risks and their likelihood, acceptability and potential impact. **Internal control systems** could assist with this risk management process.

(d) Risk may be viewed by different stakeholders in different ways. You may incorporate risk into **project appraisal**.

(e) You should have enough data from your previous analysis and working papers.

(f) Here is a checklist.

Risk type	Consequences (quantify if useful)	Possible cost	Importance, likelihood and seriousness H = over 70% M = 30–70% L = up to 30%
Business			
Political			
Financial			
Exchange			
Operational gearing			
Other			

(g)   Obviously, something that affects the long-term survival of the business is highly important. The reason for identifying the stakeholders affected is that the objectives of stakeholders differ. If you are given probabilistic data, you may use **decision trees.**

Here is some data about *Boo.com.*

Boo.com was an **Internet-based** fashion and sports goods retailer which invested $120m of venture capital. Set up by two young entrepreneurs, Boo hired staff from university, but apparently had difficulty holding on to its Finance Director. Boo developed an innovative website and hoped to introduce its services at once in 18 different countries. There was a strong corporate culture, but staff numbers expanded rapidly.

Required

Identify business risks in Boo.com.

Answer

Fact	Risk?
Most of Boo.com's staff were fresh from university	Little management experience, although lots of good ideas.
Boo.com wanted to sell in 18 countries at once	The risk was that Boo.com would **fail** to fulfil on its promises to its customers. Few normal retailers would be so ambitious. The mechanics of fulfilment, such as delivery and logistics, were as critical as the front end.
Staff were highly paid and hard working, but staff numbers were growing all the time	These were probably not used effectively.
Fashion	This industry can be inherently volatile.
New, innovative technology	Boo's website only really started to work five months after launch.
No finance director	Poor controls over the cash – many internet companies have gone into receivership.

Step 3.5   Carry out a graded SWOT analysis

SWOT is another useful framework to integrate and synthesise the different elements of the case study and the results of your analysis. This is invariably subjective, but it enables you to prioritise effectively.

(a)   Strengths and weaknesses are internal. Opportunities and threats are external.

(b)   A strength can turn into a weakness in some circumstances. For example, organisational culture can be a strength, but it can be inappropriate in the wrong environmental conditions.

(c)   Categorise all items by areas of the business. It might then emerge that there may be particular weaknesses in particular areas (eg weak in production, strong in marketing).

(d)   You can use other business models to help you determine what are opportunities for example. The Ansoff matrix from the Business Strategy paper can structure your thinking here.

(e)   You should indicate whether these are high, medium or low in importance.

STRENGTHS	Ref	Function	WEAKNESSES	Ref	Function
1			1		
2			2		
3			3		
4			4		
5			5		
6			6		
7			7		
8			8		
9			9		
10			10		
OPPORTUNITIES	Ref	Function	THREATS	Ref	Function
1			1		
2			2		
3			3		
4			4		
5			5		
6			6		
7			7		
8			8		
9			9		
10			10		

Step 3.6   List key business issues

You should be able to identify six to ten **key issues** for the business, ranked in order of significance. Why?

(a)   They reflect what is of concern to the business, irrespective of what turns up in the unseen. For example if **cash flow** is a key issue (from Step 2.1 Analyse the numbers), you will be alert for cash flow implications in the unseen data in the exam room. You can also mention some key business projects.

(b)   A list will be easy to remember and it will help you prioritise.

(c)   It might help you a great deal if you are able to compare notes with a colleague.

(d)   Finally, you need to give the key issues a time horizon, to differentiate between **urgency** and importance.

Issue in order of importance	Description	Time scale (years)
1		
2		
3		
4		
5		
6		
7		
8		
9		
10		

Let us return briefly to the example of Virgin (see Question on Competences). Obviously, the management has an objective for each of the businesses, but there may be key issues for the **Virgin group** as a whole. Here are some facts.

Virgin took control of Our Price in 1998 with debts of £115m. In accounts filed in January 1999, Our Price owed £172m. Our Price has suffered losses because of sales of CDs over the Internet. 'But as Sir Richard points out, he cannot contemplate the bankruptcy of **any** business of his, let alone such a prominent business' *(The Economist)*. As indicated earlier, there are other facets to the Virgin group. (You could almost describe them in portfolio terms. The **airline business** could be a cash cow, for example, to invest in **Internet start ups** and other business areas.) Identify **key** issues from the data above.

Answer

For the group as whole, the key issue at that time is to raise cash to deal with **the banks**. This was both urgent and important. Other key issues are to return Our Price to profitability and to develop the Internet business. In this instance, repayment of cash comes as a priority. Internet development is also key, as a further branding exercise.

Step 3.7 Draw up a balanced scorecard

The balanced scorecard is another technique you can use to draw your analysis together. It identifies key performance measures – perhaps you could relate these to critical success factors and the links between them. **Remember that there are four perspectives.** Again, the issue is to identify the linkages between factors.

↑ market share ⇒ ↑ capacity utilisation

Financial	Internal process
• Profitability • ROCE • Cash flow • Share price, P/E ratio	• Efficiency • Capacity utilisation
Customer	Innovation and learning
• Market share • Complaints	• New product/service development

Linking issues

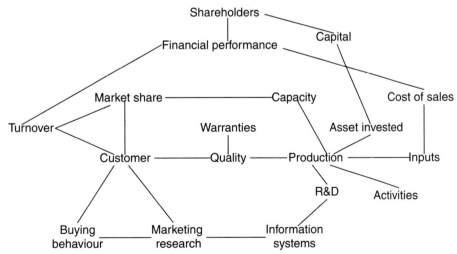

Step 3.8 Prepare a one-page business summary

This step requires you to **synthesise** and select the really **key data** of all the work you have done so far – the data which, in the exam room, you would be kicking yourself if you had forgotten or had to re-calculate or re-analyse – in other words, items of **high importance**. Remember that **synthesis** is a higher level skill.

(a) A **final synthesis of all the work** you have done so far in one document.

(b) **A one page note of all the key facts** and issues that you need to remember so that you are **not completely taken aback by the unseen data** and forget all the analysis you have done. **In the exam, you will have the case data, but none of your notes**. A lot depends on how thorough your preparation has been and your ability to remember key facts.

(c) A suggested format for the summary is given but you **should invent your own**, depending on the circumstances of the case and how easy it is **for you** to remember.

(d) Only transfer those items you think to be of **high** importance to the summary document. This does not mean that everything else is irrelevant – far from it – but you should really try to remember the key lessons you have drawn from the exercise.

(e) Alternatively you can draw a **mind map**, similar to that given in the section covering the environmental analysis. **The key is to get everything on to one page** which you can easily revise from.

Report writing and the TOPCIMA paper

6

Introduction

You really do need to practise here. Your ability to communicate clearly in writing is vital.

Topic list
1 Report writing and the assessment matrix
2 Structure
3 Language
4 Example report
5 Other formats

1 Report writing and the assessment matrix

1.1 The report format

A number of formats may be required but **report format is the most likely**. Even when not specifically asked for, report format is still a good idea, as it focuses your mind on structure and layout, making it easier to mark. Read the **question requirement** carefully.

Question

Report format

Put what follows into report format.

'The first criterion is whether this will be profitable over the estimated life cycle of product A. Another criterion which is related to the first criterion is that of estimated volume sales at the proposed price. A third criterion which needs to be considered when deciding whether or not to launch Product A is....'

Answer

(a)   Decision criteria in rank order

    (i)   Profit (ROI) over product life cycle
    (ii)   Sales volume at proposed price
    (iii)   ...

This is just an example. We have tried to get you to use report format in the analysis and synthesis stages at various times.

When writing a report, there is a clear need for appendices, workings and structure. We will cover each of these, but here is a step by step guide.

Exam focus point

> The examiner has given some guidance on reports. The key requirements are that a report should be in a recognisable format and should be easy to navigate. There should be a clear and logical table of contents and each part of the report should be clearly headed and identified. Do not go over the top. There is no need for an executive summary if time is short.
>
> Finally:
>
> 'DO NOT WASTE TIME ON EXCESSIVE PRESENTATION AT THE EXPENSE OF DETAILED CONTENT'

2 Structure

2.1 A design suggestion

The examiner has suggested the following overall design for your report.

Page 1	**Title block** • Who the report is written for (eg 'Board of XYZ plc') • Who has written the report (eg Independent Consultant') • Date • Title
	Table of contents • Outline the contents of the report in numbered sections • Give titles of Appendices • Can be used to manage your time by allocating minutes to each section/subsection you plan to include within your report.
Page 2	**Section 1 – Introduction** • 5 to 10 lines introducing background to situation of the organisation. Incorporate Unseen data if it changes the situation • Avoids explaining or evaluating issues **Section 2 – Terms of reference** • Five lines to set the scene of who you are, who the report was commissioned by and who it is aimed at
Pages 3 to 4	**Section 3 – Review and prioritisation of main issues facing the management of the organisation** • Based on SWOT analysis in Appendix 1 • Places top five issues in priority order with numbered subheadings (eg '3.1 Cash Flow Crisis – Priority 1') • Justifies the sequence of priorities in terms of consequences for organisation • Less important issues grouped as 'other issues' at end • Does not explain the background to the issues nor provide recommendations.

Few potential marks
• Integration

Crucial section that carries up to 30% of marks
• Focus
• Judgement
• Prioritisation
20% of script length

Pages 5 to 8	**Section 4 – Discussion of the main issues facing the management of the organisation**	Important section that carries up to 30% of marks
	Numbered paragraphs each dealing with an issue from Section 3 (eg 4.1 Cash Flow Crisis – Priority 1')	• Technical
	• In the same sequence as issues in Section 3	• Application
	• Explains background and potential consequences of each issue	• Focus
	• Less important issues shown under ;'other issues' heading but only written about if time allows	• Judgement
	• Numerical values stated and referenced to Appendix where they can be found (eg 'the maximum amount that should be paid for the new business has been calculated at £3.6bn (Appendix 3 line 7')	• Diversity 40% of script
	• Reference to technical theories in Appendix (eg 'XYZ plc is following a stuck in the middle strategy – see Appendix 2')	
	• Avoid putting recommendations here	
Pages 9 to 10	**Section 5 – Ethical issues to be addressed by the management of the organisation**	Mini report within a report. 10% of marks, majority for recommendations 20% of script
	• Identifies up to four issues and ranks in priority order	
	• States the ethical principles and duties involved	
	• Recommends appropriate action for each	
Pages 11 to 13	**Section 6 – Recommendations**	Most important section worth up to 30% of the marks
	Regarded by the Examiner as *'the most important part of the report'*	• Logic
	• Numbered sections corresponding to each of the numbered sections from Section 4 (eg '6.1 Dealing with cash flow crisis')	• Integration
	• Each section states **what decision you recommend,** explains **why you recommend it**, and then **tells management how to do it** (eg *'This report recommends management rejects the new contract in its present form. The contract is insufficiently profitable and has the following unacceptable features ... etc. A formal letter should be sent to the management of XYZ Ltd rejecting the contract and stating the areas of concern This would leave the door open to XYZ Ltd submitting an improved offer'*)	• Judgement
	• As a minimum, recommendations must be given for each of the prioritised issues identified in Section 3	
	• Not acceptable to dodge making recommendations on grounds such as 'need more information' or 'firm needs a strategic plan to deal with this'	

Page 13	**Section 7 Conclusion**	Very few
	• Brief five lines for closing comments	marks here
	Appendices	Essential for
	Put at back of answer booklet/Word document and on Excel spreadsheets	justification of analysis and
	Appendix 1: SWOT analysis	recommendations
	Appendix 2: other theory (PEST, 5 forces, Ansoff, Stakeholder Map)	• Technical • Application
	Appendix 3 etc: numerical workings	Up to 15 marks
	Key data and analysis given in appendices should also be discussed within the body of the report	

3 Language

3.1 Stylistic requirements

Consider the following actual extract from an exam script submitted for a past exam paper for the Chartered Institute of Marketing (cited by Dr David Pearson in *Strategic Marketing Management: Analysis & Decision,* BPP). Note in particular the writing times.

(a) Proposals for change in the organisational structure
(b) Creation of 'strategic business units' centred around each terminal

This would allow each terminal to be represented at board level with each managers having his own operational and commercial staff beneath him. This will involve a huge restructuring of the organisation and individual job roles/responsibilities, however this move is necessary in order that commercial and operations staff work alongside each other and cooperate to solve problems in the most effective way, to the benefit of EAL in serving the needs of its customers. All commercial versus operations conflicts would be solved lower down the hierarchy which will in turn be flattened out as a result of restructuring. Each terminal general manager must have beneath him his appropriate support staff for his commercial and operations roles eg catering manager, retail operations manager, quality control engineers.'

Total words = c 140 **Total time = 8 minutes**

Keeping the same heading, we might change the section to read as follows.

Each terminal to become an SBU under a general manager with his own support staff (catering, retail operations, quality control etc).

BENEFIT

Although requiring much restructuring and reformulation of job descriptions:

(a) Commercial and operations staff would work together in meeting the needs of the customer
(b) All commercial v operations conflicts would be solved lower down the hierarchy
(c) Each terminal would be represented at board level

Total words = c 70 **Total time = 4 minutes**

Exam focus point

The re-wording cuts the original word length in half.

•   It is easier to understand and mark.
•   It takes half the time to write. There would be extra time to make extra points and gain extra marks.

3.2 'Less is More'

Rule	Example		
	No		Yes
Keep words simple	Expenditure	vs	Cost
	Aggregate	vs	Total
Short words are quicker to write	Terminate	vs	End
Avoid words you don't need to write	I would be grateful		Please
	Due to the fact that		Because
	In the not too distant future		Soon (better: say when!)
	At this point in time		Now (or currently)
	In the majority of instances		In most cases
	It is recommended that A Ltd should consider		A Ltd should consider
Total	36 words (55 syllables)		14 words (18 syllables)

Be careful of jargon: jargon is technical language with a precise meaning and therefore has its uses. Keep in mind the needs of your audience. If your report is addressed to the finance director you can make more use of accounting jargon than you would to the marketing director. Remember that some industries have their own jargon.

Be precise. Be careful of 'very', 'fairly', 'partly', unless you are unable to state facts.

Do not criticise the reader. Your reports will be advising management or others, who may not be financial specialists. You will have no friends if you say to them they are useless or incompetent. That will blind them to your message. After all, if they are seeking your advice, they know that there are issues to be investigated.

Remember your audience. Remember who the report is directed to.

4 Example report

You are the management accountant of a company which specialises in producing dairy products for the slimming market. The results of your latest research have just been published (see below).

Data

Market Research Results

This research was carried out from January to June 2004, using in-depth interviews in the respondents' homes, recorded on tape and interpreted by ourselves, 'The XYZ Research Agency', specialists in market research for the food industry.

Sample size: 500
Age range: 15-55
Socio-economic groups: ABC1*
Locations: Bristol, Manchester and Greater London
Sex: Males and Females

Three broad categories were tested and the results are as follows:

Motives for wanting to lose weight	*% of respondents with weight problems mentioning*
To feel good physically	68
For health reasons	67
To stay fit	43
Because I want to live longer	25
To stay mentally alert	23
To be more attractive	21
To be more popular	15
Methods for weight control	
Avoid certain foods, eat 'slimming items'	32
Eat and drink less	23
Play sports, keep 'fit'	22
'Have certain diet days'	7
Take medicines, stimulants	3

Food which people dislike giving up	*% of respondents with weight problems mentioning*
Cakes, pies, bakery products	31
Sweets, sugar	23
Beer, alcoholic beverages	17
Meat, sausages etc	15
Chocolate	13
Cream	9
Fruit juices	9
Potatoes	9
Pasta	9

In general, the comments also revealed that dieting means a loss of pleasure at mealtimes, causes problems when one can't eat the same as the family and also one is regarded as being 'ill' when dieting.

* Socio-economic groupings:

A   Higher managerial, Chief Executives etc
B   Managerial, Executives etc
C1   Higher clerical, Supervisory etc

Required

Write a short formal report to the marketing director, Mr David Forsythe, highlighting the conclusions drawn from this research. Your recommendation will be used to help identify new products for possible development in this market

To: Marketing Director
From: Management Accountant
Date:

REPORT ON NEW PRODUCT DEVELOPMENT

1	The survey
2	Findings
2.1	Motives for losing weight
2.2	Methods of weight control
2.3	Foods respondents disliked giving up
2.4	General comments
3	Conclusions
4	Recommendations

Appendix A: Motives for weight loss
Appendix B: Methods of weight control
Appendix C: Foods which people dislike giving up

1   THE SURVEY

1.1   This report has been compiled from research findings designed to show:

(a)   Respondents' motives for losing weight
(b)   Respondents' methods of weight control
(c)   Foods which respondents were reluctant to give up

1.2   Respondents were a sample group of 500 ABC1s aged 15-55 of both sexes in the Bristol, Manchester and Greater London areas. In-depth interviews were recorded in the respondents' homes, and analysed by XYZ Research: see Appendix A.

2   FINDINGS

2.1   *Motives for losing weight* (see Appendix A)

Most respondents expressed their motives for losing weight as the desire for physical well-being (68%), health (67%) and fitness (43%), with related concerns, such as longevity and mental alertness, also scoring over 20%.

Perhaps unexpectedly, the motives most commonly associated with 'slimming' – increased attractiveness and popularity – scored comparatively low, with 21% and 15% respectively.

2.2   *Methods of weight control* (see Appendix B)

The most frequently-stated method of weight control (32%) was based on food selection: consuming 'slimming items' and avoiding certain foods. Reduced consumption in general (23%) and increased physical activity (22%) featured strongly, however, compared to the use of medicines and stimulants, mentioned by only 3% of respondents.

2.3   *Foods respondents disliked giving up* (see Appendix C)

A significant proportion of respondents were reluctant to give up foods in the high-calorie 'snack' categories: cakes, pies and bakery products (31%), sweets and sugar (23%). Alcohol (17%), meat (15%) and chocolate (13%) also featured significantly, compared to the more 'healthy' food groups such as fruit juice, potatoes and pasta (9% each). Cream was the only dairy product mentioned, (9%).

2.4   *General comments*

Respondents experienced 'dieting' as a loss of pleasure, an inconvenience when it comes to family meals, and a social stigma.

3   CONCLUSIONS

The prime reason for losing weight was health and fitness, mainly achieved through regulated food intake and increased activity. However, respondents felt deprived in general by the dieting process, and particularly disliked giving up snack foods and food generally regarded as 'unhealthy': processed foods, high in fats and sugars, low in fibre.

4   RECOMMENDATIONS

These findings present opportunities in several areas.

4.1   In order to maximise sales of our existing products, we should reappraise our promotional strategy in the light of these findings, to ensure that:

(a)   The health rather than the cosmetic benefits of our products
(b)   That our products are tasty, convenient and normal: not like dieting

4.2   We may also be able to widen the market for our existing products. Since health and well-being was the most common reason for losing weight, we might extend our marketing message to include non-dieters: emphasising the healthy image of dairy products in general and low-fat alternatives in particular.

4.3 Respondents' desire to eat normally while dieting suggests a continuing market for low-fat, low-calorie adaptations, especially of those food which people dislike giving up. Since dairy products currently feature quite low on this list, however, we should consider diversifying into the most significant areas highlighted by the research. Chocolate products may be an initial avenue, being closest to our existing product portfolio, but we may need to look at bakery and confectionery products. This would offer the potential to develop a more extensive brand, and to capture a larger share of the wider slimming market.

APPENDIX A: MOTIVES FOR WEIGHT LOSS

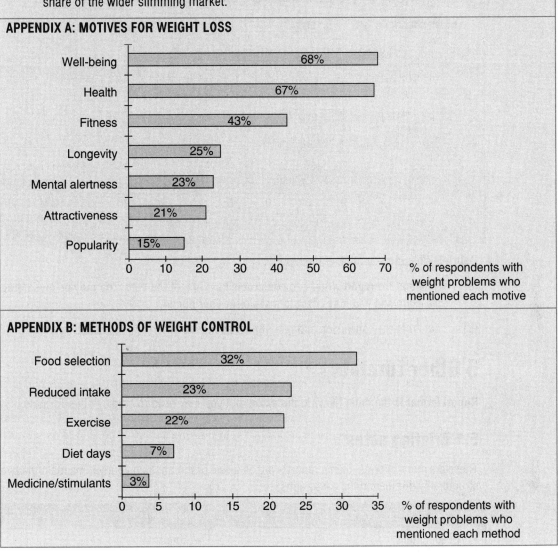

APPENDIX B: METHODS OF WEIGHT CONTROL

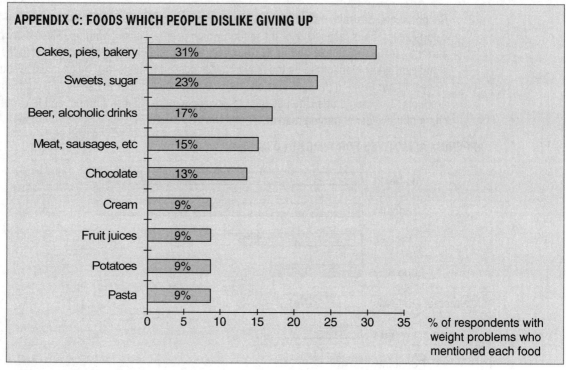

APPENDIX C: FOODS WHICH PEOPLE DISLIKE GIVING UP

Food	% of respondents with weight problems who mentioned each food
Cakes, pies, bakery	31%
Sweets, sugar	23%
Beer, alcoholic drinks	17%
Meat, sausages, etc	15%
Chocolate	13%
Cream	9%
Fruit juices	9%
Potatoes	9%
Pasta	9%

Debrief. What did you think of the report?

(a) Note that the report writer had constructed a graph of the data. You **may** be given graph paper in the exam and you **may** use it to make clear your points.

(b) Note that the conclusion and recommendations are different and are separate.

5 Other formats

Report format is the most likely in the exam, but you may need to employ other formats.

5.1 Briefing notes

These are more informal than a report – but as a rule of thumb, help yourself maintain the overall structure by numbering the paragraphs.

Structure	Features
• Heading/title • From/To/Date • Indication of content • Summary of key points/recommendations • Suggested agenda (if addressee is preparing for a meeting) • Main text of document • Concluding paragraph • Appendices	• Informal • Short sentences, short paragraphs • Concise • Not necessarily numbered

5.2 Letter

This is far less likely.

Structure	Features
• Letter heading • Introductory paragraph outlining purpose of the letter and indicating content • Summary of key point/recommendations • References to detailed text in attachments • Concluding paragraph indicating the next action to be taken • Sign off • Attachments/appendices	• Formal address • Unlikely to have paragraph numbering • Report may be attached • Generally for external communication

5.3 PowerPoint

These slides could be asked for, or **notes for a presentation**. Again you need to keep track of where you are and to show that your data is organised clearly.

Structure	Features
• Title • Summary • Topic slides in a recognisable sequence • Conclusion plus notes	• Slides themselves should be brief: eg a list of six points • Most slide presentations feature the slides and supporting notes offering more detail

5.4 Memo

Structure	Features
• Distribution (To/From/Date) • Special features (eg confidential) • Topic sections	• For internal use • A very flexible means of communication – from simple paragraphs to detailed prescriptions (eg instructions)

The exam

Introduction

You have three hours (after 20 minutes reading time) to satisfy the examiner that you have achieved the requisite standard, overall, as required by the assessment matrix.

- You will be faced with some unfamiliar information.
- You will have to integrate this with what you already know about the business.

Topic list
1 Before the exam (Step 5.1)
2 The reading time (Steps 5.2 to 5.3)
3 Your answer (Steps 5.4 to 5.9)

1	Tools to approach the case: Chapter 4	Time	Criteria of the assessment matrix
1.1	Read the case quickly twice without taking notes	1 hour	
1.2	Quickly re-read the case after a day	30 mins	
1.3	Mark up the case slowly, taking notes	2 hours	
1.4	Summarise the data in précis	1 hour	Diversity, Logic, Judgement
1.5	Carry out an information audit	1 hour	Diversity, Integration, Prioritisation
1.6	Research the industry and company	-	Diversity
1.7	Identify relevant knowledge	30 mins	Technical, Application, Focus

2	Tools to explore the case situation: Chapter 4		Technical, Application, Focus, Logic
2.1	Analyse the numbers	Depends	Diversity, Technical, Application, Focus, Logic, Ethics
2.2	General environmental analysis (PEST) and trends	1 hour	Diversity, Technical, Application, Focus, Logic, Ethics
2.3	Analyse the business environment and competitive strategy	1.5 hours	Technical, Application, Focus, Logic, Ethics
2.4	Audit the product/service portfolio	1 hour	
2.5	How does the business add value?	1 hour	Integration, Ethics
2.6	Identify information systems and processes	1 hour	Technical, Application, Focus
2.7	Identify key issues in structure, culture and personnel	1 hour	Technical, Application, Focus, Prioritisation, Ethics
2.8	Identify investor objectives, capital structure and other stakeholder objectives	1 hour	Technical, Application, Focus, Ethics
2.9	Identify and analyse possible business projects	1 hour	Integration, Technical, Application, Focus, Ethics

3	Tools to synthesise what you know: Chapter 5		
3.1	Summarise your findings in an interim position statement	1 hour	Prioritisation, Logic, Judgement, Technical, Application, Focus
3.2	Draw up a mission statement for the current business from the pre-seen data	30 mins	Logic, Prioritisation
3.3	Relate the business's distinctive competences to the critical success factors for the industry	30 mins	Logic, Judgement, Prioritisation
3.4	Identify and analyse risks, internal and external	1 hour	Diversity, Technical, Application, Focus, Prioritisation, Ethics
3.5	Carry out a graded SWOT analysis	1 hour	Prioritisation
3.6	Identify key business issues	1 hour	Prioritisation, Integration, Diversity, Ethics
3.7	Draw up a balanced scorecard	1 hour	Integration, Logic, Judgement, Prioritisation
3.8	Prepare a one page business summary	1 hour	Logic, Judgement, Prioritisation, Diversity, Integration

4	Practise report writing before the exam: Chapter 6		

5	The exam – three hours: Chapter 7	Time
5.1	The night before: review your business summary and the pre-seen	
5.2	• Review the unseen and requirement • Skim read the data • Read the requirement carefully, making a mental note of the recipient of the report, the required format and what you have to do	Reading time 20 mins
5.3	Read the unseen data in depth. Be sure to identify what has changed. Make notes on the question paper identifying the key issues.	
5.4	Consider the big picture and plan your answer. Do the calculations	45 mins
5.5	Draw up the appendices, terms of reference and introduction	10 mins

5.6	Prioritise the issues	15 mins
5.7	Write the main body of the report	55 mins
	Write the ethics section	15 mins
5.8	Write up your recommendations	35 mins
5.9	Write the conclusion and review your work	5 mins

1 Before the exam

The TOPCIMA exam is the culmination of all the work you have put in over the past six weeks. You have done a great deal of analysis and synthesis, using a number of different techniques. You should be able to live and breathe the life of the company.

In the exam, **you cannot take any notes with you**. All you will see is the case study data you received before your work began, some new data (unseen) and the requirement.

Step 5.1   Review your business summary and the 'pre-seen' material

It is vital, therefore, that you review the **business summary** as this contains in a brief form all the work you have done already. Even if you can remember **one** fact, such as the ROCE for the latest year, you will not have to recalculate it.

Have another look at the 'pre-seen' material. You will encounter it again, in its unanalysed form, in the exam. You might want to link it, in your mind, to the business summary.

By now, you should be well versed in taking exams and should not need any further advice about getting there on time, making sure you have live batteries in your calculator and so on. We would, however, advise you to bring **coloured highlighter pens**.

2 The reading time (Steps 5.2–5.3)

In the exam room you will find:

- A **copy of the pre-seen case** data you have been working on in the past six weeks
- Up to six sides (A4) of other data – the **unseen** data
- A **requirement**, which will describe one or more tasks you must complete
- A blank answer booklet for your answer and another one for appendices **or** a computer, specially adapted for the exam.

You cannot bring textbooks or other materials into the room.

Step 5.2   Review the unseen and read the requirement

Firstly, don't panic. You have spent at least six weeks looking at the data, and analysing it ad nauseam. However, it is quite possible that the new 'unseen' data will surprise you or seem unfamiliar. It might put you off. You cannot question spot from the case so it may be what you do not expect.

You have 20 minutes reading time and you need to use it wisely.

Just as at the start of the pre-seen, you need to **skim read** the new information to get an idea as to what it is telling you, before going into the detail.

Then read the requirement thoroughly and make a mental note of the role you must adopt, the recipient of the report, what you have to do, and the required format.

(a)   What will the requirement look like?

     CIMA has said that the requirement will contain **one or more tasks**. However, it is likely there will be only one requirement.

(b)   You are also asked to **adopt a particular role**. This is important to keep in mind as this will determine the type of report you will write and how you present your data.

(c)   To make absolutely sure, use the requirements to head up your report. Here's an example.

Requirement

Hugh Mountolive the Chief Executive Officer can see both sides of the arguments presented by Melissa and Clea regarding closing down the Alexandria factory and moving to Port Said, but is uncertain about how to evaluate such an important issue.

He has asked you, Justine Nessim, the management accountant, to write a report covering all the major factors that need to be considered in relation to the closure and move, with a recommendation.

You can turn this into **a title page,** as follows.

To: Hugh Mountolive, Chief Executive Officer

From: Justine Nessim, management accountant

Date:

Re: Analysis and recommendations regarding the proposed closure of the factory in Alexandria and the move to Port Said

You have clearly identified the recipient of the report (the managing director), the role you must adopt (management accountant) and what you must do.

(d)   If you analyse the requirement in (c) above this is what you might infer:

		Implications
Your role	Justine Nessim Management accountant	Adjudicating between Clea and Melissa?
Recipient	Hugh Mountolive	He cannot make up his mind and wants you to make a recommendation.
All the **major** factors		Not just financial issues but other considerations. **Major** factors are asked for, so you will have to prioritise here.
In relation to the **closure** and **move**		Two separate items are under review.
With a recommendation		This implies a choice between options, and your own recommendation. You will need a rationale for this.

Exam focus point

The requirement is likely to be 'Prepare a report that prioritises and advises on the main issues facing XXXX and makes appropriate recommendations'.

Step 5.3 Read the unseen data in depth

Now you have firmly fixed in your mind what you have to do, you can start to read through the unseen data, looking for key words.

(a)   As you go through the unseen data, **highlight key facts** and mark them as High, Medium or Low importance. You are aiming to create an **issue list.**

(b)   **Then identify further information that you might need**. You may have to calculate some more ratios, for example, from the data provided.

(c)   If new financial data is given, think about how you will use it.

(d)   Think about which business strategy models you will use.

(e)   Consider any real-life examples you could use.

(f)   Remember, you need to be clear in your mind about **what has changed.** It is vital that you take this on board.

3 Your answer

Step 5.4   Consider the big picture and **plan**

(a)   Decide on the five key issues, the rationale and justification for your choice.

(b)   You might benefit from drawing a spider diagram or mind map.

(c)   Do the calculations. These will be included in the appendices. Make your assumptions very clear and do not get too involved, you do not have much time. The maximum amount of time you should spend will depend on the technical marks available, but more than 20 minutes will be too much.

(d)   Plan your recommendations.

(e)   Plan your writing time. Give approximate timings to each section of the report.

<table>
<tr><td>**Exam focus point**</td><td>Make sure at the planning stage you think about real life examples and the impact of one issue on others.</td></tr>
</table>

Step 5.5   Draw up the appendices, terms of reference and introduction.

(a)   Produce your appendices. You should start with a SWOT analysis with all five key issues included.

(b)   Write one sentence for the terms of reference.

(c)   Write the introduction. Identify and prioritise the main issues facing the organisation, showing the top five items in order of priority.

Step 5.6   Prioritise the issues

Write the section on the prioritisation of the issues.

(a)   Prioritise the top five issues. Remember to justify your choices: 'this is important because….'

(b)   The remaining issues should be listed as bullet points.

(c)   Make sure you refer to the business strategy models you have included in the appendices eg SWOT, PEST.

Step 5.7   Write up the main body of the report and the ethics section

(a)   Write up the main discussion sections using technical knowledge, real life examples and calculations to illustrate your points in sufficient **depth**.

(b)   Make sure you follow your plan.

(c)   Write up your ethics section.

Step 5.8   Write up your recommendations

<table>
<tr><td>**Exam focus point**</td><td>You must stop with 40 minutes to go and produce an exit strategy. You **will not pass** this exam without detailed recommendations.</td></tr>
</table>

(a)   You need to write a recommendation for **each** issue.

(b)   The main issues should have a number of recommendations.

(c)   Al recommendations must have a **justification**. '**Because**' is essential.

(d)   Recommendations must be sensible, commercial, practical and cover human resources, information technology and operational issues.

Step 5.9   Write the conclusion and review your work

Have you written a commercial, comprehensive report? Congratulations, you have probably passed!

Teaching case: Zubinos

Zubinos: pre-seen data

Introduction

This chapter includes the pre-seen case study data for the case that we are looking at in detail.

You will see that we have numbered the paragraphs and have shaded various key words and phrases in the data. This indicates the sort of highlighting that you are likely to do while carrying out your in depth read through and analysis.

P10 – Test of Professional Competence in Management Accounting

Monday 6 March 2006

PRE-SEEN MATERIAL, PROVIDED IN ADVANCE FOR PREPARATION AND STUDY FOR THE EXAMINATION TO BE HELD ON MONDAY 6 MARCH
INSTRUCTIONS FOR POTENTIAL CANDIDATES
This booklet contains the pre-seen case material for the March 2006 examination. It will provide you with the contextual information that will help you prepare yourself for the examination on Monday 6 March.
The TOPCIMA Assessment Matrix, which your script will be marked against, is available as a separate document which will also be e-mailed to you.
You may not take this copy of the pre-seen material into the examination hall. A fresh copy will be provided for you in the examination hall.
Unseen material will be provided for the examination: this will comprise further context and the examination question.
The examination will last for three hours. You will be allowed 20 minutes reading time **before the examination begins** during which you should read the question paper and, if you wish, make annotations on the question paper. However, you will **not** be allowed, **under any circumstances**, to begin using your computer to produce your answer, or to use your calculator during the reading time.
You will be required to answer ONE question which may contain more than one element.

© The Chartered Institute of Management Accountants 2006

Zubinos Coffee Shops

Market overview

1 The number of chains of coffee shops in the UK has increased four-fold in the last five years, with thousands of branded coffee shops now operating around the UK. The total turnover for all branded coffee shops in the UK exceeded £1 billion (£1 billion is equal to £1,000 million) during 2005. Over the last few years a number of UK based branded coffee shops have emerged to compete with the internationally recognised coffee shop brands.

2 A further shift in the market growth is that the coffee bar culture has extended beyond the UK's major cities and is now successfully penetrating smaller towns. This has mainly been driven by the larger of the coffee shop brands. Consumer awareness of branded coffee shops has also increased in the last few years.

3 The range of products offered has also changed over the last few years and branded coffee shops are now meeting customer demand for a larger range of foods and better quality products by using premium ingredients. Furthermore, branded coffee shops are able to command a higher average price for their products by using quality and service as differentiators, as price appears not to be a particularly sensitive factor.

4 In addition to the branded coffee shops, there is a large number of non-specialist food and beverage outlets including department stores, supermarkets and bookshops, which continue to expand their own cafes. They are enjoying the success of the 'coffee culture' that has been established by the branded coffee shops.

5 Market research is very important in this fast moving consumer driven marketplace and the over-riding factor that continues to be the most important reason that consumers select a coffee shop is its convenience of location. There were over 500 branded coffee shops in London at the end of 2005.

Zubinos' personnel

6 The career histories of Zubinos' Directors and key employees are shown in **Appendix 1** starting on page 10.

The first Zubinos coffee shop

7 On returning to the UK in early 2001, Luis Zubino, the founder of Zubinos, bought a flat in London and set about locating suitable premises for his new business venture. His original plan was to have over five coffee shops opened within five years and he wanted the cash generated from each coffee shop to finance the opening costs for the next coffee shop. He had put together a business plan to get a personal loan, which was secured on both his own flat and his parents' house. This loan, together with his savings, was used to acquire £300,000 of equity in Zubinos.

8 Zubinos was formed in March 2001 with 2 million authorised shares of £1 each, of which 300,000 shares were allocated to Luis Zubino and these shares were fully paid up at par value in March 2001. At the time these shares were issued, £1 per share at par value was considered a fair value.

9 Luis Zubino opened the first Zubinos shop in June 2001 in London, in rented premises. He fully understood that it was location and convenience that would be critical to the success of the coffee shop. He had been lucky in being able to rent a large corner shop on a busy junction, which was surrounded by offices and on the route to nearby public transport, thereby having the benefit of many passers by. Luis Zubino hired a large number of staff to ensure good customer service and to minimise waiting times during peak busy periods such as lunch breaks.

10 Most coffee shops only serve a selection of hot and cold drinks and a small range of snacks and cakes. What distinguished Zubinos from many of the other branded coffee shops back in 2001, was that Zubinos also sold a range of freshly made sandwiches, with high quality fillings and other food items. Zubinos also sold a specialised brand of ice cream, which Luis Zubino imported from Italy, as he considered that the quality and taste was far superior to many other ice cream brands available in the UK. He was convinced that ice cream, which is a product that is kept frozen, could generate high margins, as it would have very little waste and none of the problems associated with the short shelf life of other foods.

11   Within six months, the first Zubinos shop was generating a high turnover and had established a high level of repeat business. Zubinos became a popular meeting place. The level of profitability was below plan as more staff had been employed to meet demand and Luis Zubino considered that he did not want to lose customers' goodwill by increasing waiting times to be served. By December 2001, he handed the day-to-day management of the shop to Val Pline, who had proved herself to be the hardest working and most trustworthy of all the staff employed at the coffee shop.

12   Luis Zubino briefed Val Pline on his plans for the shop for the next few months and agreed to pay bonuses to her when the turnover reached a certain level and again when net profit (after staff and fixed costs) reached £100,000 in any financial year. Val Pline was impressed with the business plan and her new responsibilities. Only six months previously, she had joined a coffee shop with limited experience and now she found herself running the coffee shop with the possibility of earning bonuses when it became even more successful.

The growth of Zubinos

13   Within two and a half years, by the end of 2003, Luis Zubino had opened a further five coffee shops, which was twice as fast as his original business plan had envisaged. All five shops were in rented premises to reduce the initial set-up costs, but Luis Zubino had not reduced the level of expenditure on the coffee shops design and fittings. The atmosphere that the coffee shop design had created was good, and was attractive to the target market of young people. Early on, from his market research, and from personal experience in his parents' business, Luis Zubino wanted his coffee shops to appeal to the 20-to-35 year old age range. This was for several reasons:

- The target age range market segment has more time and more disposable money;
- They attracted other people of similar ages into the coffee shops, as they become the place to meet up;
- The target age range would be attracted to the 'trendy' atmosphere that Luis Zubino has created at Zubinos.

14   Luis Zubino wanted to expand the number of Zubinos coffee shops, but could not find suitable premises to rent in the locations he wanted. By mid-2004 he appointed a management consultancy firm for financial planning advice on how he could expand the business. Zubinos had only been in existence, at that stage, for fewer than four years.

15   The consultant with whom he dealt with was George Shale, and the two quickly established good rapport and worked well together. It was George Shale's idea to open only a few more Zubinos coffee shops in the London area where sites were difficult to obtain and rent very expensive. George Shale recommended that Zubinos should start to expand into towns and cities elsewhere in the UK where shop location would not be such a problem, rather than continue to expand within the fiercely competitive London market.

16   When Jane Thorp joined Zubinos in early 2003, she could immediately see the large potential of the Zubinos brand. By the end of 2003, Zubinos had six shops operational with plans for four further shop openings in 2004. Eight further shops were opened in 2005, resulting in eighteen coffee shops in total operational by the end of 2005. The geographical split of Zubinos coffee shops was ten in London and eight coffee shops outside of London. Zubinos has not had any problems with building up its customer base after each new shop opening in the smaller towns and cities into which it had expanded.

17   George Shale also suggested that Zubinos could consider opening Zubinos coffee shops on the premises of another retailer. He undertook to try to locate a chain of retailers who would rent out part of their shop space. This has been done with other coffee shop chains, which have coffee shops located in motorway service areas and chains of bookshops. Luis Zubino liked the idea of a Zubinos coffee shop in a chain of other shops and a search for a suitable retail chain started in May 2004. However, with the expansion of Zubinos into eight provincial towns and cities, Zubinos has not yet pursued the identification of a suitable retail chain into which it could open Zubinos coffee shops.

18   The Zubinos business has a high turnover. However, profitability was still lower than some of its competitors, for several reasons as follows:

- High rental costs for three of the ten London coffee shops;
- High staff costs, as good customer service remains a high priority for Zubinos;
- Lower than average gross margins on some products due to the higher than average procurement cost of the quality ingredients that Luis Zubino has selected;
- Lower margins on coffee products as over 80% of its coffee beans are procured from suppliers who deal only with 'Fair Trade' coffee producers (see below).

Staffing issues and performance related bonuses

19   Luis Zubino was kept very busy with expanding the Zubinos business and left each of the coffee shop managers alone to run each Zubinos coffee shop. Most management responsibilities were devolved to the shop managers, who were responsible for local procurement of food supplies, staff recruitment and day-to-day staff management.

20   Vivien Zubino, Luis Zubino's wife, managed one of the London Zubinos coffee shops after they married in 2002. She also undertook much of the procurement of coffee supplies, together with Jane Thorp, until the full time Procurement Director, Maria Todd, joined Zubinos in September 2004. However, there were often duplication of orders or gaps in delivery of supplies as both Jane Thorp and Vivien Zubino were constantly busy with other responsibilities.

21   Payroll was operated by an out-sourced agency centrally and Luis Zubino managed all other staff issues. It was only with the appointment of Anita Wiseman in November 2004, that human resource (HR) matters were undertaken centrally. Zubinos employed over 360 staff (some part time) by 31 December 2005.

22   Anita Wiseman wants to formalise job responsibilities and recruitment and ensure that staff are offered promotion in newly opened branches of Zubinos. Following on from the dismissal of three employees during 2005 for minor thefts, of both produce and cash, she also suspected that staff management and the required control procedures were not in place in the coffee shops. Coffee is a high value product and one employee was dismissed for selling stolen bags of coffee beans. This theft was only identified because he had been foolish enough to steal, and then sell, the bags of coffee beans on the premises of the Zubinos coffee shop in which he worked. A fellow employee had reported the incident to Luis Zubino.

23   Anita Wiseman has introduced quarterly performance related bonuses for all employees based on the sales revenue and the net margin for each coffee shop. The bonus is paid quarterly to recognise the previous quarter's results and to motivate staff to stay with Zubinos, so reducing the high staff turnover. However, the bonuses paid for the last two quarters of 2005 were lower than previously paid, as the targets were more challenging. Some coffee shop managers and other employees were disappointed with their reduced bonus payments despite working as hard as ever over the Christmas 2005 period.

Fair Trade produce

24   Luis Zubino, having a strong social conscience, felt that the coffee beans that Zubinos coffee shops should use should be bought from suppliers of Fair Trade coffee. Additionally, from his initial research into the industry, he was convinced that Zubinos could charge a price premium for the use of Fair Trade coffee.

25   Fair Trade benefits 800,000 farmers worldwide selling a wide variety of products. Farmers are organised into small co-operatives, whereby products are procured at an agreed minimum price, which is above the price that some small independent farmers would be able to achieve for their crops on the open market. Fair Trade produce is successfully breaking the cycle of poverty for farmers in many countries and the coffee industry is one where Fair Trade has been very successful. Luis Zubino felt strongly that in today's world where consumers are demanding more humane and more environmentally sensitive products, the use of Fair Trade coffee in Zubinos coffee shops is a responsible and sensible choice of supply.

26 From the opening of the first Zubinos in 2001, Luis Zubino bought 100% of all coffee from Fair Trade suppliers. As the range of coffees expanded in Zubinos coffee shops, he found that some coffee and cocoa beans were unavailable through Fair Trade suppliers. On average, Zubinos procures over 80% of its produce from Fair Trade suppliers. Luis Zubino would still like this to be 100%. When Maria Todd joined in September 2004, Luis Zubino requested her to increase the proportion of coffee supplies procured from Fair Trade suppliers. This necessitated a change from some of its current suppliers to achieve this objective. The extensive use of Fair Trade coffee is used in some of Zubinos' marketing literature, and it has raised the profile and awareness of Fair Trade with some of its customers.

IT development

27 Jane Thorp commissioned an IT company in early 2005 to completely update the Zubinos website. The total cost of this IT work was forecast to be £220,000, but the final cost was a little over £300,000 including new hardware equipment. The new website has helped to create stronger brand awareness. The new Zubinos website also has an on-line communications area which allows users to 'chat' on line. Since November 2004, a range of Zubinos merchandise can also be ordered on-line. This range of merchandise includes coffee machines and coffee supplies, which have been selling well, despite little direct publicity.

28 George Shale is continuously frustrated by the lack of financial and business information in a usable format. The company had grown fast and he has prepared several proposals requesting that a new database financial forecasting system is implemented. He also wants the shop managers to be more involved in sales and profit forecasting and the system that he had proposed would allow shop managers to input their data for consolidation. However, Luis Zubino felt that the shop managers are already under a heavy workload and that the quality of the data that they could input into the proposed system would be little better than that currently submitted by e-mail to Zubinos Head Office. The current standard of forecasting by shop managers is not very good and has generally underestimated the growth in sales. The database proposal has been turned down previously on cost grounds, as Luis Zubino considers that the cost does not justify the slightly improved level of forecasting.

29 However, a new IT system to capture sales and product analysis data at source, which will also help with stock control, was commissioned in October 2005. This project has been scaled down from the original specification and is forecast to cost £110,000.

Introduction of a business investor

30 By summer 2004, Zubinos had eight coffee shops open and had found suitable locations for two more. However, Zubinos' bankers, Kite Bank, were reluctant to increase the level of loans. At the end of June 2004, Zubinos had three loans in place, totalling £600,000. All loans were at 12% interest per year. These were:

- An initial five-year loan for £300,000 taken out in December 2001;
- A second five-year loan for £200,000 taken out in December 2002 to fund further expansion;
- A third five-year loan taken out in April 2004 for £100,000, to cover a shortfall in working capital due to all cash resources being used for expansion.

31 Instead, the bank introduced Luis Zubino to the manager of the bank's private equity provider, who is Carl Martin. Carl Martin and Luis Zubino established a good working relationship early on in their business meetings and Carl Martin was impressed with the business plan and the growth of the Zubinos business in the last few years. He felt confident that if Kite Private Equity (KPE) were to invest in the Zubinos business, the additional private equity finance, together with less expensive loan finance, would allow the Zubinos business to expand far more rapidly.

32 After many discussions and the preparation of additional, more detailed business plans, KPE agreed to invest in the Zubinos business in January 2005.

33 KPE invested £2·4 million in equity finance initially, but the agreement was to also provide loan finance when required by expansion plans. The agreed value of loan finance was up to £5·0 million over the next 4 years at an annual interest rate of 10% per annum, secured against Zubinos assets. KPE appointed Carl Martin as its representative on the Board of Zubinos.

34 The balance sheet, income statement and statement of changes in equity for Zubinos for the last two financial years are shown in **Appendix 2**.

Shareholdings at December 2005

35   Since the formation of Zubinos in 2001, other Directors have purchased shares in Zubinos. They have paid between £2 and £5 per share, based on the agreed fair value at the time they acquired shares.

36   Luis Zubino and the rest of the Zubinos shareholders welcomed KPE into the business. KPE purchased 400,000 shares at £6 each (£1 each plus a share premium, based on an agreed fair value, of £5 per share). The shareholdings at 31 December 2005 are shown below.

	Number of shares	% shareholding %
Luis Zubino	300,000	30.0
Vivien Zubino	120,000	12.0
Jane Thorp	30,000	3.0
Maria Todd	24,000	2.4
Anita Wiseman	36,000	3.6
George Shale	90,000	9.0
KPE	400,000	40.0
Total shareholdings	1,000,000	100.0

37   The Zubinos Board comprises the above six shareholders plus Carl Martin, KPE's nominated representative. Luis Zubino is Chairman of the Board in addition to his role as Managing Director.

Analysis of gross margin

38   George Shale commissioned a new IT system in October 2005 that will capture and analyse sales and cost of sales data without all of the manual intervention and spreadsheet analysis that is currently required to produce management information. The system is due to be operational in early 2006.

39   The analysis of the gross margin across the eighteen Zubinos coffee shops for the year to 31 December 2005 is shown as follows. It should be noted that the figures below are for all eighteen Zubinos coffee shops, but eight of them were operational for only part of 2005.

	Coffee products £'000	Other drinks £'000	Sand– wiches £'000	Ice– cream £'000	Other foods £'000	Total £'000
Sales revenue	4,734	1,344	3,584	896	3,360	13,918
Cost of food and drinks	926	642	1,260	182	1,962	4,972
Gross margin	3,808	702	2,324	714	1,398	8,946
Gross margin %	80%	52%	65%	80%	42%	64%

Zubinos' expansion plans

40   The current five-year plan was approved by KPE, and subsequently the Zubinos Board, in December 2005. This plan includes the expansion of Zubinos to 75 coffee shops by the end of 2010. An extract from this current five-year plan is shown in **Appendix 3**.

41   Much of the expansion planned is due to be financed by cash generated by operations, as well as additional loan finance from KPE. The amount of loan finance will be determined by whether the new openings will be in rented premises or whether the company will be required to purchase the site. Much will depend on the location selected and the alternatives available in each town or city targeted for expansion.

42   During 2005, eight new Zubinos coffee shops were opened. Up to the end of 2004, all coffee shops, except one, were in rented premises. Zubinos has previously purchased one property in London in 2003, in which it has its head office above the coffee shop. During 2005, two of the newly opened Zubinos coffee shops were in large premises that had been purchased, as Luis Zubino was unable to locate a suitable site that could be rented. The cost of the two coffee shops that were purchased were over £1 million each, including the shop fitting costs.

43   Jane Thorp uses a number of criteria for the selection of new sites for future Zubinos coffee shops. These
      include:

      1.   *Competition* – the strength of the competition in the proposed market place and whether the competition
            will stimulate growth, but not be too strong so as to restrict profits.
      2.   *Resources.* Whether there are adequate resources, staff and supply links to set up a new coffee shop.
      3.   *Consumer demand.* Is there sufficient demand for a Zubinos coffee shop and what is the current level of
            demand and how is it being met? A further issue is whether the area has the income to create profitable
            demand for Zubinos.

44   Some relevant factors in the Zubinos expansion plan are the population size and the population density. When
      population becomes concentrated it often tends to take on a different character. Urbanisation produces the need
      for a higher level of products and services. Jane Thorp uses a number of easy measures such as the presence,
      or absence, of well-known chains of clothes retailers, to determine the potential for a new coffee shop location.

45   Jane Thorp had prepared a paper for the December 2005 Zubinos Board meeting, proposing that each Zubinos coffee
      shop should have a few computers available for customers' use, for browsing on the internet or for passing business
      people to send e-mails. The proposal is for the computers to be available free of charge for all customers. The Board
      considered the proposal, but decided against it for several reasons, not just on cost grounds, but on space
      considerations and also concerns over damage or theft. Luis Zubino stated that Zubinos did not need to offer its
      customers such facilities, as Zubinos coffee shops already were very busy at peak times. Jane Thorp is confident that
      this innovative free service is a good way of retaining customer loyalty and for attracting new customers.

Labelling of foods

46   One of the London-based Zubinos coffee shops had just broken the barrier of sales of £1 million in a rolling 12
      month period. The manager at this coffee shop decided to try to increase sales further by introducing additional
      nutritional data for some food and drink products. The coffee shop manager decided, without consulting
      anyone, to display the calorie information as a ploy to improve sales. However, when she calculated and
      displayed the calorie content of many of the coffee products and foods, she was disappointed to find the calorie
      content very high. Many customers were also very surprised and switched to other drinks and did not purchase
      any cakes or pastries. This led to a small reduction of sales revenue.

47   This Zubinos coffee shop manager then started a new initiative during summer 2005 in the Zubinos coffee shop
      in which she manages. She introduced a small range of low fat and low calorie snacks and meals, which proved
      to be very popular. However, when this was discussed with Jane Thorp in Marketing, a major disagreement
      arose concerning the range of foods that Zubinos should be offering, and Jane Thorp's view that there should be
      a standard menu at all Zubinos coffee shops. The manager was furious that Zubinos Head Office had not
      welcomed her low calorie meal initiative.

Other recent developments in the *Zubinos* business

48   In April 2005, Zubinos introduced its first delivery service from three of its central London coffee shops. This delivery
      service to local businesses provides coffee and a catering service on customers' premises. Customers place orders
      on-line to their local Zubinos coffee shop. Despite a few initial problems, the delivery service is working well, although
      sales are still very low. Customers are automatically invoiced after delivery, instead of the usual cash payments in the
      coffee shops. There has been some additional work caused by payments received not matching with the invoiced
      amounts, and shop managers have simply written off the small differences. There is no system yet in place to chase
      up payment for deliveries if the customer does not pay within Zubinos' 30-day terms.

49   Zubinos wants to continue to be innovative and to be ahead of its competitors in terms of the types of foods
      offered. Jane Thorp and Maria Todd are in contact with a number of food manufacturers to explore offering a
      wider range of foods. They need to ensure that any new food ranges fit in with Zubinos' current pricing and food
      quality levels.

Proposed expansion of Zubinos overseas

50   Jane Thorp and Luis Zubino believe that during 2007, when Zubinos plans to have over 26 shops open in the UK, it will be in a position where it could consider expanding overseas. Already, a number of contacts of Luis Zubino, who live in Europe, are keen to operate Zubinos coffee shops in Europe.

51   The current five-year plan, which was approved by KPE and the Zubinos Board in December 2005, is based on operating 50 coffee shops in the UK by 2010 and 25 coffee shops in Europe.

52   However, Luis Zubino would like to have more than 25 coffee shops operating in Europe by 2010. There are a number of reasons why Zubinos should consider expanding abroad and these include:

- Saturated home market where competition is so intense that it can no longer gain any significant market share improvement
- Competition may be less intense in a different market
- Comparative advantage in product against local competition, particularly in areas dominated by British people living and holidaying abroad, which is becoming increasingly popular in some areas of Europe, especially Spain

Appendix 1

Zubinos' personnel

Luis Zubino – Chairman and Managing Director

Luis Zubino, now 29, had worked in his parents' café for two years after he left school. He did not want to go to university and instead saved enough money to travel extensively. He is an intelligent man, who has his father's entrepreneurial spirit. After spending several years abroad, he returned to the UK in 2001 and established Zubinos.

Vivien Zubino – Director

Vivien Zubino, now aged 30, married Luis Zubino in 2002, after the opening of the first Zubinos shop. She is a director of Zubinos and now works part time at one of the Zubinos coffee shops in London. She has assisted her husband in achieving his ambitious plans and has helped to create the designs for the Zubinos coffee shops and also some of the innovative menus available at Zubinos coffee shops. She has always supported her husband and his ideas, which has contributed to the high growth achieved to date. Vivien Zubino purchased shares in Zubinos during 2002.

Jane Thorp – Marketing Director

Jane Thorp was the first professional appointment that Luis Zubino made in early 2003. He knew by then that Zubinos had the potential to be successful, and understood the importance of branding, and the company needed a strong Marketing Director. Jane Thorp had previously worked in marketing for a mobile phone company and more recently for a leading high street fast food chain, which she did not like. Jane Thorp, aged 32, relished the challenges that Zubinos posed and was determined to help both Luis and Vivien Zubino to create a successful business. She invested personal funds into the company in 2003 when she bought 30,000 shares, which was then nearly 7% of the issued share capital.

Maria Todd – Procurement Director

Maria Todd, now 35, had worked in procurement for an international food retailer and was frustrated with the lack of initiative she was allowed to use. She had extensive procurement and contract experience and welcomed the challenges that a growing company, such as Zubinos, could offer her. Maria Todd invested £120,000 of personal funds to buy shares in the company.

Maria Todd joined Zubinos in September 2004 and is based in its Head Office, which is located above one of the London Zubinos coffee shops. The first floor above the shop accommodates around 28 employees including two junior procurement staff. Prior to Maria Todd joining Zubinos, most of the procurement decisions were made by a variety of people. She is frustrated by the lack of discipline in the company, as many coffee shop managers still order some supplies from local food wholesalers to meet demand. The coffee shop managers state that they need this flexibility to provide customers with the foods in demand. However, Maria Todd considers that the coffee shop managers are simply not planning their food ordering very well and are continuously running out of a variety of products. One shop even ran out of the specially mixed Zubinos coffee beans recently.

Anita Wiseman – Human Resources Director

Anita Wiseman, now 29, has known Luis Zubino since their school days. She has a degree in Human Resource management and has worked in human resources (HR) for a chain of department stores before joining Zubinos in November 2004. Prior to Anita Wiseman joining the company, much of the HR management work had been out-sourced or handled by Luis Zubino, who had delegated authority for hiring new employees to each coffee shop manager.

George Shale – Finance Director

George Shale, aged 39, had worked for a leading audit group for over 10 years before he moved into management consultancy. Zubinos appointed the consultancy firm that George Shale worked for in mid 2004 for financial planning advice. George Shale was the consultant in charge of the Zubinos case and worked closely with Luis Zubino on a new five-year plan. George Shale was so convinced by the business plan that he had helped to produce, and in Luis Zubino's ability to grow the Zubinos business, that he joined Zubinos in December 2004. He bought 90,000 shares in Zubinos. Prior to George Shale joining the company, much of the finance work was managed by Zubinos' external auditors, and supplemented by temporary finance staff. Since joining Zubinos, George Shale has recruited a small team and has taken all accounting and finance matters in-house.

Bob West – Business Planning Manager

Bob West, aged 35, used to work for George Shale at the management consultants and was recruited by George Shale to fill the new post of Business Planning Manager at Zubinos in June 2005. Bob West has always worked as a consultant and been involved with many young start– up business ventures, and has a lot of experience. However, he has not been involved in the food retailing business before joining Zubinos.

Jack Rayfield – Shop management and security

Jack Rayfield, aged 52, joined Zubinos in 2003 having worked in retail management for the past 20 years. He was recruited by Luis Zubino who considered him to be a reliable hard working manager who could take care of the day-to-day operations involved with the shops. Since Jack Rayfield joined, he has introduced many new procedures and tightened up some poor business practices. One of the procedures that he has introduced is daily banking of cash and reconciliations to records of revenue for each shop.

Jack Rayfield is very good on HR matters and has played an active role with shop managers in the recruitment of staff, particularly for new Zubinos coffee shops. However, recently he has clashed with Anita Wiseman over many issues.

Val Pline and Sally Higgins – Zubinos' Area Managers

Both Val Pline and Sally Higgins had originally joined Zubinos in junior supervisory roles in its early days and then progressed to coffee shop managers. In September 2005, they were both appointed to the new roles of area managers. Val Pline is responsible for all London and the South East-based Zubinos coffee shops and Sally Higgins has responsibility for all other UK coffee shops.

They have both received management training and have been rewarded with performance related bonuses linked to sales revenue and net margins. They are now responsible for the recruitment and management of all staff for the coffee shops that they manage. Due to high staff turnover, which is not unusual in this business sector, they have spent much time on staff recruitment and on staff training issues.

Carl Martin – Investment Director, Kite Private Equity (KPE)

Carl Martin, aged 39, is the liaison manager at KPE who is responsible for a range of clients into which KPE has invested equity and loan finance. The companies that KPE has invested in vary greatly and are operating in a wide range of industries, including manufacturing, service and retail sectors. Carl Martin was appointed to the Zubinos Board in January 2005, to manage KPE's shareholding.

Due to Carl Martin's demanding role in many other companies, he has left the Zubinos management team to manage the Zubinos business. He is content that the monthly sales and profits that had been achieved during 2005 were ahead of the agreed forecast. Therefore, he has not been as 'hands on' as he would have been if targets had not been met. Carl Martin gets on very well with Luis Zubino, and they both have much mutual respect for each other's roles. Luis Zubino appreciates that Zubinos would not have been able to grow as quickly without the KPE finance and is very pleased that Carl Martin has not really interfered with the way that Zubinos is run.

Appendix 2

Zubinos' Balance Sheet, Income Statement and Statement of changes in equity

Note. All data in this appendix is presented in international financial reporting format

Balance Sheet

	As at 31 December 2005		As at 31 December 2004	
	£'000	£'000	£'000	£'000
Non-current assets (net)		7,025		2,958
Current assets				
Inventory	420		395	
Trade receivables and rent prepayments	209	124		
Cash and short term investments	391		85	
		1,020		604
Total assets		8,045		3,562
Equity and liabilities				
Equity				
Paid in share capital	1,000		600	
Share premium reserve	2,630		630	
Retained profits	1,751		854	
		5,381		2,084
Non-current liabilities				
Loans				
Bank loan at 12% (repayable in 2006)	300		300	
Bank loan at 12% (repayable in 2007)	200		200	
Bank loan at 12% (repayable in 2009)	100		100	
KPE loan at 10% (repayable in 2010)	300		–	
		900		600
Current liabilities				
Trade payables	1,367		689	
Tax	283	160		
Accruals	114		29	
		1,764		878
Total equity and liabilities		8,045		3,562

Note. Paid in share capital represents 1 million shares of £1.00 each at 31 December 2005

Income Statement

Year ended 31 December

	2005 £'000	2004 £'000
Revenue	13,918	7,962
Total operating costs	12,651	7,225
Operating profit	1,267	737
Finance costs	(87)	(69)
Tax expense (effective tax rate is 24%)	(283)	(160)
Profit for the period	897	508

Statement of changes in equity

	Share capital £'000	Share premium £'000	Retained earnings £'000	Total £'000
Balance at 31 December 2004	600	630	854	2,084
New shares issued during 2005	400	2,000	–	2,400
Profit for the period	–	–	897	897
Dividends paid	–	–	–	–
Balance at 31 December 2005	1,000	2,630	1,751	5,381

Note. For the purpose of the case, it should be assumed that the accounts for the year ended 31 December 2005 are final and have been audited.

Appendix 3

Extracts from Zubinos 5-year plan

	Actual	Plan				
	2005	2006	2007	2008	2009	2010
Number of coffee shops:						
Start of the year	10	18	26	36	48	60
New openings	8	8	10	12	12	15
End of the year	**18**	**26**	**36**	**48**	**60**	**75**
Average number of coffee shops for the year	14	22	31	42	54	68
Analysis of new shop openings:						
UK	8	8	9	5	5	5
Overseas	–	–	1	7	7	10
	£'000	£'000	£'000	£'000	£'000	£'000
Coffee shops revenue	13,498	22,176	37,072	57,378	82,553	110,751
Revenue from new product launches in each year	420	1,560	2,200	2,900	3,800	4,800
Total revenue	13,918	23,736	39,272	60,278	86,353	115,551
Pre-tax operating profit	1,267	2,160	3,613	5,606	8,203	10,977
Capital expenditure	4,800	2,700	3,400	3,800	4,100	5,000

Note. The extracts from the 5-year plan shown above were approved by KPE and the Zubinos Board in December 2005.

UK National News

TUESDAY DECEMBER 20 2005

ZUBINOS is winning a share of the coffee wars

THE coffee shops chain, Zubinos, renowned for its choice of coffees and fresh foods, today opened its eighteenth coffee shop and is now expanding nationwide.

Managing Director, Luis Zubino commented 'our customers are very important to us and we provide them with the coffees that they want and a wide variety of top quality foods in an appealing atmosphere'.

Zubinos has eight coffee shops outside the capital. They are much larger than many of its competitors' coffee shops. Zubino stated, 'our customers want to feel as if they are at home and we have created the authentic European coffee house atmosphere. Our sales are growing rapidly, which confirms to us that our customers like what we provide'.

It is forecast that sales for 2005 will be over £14 million, which is nearly 75% up from sales of around £8 million during 2004.

Zubinos appears to have managed to compete effectively against the many coffee shops chains, most of which have nationwide coverage. However, as Zubinos expands, the market expects there to be some consolidation. A leading UK coffee shop chain, Café Café, recently bought 12 coffee shops from the global coffee shop chain Whistle.

When asked about Zubinos expansion plans, Luis Zubino stated, 'it is our intention to continue to expand within the UK and to open Zubinos coffee shops overseas in the next few years'.

KPE, the private equity arm of Kite Bank, is financing much of the Zubinos expansion. KPE is quoted as being 'very pleased with Zubinos operational and financial performance to date'.

End of pre-seen material

Zubinos: approach and explore the case situation

Introduction

This chapter covers steps 1 and 2 of the case study approach that we discussed in Chapter 4 of this Study Text.

Topic list
1 Approach Zubinos (Steps 1.1 to 1.7)
2 Analyse the numbers (Step 2.1)
3 General environmental analysis (PEST) and trends (Step 2.2)
4 Analyse the business environment and competitive strategy (Step 2.3)
5 Audit the product/service portfolio (Step 2.4)
6 How does the business add value? (Step 2.5)
7 Identify information systems and processes (Step 2.6)
8 Identify key issues in structure, culture and personnel (Step 2.7)
9 Identify investor objectives, capital structure and other stakeholder objectives (Step 2.8)
10 Identify and analyse possible business projects (Step 2.9)

1 Approach Zubinos (Steps 1.1 to 1.7)

Read, re-read and mark up the case (Steps 1.1 to 1.3)

This is just a reminder – **skim reading** the case twice at the outset enables you to get a better grasp of the big picture.

Quickly re-read the case after a time (Step 1.2) – perhaps the day after you first received it – an important part of the review process.

Mark up the case slowly, taking notes (Step 1.3), is your first detailed reading of the case. The purpose of this stage is to get you set up for writing a précis. You are not going into decision making mode here, just noting and summarising the data so you make sure you are covering everything. So, put away your calculator.

Summarise the data in a précis (Step 1.4)

In Chapter 4, we showed you how to do a précis. Go back to Chapter 4 Step 1.4 for the details. Once you have refreshed your memory, write your précis of Zubinos.

(a)   **Look at our précis below.** Do you think it is any good? Yours may well be better.

(b)   **Sample précis 1**. Give marks out of ten to your précis and ours. Someone else you know who is doing the exam may also be willing to mark it.

Give marks out of ten	Your précis	Our précis
Q1 Does the précis cover the key points at the right level of detail?		
Q2 Does the précis avoid analysis at this stage?		
Q3 Is the précis clearly structured?		
Q4 Is the précis well written?		

BPP précis	Chapter para reference
Market overview	1-5
Zubinos is a UK chain of coffee shops. Service marketing is an important consideration. There is strong competition and low barriers to entry. Location is critical, brands enable higher prices to be charged and coffee is an 'affordable luxury' purchase.	
The first Zubinos coffee shop	
Luis invested £300,000, using his own savings and borrowing money. Later investors have had to pay more for their shares, suggesting that wealth is being generated.	8
Luis knows the importance of location and convenience, although he later understands the significance of the **brand** for further expansion.	9
Note that demand peaks at different times: time of day could be used for **segmentation**.	
Zubinos' strategy of offering freshly made sandwiches and ice cream **differentiated** it against other branded coffee shops. There is a high level of repeat business.	10-11
People joining at the bottom could be given management positions quickly.	12
The growth of Zubinos	
There has been rapid expansion. **Segmentation** and **targeting** are mentioned with the 20 to 35 market. The main objective is growth. The rapid expansion shows evidence of low entry barriers.	13-15
By appointing George Shale, Luis is professionalising the management of the business. George recommends a strategy of market development (Ansoff), believing that other parts of the UK are less competitive.	
Jane Thorp is marketing director. She sees the potential of the **brand**.	6

BPP précis	Chapter para reference
Zubinos could consider opening coffee shops on the premises of another retailer.	17
Profitability is lower than some of its competitors.	18
Staffing issues and performance related bonuses	
Is Zubinos going through a crisis of delegation?	19-23
Zubinos is centralising certain management functions, such as procurement, marketing and HRM, thereby reducing the autonomy of local shops and instituting stricter control measures.	
The performance related bonuses seem to rely on financial measures. Lower bonus payments may be demotivating.	
Fair trade produce	
Luis believes coffee beans should be bought from Fair Trade suppliers, justifying a price premium and the policy is marketed.	24-26
IT development	
Zubinos is building a 'community' of people using its website, which might build loyalty. Also, the website allows brand extension – sale of coffee direct – a type of product development	27
There is a lack of financial and business information in a usable format. A new IT system will cost £110,000.	28-29
Introduction of a business investor	
The loan finance of 12% is expensive. Zubinos has been astute in obtaining long term investment resources to put its finances on a more secure footing 10% is still high.	30-34
Although the third 5-year loan is supposed to fund 'working capital', in effect it replaces money used for expansion. The expansion is to be rapid: this creates certain kinds of risk, eg overtrading. However, the professional management structure seems designed to take the company forward.	
Shareholdings at December 2005	
KPE paid £6 per share. This effectively values the company at £6m, or £5.4m if we deduct the loans. KPE has 40% of the shares but, critically, is offering a line of credit. This investor has power.	35-37
Luis and his wife own 42% of the shares. Luis is Chairman and Managing director.	
Analysis of gross margin	
A new MIS is planned to be operational in early 2006.	38
Only 34% of turnover is made up by coffee products or only 43.6% for all drinks. Drinks provide just over 50% of the gross margin, however. Even so, more than half of revenue, and just under half of gross margin, is accounted for by food.	39
Zubinos expansion plans	
The five year plan involves rapid expansion, financed by cash generated from operations and additional loan finance from KPE.	40-41
There is a problem with finding suitable properties to rent so shops have been purchased at over £1m.	42
Criteria for the selection of new sites are strength of competition, adequate resources and sufficient consumer demand. Presence of well-known chains is another factor.	43-44
Jane Thorp has proposed setting up cyber cafes.	45

BPP précis	Chapter para reference
Labelling of food	
There are no formal procedures for innovation and for piloting new products. Local initiatives have been discouraged. There is a potential market for low calorie products	46-47
Other recent developments	
A delivery service to local businesses has been started.	48
Zubinos could offer a wider range of foods.	49
Proposed expansion overseas	
Luis has European contacts keen to operate Zubinos coffee shops, growth overseas is included in the 5 year plan.	50-52
Reasons for expansion overseas include a saturated home market, less intense competition and comparative advantage against local competition.	
Appendix 1 Personnel	
There is no organisation chart.	
Luis is young and appears committed to the business.	
Vivien has been at the heart of new product development although she only works part time.	
Jane is used to consumer marketing and knows about fast food chains.	
Maria is in charge of procurement which Zubinos has had problems with. Local managers need help in forecasting.	
Anita has taken HR back in-house, there is no strategy for HRM.	
George helped put together the business plan and is emotionally committed to it. Accounting and finance matters have been taken back in-house.	
Bob knows about startups, although not about food retailing.	
Jack has introduced new procedures but has clashed with Anita on HR issues.	
Val and Sally are area managers for coffee shops – defined as 'new roles'. They are also responsible for recruitment and management of all staff.	
Carl represents 40% of the shares. He will get more involved if Zubinos does not hit its target.	
Appendix 4 Newspaper reports	
Zubinos coffee shops are larger than their competitors.	
Zubinos competes effectively: yet the industry is consolidating and other firms are growing by acquisition.	
KPE is pleased with 'operational and financial performance'	

So, what do you think about the précis above? Remember the point of the exercise is to assimilate information.

Carry out an information audit (Step 1.5)

We suggest you enlarge and photocopy the schedules already provided in Chapter 4 and mark them up (✓, X or P) with the information you have. The purpose of this is to go over again what you have after your précis, and to analyse more precisely what you are missing. It also enables you to start classifying the information into frameworks that can be used.

Research the industry (Step 1.6)

We chose Zubinos for our teaching case because it is the most accessible of the case studies to date. You can visit coffee shops and read about them very easily. You may already have a good knowledge of the business sector in which they operate, how they sell their products and how they compete.

You can use the internet to look up information on their likely rivals in the real world and topical issues such as fair trade.

Identify relevant technical knowledge (Step 1.7)

The following table lists possible technical knowledge issues for you to consider. Not all of these will need pursuing further. Most of these are covered in the other steps in the BPP approach.

Knowledge area

- Objectives and goal congruence
- Internal controls
- Ways to deal with risk:
    - Accept, insure, control, manage, transfer
- Greiner's organisational life cycle
- Service marketing mix
- Ansoff matrix
- Shareholder value analysis
- 5 forces/competitive strategies
- Corporate governance
- Ethics
    - Personal/professional ethics as a management accountant
    - Business ethics
    - Corporate social responsibility
- Project appraisal techniques
- Benchmarking
- Customer profitability analysis
- Supply chain management
- Motivation theory
- Mendelow's stakeholder matrix
- Sources of finance
- Business valuation
- e-commerce and McFarlan's grid
- Branding
- WACC
- Segmentation
- Boston matrix

In practice, most of the knowledge elements you cover will be drawn out from the specific steps we take to explore the case, analyse the case and synthesise our results.

2 Analyse the numbers (step 2.1)

In the exam, you will only have a limited amount of time, so try to get to the heart of the data now. In our guide to the BPP approach, we gave a **checklist** of possible items to be considered, but **you should always add other numerical analysis that you consider useful.** You are very interested in future trends, which is why Zubinos' five year plan is useful.

Below we have calculated a table of ratios. We have not calculated every ratio in the list in Chapter 4 and we have added a few others. **You may have calculated a different set of ratios or gone into more detail.** Remember, you are using ratio analysis to **become more familiar with the case** – all the knowledge and technical abilities you now possess are tools to use.

Table of ratios

Actual vs forecast	The forecast is ambitious. There is no evidence yet that it is not being met, the 2005 figures are favourable.
Turnover	Turnover rose 75% last year Turnover is forecast to rise at 56% pa over the next 5 years There is no breakdown of turnover growth by store or product
Cost of sales	Gross margin in 2005 (weighted for sales mix) was 64.3%. Net margin in 2005 was 9.1%. Therefore, overheads to sales in 2005 was 55.2%.
Gross profit percentage	64.3% overall in 2005. No year to year comparators are available.
Expenses	Not separately available.
Net profit	There has been a slight reduction in net margin from 9.3% in 2004 to 9.1% in 2005. The pre-seen suggests this may be due to new stores.
Interest cover	Loans at between 10% and 12% Interest cover in 2005 = 14.56 times
Dividend cover	No dividends have been paid since 2001.
ROCE	Taking profits pre interest and tax over equity plus loans: 2004 = 737/2,684 = 27% 2005 = 1,267/6,281 = 20% Although falling, the ROCE is in excess of the cost of debt, at least. Also, ROCE will be low due to the expensive stores purchased during the year and the fact that new stores do not have the benefit of an entire year's earnings.
Retained profit/assets employed	Zubinos retains all its profits at present.
Non-current assets	In 2004 Zubinos generated £2.69 or revenue per £1 of non-current assets. In 2005 it generated £1.98 per £1. Could suggest that it overpaid for the most recent shops, certainly a worrying trend if more shops are to be acquired.
Turnover/current assets	2004 = £13.18 2005 = £13.64 This is a marginal improvement but not significant
Turnover periods Inventory, Receivables, Payables	Main point here is the greater use of trade credit. 2004 = 31.59 days 2005 = 35.8 days As the number of shops increase so does the amount of credit (from £689,000 in 2004 to £1,367,000 in 2005). It can be seen that credit taken is being extended too although it is not excessive.
Working capital/assets employed	Not relevant
Current/quick ratio	2004 = 0.23 2005 = 0.34 Given that this is a cash business this apparent lack of solvency is not an issue and is common in retail businesses.

Gearing	2004 = 600/(2,084 + 600) = 22%
	2005 = 900/(5,381 + 900) = 14%
	Zubinos is low geared.
Earnings per share	2004 = 508,000/600,000 = £0.85
	2005 = 897,000/1,000,000 = £0.90
	Forecast EPS 2010 = (10,977000 × 0.76)/1,000,000 = £8.34
Price/earnings ratio	Not available using market values. KPE paid (2.4/0.4) £6 per share in 2005 which, using 2004 EPS, gives PE of 7.
Cost of capital	Not possible to calculate without making complex assumptions about future dividends.

These ratios are a useful starting point but we need to look at some areas of the financial data in more depth.

Gross margin analysis

	Coffee products	Other drinks	Sandwiches	Ice-cream	Other foods	Total
Sales revenue £'000	4,734	1,344	3,584	896	3,360	13,918
% of sales revenue	34%	10%	26%	6%	24%	100%
Gross margin £'000	3,808	702	2,324	714	1,398	8,946
Gross margin %	80%	52%	65%	80%	42%	64%
% contribution to gross margin	42%	8%	26%	8%	16%	100%

Valuation of shares

(a) **Net assets method**

On the basis of 2005 figures $\dfrac{\text{Equity}}{\text{Number of shares}} = \dfrac{5,381,000}{1,000,000} = £5.38$ per share

(b) **Price/earnings method**

Post tax earnings = £897,000

P/E Sector ratio = 20

Adjustment for Zubinos not being listed = 1/3

Valuation = $\dfrac{897,000 \times 20 \times (1 - 1/3)}{1,000,000} = £11.96$ per share

(c) **Earnings flow valuation**

	2006 £'000	2007 £'000	2008 £'000	2009 £'000	2010 £'000
Pre-tax operating profit	2,160	3,613	5,606	8,203	10,977
Less: tax 24%	(518)	(867)	(1,345)	(1,969)	(2,634)
Post-tax earnings	1,642	2,746	4,261	6,234	8,343
Discount factor 12%	0.893	0.797	0.712	0.636	0.567
Discounted earnings	1,466	2,189	3,034	3,965	4,730

Value of discounted earnings = 15,384,000

Value per share = $\dfrac{15,384}{1,000} = £15.38$ per share

2.1 Financial analysis report

You are the business adviser of Charles Frere, a rich friend of Vivien Zubino. Vivien has discussed with Charles the possibility of Charles purchasing 50,000 of the unissued shares of Zubinos, at a price of £7 per share. Charles is unsure whether this price is really a fair price and would like your comments on a fair valuation for the company, also the company's future prospects and financial risks.

Requirement

Prepare a report for Charles, discussing the principal features of Zubinos' most recent accounts and forecasts and advising him on a range of possible values per share. Your report should indicate what further information would be helpful for your analysis.

Report

This report comments on the main features of the most recent accounts and forecasts, suggests possible fair values under a range of methods and lists further information that would assist in valuing Zubinos.

1   **2005 accounts**

(a)   **Profitability and returns**

Zubinos' **profit margin** and **increases in revenue and profit** appear to be **much better** than for many other coffee shop chains. Despite the significant increase in shop numbers, revenues, costs and operating profits have all increased at roughly the same rate in 2005, indicating that the expansion in 2005 appears to have been **well-controlled.** The breakdown of gross margins indicates that coffee sales only contribute about a third of revenues, though just over 40% of profits due to high mark-up. The amount of revenues generated by food may have implications for the forecasts (discussed below).

The significant increase in earnings has boosted **earnings per share** by 6%, but the overall increase in finance has caused **return on capital employed** to drop from 27% to 20%. This figure is dependent on how much extra capital will be required over the next couple of years. Revenues generated by non-current assets have fallen significantly due to the investments in freehold rather than leasehold property in 2005.

(b)   **Liquidity and working capital**

Both **current and quick ratios** are low, although for a consumables retailer this is not uncommon. The **fall in the current ratio** has been largely due to the much smaller increase in inventory (6%) than would be suggested by the expansion of shops, suggesting better control. The **increase in receivables** will mostly be due to prepayments on rentals, but may be partly due to problems collecting debts on the delivery service.

The main concern is the **rapid increase** in **trade payables**, with Zubinos now taking somewhat over a month on average to pay suppliers. Further increases may not only jeopardise Zubinos' **relations** with its suppliers, but also Zubinos' **reputation** as a Fair Trade customer. Zubinos' dependence on short-term finance appears to be increasing, which is rather worrying as the last bank loan was required to cover **increases in working capital.** Another concern is how well shop managers are carrying out **cash flow planning.**

(c)   **Gearing**

It seems that Zubinos has potential to obtain extra loan finance as gearing at 14% has fallen as a result of the **venture capital investment** and the venture capitalist is happy to provide more loan capital. The interest cover of 14.6 suggests there is no problem meeting commitments.

However over the next couple of years retained cash earnings will not be enough to meet capital expenditure requirements and monies will be required to repay the loans repayable in

---

2006 and 2007. As mentioned above, **reliance on short-term finance** appears to be **increasing**. In addition the directors may intend Zubinos to start paying dividends; if it does, this will limit the retained funds available for investment.

2 2006 – 2010 Forecast

The rapid expansion planned makes the production of a reliable forecast very difficult. The forecast produced represents only one set of figures, based upon a number of assumptions some of which are **not clear** (see further information required) and which may differ significantly from the actual figures. In addition the company's forecasting has not been **very accurate** in the past, with under-estimation of the expansion in the early years, and the failure of staff to meet targets in late 2005 possibly being the result of over-optimistic recent forecasts.

In addition Zubinos' ability to meet the forecast will not only depend on the predicted demand levels being reached, but also the **finance** being available to support the required expansion and the **management and infrastructure** being further developed.

The following areas of the forecasts are particularly significant.

(a) Revenues – coffee shops

Most of the forecast growth is dependent upon the success of the new coffee shops opened after 2005. The figures suggest that saturation point will not have been reached in the **UK market** by 2010 as Zubinos is continuing to open shops in the UK up until that date. However the company appears to be expecting a **peak** to **be reached** in 2007, as the number of UK openings and the rate of growth in revenue per shop fall after that. This may reflect **expectations of UK market trends** that may not be very predictable, also expectations that shops opened abroad will have to **limit prices** whilst Zubinos establishes itself. Also by 2007 Zubinos may be located in all places with **most potential** in the UK, and after then will be choosing from locations with less promise.

In addition the forecast increases will also depend on being able to increase revenues from the product range in existing and new shops. As the products Zubinos already offers appear to be well-diversified, there may not be much scope for introducing new high-revenue earning products, even though the possibility of offering a wider range of foods is currently being investigated. Thus Zubinos' ability to increase revenue per shop appears to be dependent on its ability to **increase prices** without suffering a fall in demand, the effect of which matches or outweighs the rise in prices.

(b) Revenues – other products

The forecast suggests a very major expansion in new products over the next year or so with significant increases in following years. It is difficult to say how realistic these expectations are, as there is no detailed information about what these products are likely to be, or whether the category includes products that will be sold in coffee shops or is limited to products sold by other means. The forecast may be based on expansion of **on-line merchandise**, with the increase in sales fuelled by better publicity as well as more products.

(c) Costs and profit margins

Although operating profit margin dropped between 2004 and 2005, the directors expect that margins will gradually improve between 2005 and 2010. This suggests that the board expects **costs** to be kept under **reasonable control**, even if the increase in margins is mainly driven by enhanced revenues.

Costs may be limited by **centralising activities** such as **ordering**, also **rentals** on shops outside London being lower than for shops within the city. In addition the board appears to be taking a cautious attitude to initiatives involving significant expenditure, refusing to invest in on-line facilities for the cafes and scaling down the level of IT expenditure.

However there are a number of reasons why Zubinos may have difficulties limiting expenditure, although some of the items listed below will be capitalised rather than affecting profit margins.

(i)   Zubinos is continuing to rely on **Fair Trade suppliers**

(ii)   Zubinos has historically operated a policy of **significant investment** in **staff** and **fixtures and fittings**, and commercial pressures are likely to mean that this policy has to continue

(iii) **Increased expenditure** on **central functions** such as human resources will be necessary as the company expands

(iv)   **Further investment** in **information technology** may also be required

(v)   **Distribution costs** may **increase** significantly as Zubinos expands over the UK and into Europe

(d)   Capital expenditure

The predicted level of capital expenditure per new shop opened drops significantly from £600,000 in 2005 to between £317,000 and £342,000 over the 2006 – 2010 period. In 2005 significant expenditure was needed to acquire the two freehold sties. The assumption appears to be that the great majority of new shops will be **leasehold sites**, but this will depend on what is available in the desired locations. It is also unclear how much capital expenditure will be needed to **refit** and **upgrade** existing stores, or how capital expenditure will be financed, as post-tax operating profits (and presumably retained cash) will not exceed capital expenditure until 2008.

3   Valuation methods

(a)   Net assets method

The net assets method is based on the **current book value** of assets and takes no account of the future earnings potential of the company. It is generally used as a floor value in share purchase and acquisition negotiations. However the most recent value of shares in 2005 at £6.00 was rather closer to the net assets value of £5.38 based on the 2005 accounts than the other methods based on **earnings potential** that give higher values.

(b)   Price-earnings ratio

This value has been calculated on the following basis.

(i)   Taking **Zubinos' earnings in 2005**

(ii)   Multiplying by a broad **average price-earnings ratio** of 20 for listed companies in the beverages sector

(iii) **Scaling down the valuation by 1/3** to take account of the fact that Zubinos' shares are not listed and hence are more difficult to sell

This method suggests a fair value of about £12 per share, and suggests the asking price of £7 is an undervalue. However, the following points should be kept in mind.

(i)   The 2005 earnings figure is a snapshot in the middle of a period when Zubinos is expanding rapidly.

(ii)   20 is an **average** that does not take into account wide variations in the sector; other data suggests that the sector is becoming increasingly polarised between companies that are doing very well and companies that are seriously struggling.

(iii) More **sector-specific data** than for the whole beverages sector would be useful.

(iv)   The **reduction of 1/3 in value** is fairly **arbitrary**.

(c) **Earnings methods**

This method takes operating earnings after tax and discounts them at a factor reflecting the company's weighted average cost of capital to approximate to a present value of future cash earnings. The forecast figures up to 2010 have been used; the cost of capital used is 12% on the basis that the **cost of debt** is lower than the interest rates charged because of tax relief on debt, but the **cost of equity** is rather higher than the cost of debt, because equity investment is riskier.

The value calculated per share, £15.38, is more than double the existing asking price. However there are a number of problems with this figure.

(i) It is dependent upon the **quality** of the **forecasts**.

(ii) The cost of capital figure chosen is an **approximation**, and a true figure might be higher, implying a lower valuation.

(iii) No account has been taken of earnings flows after 2010.

(iv) The figures have not been adjusted for **depreciation** or for **capital expenditure**.

(d) **Other comments**

The following **other reservations** apply to the valuation exercise.

(i) The **dividend valuation model** cannot be used to value the shares because Zubinos has not paid any dividends. The dividend valuation model is argued to be often the best method of valuing small % holdings of shares since shareholders holding small quantities of shares have **little control** over the **policies that determine earnings**.

(ii) Bringing **risk** into the valuation exercise is difficult but there clearly are risks in investing, as many companies in this sector are in financial difficulties, and if problems arise the bank and venture capital company will have first claim on the company's assets.

(iii) At present it appears that any **returns** from the shares will have to be realised in the form of **capital gains** as Zubinos is not paying any dividends. These can best be realised by Zubinos being listed on a stock exchange, but at present there are no plans to seek a listing.

4   **Other information required**

There are a number of issues concerning the forecasts on which more information would be helpful. It would be useful to know the **sources** of the data used, as if the forecasts were largely based on data supplied by **current shops**, these forecasts have not always been very accurate in the past. Another key issue is whether the forecasts are based on the assumption that growth will continue to be **organic** (that is not boosted by acquisitions) and new shops opened mainly in **leasehold** premises, also whether the forecasts assume that some of the new shops will be in the premises of another retailer.

More details would be helpful in the following areas.

(a) What will the impact, if any, on the forecasts of any predicted economic/ industry/ market/ social **trends** over the next five years?

(b) The UK locations or geographical areas into which Zubinos is likely to expand in the next couple of years need to be considered. Bear in mind that the shops opened during this time period are expected to deliver **high growth**, despite **competition** that Zubinos is likely to face in those locations.

(c) From 2008, what will be the **split in** expected revenues and profits **between** UK **and** overseas **shops**?

(d) Any **expected changes** in the **product mix** offered by the shops need to be factored in?

(e) Which **new products** are meant to be the most substantial contributors to the growth in new products?

(f) Will there be any changes in the way the company operates that will have a **significant influence on cost patterns**? Examples include quality standards, staffing of new shops, use of suppliers and development of centralised functions.

(g) Is capital expenditure is solely expected to be on **new shops**? or will existing fixtures and fittings will have to be replaced or a larger refit be required in order to maintain Zubinos' reputation for being trendy?

(h) Is Zubinos is likely to pay any **dividends** over the next few years?

5 **Conclusion**

The value of the investment depends on how the forecasts are viewed. Whilst Zubinos has exceeded forecasts in the past, its forecast expansion over the next few years is on a much greater scale than before. The price asked for appears reasonable in the light of what the venture capitalist paid a year ago and Zubinos' results in 2005. However I recommend that further details should be sought about the assumptions made in the forecast before a final decision is taken on whether to invest.

Appendices

Note that the financial data that we have included earlier in this section would be inserted as appendices to a report.

3 General environmental analysis (PEST) and trends (Step 2.2)

PEST analysis is familiar to you from Business Strategy, but is a good test of your commercial awareness. PEST feeds into the **analysis of the risks** the business is facing.

PEST

Political and legal factors

General 'political' factors have very little impact on Zubinos. Its main resource, coffee, is widely available and is a traded commodity. However, government decisions on personal and business taxation, employment regulation and so on will affect Zubinos, as is the case with other business.

Legal and regulatory factors have a significant impact. Environmental health and food safety are enforced by local government through inspection. Local government officials can order Zubinos to close its coffee shops if the premises are not clean. Local authorities also grand planning permission (eg if a building's use changes) and, should Zubinos wish to sell alcohol, grant licenses.

Because Zubinos is a limited company, it is regulated by company law. It must keep suitable accounting records. It collects VAT and PAYE for the government.

Government regulations on labour may differ from market to market. When expanding into France and Spain, full account needs to be taken of local employment laws, which vary from country to country. The growth of the EU should make it easier to do business in these countries.

If the company decides to float on a Stock Exchange, then the regulatory burden will grow.

Economic factors

As a discretionary purchase, coffee might be affected by a downturn in the economy. If people have less to spend, for example if interest rates on mortgages rise, they are likely to give up luxuries or switch to cheaper products. If unemployment rises, fewer people will visit Zubinos on the way to work. On the other hand, there will be downward pressure on wages, so the firm will be able to contain its costs.

The exchange rate might affect the cost of some inputs. Net margins are relatively low, so a significant rise in input costs – unlikely though this is – could hurt margins.

Local economic factors, as suggested in the case, are very important for each shop.

Social and cultural factors

This is critical. The company is targeting a demographic segment, and so needs to be in tune with the feelings and aspirations of that segment. To what extent is the coffee culture a permanent feature of the UK landscape? Other branded formats have flourished and declined owing to changing fashions and change in buyer behaviour. Fewer people are visiting pubs, for example, that was the case 20 years ago.

People are becoming more health conscious, and if caffeine is associated with ill health, Zubinos will have to respond: but there are alternative beverages, decaffeinated versions and so on. (Green tea, for example, is being promoted as a healthy beverage.)

Technology

It is unlikely that there will be any replacement for 'eating out' or cafés. However, as suggested in the case, Internet access can be an additional service that is offered to customers. Technology can be used for marketing (eg website, text messages on mobile phones and so on).

Technology is also influential in the operational management of the business, and the collection of management information. Developments in this respect (eg linking the stores to a central procurement system, perhaps linked electronically to suppliers) will be helpful.

4 Analyse the business environment and competitive strategy (step 2.3)

Compare your completed checklists below with ours and summarise them in a five forces analysis.

4.1 Five forces and industry analysis

Step 1 Identify the type of industry

What industries does the company operate in?		Classify as **emergent**, **mature** or **declining**
1	Coffee shops	Mature
2		
3		

Step 2 Threat of new entrants

	Item	Comment
1	High capital costs to enter	No
2	Is there a strong brand?	No
3	Is the industry attractive?	Yes
4	Does the case suggest new entrants?	Yes
5	Ease of exit (if declining sector)	Yes
	Threat of new entrants: high, medium or low (H/M/L)?	H

Step 3   Substitute products

	Item	Comment
1	Can other industries provide the same benefit?	Yes
2	Does the case evidence any threats?	Yes
3	Other considerations	
	Threat of substitute products: high, medium or low (H/M/L)?	H

Step 4   Customer bargaining power (and marketing issues)

	Item	Comment
1	Consumer or business to business?	Both
	If B-to-B, any issues in customers' own markets?	
2	Total revenue	£13.9 m
3	Market size	£1 bn
4	Market share	Small
5	Does the organisation really understand its customers and their needs?	Yes
6	Can key segments be identified in the data? If yes, what are they and what percentage of sales do they represent?	No
7	Trends in revenue and other sales performance indicators	Rapid growth
8	Does the case identify any Key Customers who account for a significant proportion of revenue? If Yes, note details Is it possible to do a customer profitability analysis? If so, are there some customers who are not profitable?	Yes 20-35 age group seen as the target market • No • Not known
9	Are current customers loyal or beginning to defect? How serious is this?	Customer loyalty is likely to be low given the number of substitutes
10	Are customers price sensitive?	Possibly
11	Does the case identify customers and markets not served?	Outside the UK
12	Can customers obtain the same benefits elsewhere?	Probably
13	Does the organisation have a coherent marketing strategy based on the 7Ps? Product – Price – Promotion – Place – People – Process – Physical evidence	Probably
14	Does the organisation consider building long-term customer relationships?	Possibly
15	What is the branding policy?	Brand is important but hard to compete with other global brands
	Customer bargaining power? high, medium or low (H/M/L)?	H

Step 5 Suppliers and resources

	Item	Comment
1	Supplier industries – what resources does the business consume?	Coffee, other foodstuffs
2	Are key suppliers identified? How close is the relationship?	No
3	Trends in input costs – and volatility See analysis of ratios	Not known
4	Is there a supply policy?	No
5	Ease of sourcing supplies from others/new suppliers	There are problems with supply
6	Can firm easily pass on increases in prices to customers?	No
7	Is the supply chain managed strategically?	No
	Supplier bargaining power: high, medium or low (H/M/L)?	M

Step 6 Questions about competitors

	Item	Comment
1	Does the case identify particular current competitors? If yes What are their goals and competitive strategy?	No Coffee shops are very competitive, but competition is very local
2	Does the case suggest potential competitors in the current industry?	Yes
	Competitive rivalry: high, medium or low (H/M/L)?	H

Now let us produce a specific competitive forces checklist.

Competitive forces checklist

Existing competition and competitive rivalry: intense

- There is intense competition
- Further differentiation is difficult to secure (quality and ethics are already catered for)
- The saturated home market may lead to consolidation in the industry
- Economies of scale enjoyed by large global brands may be difficult to match

New entrants

- Barriers to entry are low (Luis started successfully with a £300,000 loan)
- Bookshops, pubs, even petrol stations (BP's 'Wild Bean café') can offer coffee
- While it is easy to open a coffee shop, building a **brand** is harder
- Sandwich bars can compete

Substitutes

- Flasks – people can make coffee or other drinks at home
- Vending machines are getting better (Klix)
- Free water dispensers are provided in many offices
- Other meeting places include pubs and clubs for entertainment

Buyers

- Individuals exercise buying power through choice
- Companies (deliveries) may have high buying power

Suppliers

- Coffee is a widely traded commodity so supplier power is low: hence fair trade
- Suppliers of rental property have high buying power

The industry would appear to offer low profitability: brand building and scale economies would appear crucial for the long term.

---

5 Audit the product/service portfolio (Step 2.4)

Step 1 Define the product in terms of customer needs satisfied

Customers want to buy coffee and food products in a convenient location in shops with a good atmosphere. They are increasingly demanding a wide range of foods using premium products.

Step 2 Identify product and service elements

Product	Good coffee and food with an emphasis on Free Trade ingredients
Price	Premium pricing due to association with coffee culture and ambiance of shops
Promotion	Only the website is mentioned
Place	Key criterion in growth is the selection of sites in proximity to travel hubs and offices employing the target customers
People	Given that production of the drinks and management of the shops must take place with customers present, it is vital that the appearance and manner of the staff communicates the service values of Zubinos.
Physical	The appearance of the shops, their layout, furnishings, lighting and music will all be critical to making them somewhere that people want to meet, or to relax. To a lesser extent the crockery and cartons in which food and drink is provided will be an element here
Process	For take-away customers the speed of service is likely to be a key criterion. For the eat-in customer it is likely that an ability to linger will be important. Blending these two different service requirements will be essential

Step 3 Use the Boston matrix to identify how the product or service is positioned

Not presently relevant as Zubinos has only one line of business. Clearly individual stores may be classed as cash cows or problem children to assess cash flows in the company. The low relative share of Zubinos can be interpreted through the matrix as a possible weakness due to lack of economies or scale, lack of experience effects and lack of brand penetration.

Step 4 Product costs and profitability

We know that in December 2001, profitability was lower than that of its rivals. In Paragraph 18 of the pre-seen, we note that profitability was lower than **some** of its competitors, not all.

The gross margin is 64% (Para 39), the operating profit margin before tax is 9.1% (£1,267/£13,918). Costs in 2005 were £12,651, of which food and drink accounted for £4,972. The other expenses must relate to premises costs and overheads, including depreciation, or over 60% of total costs. 42.5% of the gross margin is accounted for by coffee (Para 39: £3,808/£8,946).

6 How does the business add value? (Step 2.5)

The value chain is another useful model for identifying what the business does and its strengths and weaknesses.

Value chain

Inbound logistics	• Quality ice cream • Fair trade coffee beans	• Duplicated/inconsistent ordering (customers do not receive high quality as standard) • Only 80% of the coffee is 'fair trade'. This undercuts the positioning. • There is a lack of planning and discipline in procurement.
Operations	• Staffing levels are suitable • Locations are good • Expensive fixtures/fittings • Internet access/ordering	• Thefts – possible stock-outs/disruption to service • Low-cost 'scaled down' internal IT systems • No customer focused innovations allowed
Outbound logistics	Delivery service/catering	No post-sale liaison with customers re: payment for deliveries
Marketing	Little known	Little known
Service	Incorporated above	Incorporated above

7 Identify information systems and processes (Step 2.6)

	Issue	Comment
1	**Information technology**	
1.1	What are the structural arrangements for IT? (eg IT department, delegated to users, information centre, outsourced)	Not clear
1.2	Who looks after IT strategy and security?	No clear role but Jane Thorp and George Shale have an input
1.3	What is the role of IT in the development of the company? (McFarlan's grid) • Factory • Support • Turnround • Strategic	Support
1.4	Is IT use considered within the business strategy and is it implementation harmonised with it?	No
1.5	Is e-commerce relevant and does the firm have a stance towards this development?	Yes, Zubinos website recently updated
1.6	Main packages • Operational reporting • Corporate reporting	Unknown

	Issue	Comment
2	**Knowledge and information**	
2.1	What internal communication systems are in use – eg paper, email, intranet?	Unknown
2.2	Do managers receive good information in terms of the performance of the business (ACCURATE mnemonic)?	No
2.3	Knowledge management – is information shared or hoarded?	Unknown
3	**Risk**	
3.1	Does current IT set up involve business or security risk?	Yes • Lack of appropriate management information • Risks from website
4	**Management and internal control systems**	
4.1	How are activities and resources controlled in the organisation?	Rather chaotic with weaknesses apparent in internal control
4.2	Is the management accounting system well designed and operated?	No
4.3	Who sets performance targets, and are they effective?	There is a bonus scheme but it has caused problems
4.4	What is the extent of centralisation versus decentralisation?	Some attempt at centralisation but not particularly effective
4.5	Is reporting timely?	No
4.6	Are management accounting and information systems regularly audited?	No evidence.
4.7	Generally, are principles of good corporate governance followed (eg separation of chairman and chief executive?)	No
4.8	Is the business susceptible to fraud (computer-based or otherwise?)	Yes

8 Identify key issues in structure, culture and personnel (Step 2.7)

Fill in the checklist in Chapter 4 to marshal your thoughts.

(a) **Structure**

Item	Comment
Step 1 Draw an organisation chart, if the case has not already provided you with one.	
Step 1.1 What sort of departmentation approach is used (eg functional, matrix)?	Functional but with some overlaps of responsibility for recruitment

Item	Comment
Step 2 Does the case data indicate any problems with the current organisation structure, such as reporting/communication, corporate governance, co-ordination, focus on the business?	Yes • Corporate governance • Weaknesses in internal controls
Step 3 Does the case data offer opportunities for you to benchmark the performance of different departments with other firms? If so, how does the firm compare?	Yes With 18 shops already there are opportunities for identifying and disseminating best practice.
Step 4 Identify any outsourcing arrangements currently in force, and arrive at a reasoned judgement as to how effective they are in terms of operations, risk and financial security.	Payroll No information on effectiveness
Step 5 Identify any possible opportunities for outsourcing and note feasibility.	IT?
Step 6 In your opinion, is the structure a strength or a weakness in the light of the situation facing the business and why?	Lack of clarify of roles is a weakness.
Step 7 Recommend improvements: what structure (in brief) would you consider better?	Need to adopt a formal structure suitable for their strategy.

(b) **Culture**

Item	Comment
Step 1 What does the case tell you about the culture of the organisation and its management? Classify it, if you can, according to a framework used in your earlier studies.	A mix of the rational model, freewheeling opportunism and incrementalist
Step 2 Is it a strength or a weakness?	

(c) **Personnel**

Item	Comment
Step 1 Who are the key people?	Luis Zubinos and a committed management team
Step 2 Do they have objectives which can affect the performance of the firm?	Luis is an entrepreneur, driven by a sense of mission
Step 3 What influence do key personnel have? • Internally • Externally	Extremely influential
Step 4 Does the firm have a succession plan?	No
Step 5 Is there any evidence of poor industrial relations?	Bonus scheme is not motivating and is not rewarding performance.
Step 6 Is there a strategy for HRM and is it aligned with the business strategy?	No. HR policy is vague and there are overlapping responsibilities
Step 7 What are its employment policies (contracts, rewards, performance appraisal)?	Relatively high staff costs. Problems with the bonus scheme

Item	Comment
Step 8 Does the firm invest in training?	Area managers have had management training
Step 9 Is there evidence of high staff turnover?	Nothing in the case.
Step 10 Does the firm have skills base and competences needed for the future?	No current evidence of problems.
Step 11 What is the quality of the management team, given the challenges facing the business?	Good
Step 12 Do managers have a shared vision?	
Step 13 Do they understand their rules and responsibilities under corporate governance regulations?	No evidence

9 Identify investor objectives, capital structure and other stakeholder objectives (Step 2.8)

Fill in the checklist below.

	Investors	Comment
Step 1	Identify share owning structure: • Privately owned? • Publicly traded?	A private limited company with 40% of equity externally owned by KPE
Step 2	Note information as to the return shareholders and investors are expecting from the company – use comparative information?	Rapid expansion is planned. Possible future exit strategy for KPE but no details
Step 3	Note trends in the share price, if this information is given.	NA
Step 4	If you have a P/E ratio and a market value, calculate a possible value for the business.	Post tax earnings = £897,000 P/E Sector ratio = 20 Adjustment for Zubinos not being listed = 1/3 Valuation = $\dfrac{897{,}000 \times 20 \times (1-1/3)}{1{,}000{,}000}$ = £11.96 per share
Step 5	Do you have information to calculate the WACC? If yes, do so.	No.
Step 6	Note comparative information about other companies for a benchmark as to shareholder expectations.	None
Step 7	Note data as to the risk of the company (eg the beta)	No data available.

	Investors	Comment
Step 8	Review gearing ratios	2004 = 600/(2,084 + 600) = 22%
		2005 = 900/(5,381 + 900) = 14%
		Zubinos is low geared.
Step 9	Would you invest in this company?	
Step 10	Objectives Remuneration Performance	Already shareholders Bonus scheme issues
Step 11	*Employees* Objectives	*Comment* Unknown
Step 12	*Lenders* Exposure Relationship	*Comment* KPE are happy to provide more loan capital
Step 13	*Government* Power of influence	*Comment* Low
Step 14	*Customers and suppliers*	*Comment* See '5' forces analysis
Step 15	*Community*	*Comment* Ethical trading – Fair Trade issues

10 Identify and analyse possible business projects (Step 2.9)

The overall impression of Zubinos is that of a young company under-going rapid growth. The key question is how should the business expand further? This is possibly the nearest you will get to question spotting.

No.	Project – rationale	Main para refs in case
1	New shop openings in UK	15–17, 40–45
2	New product launches	49
3	Overseas expansion	50–52

10

Zubinos: synthesise what you know

Introduction

This chapter completes the work you will be doing on the pre-seen material.

Do remember that each case is different, there may be further analysis or synthesis work you could do suggested by the data in each individual case.

Topic list
1 Summarise your findings in a position statement (Step 3.1)
2 Draw up a mission statement (Step 3.2)
3 Relate the business's distinctive competences to the critical success factors for the industry (Step 3.3)
4 Identify and analyse risks (Step 3.4)
5 Carry out a graded SWOT analysis (Step 3.5)
6 Identify the key business issues (Step 3.6)
7 Draw up a balanced scorecard (Step 3.7)
8 Prepare a one-page business summary (Step 3.8)

1 Summarise your findings in a position statement (Step 3.1)

As described earlier, this stage may involve updating your précis and summarising your analysis so far. It is your first chance to start identifying connections between the various aspects of the case. You may prefer to do so using a mind map.

Note that one of the purposes for doing this is to enable you to tell yourself a story to fix the case situation in your mind. Here is a possible position statement for Zubinos.

What Zubinos does and how its structured

Zubinos Coffee Houses is a five year old private company that presently operates 18 coffee houses. There are 10 shops in London and the South East of England and a further eight in the rest of the country.

It has featured very rapid growth with store openings accelerating from the original plan of one a year to eight new stores during 2005.

Zubinos has few distinctive characteristics to set it apart from rivals. One potential factor is its use of Fair Trade produce which accounts for 80% of its produce. (*BPP comment: by 'produce' we assume the pre-seen means just coffee and cocoa beans and does not include foods and ice cream*).

The operation of the coffee houses was regionalised in mid-2005 with two Area Managers, Val Pline and Sally Higgins, taking responsibility for London and South East and Regions respectively. The responsibilities of Area Managers are not stated clearly beyond those of assisting store managers with recruitment.

Senior management is structured by function, seemingly following consultancy advice in 2003 with several appointments being made in 2004. The functional responsibilities of Marketing, Procurement, Human Resources and Finance are covered, but there are no board level directors of operations nor information technology.

The board features six directors of whom four have functional responsibilities. There are two Non-Executive Directors, Carl Martin, nominee of Kite Private Equity, and Vivien Zubino, wife of the Luis Zubino the CEO. Neither of these NEDs can be regarded as independent. Luis Zubino combines the roles of Chairman and CEO.

Zubinos is 42% owned by Luis and Vivien Zubino and 40% owned by Kite Private Equity (KPE) with the remaining 18% of shares spread between the remaining directors. KPE will presumably be looking for an exit route to realise the capital gain on its shares.

Zubinos' present financial and competitive performance

In London, Zubinos has 10 out of the 500 branded shops operating, a market share (by location) of 2%. Therefore compared to major operators, it is very small.

Zubinos is profitable. Post tax profits grew 76% in 2005 against turnover growth of 74%. ROCE fell in 2005 to 15.7% compared to 20.7% for 2004 although this may be distorted by many of the eight shops opened in 2005 and included in year-end assets not having yielded a full year's earnings.

Capital gearing has fallen from 22% in 2004 to 14% in 2005 due the present policy of not paying a dividend and instead retaining profits.

Gross margins are strongest in coffee and ice cream (80%) but lower on sandwiches (65%), other drinks (52%) and other foods (42%). The wastage rate on perishable products may be a contributory factor here. However at present Zubinos margins are less than those of its rivals.

Key issues faced by Zubinos: its opportunities and its problems

The main issue facing Zubinos is how to realise the targets in its five year plan in a market that may be becoming mature. This plan shows ambitious growth over the next five years of **outlets** from 18 to 75 (417%), **turnover** by 830% and **profits** by 867%.

The methods by Zubinos will do this have yet to be confirmed. Options include the following.

- Expanding the range of products sold in the shops (for which there is a separate revenue line showing that the percentage of revenue from new products will grow from 3% to in excess of 4% in future years).

- Striking a deal to open Zubinos branches inside the stores of other retail chains.

- Opening more branches in London but also throughout the country, these are included in the 5 year forecast. Part of this issue is whether to rent or buy freehold properties in future.

- Opening stores outside the UK of which the plan forecasts25 by 2010.

- Increasing its web-based business.

Decisions need to be taken on these issues.

There are problems in forecasting business which is leading unplanned procurements and other costs being incurred.

There seem to be some **overlaps in responsibilities** that could cause tensions. One is in the hiring of staff which presently involves the HR director (Anita Wiseman) and the Area Managers. Another is between Anita Wiseman and Jack Rayfield (shop management and security).

There could be some control problems. Financial control seems weak and one fraud has been discovered already.

Information or meetings forthcoming which may affect Zubinos' future.

These are the main outstanding issues.

- The new IT system commissioned in 2005 is due to become operational during 2006. The management information provided by this may help Zubinos to assess the profitability of its stores and products better. It may also improve margins by allowing better forecasting.

- Luis Zubino has been in discussions with other retail outlets to develop shop-in-store opportunities. The results of these discussions are still outstanding.

Debrief

- You have to make judgements. You have only so much data to go on.
- You will be able to develop your thinking when you draw up your business summary. A mind map can help link the issues.

2 Draw up a mission statement (Step 3.2)

The purpose of drawing up a mission statement is to **guide your decision-making** when looking at the unseen data and to **help you prioritise.**

You should be able to say with confidence what the business is for, or who it is for. Your mission statement should reflect the actual mission of the organisation.

Here is a possible **mission statement** for Zubinos.

We aim to provide excellent coffee shops in the UK and Europe, delighting our customers with food as well. We aim to be the best, being welcoming as well as selling the best coffee and food. We support ethical treatment of our suppliers, staff and other stakeholders.	What is missing? (a) Financial targets (b) Behaviour standards and values

3 Relate the business's distinctive competences to the critical success factors for the industry (Step 3.3)

These two models can get you thinking in broad terms about the business and the industry.

Current distinctive competences

A **distinctive** competence has to be distinctive – in other words, something unusual in the market place. It is difficult to see that Zubinos has distinctive competences nor that it has unique resources other than its locations.

CSFs

	CSFs	Does Zubinos have the competences to satisfy them?
1	Brand awareness	Marketing director has experience but needs a congruent strategy.
2	Human resource management	Individuals have human resources capability but needs a clear structure and policy.
3	Supply chain management	No procurement or information systems in place.

Debrief

You may disagree with our assessments of the CSFs in this industry.

4 Identify and analyse risks (Step 3.4)

Risk type	Consequences (quantify if useful)	Importance, likelihood and seriousness
Business		
1 Competitor action	• Increased competition in the locations in which the company operates shops, or changes in the products or facilities offered by existing competitors • Mergers resulting in competitors becoming larger and being able to benefit more from economies of scale, and being in a stronger negotiating position with suppliers	H
2 Property costs	Having to invest in freehold property (and hence incurring higher costs than currently planned) in order to be able to open shops in desirable areas	M
3 Falling returns	From shops in areas experiencing economic downturn, particularly in the retail sector	M
Operational		
1 Procurement problems	Shops could run out of inventory	H
2 Health and safety	Shops could be closed or products not offered	M
3 Quality issues	Failure of products to reach required quality standards could lead to loss of business	M
4 Staffing problems	Dissatisfied staff providing a lower standard of service and increased staff turnover resulting in more mistakes being made by inexperienced staff	H
5 Fraud	Vulnerable to losses because of employee theft of stock or cash	M

Risk type	Consequences (quantify if useful)	Importance, likelihood and seriousness
Financial		
1 Cash shortages	May require finance at possibly high cost to resolve cash shortages arising from expenditure required to finance expansion	M
2 Loss of supply sources	Supplier dissatisfaction may result from length of time taken to pay bills	M
3 Credit risk	Loss of revenue from delivery service through smaller amounts being collected than billed, and customers not paying at all because there is no system for chasing up slow paying debtors.	M
4 Interest rate risk	Zubinos will suffer increased finance costs if interest rates rise, and it has to take out new loans at higher fixed rates or take out loans at floating rates.	M
Exchange		
1 Currency	• If the £ moves adversely against the currencies of the countries where its significant suppliers are located • Currency risk if it expands into Europe and receives revenues in currencies other than £	M
Other		
Information risks	• Inappropriate decisions may be made because of the information systems not providing sufficient information or providing poor quality information • At a shop level, consequences could include ordering insufficient inventory; at a company level inaccurate information about profit margins and unrealistic forecasting could result in poor decisions being made about which products to offer and what prices to charge • Poor information could also lead to underestimates of the amount of cash that will be required, leading to an increased risk of cash shortages	H
Information technology risks	• Problems with the website could result in customers being unable to order products online and being unable to use the chatroom • Unauthorised users may be able to access customer data	M
Economic risks	• Changes in the economic environment such as an economic downturn leading to a fall in demand for expensive coffee as a luxury good • Fall in profits if there was an increase in commodity prices	M
Legal risks	• Stricter employment regulation may limit the hours employees can work and enhancing the protection employees have • Tougher health and safety regulations result in increased compliance costs and legal costs if Zubinos does transgress • New food labelling laws may force Zubinos to label products with nutritional data and threaten demand, as has happened in one London coffee shop • Changes in local planning laws may restrict what Zubinos can do with its buildings	M

Risk type	Consequences (quantify if useful)	Importance, likelihood and seriousness
Social and cultural risks	• Pubs are open for longer hours, leading to pubs rather than coffee shops being seen as places to congregate during the day • Changes in taste may lead to an increased demand for lower calorie foods than Zubinos is currently offering • Decreases in demand for coffee may result from increased fears of the consequences of excessive caffeine intake • As Zubinos has built its business on being fashionable, failing to keep up with changes in fashion, for example in terms of the 'look' of its coffee shops	M
Reputation risks	• Breaches of health and safety regulations and consequent legal action leading to customers believing that Zubinos' products are unhealthy • The ethical stance it has taken over Fair Trade; its marketing literature could be seen as misleading if it decides to use more suppliers who are not Fair Trade, or if it is believed to be exploiting Fair Trade suppliers, for example by slow payments of amounts owed	H

Debrief

(1) You may need to revisit your views in the light of the unseen data in the exam. The fact that a risk is **low** does not mean that it won't happen. It is just to help your decisions regarding your estimation of the **likely** risk.

(2) There is **no probabilistic data** in the pre-seen material so you cannot do more than a fairly simple analysis.

5 Carry out a graded SWOT analysis (Step 3.5)

The list below was the result of a brainstorming session. You may have thought of others.

Strengths	Weaknesses
1 Some good locations, some owned shops bigger than competitors' so higher peak usage capacity 2 Financial position 3 Top management commitment, improved team 4 Better service formula than competitors (App 4) 5 Bigger shops, hence more flexible 6 Good reputation (press release) as a coffee bar 7 Brand, potentially, with strong values (fair trade) 8 Website is successful 9 Some dynamic staff. 10 A variety of food/drink is offered 11 Increasing profitability 12 Zubinos is not running the risk of overtrading, as it is investing and can use long term loan	1 There is confusion in the management structure 2 Poor financial controls 3 Poor planning, poor stock control 4 Lower profits than competitors 5 Difficulties in managing growth. There is internal conflict: head office vs shops, there is conflict within senior management; centralisation stifles local initiative: poor management of innovation 6 Still small, few scale economies of scale 7 Bonus scheme is not motivating, and is not rewarding performance 8 Not diversified (BUT sticking to the knitting) 9 High interest on bank loans

LEARNING MEDIA

Strengths	Weaknesses
13 Zubinos has a generic strategy (differentiation, not clear, location) – but this is not fleshed out (eg targets), not detailed	10 Poor systems and IT– no strategic view, of this resource; not spending enough, given expansion plans
14 Place – good locations	11 HR policies/practices: vague, overlapping responsibilities
15 Product assortment, seasonality	12 It is not clear about the ability to finance FUTURE growth, from existing stores
16 Price premium	13 No contingency plans
17 Promotion/marketing; word-of-mouth	14 The assumptions in business plan are unclear
18 People	
19 Process: in store, the customers are happy	
20 Physical evidence. Ambience is good	
21 Repeat business is achieved (but not measured)	

Opportunities	Threats
1 Alliance with another retail outlet	1 Property costs; lease price hike (upwards only)
2 Internet café	2 Industry consolidation: strong venture capitalist wanting to exit in 2010?
3 Industry consolidation in UK (eg take over a company)	3 Downturn in economy: cut in discretionary consumer spend
4 Overseas – growth for branded coffee shops	4 Commodity pricing (minor threat)
5 Expatriates in Spain/France	5 Employment regulation (eg opt out) in UK and EU
6 Locations outside London & SE	6 Local planning regulations, zoning
7 Franchising!	7 Low barriers to entry
8 Non-food products (eg Starbucks offers music downloads)	8 'No logo' protests
9 Alcohol: 24 hours opening	9 Different food cultures
10 Food innovation	10 Food scares, faddishness, diet, substitutes
11 Website	11 Changing lifestyle habits of target segments
12 Railway stations (growing passenger numbers).	12 Do city centres thrive?
13 Shopping malls.	13 Substitutes eg resurgent pubs
	14 Falling retail sales
	15 Competition: Whitbred, Starbucks have lot more shops

Prioritise your SWOT

You might well have considered different strengths to be priorities. (The numbers are drawn from the brainstormed list above.)

Key SWOT item	Justification
Strengths	2 **Financial position.** Unusually perhaps for a coffee chain, Zubinos has a strong financial position, underpinned by a supportive private equity firm, whose representative has agreed and approved the five year expansion plan. Without this long term financial support, Zubinos growth would be much slower.
	3 **Top management commitment.** The senior management team appear to be fairly young, and committed, with a smattering of experienced older hands such as Jack Rayfield, Carl Martin and George Shale who provide useful perspective.

Weaknesses	1	**Confusion in management structure.** Many new, professional members of the management team have been introduced in the past few years, but responsibility for recruitment, innovation and even forecasting is not clear.
	5	Related to (1) above there are, potential **difficulties in managing growth**, given evidence of conflict between senior managers and between the centralising tendencies and local initiative: Failure to manage this will lead to demotivated staff and poor management: in a service business, staff processes are vital and staff in the shops themselves are probably much closer to customers than those secluded in head office.
Opportunities	3	**Industry consolidation in the UK.** This suggests some chains will close and there are opportunities for acquisitions: although this is not covered in Zubinos' business plan. If Zubinos has a winning formula – supported by its large shops with higher capacity – it might expect to increase market share.
	4	**Overseas growth for branded coffee shops.** Franchising – the obvious choice – does not get a mention in the case. Perhaps branded coffee shops will not do so well overseas if the concept is not established. McDonalds proves it is possible to build a business based on standard service offerings. Focusing on expatriate Britons, however, displays a poverty of ambition. Countries **other** than France, with its established coffee culture, and Spain might offer a better opportunity.
Threats	3	**Downturn in the economy** and a cut in discretionary consumer spending. The UK economy has done well since the late 1990s, with a growing service sector. However, discretionary purchases such as restaurant meals tend to suffer in a recession as people focus on essentials. This links to other changes in consumer behaviour, for example if people find other sources of entertainment, or pubs rebuild themselves.
	15	**Competition.** Barriers to entry are low as far as new entrants are concerned. Competition might also push up rents if there is competition for the best locations. Starbucks has many stores and other firms such as Costa have the flexibility to expand by franchising. Zubinos does offer other benefits, such as ice cream and fresh food, so it may be slightly better off.

6 Identify the key business issues (Step 3.6)

Issue in order of importance	Description
1	**Consolidating industry in the UK**
	Zubinos still has growth objectives in the UK, but other chains are consolidating. The competitive environment could become less favourable.
2	**Management practices, organisation structure and systems**
	Maintaining consistent product and service quality across the expanded business requires change in management. Luis has already assembled a senior management team to manage growth, but there is still plenty of work to do. Better systems (for IT) and procedures (for HR etc) need to be in place.
3	**Ability to manage and finance growth**
	Growth is financed partly by loans and partly by cash generated from operations. The business will become more complex and harder to manage. The company needs to learn how to balance local flexibility with central control.
4	**Possible cash withdrawals**
	Loans must be repaid, sooner or later dividends will be expected, and most of the management team have borrowed heavily.

7 Draw up a balanced scorecard (Step 3.7)

Financial perspective	Customer perspective
• Growth in the number of shops from 18 to 75 in five years • 830% increase in turnover • Profits of $10.98 million by 2010	• Increase in market share from current 2% • Take up of new products as % of turnover • Broaden segmental attractiveness
Internal process perspective	**Innovation and learning perspective**
• New IT system • Supply chain management • Operational management of stores	• Overseas development • New product development • Increasing web-based business

8 Prepare a one-page business summary (Step 3.8)

We proposed a format of the business summary in Chapter 4. Again, there is no need for you to follow this slavishly – it just depends on the circumstances of the case. You may feel you want to add a lot more (or less) data than what we have here.

Remember that the business summary should be **Key facts/ideas** that you have to remember, as you will not be allowed to bring this into the exam. You will have the case itself, but you will have to remember all your analysis.

BUSINESS SUMMARY: USE THIS FOR YOUR ANALYSIS AND SYNTHESIS					
	CFSs for success in industry (Step 3.3)				
Nature of business (Step 2.4): Coffee shops	Brand awareness		Supply chain mgmt		
Current mission (Step 3.2)	Human resource mgmt				
Distinctive competence (Step 3.3)					
Major stakeholder objectives: Growth; new product development					
ANALYSIS BACKUP					
Key financial data: trends (Step 2.1)	External (Steps 2.2, 2.3): 5 forces/industry				
Turnover up 75% last yr Net margin 9.1% Gross margin 64.3% ROCE 20% Est value of business (Step 2.8) £5.38 – £15.38 per share	P Regulations E Disposable incomes S Fashion, health T Internet, MIS	P o r t e R	1 New entrants high 2 Substitutes high 3 Customer B/P high 4 Supplier B/P medium 5 Rivalry high Industry: Mature		
Gearing 14% Worrying indicators: Use of trade credit increasing	Internal • Lack of management information • Internal control issues				
Competitive strategy: differentiation-focus					
Customers (Step 2.3): target age segment 20 – 35 years					

SYNTHESIS			
SWOT (Items of **high** importance) (Step 3.5)		RISKS (High importance) (Step 3.4)	
Strengths 1 Financial position 2 Top management commitment	Opportunities 1 Industry consolidation in the UK 2 Overseas growth	1 Competitor action 2 Procurement problems 3 Staff problems 4 Reputation	
Weaknesses 1 Confusion in management structure 2 Difficulties in managing growth	Threats 1 Downturn in economy 2 Competition		
Key issues (Step 3.6) (High importance)		Selection of possible business projects (Step 2.9)	
1 Consolidating industry in UK		1 New shop openings in UK	
2 Management practices, organisation structure and systems		2 New product launches 3 Overseas expansion	
3 Ability to finance and manage growth			
4 Possible cash withdrawals			

Zubinos: unseens and requirements

Introduction

This chapter contains the unseen material and requirements from the March and May 2006 exams.

We have produced an answer to the March exam in Chapter 12.

1 Before tackling the unseen material

1.1 You have three hours and twenty minutes

Firstly, don't panic. You have a lot of time, and you have the pre-seen data – without your analysis – in front of you. (CIMA will tell you if they have amended the pre-seen data in any way.)

Bear in mind that the case is not designed to help you question spot. Therefore, do not be surprised if there are issues in the unseen that you have not thought of – you have done all the analysis that you can, but you **cannot second guess the examiner**. Therefore you should **EXPECT THE UNEXPECTED.**

Now **skim read** the unseen data and read the requirement.

2 Unseen material, requirement and assessment matrix

Zubinos coffee shops – Unseen material provided on examination day

Read this information before you answer the question

Bad publicity for Zubinos

There have been several adverse national newspaper reports, as well as a national TV consumer programme, reporting that several of Zubinos' healthy food options are not what they seem. It has been reported that some of these foods, which have a low calorie count and are low in fat, contain high levels of salt, sugar and some additives which have had bad press over possible health concerns. Additionally, the calorie count on some foods sold at Zubinos has been shown incorrectly on its food label. The press has carried various reports from Zubinos' public relations (PR) company stating that "the adverse comments about Zubinos' healthy foods are mainly incorrect and minor problems have been vastly over-stated". Luis Zubino is also concerned that one of Zubinos' competitors could be trying to counter the success of Zubinos, by spreading incorrect rumours.

Zubinos out-sources its quality control to a leading food agency, QAIF, which has an excellent reputation. This agency also advises Zubinos' suppliers on the food labelling requirements and assists them with labelling when Zubinos procures food items for the first time.

The UK's Food Standards Organisation (FSO), which is responsible for all foods sold in the UK, is currently sampling a number of Zubinos food items following the recent bad press. The FSO has recently visited several Zubinos coffee shops and identified that there were several items being sold that did not have any food labels on and other food items that had incorrect or misleading data for ingredients and calorific values. Luis Zubino spoke very harshly to Maria Todd about these problems.

Maria Todd has been working very long hours and has been struggling to identify new suppliers for the planned shop openings in 2006, and was very upset by the way Luis Zubino reprimanded her over the food labelling problems. She feels that she can no longer cope with her growing role and is considering resigning.

A further embarrassing event for Zubinos occurred in early February 2006. Jane Thorp had approved each of the adverts in a routine advertising campaign promoting Zubinos. One of the adverts had stated, *"All coffee sold in Zubinos is Fair Trade coffee"*. However, a former Zubinos Head Office employee, who had been dismissed for theft, recently stated in the national press that only around 60% of Zubinos coffee was procured from Fair Trade suppliers. Even though the ex-employee's claim was not totally correct, as Zubinos use around 82% of Fair Trade coffee, the press picked up on the story. The employee also claimed that he was wrongly dismissed. His story had led to much negative publicity for Zubinos. The Advertising Standards body has investigated the false claim in Zubinos adverts and Zubinos has had to admit that the claim that all of its coffee was Fair Trade coffee was incorrect. However, the damage has been done and in February 2006, sales across all Zubinos shops were down by around 7%.

Offer to operate Zubinos coffee shops in Jibbs stores

Jibbs plc (Jibbs) is a listed company, which operates 140 do-it-yourself (DIY) retail stores in the UK and around Europe. Most of Jibbs stores in the UK are located on large out-of-town retail parks. For a number of reasons, Jibbs has seen its revenue and its EPS decline slightly over the last few years. The Jibbs Board has decided on a number of innovative ways to try to stop the decline in its business and improve the outlook for the future. This has included selling some of its smaller stores, and it also has plans for a major refit of its stores, which will be followed by advertising campaigns. Jibbs is trying to make its stores more appealing to its customers. The Jibbs Board has also decided to rent out space in its stores to a small number of other retailers and it has approached Zubinos with a proposal to open Zubinos coffee shops in some of its stores.

Jibb's Marketing Director, Jenny Wright, has put the following proposal to Zubinos, inviting it to open Zubinos coffee shops in a minimum of 20 stores, over the next 6 months. The proposal is to open Zubinos coffee shops for a two-year trial period, at a fixed rental fee of £50,000 per store per year. Zubinos average rental costs are over £100,000 per annum, but the rental space on offer in Jibbs' store is about 30% smaller than most of the existing Zubinos coffee shops, which would preclude Zubinos from offering its full range of foods and drinks.

At the end of the two-year trial period, Jibbs will decide whether to invite Zubinos to open more coffee shops in its other stores. However, Jibbs reserves the right to decline to renew the rental agreement, which would result in Zubinos having to remove all of its equipment and fixtures and fittings. It was also agreed that the rental cost would not be increased by more than the rate of inflation after the two-year trial, assuming that the trial was successful. Jibbs would not take any share of revenues, but would only charge for rent. All other costs, such as water charges and electricity, would be separately billed directly to Zubinos.

The forecast capital expenditure would be lower than currently spent on new Zubinos shops, and is forecast to be £180,000 per Jibbs store. The forecast market value of fittings at the end of the two-year trial is £90,000 per Jibbs store.

Jane Thorp has prepared the following post-tax cash flow forecast, based on twenty Zubinos coffee shops. These figures exclude capital expenditure.

Based on a total of 20 Zubinos coffee shops in Jibbs' stores	Year 1	Year 2
	£000	£000
Post-tax operating cash flows	1,250	1,500

Note: These post-tax operating cash flows include the rental fees of £50,000 per store per year.

George Shale considers a suitable risk adjusted cost of capital, for this particular proposed project, to be 14% post-tax. Jack Rayfield considers that the proposed expansion into Jibbs' stores is an easy way for Zubinos to expand its number of outlets, and could save management time that is currently spent on locating and negotiating rental agreements for High Street rented premises. Also the cost of the rent is lower. Luis Zubinos has expressed his doubts as to the validity of the cash flow forecasts prepared by Jane Thorp, which are based on throughput data provided by Jibbs.

Recent events

New HR Director
In December 2005, Anita Wiseman, Zubinos HR Director resigned and left Zubinos at the end of January 2006. She had been with the company for only a little over one year. She resigned following a series of disagreements with Luis Zubino and her frustrations with developing a workable HR policy for the company. Also, she found the overlap with the roles of the Area Managers to be conflicting with her overall HR responsibilities. She has not yet disposed of her shares in Zubinos, but **only** other Directors have a right to buy the shares from her, at a negotiated price. Until she has sold her shares in Zubinos, she has voting rights.

Zubinos has recruited a new HR Director, Kingsley Nu, who joined Zubinos in the middle of February 2006, but he has not yet bought any shares in Zubinos. Kingsley Nu immediately met with all of the coffee shop managers in the London area and is due to meet the remaining shop managers in March 2006. Kingsley Nu is impressed by the loyalty and hard work put in by almost all employees, which in most cases is far in excess of their job contracts.

He proposes that a company share ownership scheme is launched and that a monthly reward scheme for outstanding customer service is commenced. He considers that the working environment, the lack of rest periods and the poor facilities for staff should be improved immediately. He has presented Luis Zubino with a draft of some of his proposals, in advance of preparing a paper for the April 2006 Zubinos Board meeting. The proposals include the recruitment of additional staff (to reduce the hours worked by existing staff, many of which are unpaid hours worked in addition to their contracted hours). He also wants to improve staff facilities. The forecast annual cost of the proposals presented is estimated by Kingsley Nu to be around £300,000 per year, at current staffing levels. Luis Zubino's immediate reaction was that some of the proposals are a luxury that a small company like Zubinos simply cannot afford. He also considers this cost to be similar to the amount required to open a further Zubinos coffee shop, and he does not want to spend finance on staff issues which could slow down the expansion programme.

Zubinos loyalty card
Following Zubinos Board approval in January 2006, Jane Thorp is planning to shortly launch a Zubinos loyalty card. This scheme will award customers points each time they spend money at Zubinos shops and present their loyalty card to the cashier. When a regular customer has saved enough points they can be redeemed against purchases. This scheme is forecast to cost Zubinos 2% of its revenues for those customers who regularly use their loyalty card. It is expected that less than 50% of Zubinos revenue will be generated by customers with a loyalty card.

Expansion into Europe
With the successful opening of three new Zubinos shops in cities around the UK in January and February 2006, Luis Zubino is enthusiastic about opening the first Zubinos coffee shop in Europe. One of Luis Zubino's contacts has located a prime city centre site in a European city and wants to operate the shop for Zubinos. The rental agreement for this shop is currently being negotiated. The first European Zubinos coffee shop opening has been brought forward and is now forecast to open in July 2006, which is an advance of its current five-year plan.

Proposed acquisition of Zubinos

The Whistle Coffee Bar (WCB) has 180 coffee shops in the UK and 140 in Europe and is trading profitably with a P/E ratio of 18. It is listed in the UK and has a current share price of £16·80.

WCB's Business Development Director for the UK, Matt Jenkins, has contacted Luis Zubino and requested a meeting. At first, Luis Zubino thought that WCB wanted to meet to discuss the site selection for new Zubinos coffee shops. Zubinos has been successful in obtaining rented sites for the most recent three Zubinos coffee shops, despite having to outbid WCB for the locations that they were also trying to secure. This has resulted in Zubinos getting the required rental location, albeit at a slightly higher rent than was originally forecast.

Luis Zubino, George Shale and Carl Martin attended the meeting with WCB, which was held at the end of February 2006. Matt Jenkins of WCB stated that they have followed the successful expansion of Zubinos with interest and that they would like to acquire Zubinos for a cash price of £15·00 per Zubinos share. Additionally, WCB stated that it would be willing to offer senior management positions in WCB (but not WCB Board positions) to many of the Zubinos management team. Matt Jenkins made a very attractive offer of a senior finance position to George Shale, if the take-over of Zubinos is successful.

Carl Martin of KPE considers this could be a possible exit route for KPE, and has taken the acquisition proposal back to his superiors at KPE.

Luis Zubino is adamant that he does not wish to sell his shares to WCB and wants to prepare a sound case to KPE to convince it (and other Zubinos shareholders) not to sell its shares to WCB either. He stated to Carl Martin of KPE that he considered that WCB had only contacted them as Zubinos had become more successful in some city suburbs and other towns than the local WCB coffee shops.

Forecast cash flows

The forecast post-tax cash flows for the next five years, based on the agreed current five-year plan, given in **Appendix 3** to the pre-seen material, is as follows:

Approved 5-year plan cash flows	2006 £000	2007 £000	2008 £000	2009 £000	2010 £000
Operating post-tax cash flows	2,500	4,100	6,200	8,900	11,700

Note: These operating post-tax cash flows are cash generated from operations and do NOT include capital expenditure on new coffee shops and also do NOT include loan repayments.

Similar businesses to Zubinos, which are listed, have a P/E ratio of around 16. George Shale considers Zubinos overall cost of capital, to be 12%, post-tax.

Following the meeting with WCB, George Shale and Luis Zubino met and discussed how the five-year plan could be improved. Following their discussion, George Shale has prepared a draft of a new five-year plan which Luis Zubino has now discussed with other shareholders, including Carl Martin at KPE. The updated five-year plan includes a higher growth rate in sales than in the original plan and higher gross margins, based on Zubinos possible ability to negotiate further cost reductions from suppliers because of its increased level of purchasing. This revised plan also has a slightly higher growth of new Zubinos coffee shops, with a total of 80, instead of 75, by 2010.

However, the cost reductions factored into this forecast are rather optimistic as George Shale is aware that coffee prices are due to increase over the next year. Furthermore, George Shale is aware that Zubinos is likely to have an adverse currency exposure in 2006, due to changes in exchange rates, which have not been included in this updated forecast.

The post-tax cash flows generated by this updated forecast are shown below:

Updated five-year plan cash flows	2006 £000	2007 £000	2008 £000	2009 £000	2010 £000
Post-tax cash flows	2,900	5,100	7,400	11,400	14,700

Appointment of a consultant

At the Zubinos Board meeting in early March 2006, it was agreed that a consultant would be appointed to prepare a report, which prioritises and discusses the issues facing Zubinos and makes appropriate recommendations.

Requirement

You are the consultant appointed by the Zubinos Board.

Prepare a report that prioritises and discusses the issues facing Zubinos and makes appropriate recommendations.

Assessment Matrix for TOPCIMA – Zubinos

Criterion	Marks	Clear Pass	Pass	Marginal Pass	Marginal Fail	Fail	Clear Fail
Technical	5	Thorough display of relevant technical knowledge. **5**	Good display of relevant knowledge. **4**	Some display of relevant technical knowledge. **3**	Identification of some relevant knowledge, but lacking in depth. **2**	Little knowledge displayed, or some misconceptions. **1**	No evidence of knowledge displayed, or fundamental misconceptions. **0**
Application	10	Knowledge clearly applied in an analytical and practical manner. **9-10**	Knowledge applied to the context of the case. **6-8**	Identification of some relevant knowledge, but not well applied. **5**	Knowledge occasionally displayed without clear application. **3-4**	Little attempt to apply knowledge to the context. **1-2**	No application of knowledge displayed. **0**
Diversity	5	Most knowledge areas identified, covering a wide range of views. **5**	Some knowledge areas identified, covering a range of views. **4**	A few knowledge areas identified, expressing a fairly limited scope. **3**	Several important knowledge aspects omitted. **2**	Many important knowledge aspects omitted. **1**	Very few knowledge aspects considered. **0**
Focus	15	Clearly distinguishes between relevant and irrelevant information. **13-15**	Information used is mostly relevant. **9-12**	Some relevant information ignored, or some less relevant information used. **8**	Information used is sometimes irrelevant. **5-7**	Little ability to distinguish between relevant and irrelevant information. **1-4**	No ability to distinguish between relevant and irrelevant information. **0**
Prioritisation	10	Issues clearly prioritised in a logical order and based on a clear rationale. **9-10**	Issues prioritised with justification. **6-8**	Evidence of issues being listed in order of importance, but rationale unclear. **5**	Issues apparently in priority order, but without a logical justification or rationale. **3-4**	Little attempt at prioritisation or justification or rationale. **1-2**	No attempt at prioritisation or justification. **0**
Judgement	15	Clearly recognises alternative solutions. Judgement exercised professionally. **13-15**	Alternative solutions or options considered. Some judgement exercised. **9-12**	A slightly limited range of solutions considered. Judgement occasionally weak. **8**	A limited range of solutions considered. Judgement sometimes weak. **5-7**	Few alternative solutions considered. Judgement often weak. **1-4**	No alternative solutions considered. Judgement weak or absent. **0**
Integration	10	Diverse areas of knowledge and skills integrated effectively. **9-10**	Diverse areas of knowledge and skills integrated. **6-8**	Knowledge areas and skills occasionally not integrated. **5**	Knowledge areas and skills sometimes not integrated. **3-4**	Knowledge areas and skills often not integrated. **1-2**	Knowledge areas and skills not integrated. **0**
Logic	20	Communication effective, recommendations realistic, concise and logical. **16-20**	Communication mainly clear and logical. Recommendations occasionally weak. **11-15**	Communication occasionally unclear, and/or recommendations occasionally illogical. **10**	Communication sometimes weak. Some recommendations slightly unrealistic. **5-9**	Communication weak. Some unclear or illogical recommendations, or few recommendations. **1-4**	Very poor communication, and/or no recommendations offered. **0**
Ethics	10	Excellent evaluation of ethical aspects. Clear and appropriate advice offered. **9-10**	Good evaluation of ethical aspects. Some appropriate advice offered. **6-8**	Some evaluation of ethical aspects. Advice offered. **5**	Weak evaluation of ethical aspects. Little advice offered. **3-4**	Poor evaluation of ethical aspects. No advice offered. **1-2**	No evaluation of ethical aspects. Unethical, or no, advice offered. **0**
TOTAL	100						

© CIMA – January 2006

Exam focus point

The format of the assessment matrix has changed from September 2008. (See Chapter 2)

3 Review the unseen and requirement (Step 5.2)

Remember don't panic. You have three hours and twenty minutes and you have done a lot of preparation. You have also done a great deal of report practice. We are not going to cover report writing here in any more detail.

4 Read the unseen data in depth (Step 5.3)

Step 5.3 **Mark up and analyse the unseen data**

Read the unseen data carefully and mark up key points.

What has changed?

(a)   What is the unseen telling us about the firm's internal conditions?

Item	Jot down new information here
• Internal structure	
• Personnel	
• Financing	
• Resources	
Strengths	
Weaknesses	

(b)   Is the unseen telling us something new about the firm's external conditions?

Item	Jot down new information here

5 Writing your report (Steps 5.4 to 5.9)

(a)   Produce your appendices. Start with a SWOT analysis and then do the necessary calculations.

(b)   You need to choose **five** key issues and **prioritise** them.

In our suggested answer presented in Chapter 12, the five key issues identified are:

(1)   Adverse publicity
(2)   Proposed acquisition
(3)   The Jibbs offer
(4)   Expansion overseas
(5)   Human resources strategy

Do you agree with the issues chosen?

You also need to consider the ethical issues to discuss.

(c)   Produce an answer plan

Possible answer plan

Section	Suggested content
1	Terms of reference
2	Introduction and key issues
3	Adverse publicity
4	Proposed acquisition
5	The Jibbs offer
6	Expansion overseas
7	Human resources strategy
8	Ethics
9	Recommendations
10	Conclusions

(d)   Write an introduction, the terms of reference and the rationale for the prioritisation of the key issues.

(e)   Develop the key issues under each heading from your contents table.

(f)   Write your recommendations and conclusions.

6 May 2006 unseen

Zubinos coffee shops – Unseen material provided on examination day

Read this information before you answer the question

Success of new product line

In early September 2005, Sally Higgins, a Zubinos area manager, introduced a range of low calorie snacks and meals in one of the shops in which she manages. This initiative had caused quite a disagreement between Sally Higgins and Jane Thorp, who had not been consulted regarding the new food and drink items, which Sally Higgins had procured from a small local supplier.

By October 2005, it was clear that the new low calorie product line was very popular and accounted for 8% of the turnover for September 2005 in the one shop in which it was introduced. After some discussion, Luis Zubino and Jane Thorp agreed that the low calorie product line appealed to Zubinos customers and to offer this new low calorie food range in all Zubinos coffee shops. Maria Todd was requested to organise central procurement for all the low calorie food and drink products. Jane Thorp recommended that a suitable marketing strategy for the low calorie foods would be to have a range of takeaway calorie-controlled meal boxes, under the brand name of "Zubinos Light" retailing at £3·00 each.

The first "Zubinos Light" meal boxes were available in all eighteen Zubinos coffee shops during November 2005 and immediately became popular. Furthermore, some limited market research of the customers who bought the "Zubinos Light" meal boxes established that over 95% of these customers were new Zubinos customers. Jane Thorp was delighted that this new product was also bringing new customers into Zubinos.

In January 2006, a major advertising campaign, using radio and posters, was commenced, and was due to run to the end of June 2006 at a total cost of £425,000. By the end of February 2006, Zubinos found that it had become the victim of its own success. All eighteen shops were almost always sold out of the "Zubinos Light" meal boxes and Maria Todd had been having numerous procurement problems. The original supplier, ART, was unable to increase the quantity beyond its contract level of 2,000 boxes a day. A new supplier, BBK, was introduced in late January 2006, despite Maria Todd's concern over quality. By the end of April 2006, it was estimated that over 5,000 boxes per day were in demand and Zubinos was again almost always sold out. (Note: it should be assumed that there are only 20 days per month for which "Zubinos Light" meal boxes will have this level of demand, to coincide with normal working patterns).

A further two suppliers are being considered, CCV and DTY. The results from the initial inspections by Maria Todd and Zubinos' food agency, and the cost per box quotes, are shown below, compared to existing suppliers:

Supplier	ART	BBK	CCV	DTY
Food quality	Excellent	Below expectations	Below expectations	Excellent
Cleanliness of food preparation areas	Excellent	Below expectations	Very good	Excellent
Cost per meal box	£1·20	£1·60	£1·10	£2·00
Maximum daily capacity	2,000	2,000	5,000	8,000
Initial contract period	12 months	6 months	6 months	3 months

Supplier CCV would be only able to supply meal boxes to Zubinos in one geographic area of the UK, whereas DTY has a supply chain established for nationwide delivery. Maria Todd has not identified any other suppliers at this time and needs to urgently select a further supplier for the "Zubinos Light" meal boxes.

Luis Zubino's planned three month absence

Luis Zubino informed his fellow directors at the end of April 2006 that he is planning to take a three-month break from the business, following his recent split from his wife, whom he married four years ago. Luis Zubino's absence from the business is planned for June, July and August 2006.

Luis Zubino was clearly upset with the break-up of his marriage, which he felt was partly due to the very long hours that he has spent building up the Zubinos business. Luis Zubino discussed with George Shale his concern, that if his marriage is not reconciled, his ex-wife could demand a payment potentially amounting to several million pounds, if they were to get divorced. Any divorce settlement is likely to be sometime within the next two years.

Management Information

George Shale and Bob West are continually frustrated by the lack of management information in a usable format. Over the past two years a few new IT systems have been introduced but there are several inconsistencies between the systems. The monthly management accounts are prepared using financial data for each shop, but there is little statistical information on customers, such as repeat customers and customer profile. Also the analysis between main product types (coffees, food, ice creams, "Zubinos Light" meal boxes) cannot easily be obtained. George Shale recruited two accountants, on six-month contracts, at the end of March 2006 to analyse information on a weekly basis, so that trends in customer spending can be tracked.

Bob West has discussed with Luis Zubino several times the introduction of a data based management information system that would capture all of the required information at source. However, the proposed cost of the database is over £800,000 and Luis Zubino considers that the cost could escalate to over £1,000,000 and he is adamant that the administration systems, although basic, can manage at present.

Staff issues and extended opening hours

Due to the rapid expansion and the popularity of Zubinos, many of the staff have been working very hard and working long hours and they report that they feel under too much pressure. Furthermore, due to the popularity of Zubinos, it was decided to extend the opening hours, into the evening and instead of closing at 7pm, they are now open until 11pm each night, seven days a week. Many of Zubinos staff have complained about later working and this has resulted in some employees leaving the company, despite Zubinos pay being a little higher than the market rate.

Over the last few months, Zubinos has employed many European Union (EU) immigrants on temporary short-term contracts. Zubinos is paying below the market rate in this industry for these employees, but slightly above the legal minimum wage rate. The cost of these employees is approximately 12% below other Zubinos staff. The EU immigrants are also prepared to work long hours. The EU immigrant workers have accepted the shift patterns given to them, which often involve early morning shifts to accept deliveries from 5 o'clock in the morning. While these employees are given time off during the day, they are often scheduled to work a further shift later in the day, right up to closing time. Some of the EU immigrant employees choose to work straight through from early morning to closing time with very few breaks. These employees speak English poorly and offer poor customer service. Many Zubinos coffee shop managers have now noticed that the level of customer complaints has increased.

There have been several complaints and some adverse press coverage concerning disturbances to neighbours and people whose flats are above Zubinos coffee shops because of Zubinos' later closing time at night. However, the rental agreements for the rented shops allow this late closing time. Another factor that has caused problems to Zubinos' neighbours is the deliveries from its food suppliers between 5 and 6 o'clock in the morning to Zubinos coffee shops in some city centres. The parking of large delivery vehicles and the noise caused by unloading has led to several complaints, including a pending legal action for noise nuisance.

New Zubinos coffee shops in 2006

Luis Zubino wanted to open the planned eight new coffee shops in 2006, partly financed from the approved £5·0 million loan finance that KPE has made available to Zubinos. During January to May 2006, there have only been two new coffee shops opened. There are plans already in place for a further two openings later this year. The number of new Zubinos coffee shops has fallen behind schedule, as Luis Zubino, who plays a crucial role in the site selection process, has not pursued the expansion programme, as he usually would have done, due to his personal problems with his marriage breakdown.

Bob West is now trying to secure rental agreements on a further four shops. He has been unable to find suitable rental sites for two of them. He has drafted a proposal for the June 2006 Zubinos Board meeting, requesting approval to purchase two retail premises at a total cost of £2·2 million for both sites.

The capital cost and shop fitting costs are also forecast to exceed the current planned capital expenditure budget during 2006, due to two reasons:

- All four of the new coffee shops that have been opened or are currently being prepared for opening, are in larger premises, with higher fittings costs;

- The latest, more expensive, refrigerated display units have been ordered for the new Zubinos shop openings in 2006, which are far superior to those in other Zubinos shops.

The average capital expenditure for each new Zubinos coffee shop in 2006 is now forecast to be £330,000, compared to an average of £250,000 in 2005.

The latest forecast for 2006, prepared at the end of April 2006, assumes a total of only 6 new shops opening during 2006. The forecast cash which will be generated from operations for 2006 is £2·2 million. This will be used to partially fund the planned capital expenditure which is currently forecast for 2006 to be £4·7 million (and this capital expenditure forecast assumes the purchase of the two retail premises, as detailed above).

Operating costs

In an attempt to reduce operating costs, Maria Todd has chosen to change a few suppliers who are providing high cost food items, and has managed to procure very similar food items at a lower cost. She has also chosen to procure a higher proportion of coffee from UK wholesalers, which has resulted in large cost savings.

The cost savings have been achieved due to two reasons. Firstly, the coffee beans are purchased from UK wholesalers who bulk buy and the cost per kilogram is lower than the Fair Trade coffee that Zubinos had previously purchased. Most of these new coffee purchases are not Fair Trade coffee. Secondly, Zubinos pays for these new coffee purchases in UK sterling and is not exposed to any risk of currency movements.

Zubinos is now considering whether its marketing literature should be changed to reflect that only 60% of its coffee purchases is now Fair Trade coffee, whereas previously it was over 80% Fair Trade.

Franchising proposal

An international franchising company, GlobalFranch (GF) has approached Luis Zubino at the end of April 2006 with a proposal to assist Zubinos to expand via franchising. The proposal was presented to the Zubinos Board in May 2006, and Luis Zubino's initial response is favourable.

GF has stated that it has over thirty franchisees ready to open franchised outlets and it considers that the Zubinos business could be a very successful franchised business. GF has also stated that it is considering offering its franchise service to two other coffee shop chains, which are based in Europe, but has decided to allow Zubinos to have first refusal. GF has therefore stated that it needs a final decision by the end of June 2006.

GF's proposal is to franchise out the Zubinos coffee shop brand and expand both in the UK and overseas, particularly in the rapidly growing Far Eastern market. GF would like to offer its services and its experience to recruit and manage franchisees, which would then operate franchised Zubinos coffee shops in the UK, Europe and the Far East. GF insists on a minimum contract period of 5 years, with a one-year notice period. GF also stipulates that in order to allow the franchisees to build up their business, Zubinos should limit the number of its coffee shops which it operates to no more than 40% of the planned franchised coffee shops by the end of 2009.

The financial forecast shown below is based on the following number of franchised shops:

Number of forecast franchised shops	2007	2008	2009	2010	2011
New openings in year	20	30	50	80	120
Cumulative franchised shops	20	50	100	180	300

The proposal is that for each new franchised shop, Zubinos would receive 9% of the gross sales revenue. Zubinos would also supply all of its regular coffees and own brand product lines to franchised shops at agreed prices, which would include a mark up of around 6% on cost.

GF has stated that its fees for locating franchisees and managing the franchising business for Zubinos would be a fee of £20,000 for each new shop opened plus a fee of 6% of the franchised revenue for the first year of each shop opening. After the first year of each shop opening GF would charge a flat fee of 2% of the franchised revenue for the contract period. GF has prepared the following forecast cash flows (pre-tax) for the next 5 years:

Franchise income payable to Zubinos:	2007 £million	2008 £million	2009 £million	2010 £million	2011 £million
Revenue	0·9	3·5	8·2	16·9	31·9
Mark up on supplies to franchisees	0·2	0·7	1·5	2·7	4·4
Total Franchise income	1·1	4·2	9·7	19·6	36·3
Franchise fees payable by Zubinos to GF:					
£20,000 for each new shop	0·4	0·6	1·0	1·6	2·4
6% of revenue for first year	0·6	1·6	2·8	5·0	8·5
2% of total franchised revenue	0·0	0·2	0·9	2·1	4·3
Total franchise fees payable	1·0	2·4	4·7	8·7	15·2

Zubinos exclusive coffee machines

Jane Thorp launched a new product line in November 2004, selling exclusive coffee machines to customers for their homes or offices. These are sold on Zubinos website and also in Zubinos coffee shops. Until the summer of 2005, they were not well-marketed, but following a promotional campaign, the coffee machines have sold particularly well, and customers have repeatedly bought further coffee supplies from Zubinos.

The coffee machines have been procured from a leading coffee machine manufacturer on an exclusive contract for Zubinos. The coffee machines use specially designed sachets of coffee that can only be bought from Zubinos coffee shops, or available from Zubinos website. The unique selling point is that customers can enjoy their favourite type of Zubinos cup of coffee in the comfort of their own homes. The projected cash flows for the next three years for the sale of the coffee machines and coffee supplies are as follows:

	2006 £million	2007 £million	2008 £million
Sales - Coffee machines	1·1	1·3	1·7
- Coffee supplies	1·1	2·9	7·1
Costs - Coffee machines	1·2	1·4	1·9
- Coffee supplies	0·2	0·6	1·4

There have been a significant number of dissatisfied customers who have returned faulty machines over the last few months. Originally, as a gesture of goodwill, Jane Thorp had instructed all shop managers to give customers with faulty machines, a free replacement machine and free samples of coffee sachets. However, the number of faulty machines has increased in March and April 2006. The manufacturer has examined a number of returned machines, and has identified a design fault. All new manufactured coffee machines from May 2005 will have this fault corrected.

Appointment of a consultant

At the Zubinos Board meeting in the middle of May 2006, it was agreed that a consultant would be appointed to advise the Board on the issues facing Zubinos.

Zubinos: answer

12

Introduction

This answer to the **March** 2006 exam was written by a TOPCIMA student under exam conditions in 3 hours. All the analysis was her own. You might, on reading this answer, find material you had not considered or may disagree with some aspects. This is as it should be: everyone will approach the case in a different way.

We have also included a suggested marking scheme developed by BPP Learning Media from the Post Exam Guides and Script Reviews following the exam.

1 Report

To   Zubinos Board
From   Consultant
Subject Issues facing Zubinos
Date   xx xxx 2006

Section	Content
1	Terms of reference
2	Introduction and key issues
3	Adverse publicity
	3.1 Quality control
	3.2 Fair Trade coffee
4	Proposed acquisition
5	The Jibbs offer
	5.1 The strategic fit of Jibbs and Zubinos
	5.2 The financial aspects
6	Expansion overseas
	6.1 European expansion
	6.2 Other overseas expansion
7	Human resources strategy
	7.1 Policies and procedures
	7.2 Reward scheme
8	Ethics
	8.1 Fair Trade
	8.2 Inflated forecast
	8.3 Competitor rumours
9	Recommendations
10	Conclusion
	Appendices

1　Terms of reference

This report has been prepared for the Board of Zubinos to prioritise and discuss the issues facing Zubinos and make appropriate recommendations.

2　Introduction and key issues

Appendix 1 shows the inherent strengths and weaknesses of Zubinos and the opportunities and threats currently facing them. From this it can be seen that a key strength identified is the Zubinos brand image and the threat from the adverse publicity, together with the weaknesses in procurement and quality control, is therefore the first priority issue to be addressed.

The proposed acquisition by WCB is identified as the main threat to the current senior management and is therefore the next issue to be dealt with in this report.

The Jibbs offer is the most significant opportunity currently identified and requires careful consideration by the Board. Another business opportunity is the proposed expansion into Europe and this is also analysed and evaluated.

Lastly, the problems with human resources are identified as a weakness in Appendix 1 and this report will suggest how these can be overcome.

3 Adverse publicity

It can be argued that there are a number of key reasons why consumers choose to spend their money at Zubinos. The shops are in prime locations and have an agreeable ambience, the service is good and the coffee and other products sold are perceived to be of a high quality and from Fair Trade sources.

However, there are numerous competitors as evidenced by a recent newspaper article concerning the 17 places where it is possible to buy coffee in Fleet Street, London. Bad publicity will therefore have an adverse impact on sales as customers may quickly choose to spend their money elsewhere. The bad publicity has not only been in newspapers, but also on a national TV consumer programme and such programmes have considerable influence and power over consumer choices. Sales have already fallen by 7% in February and this decline must be halted as a matter of urgency if financial and growth targets are to have any chance of being met. There are two distinct areas of concern.

3.1 Quality Control

The UK Food Standards Organisation has identified problems with quality control so action does need to be taken urgently. This area is outsourced to QAIF, which has an excellent reputation. However, Zubinos may have been relying on its reputation and not properly controlling and auditing its activities. Luis has blamed Maria Todd, but should perhaps be focusing more on QAIF and ensuring that proper systems of control are in place.

Maria Todd is overloaded and in need of support. Procurement in a business such as Zubinos is a key function and should be given more of a priority. There is an urgent need to find new suppliers, particularly of Fair Trade coffee.

3.2 Fair Trade coffee

It is clear that Zubinos have made a false claim in recent advertising claiming that 'all' of their coffee is sourced from Fair Trade suppliers. This is a hot topic as Marks and Spencer have been running a big campaign concerning their use of 100% Fair Trade coffee in their Café Revive shops and their commitment to increased availability of Fair Trade products. This has led to numerous newspaper articles on the subject.

Zubinos should have been in an ideal position to capitalise on this publicity instead of having to deal with the embarrassment and negative impact of their incorrect adverts. Immediate action needs to be taken to counteract this negative publicity.

4 Proposed acquisition

Appendix 1 identifies the bid from WCB as a threat to the current management team, and Luis Zubino is adamant that he does not want to sell his shares to WCB. Presumably, but not necessarily, his wife Vivien agrees with his views and their joint 42% holding of Zubinos shares is a bigger holding than anybody else's. However, KPE holds 40% of the shares and their main objective is to achieve growth in the value of their shares. The recently departed HR Director, Anita Wiseman, still has voting rights over her 36,000 shares and if she were to side with KPE, their joint 43.6% holding will be bigger than that of Luis and Vivien Zubino. It is therefore crucial to analyse whether shareholder value will be maximised by accepting the £15 per share offer or by continuing with the present management.

Appendix 2 contains an updated cash flow forecast from which an estimated valuation of £8.71 per share has been derived. The figures used are from the original 5 year plan, which was approved by KPE and the Zubinos Board, with downwards adjustments of 10% in 2006 made for the recent fall in revenue. It has been assumed that the more optimistic predictions of growth, revenue and cost reduction made by George Shale will be counteracted by the effects of the negative publicity, coffee price increases and adverse exchange rate movements. This method does not consider free cash flow arising from trading activities beyond the period of the 5-year plan, therefore it can be viewed as a very prudent estimate of share price.

An alternative valuation can be made using an adjusted P/E ratio of 11 multiplied by the 2005 post-tax profit to give £9.87 per share.

A third valuation of £5.38 could be given by the net assets method but this ignores the significant value of the intangible assets, for example staff, brand, location, in a service organisation such as Zubinos.

WCB's offer therefore looks to be acceptable. However, the assumptions behind all of these valuations can be questioned and much higher growth could be achieved under the management of Luis Zubino than that of WCB. It is worth noting that WCB have recently sold 12 coffee shops to a rival chain so it seems strange that they should be seeking to expand by acquiring Zubinos. It could be a defensive strategy as Zubinos has become more successful in some areas and has outbid WCB in location acquisitions.

KPE would make a profit on their investment at this price but their expected exit was 2010 and they may be prepared to take an optimistic longer term view of Zubinos' growth prospects under Luis Zubino.

A realistic and achievable 5 year plan should be developed and agreed with KPE with assumptions clearly explained.

5   Jibbs offer

Jibbs is a chain of DIY stores who have proposed that Zubinos open coffee shops inside its retail park stores. Jibbs has seen its revenue and EPS decline recently and is looking for ways to halt this decline. There are two key issues to be examined.

5.1   The fit of Jibbs with Zubinos

The average customer of an out-of-town DIY store is likely to be time pressured and cost conscious. The stores are not designed for customers to linger, although there are plans for major refits. The rental space on offer is 30% lower than the existing Zubinos shops. The desired customer at Zubinos is prepared to pay a premium for its products and views the larger than average shops and the ambience as a reason to choose to purchase. The fit of these two organisations is therefore questionable.

5.2   The financial aspects

The post-tax cash flow forecast has been prepared by Jane Thorp, a marketing specialist, and is based on throughput data provided by Jibbs. It is therefore likely to be over optimistic.

There is a significant risk involved in this project, which George has recognised in his higher risk adjusted cost of capital of 14%. At the end of the two-year trial period, Jibbs could decline to renew the rental agreement and Zubinos would incur a loss of £1.8 million on the fittings, together with the costs of their removal. The assumed residual value of £90,000 per store for fittings may be an over-optimistic estimate of the realisable value. This is a large amount for a company whose current annual post-tax profit is only £897,000.

These factors mean that the Jibbs offer should be rejected and Zubinos should continue to look for a more acceptable retail chain in which to open coffee shops.

6   Expansion overseas

Luis Zubino has identified overseas expansion as a potential area for growth.

6.1   European expansion

A contact has located a prime site in a European city and wants to operate the shop for Zubinos. A rental agreement is being negotiated but all aspects of this transaction need to be carefully examined and evaluated.

The proposal is effectively a franchise agreement, as the contact will be operating the shop. This is potentially a lucrative engine for growth and a strategy for franchising should be developed. Aspects such as protection of the brand, procurement and control should be looked at as well as the financial implications. The European contact can then be used as a pilot and if it proves successful, franchising could be used as a future growth strategy.

6.2   Other overseas expansion

Europe is a mature market for coffee shops with established competitors who would have excellent knowledge of local customs and culture. Zubinos should consider other countries with more rapid economic growth and potential for a new entrant to establish themselves. Starbucks are looking to expand into China and India and Zubinos could consider following them, a strategy which can often be lucrative in emerging markets.

7 Human resources strategy

Appendix 1 identifies the lack of coherent human resources policies and procedures as a key weakness of Zubinos. In a service sector business, well motivated and trained quality staff are an essential intangible asset that needs to be nurtured and controlled. Human resources have not been a priority as evidenced by Anita Wiseman's resignation following a series of disagreements with Luis. Two aspects for consideration in particular can be identified.

7.1 Policies and procedures

A disgruntled former employee has created bad publicity for Zubinos and is claiming wrongful dismissal. Dismissal is a legal minefield and procedures need to be carefully followed to avoid such a problem. Effective recruitment and following up of references will help to avoid the employment of dishonest employees.

Zubinos needs to have an agreed human resources strategy, policy and associated procedures to ensure that such problems are avoided in the future.

7.2 Reward scheme

The current reward scheme is based on the achievement of financial targets and has proved problematic. The new HR director has proposed a share ownership scheme. This however is unlikely to achieve increased employee motivation as Zubinos shares cannot be traded in an open market and no dividends are paid.

A reward scheme based on balanced scorecard measures such as customer satisfaction, speed of service and so on would be more effective and should be developed.

It is essential that Luis Zubino recognises the vital role of human resource management and supports Kingsley Nu in his new role.

8 Ethics

There are three areas where ethical issues need to be analysed.

8.1 Fair Trade

Consumers increasingly expect companies to be socially responsible and will be very unimpressed if a company is found to have made incorrect ethical claims. As mentioned in section 3.2, Fair Trade is a hot topic, which is gaining a great deal of publicity, and the number of Fair Trade suppliers is increasing. Zubinos should capitalise on this publicity and source 100% of its products from Fair Trade suppliers.

8.2 Inflated forecasts

Senior managers of a company have a duty to ensure that forecasts and other financial information are accurate and reliable. The updated five-year plan looks to be over optimistic and should be re-examined to ensure it is presenting a true and fair picture of Zubinos' prospects to its stakeholders.

8.3 Competitor rumours

Luis is concerned that a competitor has been spreading incorrect rumours. This is unethical behaviour and should be investigated. The way to counter-act such rumours is with positive publicity and the temptation to compete via the same underhand methods should be avoided.

9 Recommendations

To remedy the difficulties identified in this report and exploit the opportunities presented, the Board is advised to action the following recommendations. They are presented in accordance with prioritisation rationale expressed in the introduction to the report:

1   To avoid any recurrence of quality control and incorrect labelling of products sold Zubinos should immediately initiate an audit of the services provided by QAIF and take immediate action to resolve problems identified. Following this a robust system of performance monitoring and internal controls of the outsourcing contract with QAIF needs to be established, effectively managed and periodically reviewed.

2   To alleviate the pressure of work currently suffered by Maria Todd, the firm should recruit an experienced assistant for her. The prime function of this new role should be to identify more suppliers, particularly of Fair Trade coffee, thus allowing the Procurement Director to focus on the more strategic aspects of supply chain management and inventory control. Only when 100% Fair Trade coffee sources can be established and supplies guaranteed should this fact be advertised widely.

3   The acquisition offer from WCB should be rejected, for the reasons identified in the report. A more realistic and achievable 5 year plan should be produced, based on reliable and authoritative planning assumptions, which should be presented to the Board and KPE at the first opportunity.

    The plan should be able to illustrate that the growth potential of Zubinos over the next 5 years (and beyond) makes the £15 share price offer from WCB less attractive to those viewing their interest in Zubinos as a long term investment.

4   The Jibbs offer should be rejected as the business risks involved are too great, there is no recognisable strategic fit, and the financial returns are unsubstantiated. However Zubinos should still continue to identify other more acceptable retail chains where profitable joint development opportunities to open coffee shops can be identified.

5   In order to expand into the European market Zubinos should establish a franchising strategy, and use the European contact identified as a pilot. Franchising represents a low risk market development opportunity for Zubinos, and if successful could establish the Zubinos brand across Europe very rapidly and with a relatively low investment required.

    Over the next year it would be advisable to examine the suitability of other countries as potential locations for coffee shops, so that the franchising strategy could be directed most effectively and profitably.

6   Zubinos being a service business, and one that has experienced a number of personnel problems, needs to develop coherent human resource policies and procedures. This will help retain staff and motivate them to deliver better performance. The implementation of a new employee reward scheme using balanced scorecard performance measures rather than short term financial results may help to achieve this.

10 Conclusion

Zubinos is in a strong position but faces a number of significant threats, which need to addressed as a matter of urgency. Several internal weaknesses have also been identified and action suggested to overcome them. Acting on the recommendations contained in this report will then allow the company to capitalise on the opportunities presented and achieve its targets for growth.

Appendix 1: SWOT Analysis

Strengths	Weaknesses
• Zubinos Brand • Good shop locations • Retail space larger than average • Loyal staff • Entrepreneurial leadership • Strong finances	• Procurement problems • Quality control issues • Lack of human resources policies and procedures • Ineffective internal controls
Opportunities	**Threats**
• Jibbs offer • Expansion into Europe and potential franchising • New product innovation	• Bad publicity • Hostile takeover bid • Increase in coffee prices • Adverse currency movements • KPE selling its shares

Appendix 2: Zubinos business valuation

	2006	2007	2008	2009	2010
	£'000	£'000	£'000	£'000	£'000
Post tax cash flows	2250	4100	6200	8900	11700
Capital expenditure	(2700)	(3400)	(3800)	(4100)	(5000)
Free cash flow	(450)	700	2400	4800	6700
Discount factor @ 12%	0.893	0.797	0.712	0.636	0.567
Present value	(402)	558	1709	3053	3799

Total present value	£8,717,000
No of shares	1,000,000
Share price	£8.71

Assumptions

1   Post tax cash flows in 2006 (£2,500,000) will be 10% lower than originally forecast due to the adverse publicity

2   This fall will be reversed in 2007 and revenue will then be as per the original 5 year plan

2 Suggested marking scheme for Zubinos March 2006

Note: this would be marked differently under the new assessment matrix which applies from September 2008 (see Chapter 2).

Criteria	Issues to be discussed	Marks	Total Marks available for criterion
Technical	SWOT/PEST/Ansoff/Porter's 5 forces/Porter's generic strategies/ Mendelow/Suitability, Acceptability, Feasibility/BCG matrix/ Balanced Scorecard/Life cycle analysis 1 mark for EACH technique displayed *Note.* 0 marks for 'name dropping' without explaining the relevant technique	1 each	5 marks
Application	SWOT – to get full 3 marks must include WCB bid in Threats	1–3	
	PEST	1–2	
	Other Technical Knowledge applied to case material in a meaningful relevant way – on merit	1–2	
	Calculations		
	NPV analysis of Jibbs proposal	1–2	
	Valuations of Zubinos in respect of WCB bid:		Max = 10
	• Based on cash flows	1–2	
	• Additional marks for cash flows into perpetuity	1–2	
	• Valuation based on P/E ratio	1–2	
	Other relevant calculations, such as loyalty card	1	
	Relevant ratios (1 mark for calcs + 1 mark for discussion of relevance of ratio)	1–2	
	Total available marks (but max = 10)	**18**	
Diversity	Display of sound business awareness and relevant real life examples	1–3 on merit	
	Relevant discussion on exit strategies for KPE	1–2 on merit	Max = 5
	Other relevant knowledge displayed	1–2 on merit	
	Total available marks (but max = 5)	**7**	
Focus	**Issues to be discussed**		
	Discussion on WCB bid	1–4	
	Discussion on KPE view of the WCB bid	1–2	
	Discussion of HR issues	1–2	
	Discussion on bad publicity and falling sales in Feb 2006	1–2	
	Discussion on Jibbs proposal	1–2	
	Discussion on overseas expansion	1	Max = 15
	Discussion on other relevant issues (on merit)		
	• Loyalty card	1–2 each up to max of 6	
	• Control of operating costs		
	• Zubinos Board		
	• Whether Zubinos should consider franchising		
	Total marks available (but max = 15)	**19**	

Criteria	Issues to be discussed	Marks	Total Marks available for criterion
Prioritisation	Full 10 marks if 5 issues prioritised and rationale for ranking good and top priority of WCB is included in top 2 priorities.	Full 10	Max = 10
	The WCB bid should be in top 2 priorities on the basis that there is no greater threat to a company's very existence than a hostile take-over bid. OR		
	6–9 marks if top priority of WCB bid is in top 2 priorities but ranking rationale is weak OR	6–9	
	4 marks maximum (marginal fail) if WCB bid is not in top 2 priorities (irrespective of quality of rationale for ranking of other priorities)	Up to 4	
Judgement	**8 key issues requiring analysis in this case:**		
	Marks on merit based on depth of analysis and commercially realistic comments (not just 1 mark for each point made). Full marks could be awarded even if all of the issues listed have not been analysed, although it is unlikely that high marks would be awarded if the analysis did not include most of the issues shown below.		
	1. WCB bid Analysis to include that the £15 is an initial bid an that there could be higher offers or other bidders, the trade off of risk of high values in the future versus cash now and that Zubinos shareholders are looking for substantially higher gains in the future	1–4	
	2. Need to stop current downfall in revenues Analysis that identifies that urgent action is required to stop revenue decline & need to be customer focussed	1–2	
	3. HR issues and quality of customer service Analysis to include a clear understanding between HR issues and the quality of customer service provided. Max 1 mk if customer service not discussed.	1–3	Max = 15
	4. Jibbs proposal Analysis of the proposal should include identification that this is not a good strategic fit for Zubinos, that it is a different target audience and that the investment would not be a good use of the scarce loan facilities (as it would require £3.6 million of the total loan of £5 million)	1–3	
	5. Zubinos 5 year plan and the need to achieve this to keep investors content	1–2	
	6. Advice to the Zubinos Board on the timing and alternative exit strategies for KPE (this could include a MBO or a listing around 2009)	1–2	
	7. Recognition of possibility of other take-over bids in the future.	1–2	
	8. Franchising – recognition that this is a common method of expansion in this industry	1–2	
	Total marks available (but max = 15)	**20**	

Criteria	Issues to be discussed	Marks	Total Marks available for criterion
Integration	Judge script holistically and whether recommendations follow on logically from analysis of the issues in the report and refers to data in appendices	1–4 if weak or 6–10 if good	10
Logic	General presentation and EFFECTIVE business communication. If report format and business English is good and all data in appendices are fully discussed in the report = full 5 marks. More usual to award 3 or 4 marks, depending on quality of report format and communication skills.	1–5	Max = 20
	Recommendations		
	(Marks on merit. Max 1 mark if only an unjustified recommendation is given)		
	Accept or reject WCB bid with supporting reasons	1–4	
	Ways to increase revenues after bad publicity	1–2	
	HR issues	1–2	
	Jibbs proposal (Max = 1 if rec is to accept)	1–2	
	Ways to achieve 5 year plan	1–2	
	Whether to franchise in future	1–2	
	KPE exit plans	1–2	
	Other recs (on merit)	Up to 5	
	Total marks available (but max = 20)	26	
Ethics	**Ethical issues in case include:**		
	Unhealthy low calorie foods Wrong labelling Incorrect marketing of volume of Fair Trade coffee HR issues including long hours worked Overstated 5 year plan is misleading to investors	1–5 each including advice	
	1–5 marks (on merit) for each ethical issue including detailed advice on each ethical issue as follows:	Max = 4 if no advice	
	• 1–2 marks for identification and justification of why an issue has an ethical dimension		Max = 10
	• +1–3 marks for detailed recommendations of actions (including when and by whom) to overcome the ethical dilemma		
	Therefore if an ethical issue is fully discussed and clear recommendations made = full 5 marks for each ethical issue, although if the identification of the ethical aspect of the issue is not well discussed and the recommendations are weak, marks will be 2–3 for each issue.		
	However, maximum of 4 marks overall (marginal fail) if several ethical issues discussed but no meaningful or sensible advice given.		
Total			100

P
A
R
T

C

Previous TOPCIMA cases

Merbatty
September and November 2007

13

Merbatty: pre-seen data

Introduction

This chapter includes the 'pre-seen' data for Merbatty, examined in September and November 2007.

P10 – Test of Professional Competence in Management Accounting

For examinations on Tuesday 4 September 2007 and on Thursday 22 November 2007

PRE-SEEN MATERIAL, PROVIDED IN ADVANCE FOR PREPARATION AND STUDY FOR THE EXAMINATIONS IN SEPTEMBER AND NOVEMBER 2007.
INSTRUCTIONS FOR POTENTIAL CANDIDATES
This booklet contains the pre-seen case material for the above examinations. It will provide you with the contextual information that will help you prepare yourself for the examinations.
The TOPCIMA Assessment Matrix, which your script will be marked against, is available as a separate document which you should download.
You may not take this copy of the pre-seen material into the examination hall. A fresh copy will be provided on the examination day.
Unseen material will be provided on the examination day; this will comprise further context and the examination question.
The examination will last for three hours. You will be allowed 20 minutes reading time **before the examination begins** during which you should read the question paper and, if you wish, make annotations on the question paper. However, you will **not** be allowed, **under any circumstances**, to either begin writing or using your computer (September examination only) to produce your answer or to use your calculator during the reading time.
You will be required to answer ONE question which may contain more than one element.
September examination only: Your computer will contain two blank files – one Word and an Excel file. Please ensure that you check that the file names for these two documents correspond with your candidate number.

TURN OVER

© The Chartered Institute of Management Accountants 2007

Merbatty Boat Case

Market overview

1   The developing luxury boat building industry is one with a growing customer base of wealthy, successful individuals and corporate clients. The industry is mostly concentrated in Europe and the USA, although new boat building companies have recently entered the market in Australia and some areas of Asia. Classification of the market and its products can be done in different ways, but the most common are by boat length, engine performance or by hull type. In 2006, the luxury boat building industry generated approximately $5 billion in revenues and delivered nearly 3,500 engine-powered boats globally.

2   The material in this case is confined to boats powered by engines and does not include sailing yachts, which are a completely separate market segment.

3   There are a number of major international builders of luxury boats, which together produce a range of over 150 different models. Most luxury boats have living accommodation and crew quarters. The selling prices for these luxury boats range from around $0·4 million to over $9 million. Each boat type has a choice of different cost options, depending on customers' specifications and engine size.

4   Boat building companies typically appoint agents to secure sales from the end customer. The sales agent is the ongoing link with the customer from initial contact until delivery of the boat. Most boat building companies have agents in a wide variety of places globally, in order to secure sales, even though they have boat building facilities in only one or two locations. Completed boats are tested, then inspected and then delivered to wherever customers want, with the sales agent fully involved.

5   The individuals and corporate customers who buy these luxury boats are successful, wealthy individuals who expect the highest standards of quality and customer care. As the market has become more competitive, the need to live up to *"what the customer wants, the customer gets"* has become even more important. Boat building companies are facing the difficult task of balancing the need to deliver customer choice and a high specification at a price that is competitive. In addition, boat building companies need to generate sufficient profitability to invest in research for future designs in order to stay competitive and to give a return for their shareholders.

Merbatty

6   Merbatty was formed 33 years ago by its current Chairman and is based in a northern European country. Merbatty has enjoyed rapid growth in sales and profitability in recent years. Merbatty became listed on a European stock exchange in November 2006.

7   It currently has two boat building facilities, one at its Head Office base in Europe and a second on the West Coast of the USA. It has sales offices at the two boat building locations, staffed by Merbatty employees. The majority of Merbatty sales worldwide are secured through sales agents appointed by Merbatty.

8   Sales revenue is paid to Merbatty in three instalments. A deposit of 20% is paid by the customer on signing a binding contract for a boat as specified by the customer. A second instalment of 30% is paid when the boat's engines are delivered to the boat building facility. The final 50% is paid on completion of the boat only after inspection by the customer. Delivery to the customer's choice of location is at an extra cost. Merbatty's price list is in Euros for European sales. Due to pressure from customers in the USA, sales there are priced in US Dollars. Sales to other parts of the world are in either Euros or US Dollars.

9   Merbatty currently has a range of 15 boats varying in price from between €0·4 million for a 5 metre boat to over €4 million for a 35 metre boat. The selling prices of Merbatty's range of boats are shown in **Appendix 1** and relate to the basic model specification, as prices may vary depending on the customer's own selection of the specification for interior design and accommodation facilities.

10   Customers usually choose from a range of additional features, to enable them to make the boat very individual to personal requirements. To facilitate this choice, Merbatty offers a full interior design service. In 2006 these additional features generated €50 million of additional revenues. This represents a further 11% on top of basic selling prices.

The operating profit achieved for Merbatty's current range of boats in 2006 was as follows:

	Small boats (up to and including 24 metres)	Large boats (25 metres and over)	Additional features selected by customers	Total 2006 operating revenues and costs
Number of boats	223	57	-	280
	€ million	€ million	€ million	€ million
Revenue	256	196	50	502
Operating costs (including allocated overhead costs)	222	163	41	426
Operating profit	34	33	9	76
Operating profit %	13·3%	16·8%	18·0%	15·1%

12 During 2006, Merbatty commenced production on a record number of 280 boats, representing a global market share of around 8%. Merbatty's statistics for boat construction are based on the number of boats **commenced** in a year.

13 Depending on the model and the size of the boat, the time taken to build a boat varies from 3 months to around 10 months. This time represents the period from the date of the customer signing the order contract to delivery of the completed boat. The boat is only delivered to a customer after successful completion of its sea trials and subsequent inspection by the customer.

14 The geographical analysis of sales according to the home base of the customer in 2006 and by the target markets for 2011, is shown in **Appendix 2**.

15 Merbatty currently has sales agents worldwide who generate sales. Most of Merbatty's agents worldwide work exclusively for Merbatty except in a few locations, where the agents also sell boats built by several other boat building companies. The agents receive a fixed percentage of the final revenues of around 4%, including any additional features that the customer orders for the boat. The agent's fee is paid in two instalments for each sale, 50% of the agent's fee at the point of signing a sales contract with the customer and the final balance on delivery of the boat to the customer. This split in the agent's fee creates an incentive for the agent to maintain close contact with both the customer and Merbatty's boat building facility in order to monitor progress and delivery details.

16 Market research has established that there is a growing market for luxury boats. Recent orders from both new and existing customers have supported this research. Indeed Merbatty has several customers who regularly replace their boats every few years. It also has other customers who have bought two or three boats to keep in different locations round the world.

Merbatty's personnel

17 The career histories of Merbatty's Directors are shown in **Appendix 3**.

18 Merbatty employs almost 2,200 employees at the two boat building facilities which are currently operational. The total staff costs were €87 million in 2006. However, additional employees will need to be recruited later in 2007 when Merbatty opens its third boat building facility (see page 7).

The table below shows an analysis by function of Merbatty employees at the end of 2006:

	Number of employees at 31 December 2006
Skilled boat building technicians (includes supervisory staff)	1,940
Office and administration staff	188
Senior management staff	22
Sales staff (excluding external sales agents)	17
Total employees	2,167

20 The employee numbers shown above exclude outsourced processes. In addition to using sales agents to secure the majority of sales, Merbatty chooses to outsource several elements of its boat construction process. These include the use of an interior design service, which Merbatty uses for all interior fittings.

Merbatty's recent history

21   Merbatty's sales have risen by over 10% each year for the last 12 years. The founding shareholder, Alberto Blanc held the roles of Chairman and Chief Executive until September 2005, when the management team was strengthened in the lead up to the flotation of Merbatty in November 2006. The flotation issued 120 million new shares, each at a nominal value of €0·50 each. The flotation price was €2·80 a share and all shares were fully subscribed and generated a cash inflow to Merbatty of €336 million (before issue costs) in November 2006.

22   At the point of flotation Merbatty repaid its then existing bank loan of €120 million and its bank overdraft, which had reached over €120 million. Andreas Acosta also renegotiated a new loan at a more competitive interest rate. This new loan is for €200 million, at an annual interest rate of 7%, and is secured on Merbatty's assets. This new loan, together with some of the equity raised in the listing will finance Merbatty's capital expenditure programme over the next few years, as well as finance the increase in working capital in order to achieve the growth targets planned.

23   To meet the growing demand, and due to capacity constraints at its boat building facility in Europe, Merbatty acquired some land in the USA in 2002 and developed a totally new purpose-built boat building facility. This has been operational since early 2004. There were some initial operational problems but Merbatty has been able to put in place experienced and committed employees who have the required skills to meet the exacting demands of Merbatty's growing customer base. The European and USA based boat building facilities both produce all 15 of the models currently offered by Merbatty, although the USA boat building facility rarely produces boats smaller than 20 metres.

24   Merbatty's profit, before dividends, was €40 million for 2006, a record profit level, as shown in the extract from the accounts in **Appendix 4**. The country in which Merbatty is based charges tax at 35% of operating profits less finance costs.

25   Merbatty's Chairman Alberto Blanc was awarded the "Business Person of the Year" in a European awards ceremony in 2004 and this, together with Merbatty's listing, has raised the global profile of Merbatty.

Merbatty's current position

26   Merbatty had signed contracts, and received the required 20% deposits from customers, on future orders for 39 boats (building of which has not yet commenced) at the end of June 2007. The lead time from contract signing to start of construction usually averages six weeks. Sales are on target for Merbatty to meet the planned 300 boats commenced in 2007.

27   As soon as an order is contractually placed, Merbatty will order the required supplies, such as the hull, engines and other major bought-in components for the boat. Merbatty will also allocate a specific building space within the agreed boat building facility. However, until it has undertaken around 20% of the construction work, a proportion of customers' deposits will remain in the Balance Sheet (as a Current Liability) and not be recognised in the Income Statement.

28   The Financial Statements for 2006 (included in **Appendix 4**) include a revaluation reserve in Merbatty's Balance Sheet to reflect an increase in the value of the Non-current Assets, which had been valued in 2006 prior to Merbatty's flotation.

Merbatty's shareholders

29   Merbatty was listed in November 2006 when a major change in the shareholdings took place. Most executive directors acquired shares in the company. In addition, all of the executive directors have share options in order to encourage them to achieve the planned results, which would lead to growth in Merbatty's share price. The share options allow all directors to purchase up to 5 million shares each, any time up to 30 November 2012, at a price of €5·00.

30   Alberto Blanc had previously held 90% of shares and chose to retain the same number of shares (54 million shares) but after the flotation, his shareholding was reduced to 30%. The new issue of shares brought in external investors and much needed finance in order for the company to expand. Alberto Blanc believes in the huge potential of the Merbatty brand and aims to achieve the five-year plan. He then intends to retire.

31   Prior to flotation, Merbatty had 60 million shares at a nominal value of €0·50 each in issue and had a total of 500 million authorised shares. At flotation, in November 2006, Merbatty issued a further 120 million shares at a price of €2·80. At the end of 2006, Merbatty had 180 million shares in issue. The shareholdings at the end of 2006 were as follows:

	Shareholding at 31 December 2006
Directors:	
Alberto Blanc	30%
Jesper Blanc	8%
Henri Gaston	3%
Stefan Gil	3%
Andreas Acosta	3%
Tobias Houllier	2%
Lukas Dian	2%
Alain Mina	2%
Marie Lopp	1%
Bernie Ritzol	1%
Investors:	
JKL (has Board representative)	28%
Corporate fund investors	12%
Other shareholders:	
Small investors	3%
Employee-held shares	2%
Total shareholdings	100%

33   JKL is a listed company with a varied portfolio of investments in a range of international companies, mainly in the construction, engineering and maritime industries. At Merbatty's flotation, JKL purchased 50·4 million shares at a cost of over €140 million as it considers that Merbatty's growth to date and its range of products, together with its potential for the future, will lead to a substantial return on its investment. Following discussions prior to flotation it was agreed that JKL's Investment Director, Simone Lellet would have a seat on the Board of Merbatty and would be involved in helping Merbatty to achieve its five-year plan. Simone Lellet has been involved in some operational planning meetings and she has proved to be a useful management resource.

34   Merbatty's shares initially traded at €3·48 shortly after flotation and Merbatty's directors are pleased with the market's confidence in the company. By 30 June 2007 the share price had risen to €3·65.

35   The market sector average P/E ratio at 30 June 2007 is 15.

Future plans for expansion

36   As a result of the company becoming listed in 2006, the Board of Merbatty was expanded with a number of new Board members. With the input of fresh ideas from the new members of the management team, a number of options have been put forward for expansion of the business. These include producing a much wider range of new models, which would enable Merbatty to offer customers a wider selection of boat sizes and engine capabilities than that currently produced.

37   Merbatty's five-year plan for the period up to and including 2011 is shown in **Appendix 5**. It is this five-year plan on which the prospectus forecast was based.

38   Currently, Merbatty produces 15 different models of boat (ranging from 15 metres to 35 metres in length). One new model is due to be introduced early in 2008 and there are possible enhancements to existing models by the middle of 2008. Lukas Dian, the Technical Director – Design, believes that there is a strong opportunity to build larger boats which would be in the range of 35 to 40 metres in length. The main market for these very large boats would be in the Middle East. The press launch of Merbatty's first 38 metre boat in May 2007 had a good response and this new model will go into full production shortly.

39   In the past, Merbatty has always been very cautious and produced boats when specific orders have been placed, except for a small number of boats built for demonstration purposes. However, after talking to some of Merbatty's agents in the Middle East, Jesper Blanc is confident that the demand in this region will be so great that Merbatty could sell any large boat that it builds. He has proposed that Merbatty should begin production on a range of large boats before any definite orders are placed, in order to capture sales from customers buying impulsively.

40   Stefan Gil is working on a proposal for Merbatty to open sales offices in over 20 locations worldwide. This would result in the termination of some sales agents' contracts. He considers that this will be needed to generate the additional sales required in order for the five-year plan to

be achieved. Additionally, it would allow Merbatty to save costs, as it is anticipated that the costs of running Merbatty's own sales offices would be lower than that paid in agents' commissions.

41 Detailed operational plans were prepared in the form of Merbatty's current year budget for 2007, in order to ensure that the planned level of growth in sales and profitability is monitored and achieved. Merbatty is currently on target to achieve the budgeted number of 300 new boats to be commenced in 2007. This is the highest number of new boats Merbatty will ever have commenced building in one year.

42 The company currently has two boat building facilities, in Europe and on the West Coast of the USA. The maximum annual capacity for these two facilities will depend on the mix of boat models ordered, as several smaller boats can be built in less time than one larger boat. There is an increasing demand for larger boats. Based on Merbatty's current product mix during 2006, the existing two boat building facilities have a maximum capacity, in terms of space, of 320 boats in total each year.

43 The five-year plan includes forecast capital expenditure for the opening of Merbatty's third boat building facility in September 2007. Additionally, the five-year plan includes capital expenditure that would be required for a fourth boat building facility planned to be built during 2010 and 2011. Bernie Ritzol considers that this may be located in a new target market, perhaps in Asia.

Planned opening of third boat building facility in Surania in 2007

44 In March 2006, the Merbatty Board approved the proposal to open a third boat building facility. This is located in Surania (a fictitious country) which is a thriving country in the Middle East. The boat building facility is being constructed to meet Merbatty's exact specifications and is due to be opened in September 2007.

45 The decision to open a third facility was taken in preference to extending either, or both, of the existing facilities for several reasons. First, the five-year plan is based on strong growth in revenue from customers based in the Middle East, with revenue growing from €40 million in 2006 to €180 million in 2011. Revenues from sales generated in this region are forecast to grow from 8% of total revenue to 18% by 2011. Furthermore, there is an increasing trend for the boats ordered by customers in the Middle East to be for the larger models, so this new facility will specialise in building larger boats.

46 Merbatty's research also shows that skilled labour is available in Surania and also that there are sufficient skilled employees at Merbatty's existing boat building facilities who are willing to be seconded to the new facility.

47 Merbatty already has a sales agent located in Surania who has been selling Merbatty boats for over 15 years, who will continue to generate sales through his established reputation and contacts. In addition, Merbatty has recently appointed four additional sales agents in other countries in the Middle East region.

48 The Suranian boat building facility will enable Merbatty to build approximately 180 additional boats each year, depending on their size. However, if the number of large boats in the mix were to increase to a higher proportion than in the agreed five-year plan, it is estimated that the Suranian facility would only have the space to build 140 boats (albeit larger boats) each year.

Merbatty's development plans

49 Bernie Ritzol, the Global Market Development Director, would like to expand the range of models that Merbatty builds and considers that there is demand for a greater variation of designs within the range of hull sizes that are currently built. He is investigating the possibility of expanding the range of boats Merbatty builds, to have 10 new models over the next two years, instead of the planned three new models per year. He has asked Lukas Dian, the Technical Director - Design, to prepare a proposal for investment in research and development needed for this expansion, for the Board meeting in September 2007.

50 Lukas Dian has identified the need for €10 million expenditure on the design of new IT systems, including state of the art boat building CAD and CAM systems, both of which would minimise man hours and thus increase net margins. A further €15 million of expenditure would be required to improve Merbatty's existing boat building facilities, especially to accommodate large boats and the planned 3 new models each year. This capital expenditure is included in the five-year plan which is shown in **Appendix 5**.

Current use of new technology

51 Merbatty currently uses the latest in modern marine production technology, including Computer Numerical Controlled (CNC) machining and robotic spray systems for automated precision spray painting for maximum hydrodynamic efficiency. Investment in technology in the last two years has increased by 10% and has cost the company a total of €10 million.

52 Merbatty has also spent over €4 million on technology to apply glass re-enforced plastic onto each hull to add an external enhanced performance gel coat to increase hull durability and strength. This process was introduced in the USA boat building facility earlier in 2007 and is proving successful in speeding up the time taken at this stage of production of the boats. The previous hull coating technology was very labour intensive, requiring a number of skilled operators using hand-held machines to apply the external gel coating. The old technology is still used in the European boat building facility and for smaller boats built in the USA facility.

Merbatty sponsorship contracts

53 Merbatty has signed two different sponsorship contracts which both generate a lot of positive public relations (PR) and have helped to increase Merbatty's brand recognition. The sponsorship contracts are as follows:

54 • €5 million per year for three years from July 2006 to June 2009 payable to a major global speedboat race organiser which generates significant publicity for Merbatty through advertising and TV coverage of the race events. The races are also sponsored by a number of other global brands, but Merbatty is the principal sponsor.

55 • €5 million per year for five years from January 2007 to December 2011 to a global travel and high quality hotel chain. This company promotes Merbatty boats in a variety of ways, including advertising on all of its websites worldwide, and through promotional information at all of its hotels. Merbatty also works with this company to arrange travel for its customers to inspect their boats.

Merbatty's supplier relationships

56 Merbatty has a number of key suppliers. There has been a trend for more professional relationships with suppliers in Merbatty since Paul Lavie, Merbatty's new Procurement Director, joined the company earlier in 2007. Merbatty has introduced supplier rating systems and Key Performance Indicators (KPI's) for all suppliers. Paul Lavie would like to see Merbatty work more closely with a few key suppliers and to build long standing supplier relationships.

57 Merbatty's ability to work closer with its key suppliers has also been facilitated by the recent development of an on-line order tracking and processing system between Merbatty and two of its key suppliers, which are MNE and Marinatron (see below). This system allows Merbatty to place specific orders for standard engines and satellite control panels to be delivered to Merbatty's boat building facilities and to track the orders right through from the early stages of the boat building process to delivery and installation.

58 Marinatron is Merbatty's key supplier of radar and satellite navigation systems. This USA based company supplies over 30% of the market for marine satellite navigation systems and they are used in all of Merbatty's boat models. It also supplies to a number of Merbatty's competitors in the USA.

59 Topcrest is a manufacturer of boat hulls and is based in the same European country as Merbatty's European boat building facility. Merbatty has been a long standing customer of Topcrest and has built up a very strong relationship with Topcrest's design and manufacturing team. Topcrest has a reputation as one of the top three hull manufacturers in the world and demand for its hulls (ranging from 12 metres to over 40 metres long) has been growing rapidly in the last five years. Merbatty is a key customer of Topcrest and both companies recognise the importance of working closely together on future designs. The lead time for hulls varies from two to six weeks depending on the size of the hull and the design specifications.

60 Sea Safety Equipment (SSE) is a European based company, which supplies most of the on board safety equipment such as inflatable life boats and life jackets.

61 MNE Engines, based in Europe, is a large manufacturer of nautical engines for both commercial and military purposes and it supplies engines worldwide to a wide range of customers. MNE is one of only five specialised nautical engine manufacturers in Europe. MNE supplies all of the diesel engines for all models of Merbatty boats. The order value of engines in 2006 was approximately €38 million.

62 Aqua Designs is an internationally renowned firm of interior designers which specialises in the design and interior fittings for luxury boats. This includes all of the teak wood panelling to cabins and decks, air conditioning, interior furnishings, on board entertainment systems, satellite telephone systems and underwater lighting facilities. All Merbatty boats have a standard specification for interior design but customers can opt to add to this specification from a vast range of options provided by Aqua Designs. These additional internal specifications can add around 11% to the price of a boat, depending on customers' preferences. Aqua Designs operates throughout Europe and the USA, but it does not have operations in the Middle East. Aqua Designs has declined all requests from Merbatty to provide the same interior design service for Merbatty's new Suranian boat building facility. Merbatty is currently finalising

63 In 2006, Merbatty invested in a newly released "off the shelf" state-of-the-art production management software system. This software system is designed to improve productivity and increase resource utilisation. Its most significant advantage is that it enables areas for improvement in labour efficiency and workforce allocation, to be easily identified. In addition, the real time information provided can be used to manage production more effectively by providing clear information on Work-In-Progress. The result has been on-time delivery of all boats, with no penalties for late delivery of boats to customers, since this new IT system has been operational.

64 This software allows Merbatty's management team to respond quickly to minimise potential, and actual, disruptions to production by providing real-time data on workforce utilisation and shop floor processes, material delays, machine downtime and employee idle time. This has resulted in increased productivity. This software has been installed at both the European and USA facilities and it is intended that it will also be installed within the new Suranian facility.

Charitable work

65 Alberto Blanc has been involved in charitable work for many years and feels strongly that Merbatty should continue to support a range of charities.

66 Merbatty financially supported a number of fund-raising events throughout the USA in 2006, which raised $4 million as a contribution towards a new hospital wing. Additionally, the company made donations totalling €0·5 million towards a European Child Poverty Prevention Charity.

67 Alberto Blanc spends much of his spare time advising and working for charitable organisations in Europe, as he strongly believes that those who are as fortunate as he is should do as much as possible to help those less fortunate. Merbatty receives much good publicity from Alberto Blanc's charitable work and every employee is encouraged to spend two to six months seconded from Merbatty, on full pay, to undertake a range of short assignments for charitable organisations. Every member of staff is eligible to participate in one charitable assignment every four years.

Appendix 1

Analysis of Merbatty's range of boats

68

Model	Length (metres)	Maximum speed (knots)	2006 Standard selling price € million	Units sold in 2006	Units sold in 2005
Performance Motor boats: P Series					
P- 3000	35	40	4·4	10	-
P- 2000	25	38	3·4	10	8
P- 1000	20	38	2·9	11	10
P- Gold	19	35	2·8	12	19
P - Elite	18	31	2·3	16	21
Motor boat: C Series					
C- 34	34	31	3·4	11	-
C- 31	31	31	3·2	10	10
C -28	28	31	3·0	16	13
C -23	23	30	2·5	20	29
Flybridge range					
F -1	22	30	1·0	25	22
F- 2	20	30	0·8	24	24
F- 3	16	32	0·6	27	27
Cruisers					
Z - 1	18	34	0·6	30	24
Z - 2	16	32	0·5	23	20
Z - 3	15	30	0·4	35	26

69

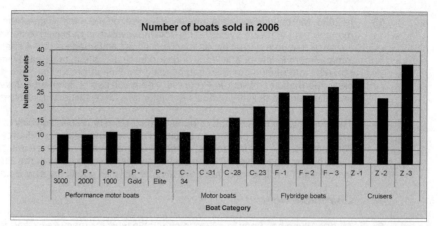

Number of boats sold in 2006

70

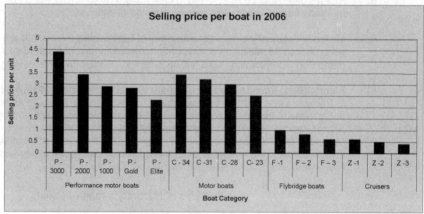

Selling price per boat in 2006

Sales Revenue analysed by home base of customers

71

	Sales Revenue 2006 € million	Planned Sales Revenue 2011 € million Note: All figures shown are based on 2006 prices
Europe	219	420
USA	148	240
Middle East	40	180
Asia	45	65
Australia	30	60
South America	18	29
Africa	2	6
Total revenue	502	1,000

Merbatty's key personnel

72 ### *Alberto Blanc - Chairman*

Alberto Blanc, now 62, had an interest in boats from an early age, when he used to spend his summer holidays at his uncle's boat building facility. Having a keen eye for design and a love of the ocean, he went to marine college in 1965 and became a marine engineer in 1968. He started Merbatty after his uncle gave up his business in 1974 and passed the boat building facility onto Alberto. He plays an active role in the business and is often seen in the European boat building facility, talking to and advising design and technical staff. He believes in a "hands on" management style and that the best way to learn what is happening in the business is to see the boats actually being built. He is also a strong believer in the importance of charity work.

73   *Henri Gaston - Chief Executive*
     Henri Gaston is a 35 year old MBA graduate who joined Merbatty in September 2005. He
     has previously worked for one of Merbatty's major overseas rivals and has a number of
     contacts throughout the industry.

74   *Stefan Gil - Sales Director*
     Stefan Gil, who is 52, has worked for Merbatty for 14 years and was previously a sales
     director of one of the main engine suppliers, where he worked for 10 years. He has a very
     strong technical knowledge and previously spent five years in the Middle East as an
     engineer. He is a keen sailor and has recently sailed single-handed across the Atlantic for
     charity. His main challenge since joining Merbatty has been to create a strong brand
     image for Merbatty in order to appeal to the wealthy European and American customer
     base. He is a great asset to Merbatty.

75   *Andreas Acosta - Finance Director*
     Andreas Acosta, aged 45, joined Merbatty in 2000. He previously worked as a
     management consultant for a large international firm of auditors. It was during this time he
     developed a keen interest in the boat building industry after being in charge of an
     international investigation of the industry. His main concern is the management of cash
     and the potential costs involved in overseas developments. Andreas leads a team of 10
     accountants in the European office and a further 8 in the US office.

76   *Jesper Blanc - Marketing Director*
     Jesper Blanc is the 30 year old son of the Chairman. He graduated from university 6
     years ago with a degree in Media Studies and has worked in the company since then. He
     has worked within the Engineering department and in the Systems and IT department for
     short periods but did not feel that his talents were in either area. His father initially
     appointed him as a Marketing Assistant, which he enjoyed immensely. His father later
     promoted him to the role of Marketing Director 12 months ago. Since his appointment he
     has visited many different countries, talking to customers and agents and establishing
     contacts.

77   *Tobias Houllier - Operations Director*
     Tobias Houllier, now aged 50, started as a junior carpenter and has now worked for
     Merbatty for the last 30 years. During his time he has worked in the engineering
     department, the design department and he has been the European boat building facility
     manager. He has held the role of Operations Director for the last 10 years and is probably
     the most experienced person in the whole company. He is very keen on training and
     encourages all of the designers and engineers to become qualified.

78   *Alain Mina - Technical Director - Systems and IT*
     Alain Mina, aged 35, has worked for Merbatty for the last 8 months. Previous to this he
     was a senior IT project manager for an organisation specialising in building and
     distributing military radar equipment. This is his first role at Director level and he is finding
     it difficult to take a less hands on role than he has previously been used to.

79   *Lukas Dian - Technical Director - Design*
     Lukas Dian aged 36, has worked for Merbatty for 5 years. He started as the Chief
     Designer, but due to his leadership and his personnel management skills he was
     promoted to Director level within 1 year of joining. He leads a team of over 20 designers
     who meet on a regular basis and he encourages an open door policy in order to create a
     feeling of freedom of thought and creativity.

80   *Marie Lopp - HR Director*
     Marie Lopp, now aged 40, has worked for Merbatty for 3 years. She is the first HR director
     as previously Alberto Blanc did not believe in Human Resource departments. However,
     as the organisation expanded and staff issues and legislation became more complex, he
     finally agreed to appoint a HR director. Marie Lopp has a difficult job persuading Alberto
     Blanc of the importance of human resource issues and in particular, she struggles to get
     him to invest in training for staff other than the engineers and designers.

81   *Paul Lavie - Procurement Director*
     Paul Lavie, aged 38, joined Merbatty in March 2007. He has many years of experience
     working for a large supplier of components to the automotive industry. He is also
     concerned that the procurement department had not established a close relationship with
     some of its major suppliers.

82   *Bernie Ritzol - Global Market Development Director*
     Bernie Ritzol, now aged 46, joined Merbatty 12 years ago and has been responsible for a
     number of strategic developments including the acquisition of land in the USA and the
     opening of Merbatty's second boat building facility. He has also worked closely with
     Tobias Houllier in the development of new boat models and also with the Technical
     Director - Design, since Lukas Dian was appointed to this new position four years ago.
     Bernie Ritzol was one of the driving forces behind Merbatty's listing, to enable the

83   *Simone Lellet - Investment Director, JKL*

Simone Lellet, aged 42, is JKL's Investment Director and she was appointed to the Board of Merbatty in November 2006, when Merbatty became listed and JKL bought 50·4 million shares, resulting in a holding of 28% of Merbatty's issued shares. Simone Lellet is very enthusiastic about Merbatty's five-year plan and wants to participate in the decision making process to help Merbatty achieve the goals set out when the company became listed. She has attended every Board meeting and has also been involved in some operational planning meetings, with the Board's permission.

84   *Non-executive directors*

Merbatty has six non-executive directors. The six non-executive directors hold various other directorships, in a variety of industries. Four of the non-executive directors are based in Europe and two hold directorships of USA listed companies and are based in the USA.

Merbatty's Balance Sheet, Income Statement and Statement of Changes in Equity

Note: All data in this Appendix is presented in international financial reporting format

Balance Sheet	As at 31 December 2006 € million	As at 31 December 2006 € million	As at 31 December 2005 € million	As at 31 December 2005 € million
Non-current assets (net)		535		362
Current assets				
Inventory (including Work-in-Progress)	165		126	
Trade receivables and accrued revenue	93		76	
Cash and short-term investments	171		7	
		429		209
Total assets		964		571
Equity and liabilities				
Equity				
Paid in share capital	90		30	
Share premium reserve	318		42	
Revaluation reserve	80		-	
Retained profits	133		113	
		621		185
Non-current liabilities				
Bank loan at 8% interest per year (repayable in 2010)	-		120	
Bank loan at 7% interest per year (repayable in 2014)	200		-	
Payables: amounts falling due after more than one year	7		2	
		207		122
Current liabilities				
Bank overdraft	-		126	
Trade payables and accruals	101		112	
Customers' deposits	13		9	
Tax	22		17	
		136		264
Total equity and liabilities		964		571

Note: Paid in share capital represents 180 million shares of €0·50 each at 31 December 2006

Income Statement	Year ended 31 December 2006 € million	Year ended 31 December 2005 € million
Revenue	502	445
Total operating costs	426	380
Operating profit	76	65
Finance costs	-14	-17
Tax expense (effective rate is 35%)	-22	-17
Profit for the period	40	31

Statement of Changes in Equity	Share capital	Share premium	Re-valuation reserve	Retained earnings	Total
	€ million	€ million	€ million	€ million	€ million
Balance at 31 December 2005	30	42	-	113	185
New shares issued during 2006	60	276	-	-	336
Profit for the period	-	-	-	40	40
Revaluation reserve	-	-	80	-	80
Dividends paid	-	-	-	-20	-20
Balance at 31 December 2006	90	318	80	133	621

Extracts from Merbatty's 5 year plan

Financial data	Actual	Plan				
		Note: All figures shown in the financial data below are based on 2006 prices				
	2006 € million	2007 € million	2008 € million	2009 € million	2010 € million	2011 € million
Revenue (analysed by home base of customers):						
Europe	219	240	275	310	350	420
USA	148	160	170	190	210	240
Middle East	40	50	80	110	140	180
Other areas	95	105	120	130	145	160
Total revenue	502	555	645	740	845	1,000
Operating costs	426	471	552	634	725	863
Operating profit	76	84	93	106	120	137
Post tax profit for the period	40	45	51	60	69	80
Dividends	20	23	26	30	34	40
Capital expenditure:						
New boat building facilities	90	30	0	0	60	100
Other capital expenditure	40	25	15	20	20	25
Total capital expenditure	130	55	15	20	80	125

Key business statistics	Actual	Plan				
	2006 € million	2007 € million	2008 € million	2009 € million	2010 € million	2011 € million
Number of boats commenced in the year	280	300	340	385	435	500
Number of new models introduced	2	3	3	3	3	3
Satisfied customers (as surveyed)	99·5%	100·0%	100·0%	100·0%	100·0%	100·0%
Staff turnover (calculated as number of staff leaving as a percentage of total employees)	20%	18%	15%	12%	12%	12%
Charity - funds donated (€ million)	0·5	0·6	0·7	0·8	0·9	1·0
- man years on secondment for charity work	3·0	4·0	5·0	6·0	7·0	8·0

End of Pre-seen material

14

Merbatty: some help from BPP

Introduction

The topic list below identifies examples of the type of activity which will be available in the BPP Learning Media Toolkit for your paper.

1 How well have you read the pre-seen information?

	Question	Answer
1	Is the luxury boat market growing?	Yes. Para 1 of the Pre-seen material says it is and para 2.2 in Chapter 2 suggests growth rates of between 12% and 28%.
2	What has been the sales growth rate enjoyed by Merbatty?	Sales revenue grew 13% between 2005 and 2006. According to para 68 total units sold grew from 253 to 280 (11%) between the same years. This is confirmed by the statement at para 21 that sales have risen at 'over 10% for the last 12 years'.
3	Name the top three markets for Merbatty's boats in 2006.	According to para 71 they are Europe, USA and Asia.
4	Name the top three markets forecast for Merbatty's boats in 2011.	According to para 71 they are Europe, USA and Middle East.
5	For how long has Alberto Blanc run Merbatty?	Para 6 tells us he has run it for the whole 33 years since its formation.
6	How many models of boat did Merbatty make in 2006?	15, according to paras 23 and 68.
7	How many models of boat will Merbatty make in 2009 if Bernie Ritzol gets approval for his plans?	Merbatty made 15 types of boat in 2006 and its five-year plan shows it intended to introduce 3 new models in 2007. According to para 49 Bernie proposes 10 new models over the 'next two years', presumably 2008 and 2009. Therefore 28 models by the end of 2009 assuming none of the present models are discontinued.
8	Which board member was appointed most recently?	Paul Lavie was appointed in March 2007 which, in July 2007, means he was appointed four months ago. By November 2007 he would have been appointed eight months ago, the same as Alain Mina. We assume the Pre-seen is the situation as at 1 July 2007 given the most recent date we are given is the share price at 30 June (para 34).
9	Who supports the development of a policy on training and staff development?	Marie Lopp and Tobias Houllier support training. There is no mention of broader staff development programmes.
10	Who will staff the Suranian facility?	This has not been revealed. Para 46 seems to offer a choice between local employees or the transfer of employees from existing facilities.
11	What is included in the capital expenditure forecast for 2007?	Of the €55m it seems €30 is for building the Suranian facility and, according to para 50, the remaining €25 is for improving existing facilities (€15m) and new IT systems (€10m).
12	How many sales agents are employed by Merbatty?	None. Sales agents are not employees and are specifically excluded from the employee data in para 19. We are not told the total number of sales agents representing Merbatty. Merbatty does have 17 sales staff of its own however.

	Question	Answer
13	How much was paid to Aqua Designs in 2006?	The Pre-seen does not reveal this. It states only that up to 11% can be added to the value of a boat due to their designs (para 62) and para 10 implies this was worth €50 revenue in 2006.
14	Which Board members support the charitable work of Merbatty?	Alberto Blanc (paras 65 & 72) and Stefan Gil (para 74) have shown active support. However, given that it is in the five-year plan accepted by the Board in 2006 it could be suggested that all Board members at this time gave support.
15	What kind of boats will be built in Surania?	The European and USA facilities build all models of boats (para 23) but Surania will 'specialise in bigger boats' (para 45).
16	What are the names of four real-world rivals to Merbatty?	Sunseeker Ferretti (Riva, Pershing and Custom Line) Princess Riviera.
17	What percentage of operating costs in 2006 were payments to MNE Engines?	Operating costs were €426m. MNE received orders worth €38m so therefore it was approximately 8.9% of operating costs.
18	How many staff did Merbatty employ at the end of 2006?	2,167 (para 19).
19	When are Merbatty's loans repayable?	€200m is repayable in 2014. The loan for €120m repayable in 2010 was refinanced in 2006.
20	Where in Asia will the new boatyard be?	There is not definitely going to be a new boatyard in Asia. Although some capex appears in the five-year plan for a boatyard the choice of Asia is just something ventured by Bernie Ritzol (para 43). No precise location given.
21	What information systems does Merbatty presently use?	CAD (assumed already something in place – para 50) CAM and CNC machines (para 51) On-line order tracking system (para 57) – therefore extranet and SCM A production management system installed on 2006 (para 63)
22	Which supplier has declined to support Merbatty in Surania?	Aqua Designs will not provide its services in the Middle East (para 62).
23	When did Merbatty open the USA facility and where in the USA is it?	The facility was opened in 2004 (para 23) and is on the West Coast (para 7).
24	If a customer places an order for a €4m boat how will the payments to and from Merbatty follow?	Customer pays 20% deposit (€0.8m) (para 8) Merbatty pays 50% of commission to agent immediately (€80,000) (para 15) Second customer instalment of 30% paid at engine delivery (€1.2m) (para 8) Final customer payment received after customer inspection (€2m) (para 8) Merbatty pays second half of agent's commission (€80,000) (para 15)

	Question	Answer
25	How long does it take to build a boat?	Between 3 and 10 months (para 13)
26	How many boats in total does the Pre-seen suggest were built in 2006?	3,500 (para 1) of which Merbatty had an 8% share with 280 boats (para 12) : *check 100/8 x 280 = 3,500*
27	Which Board members have less than a year's experience of the boat building industry?	Alain Mina Paul Lavie Simone Lellet
28	Does Merbatty support any charities in the Middle East?	Not at present. The charities it supported in 2006 are in USA and Europe (para 66).
29	Which of Merbatty's suppliers are based in the same country as its facilities?	Marinatron (USA) Topcrest Aqua Designs (operates in USA) The remaining suppliers, SSE and MNE are European, but not necessarily in the same country as Merbatty.
30	What major IT/IS projects must Alain Mina oversee in the coming 12 months?	CAD/CAM systems (para 50) Installation of the systems in Surania (para 64)

2 Financial analysis

2.1 Investors' analysis

Ratio	Calculation	Comment
Return on capital employed (ROCE), based on profit before interest and tax, and year end capital employed	See (a) below	ROCE at 31 December 2006 is significantly lower than at 31 December 2005 due to the share issue during the year.
Return on equity	See (b) below	Return on equity at 31 December 2006 is significantly lower than at 31 December 2005 due to the share issue during the year.
Earnings per share (EPS) assuming 180 million shares in issue throughout	See (c) below	Indication of how well the firm earns money for its equity holders. But again much lower in 2006 versus 2005 due to new share issue.
P/E ratio as at 30 June 2007 based on the 2006 earnings for Merbatty	See (d) below	We are told in the pre-seen that the sector average P/E ratio at 30 June 2007 is 15. So Merbatty's is slightly above the sector average.
Dividend cover as at 31 December 2006	See (e) below	The company is able to continue paying its present level of dividend.

(a)   **ROCE** $= \dfrac{\text{Operating profit (PBIT)}}{\text{Long term capital}} = \dfrac{€76m}{€828m} = \mathbf{9.2\%}$

Long-term capital = Equity + Long term liabilities

Shareholders' equity	621
Long-term liabilities	207
Long-term capital	828

(b)   **Return on equity** $= \dfrac{\text{Profit after tax}}{\text{Shareholders' equity}} = \dfrac{€40m}{€621m} = \mathbf{6.4\%}$

(c)   **EPS** $= \dfrac{\text{Profit attributable to ordinary shareholders}}{\text{Weighted average number of ordinary shares}}$

Profit after tax (€m)	40
Number of shares (m)	180
EPS (€) $= \dfrac{40}{180}$	0.22

(d)   **P/E ratio** $= \dfrac{\text{Market price of share}}{\text{EPS}}$

Market price of share (€) = 3.65

EPS (from (iii) above = 0.22

P/E ratio = 16.43

(e)   **Dividend cover** $= \dfrac{\text{Earnings per share}}{\text{Dividend per share}} = \dfrac{0.22}{0.11} = 2.00$

Dividend per share is $\dfrac{20}{180}$

2.2 Share price projection

Measure	Calculation	Comment
Projected share price at 31 December 2007	EPS(€) $= \dfrac{45}{180} = 0.25$ Price earnings ratio $= \dfrac{\text{Market price of share}}{\text{EPS}}$ $16.43 = \dfrac{\text{Market price of share}}{0.25}$ Market price of share $= 16.43 \times 0.25$ Market price of share (€) = 4.11	What could cause share price to deviate from this? • profits not reaching anticipated levels (−ve) • trading exceeds anticipated levels, and future expectations are favourable (+ve) • market anticipating a takeover bit for the company (+ve) • market feeling the company needs a change of strategic direction or management (−ve)

2.3 Liquidity and working capital

Measure	Calculation	Comment
Inventory days (Note: use total operating costs as an indicator of cost of sales)	See (a) below	Will amount of money tied up in stock continue to increase as the product range increases?
Accounts receivable period	See (b) below	
Accounts payable period	See (c) below	
Working capital cycle	See (d) below	Has risen significantly from 2005. How long could company's cash flow sustain similar increases going forward?
Ratio of revenue to working capital	See (e) below	Net working capital increased 74% from 2005 to 2006. Revenue only increased 13%.
Current ratio	See (f) below	Share issue meant overdraft was cleared and Merbatty now has cash at bank
Quick ratio	See (g) below	Share issue meant overdraft was cleared and Merbatty now has cash at bank

		2006	2005

(a) **Inventory days**

$$\frac{\text{Inventory}}{\text{Total operating costs}} \times 365$$

2006: $\dfrac{165}{426} \times 365 = 141.4$

2005: $\dfrac{126}{380} \times 365 = 121.0$

(b) **Accounts receivable period**

$$\frac{\text{Trade receivables}}{\text{Revenue}} \times 365$$

2006: $\dfrac{93}{502} \times 365 = 67.6$

2005: $\dfrac{76}{445} \times 365 = 62.3$

(c) **Accounts payable period**

$$\frac{\text{Trade payables}}{\text{Total operating costs}} \times 365$$

2006: $\dfrac{101}{426} \times 365 = 86.5$

2005: $\dfrac{112}{380} \times 365 = 107.6$

(d) **Working capital cycle**

Inventory + Receivables – Payables

2006: 122.5

2005: 75.8

(e) **Revenue to net working capital**

$$\frac{\text{Revenue}}{\text{Net working capital}}$$

2006: $\dfrac{502}{157} = 3.2$

2005: $\dfrac{445}{90} = 4.9$

(Net working capital = Inventory + Receivables – Payables)

(f) **Current ratio**

$$\frac{\text{Current assets}}{\text{Current liabilities}}$$

2006: $\dfrac{429}{136} = 3.2$

2005: $\dfrac{209}{264} = 0.8$

(g) **Quick ratio**

$$\frac{\text{Current assets less inventory}}{\text{Current liabilities}}$$

2006: $\dfrac{264}{136} = 1.9$

2005: $\dfrac{83}{264} = 0.3$

2.4 Cash flow

Merbatty – Extract from cash flow for year 2006

		€m	€m
Operating profit			76
Movements in working capital			
(Increase)/decrease in trade and other receivables	76 – 93	(17)	
(Increase)/decrease in inventory	126 – 165	(39)	
Increase/(decrease) in trade and other payables	101 – 112	(11)	
Increase/(decrease) in customer deposits and payables due after more than one year	7 – 2 + 13 – 9	9	
			(58)
Depreciation and amortisation of non-current assets			37 (W)
Cash generated from operations			55

Working

Movement on non-current assets

		€m
Net book value at 31 December 2005		362
Capital expenditure in year (Appendix 5 of pre-seen)		130
Revaluation reserve (Appendix 4 of pre-seen; non-cash item)	(1)	80
		572
Net book value at 31 December 2006	(2)	535
Depreciation for year (1) – (2)		37

2.5 Cost of capital

Merbatty – weighted average cost of capital

Cost of equity (calculated using dividend growth model)

$$k_e = \frac{d_0(1+g)+g}{P_0}$$

Where k_e =   cost equity
         d_0 =   current dividend
         P_0 =   market value of equity (ex-dividend)
         g =   expected constant annual growth rate in dividends

Based on 2006 figures

(a)   Assume share price of €3.65 (ex-dividend)

(b)   Dividend just paid of 11.1 cents $\left(\dfrac{20}{180}\right)$

Dividend growth	*2006*	*2011*
Dividend (m)	€20	€40

Doubles over five years

Therefore annual growth rate is fifth root of $2 = \sqrt[5]{2} = 14.9$

Will use 15% for calculations

$$k_e = \frac{11.1 \times (1.15)}{365} + 0.15$$

$$= 0.035 + 0.15$$

$$= \mathbf{18.5\%}$$

Cost of debt

$$k_{dnet} = \text{interest } (1 - \text{tax})$$
$$= 7(1 - 0.35)$$
$$= \mathbf{4.55\%}$$

Interest is 7% (given in pre-seen)
Effective tax rate (35% (given in pre-seen)

Weighted average cost of capital (k_0)

$$k_0 = \frac{(k_e V_E) + (K_d V_D)}{V_E + V_D}$$

Merbatty has 180 million ordinary shares

Merbatty has €200 million loan @ 7%

$$k_0 = \frac{(0.185 \times 180 \times 3.65) + (0.0455 \times 200)}{(180 \times 3.65) + 200}$$

$$= \frac{130.65}{857}$$

$$= \mathbf{15.24\%}$$

2.6 Capital gearing

	2006 €m		2005 €m	
Financial gearing = $\dfrac{\text{Long term debt}}{\text{Long term debt} + \text{Equity}}$	$\dfrac{200}{821}$	= 24.4%	$\dfrac{120}{305}$	= 39.3%

Long term capital = Equity + Long term liabilities

	€m	€m
Share capital	90	30
Share premium	318	42
Revaluation reserve	80	–
Retained profits	133	113
Shareholders' equity	621	185
Long term debt		
Bank loan	200	120
	821	305

2.7 Valuation of Merbatty

(a) **Price earnings approach** (based on December 2006 figures)

Value of firm = maintainable earnings × price earnings ratio
= €40m × 16.43 = €657 million

The business forecasts support the December 2006 net profit as a floor level of earnings which future earnings are not expected to fall below.

(b) **Dividend growth approach** (based on December 2006 figures)

$$P_0 = \frac{d_0(1+g)}{k_e - g}$$

Where P_0 = market value

          d_0 = dividend paid

          g = dividend growth rate (15%, from Activity 3.13)

          k_e = cost of equity

$$P_0 = \frac{20 \times (1+0.15)}{0.185 - 0.15}$$

P_0 = €657 million

3 Strategic analysis

3.1 Stakeholder mapping

Stakeholder	Power	Interest
Alberto Blanc	High (largest single shareholder). Has power to sell shares (affecting share price) and vote on policy even after retirement	High (still a "hands on" chairman though due to retire in 5 years)
Simone Lellet	Low (represents minority 28% shareholder but only a "participant" in the decision making process – "with the Board's permission" (p. 13)	High – keen to be involved in operational decision making; full time JKL representative on the Board
Corporate fund investors	Low – 12%	Low – as long as dividend maintained and growth delivered
Jesper Blanc	High – 8% shareholder and son of Alberto (evidence of nepotism in his appointment); key role on Board	High – executive decision maker
Henri Gaston	Low – unclear what he does; "has a number of contacts in the industry"	High – executive decision maker
Andreas Acosta	High – key role on Board, manages entire dept of 18 staff	High – executive decision maker
Stefan Gil	High – a "great asset to Merbatty" with "very strong technical knowledge" and in charge of the brand image	High – executive decision maker
Alain Mina	Low – too involved in the operational aspects of his job	High – executive decision maker
Marie Lopp	Low – finding it difficult to convince Alberto of the need for HRM	High – executive decision maker
Bernie Ritzol	High – key decision maker over Surania and a "driving force"	High – executive decision maker

Stakeholder	Power	Interest
Sales agents	High – face of the company; can influence sales; Merbatty heavily reliant upon them	Low – as long as the boats produced are sellable
Skilled boat building technicians	High – such technicians are in very short supply	High – full time employees in the company
Marinatron	High – dominant market leader with significant supplier power as a result	Low – not reliant on Merbatty
Topcrest	High – long standing supplier of hulls; Merbatty has recognized the "importance of working closely together"	High – not reliant on Merbatty but work closely together
Sea Safety Equipment	Low – not a key supplier	Low – no evidence of close working relationship
MNE Engines	High – supplies ALL Merbatty's engines – €38m per annum	Low – has a "wide range of customers" to deal with. Only interested in getting paid promptly
Aqua Designs	High – evidenced by their refusal to supply to Surania	Low – appear to have no interest in Merbatty's development in Surania

Mendelow's stakeholder mapping framework can be used to represent the stakeholders in Merbatty.

Level of interest

	Low	High
Low	**MINIMAL EFFORT** SSE Corporate Funds	**KEEP INFORMED** Simone Lellett Henri Gaston Alain Mina Marie Lopp
High	**KEEP SATISFIED** Sales agents Marinatron MNE Aqua Designs	**KEY PLAYERS** Alberto Blanc Jesper Blanc Andreas Acosta Stefan Gil Bernie Ritzol Skilled Technicians Topcrest

Power

3.2 Five forces analysis

Force	Main examples	Ability to affect profitability
Buyer power	Affluent sector can easily overcome switching costs or adopt substitutes or could afford to lose deposits and cost Merbatty a sale	High
Supplier power	Growth in the market means suppliers can flex their muscles – see pp. 8 & 9	Very high
Threat of entrants	New entrants entering market in Australia and Asia (p.1) suggests barriers are low in certain sectors.	Moderate
Substitutes	Private jets, helicopters, sailboats, luxury/sports cars	Moderate
Competitive rivalry	Merbatty has 10% market share against "a number of major international builders" (p.1)	High

3.3 PEST analysis for Merbatty

Political/legal	• Potential for international dispute to disturb trade • Changes to regulations on boats and employment (eg safety standards) • Laws on ownership of foreign subsidiary boatyards
Economic	• Rapid rise in incomes and living standards in Asia • Exchange rate volatility affecting Euro and $US • Low cost competition from Asia • Potential for lower production costs in Asia
Social	• Emergence of elite groups in emerging economies • Different employment cultures in boatyards in USA, Europe and Surania
Technological	• New materials and methods for building boats • Improvements to business IT/IS applications

3.4 PEST analysis for new Asian facility

	Opportunity	Threat
Political/legal	• Less employment legislation to comply with • Erosion of political trade barriers • Potential for overseas development grants/tax incentives	• Some threat to political stability – communist regimes etc. • Complexity of certain aspects of law, eg Land ownership • Profit repatriation rules – dividends restricted
Economic	• Largest developing economy in the world – China & Far East • Lower labour rates • Raising finance – for eg. Japanese base rate remains flat at 0.5% (July 2007) while European rates are increasing over 6.5%	• Exchange rate volatility as witnessed by "Nikkei bubble" in Japan, 1990

	Opportunity	Threat
Social	• Increasing desire to embrace and emulate Western culture and recreation activities	• Language barriers • Religious/cultural differences affecting work practice
Technological	• Lower cost computerised CAD / CAM technology	• Compliance and integration with existing technology

3.5 Porter Diamond

Source	Examples	Advantage gained in Europe	Change in Surania
Demand conditions	• Sophistication of consumer • Levels of demand • Healthy economy • "Must have" culture	• Centuries of sailing/boating experience • High demand for quality status goods • Healthy economy	• Huge rich/poor divide – may make smaller models unattractive to the mega wealthy • May be a short-term "fad" for oil rich millionaires • Lack of sophistication and customer knowledge about maritime activities
Related and supporting industries	• Harbours and marinas • Maintenance providers • Crews • Charter companies	• Plentiful harbouring sites • Easy to obtain crews from traditional sailing nations (Britain, Portugal, Spain, Italy, France etc.)	• Newer industry so perhaps lacks supporting industries • Fewer trained crews
Factor conditions	• Climate • Natural conditions • Population • Infrastructure	• Mediterranean – calm water • No extreme weather conditions (earthquakes, hurricanes, tsunamis etc.) • High education levels among population • Well developed infrastructure	• Risk of drought • Tsunamis in the Indian Ocean • Earthquake risk threatens infrastructure • Population less widely advanced
Firm strategy, structure and rivalry	• Management's attitude to risk, investment, profit etc. • Investment in people/innovation • Presence of competitors to motivate pursuit of excellence • National cultural factors related to the industry	• Many competitors to inspire ambition • European sailing history/culture • EU countries sponsor innovation, investment in people etc.	• Few competitors may lead to complacency in boat facility • Not traditionally a sailing/boating culture • Less emphasis on innovation

4 SWOT analysis

Strengths	Weaknesses
• Established global brand giving access to premium market segments • Cash positive and profitable business	• Relatively small market share (8%) leading to less economies of scale and high promotional costs per boat • Muddled roles on Board with overlap between Global Market Development Director and both CEO and Marketing Director • High proportion of sales made in lower margin products • High dependence on Aqua Designs and other key suppliers
Opportunities	**Threats**
• Global economic development creating further rich elites wishing to buy prestige products like boats • Lower costs of production available in emerging Asian economies	• Lower cost producers from Asia • Other prestige products (private jets, luxury homes, helicopters)

4.1 Prioritise your SWOT

Choose the TWO **most significant** Strengths, Weaknesses, Opportunities and Threats. Justify your choices.

Strength	
Reputation as quality airline	Reputation gains passengers, alliance partners and access to new markets.
High load factors	In a high fixed cost industry like airlines this is essential to recover the fixed costs and to make profit. It reflects good route planning and marketing.
Weakness	
Staff unrest	Staff unrest could bring an immediate halt to operations for a protracted period with consequent losses and deterioration of customer goodwill.
Lack of Board experience	FQA faces significant opportunities and challenges which represent a discontinuity from the business that the Board know how to run. This reduces FQA's ability to adapt.
Opportunity	
Growth in alternative markets	The volume of additional business will be significant if FQA can position itself to take advantage of it.
More cost effective fleet	This could raise margins significantly.
Threat	
Pressure from investors	This could trigger either a strike or a sell-off or seizure of control by investors if not satisfied.
Green legislation	This will force FQA to replace fleet ahead of time or pay high costs for 'permits to pollute'. This may affect cash flow, balance sheet values and profits.

Merbatty: unseens and requirements

Introduction

This chapter contains the unseen material and requirements from the September and November exams.

We have produced a suggested answer to the September exam in Chapter 16.

1 September 2007 unseen

Requirement

You are the consultant appointed by the Merbatty Board. Prepare a report that prioritises, analyses and evaluates the issues facing Merbatty, and makes appropriate recommendations.

Proposal to enter the boat chartering market

The boat chartering market is defined as the renting of boats, which are owned and operated by a company, and rented on a weekly basis to private individuals or companies. A boat chartering company puts its own crew on board and pays all the fixed costs. The end customer who charters (rents) a boat typically pays the fixed weekly fee plus some additional charges. There are many boat chartering companies globally.

The prospectus forecast for Merbatty at the time of flotation included a number of new areas of revenue generation, one of which was a proposal to enter the boat charter market. Bernie Ritzol, Merbatty's Global Market Development Director, is very keen to see Merbatty generate revenues from new sources. He believes that the time is right for Merbatty to enter the highly competitive boat chartering market. Bernie Ritzol has prepared a proposal for Merbatty to initially build 10 large boats specifically for chartering, all 10 of which will be based in Europe. If this initial trial into the chartering market is successful, then Merbatty will build and operate additional charter boats to meet market demand worldwide.

If the Board approves this proposal, Merbatty would need to commence the building of all 10 boats by November 2007, so that they will be available for chartering during Summer 2008.Therefore a Board decision on this chartering proposal will need to be made by mid-October 2007.

The average capital cost of each boat is forecast to be €3·2 million, post-tax. The post-tax net cash inflows (excluding the capital cost and residual values of the 10 boats) are forecast to be:

Forecast post-tax net cash inflows

(Total for all 10 charter boats)

	2008 € million	2009 € million	2010 € million	2011 € million	2012 € million
Post-tax net cash inflows (nominal values)	10·5	13·9	16·9	17·9	26·6

These post-tax net cash inflows are based on the expected number of weeks that all 10 boats would be chartered each year and represent only about 40% of the year. Andreas Acosta, the Finance Director, recommends that a suitable risk adjusted discount rate is 14% post-tax and considers that this investment should be appraised over a five year period. The post-tax residual value at the end of year five is forecast to be €0·75 million for each boat.

Shortage of skilled employees

Marie Lopp has been actively recruiting skilled boat builders during 2007. Merbatty needs more employees at its existing facilities to build the increased number of boats and also to cover for employees who have been seconded to Merbatty's new boat building facility in Surania.. However, there is a high demand for skilled boat builders in this sector and recruitment of new employees has been lower than required. Merbatty will need to recruit a total of over 100 skilled boat builders over the next two years to be ready to meet the forecast growth in the number of boats to be built.

Merbatty currently spends approximately €1 million per year on training, the majority of which is for designers and engineers. However, this is significantly less than its major competitors, two of whom spend in excess of €5 million per year. Alberto Blanc's philosophy is that too much time P10 20 September 2007 spent on training detracts from the actual boat building activity and that the best form of training is done whilst working on the job. A number of skilled employees and new apprentices have recently resigned from Merbatty. Some apprentices stated that they considered their future would be more secure if they worked for an employer who can support their studies.

Stock discrepancy

Andreas Acosta has received an internal audit report that states that there is a discrepancy of €0·2 million of electric power tools which Merbatty purchases for employees to use during boat construction work. This discrepancy was discovered at a stock take at the end of June 2007.

On investigation, it has been established that many employees have taken these electric tools for personal use over the last few years. Recently, one long standing employee was dismissed for the theft of a €300 power drill when it was discovered in his possession on a random and unannounced check of employees when leaving the boat building facility.

Problem at Merbatty's boat building facility in the USA

A serious problem has been identified in Merbatty's boat building facility in the USA. This problem has arisen from the use of new technology, which was introduced only at the USA facility in February 2007. The new technology involves the application of glass re-enforced plastic onto the hull of each boat to improve its durability and strength. The glass re-enforced plastic technology has been used on a total of 32 boats.

However, in July 2007, sea trials were held for 4 boats whose hulls had been coated with this new technology. (Sea trials are defined as a rigorous series of "in-water" tests which are designed to test the boat under a variety of sea and weather conditions and are conducted as a final test before delivery to customers). The sea trials identified cracks in the hulls and significant water leakage on all 4 boats. During earlier tests on these 4 boats at the USA boat building facility, no faults had been identified at all and therefore these boats had been completed and prepared for sea trials prior to delivery to customers. Following the discovery of these cracks, the problem was reported to Tobias Houllier. He immediately instructed a team of senior engineers be sent out to inspect the 24 boats built using this new technology which have already been delivered to customers.

These inspection tests were conducted during August 2007. All 24 boats were comprehensively inspected and 6 of these boats were found to have similar cracks in their hulls. Therefore at the end of August 2007, it had been identified that there are 10 completed boats with these serious cracks; 6 which have been delivered to customers and 4 which failed their sea trials. There are a further 4 boats that are still under construction where this technology has already been applied.

It is not yet known whether these serious cracks can be repaired, or whether the boats will have to be re-built. Andreas Acosta has estimated that if the 10 completed boats need to be re-built, then the additional cost to Merbatty, including penalty payments, would be around €11 million. Fortunately, the previous technology is still available and is used within the USA boat building facility for some of Merbatty's other boat models. The boats built in the USA facility using the previous technology have shown no evidence whatsoever of leakages or cracking.

Delayed opening of Merbatty's new boat building facility in Surania

Merbatty was planning to open its third boat construction facility in Surania at the start of September 2007. This new facility was planned to cost a total of €120 million during 2006 and 2007. However, there have been delays at the final stages of construction and also in the issue of import permits for specialised equipment. The Suranian facility was opened for trials and safety testing in August 2007 but it quickly became apparent that the air conditioning for this large building was not adequate. Therefore, the safety certificate was not issued by the relevant authorities.

Merbatty will not be able to install the remaining equipment, or install and test the more powerful air conditioning, required to ensure a safe working temperature in this hot country, until December 2007. The updated estimated date for the opening of this new facility has been put back to the end of January 2008, due to the time required for the authorities to test the working environment and to issue a safety certificate. It is also forecast that there will be cost over-runs of €20 million.

In the month of August 2007 alone sales in the Middle East region exceeded all sales targets. Sales of Merbatty's top of the range boats generated €25 million in August 2007. The total planned sales revenue for the whole of 2007 for the Middle East region was forecast to be €50 million.

At the end of August 2007, Merbatty had 13 signed contracts for large boats which were due to be built at the new facility in Surania, which was originally scheduled to open in September 2007. The latest forecast is that there will be further orders for 17 large boats in the Middle East region up to the end of 2007. Therefore there could be a forecast total of 30 large boats for the Middle East region that need to be built somewhere, as the Suranian facility has not opened on time. Tobias Houllier has stated that once construction on a boat has started in a boat building facility, it is not feasible to move the partially completed boat to another facility.

The boat building facilities in Europe and USA have the capacity to build all 30 large boats. However, if the location of the building of these boats were to be moved to Europe and the USA boat building facilities, neither of these boat building facilities would have any further spare space to commence any additional large boats until all 30 of these large boats are completed, which would be around the middle of 2008.

Therefore, there would not be any spare capacity to build the 10 large boats required for Merbatty's boat chartering proposal (detailed above). If the location of the boat building for the orders from the Middle East were to be moved to Europe and the USA, this would necessitate additional costs. These additional costs include payments to compensate customers who would need to inspect their new boats at a different location and also to pay sub-contractors additional fees to relocate their employees to a different boat building facility. The additional direct cost of moving the building of these 30 boats to either of Merbatty's other two boat building facilities is forecast to be €4 million in total.

Alternatively, Merbatty could advise its Middle East customers of the five-month delay in commencement of construction of these boats. If the building of these 30 boats were to remain in Surania and the commencement of their construction is delayed for five months to the end of January 2008, the forecast effect on the company's operating profit for 2007 would be a reduction of €9 million, as the operating profits on these boats would be recognised in the 2008 accounting year. Additionally, Merbatty would be liable to pay an estimated €2 million as penalties for late delivery if all 13 boats currently contracted for, were to be delivered five months late.

Stock market analysts have advised Andreas Acosta that it is important that Merbatty achieves its planned profit target for 2007, as well as the target of 300 boats commenced in 2007. It has come to the attention of Andreas Acosta that two new boat contracts for customers based in the Middle East have been given an immediate start date at Merbatty's boat building facility in Europe. Building of these two boats has commenced despite prior orders for other boats that should have commenced before these Middle East orders. On investigation, Andreas Acosta has established that the customers have made unofficial payments to several of Merbatty's employees and the sales agents involved, in order to speed up the delivery dates. Andreas Acosta has reported this to Alberto Blanc, who stated that payments are often made by established Merbatty customers in order to secure an earlier completion date.

Proposal to increase sales in Australia

Jesper Blanc, Merbatty's Marketing Director, has spent the last four months in Australia, reviewing the market position and meeting with boat builders and agents. He met with a very positive response to the possibility of Merbatty opening a sales office and renting space in a marina for the display of Merbatty boats in a key coastal city in Australia. This would enable Merbatty to service an ever growing market for luxury boats in this part of the world and its own sales office would replace Merbatty's current sales agent.

Jesper Blanc has proposed to the Merbatty Board that the full range of 15 Merbatty boat models should be on display within the sales marina. These boats could be sold if a customer wanted to buy a boat for immediate delivery. Usually, Merbatty only has 2 or 3 of its boats on display at any location, or at any of the international boat exhibitions. It had never before had such a large display of its range.

The total cost of the proposal is €31 million in 2008 and €10 million in 2009, including new boat models introduced. Jesper Blanc is confident that over the next few years this would increase boat sales in Australia from the 35 boats sold in 2006 to over 150 boats per year by 2011. The current agreed five-year plan only includes sales of 70 boats (generating sales revenue of €60 million) in 2011. The proposal also includes a marketing campaign, spread over two years.

If Merbatty were to be able to increase sales to 150 boats by 2011 by setting up its own sales office and undertaking the proposed marketing campaign, Andreas Acosta has calculated that this could generate a post-tax NPV of €30 million over four years. For this proposal to generate a break-even NPV, Merbatty would need to sell an average of at least 70 boats every year for four years.

Navigation control panels

One of Merbatty's major bought-in components for each boat is the navigation control panel. This is a highly sophisticated computerised system which guides a boat automatically and is linked to satellite navigation systems. At the end of July 2007, the manufacturer of this system, Marinatron, advised all of its customers, including Merbatty, that one particular model of its navigation control panels, supplied in the four-month period between March and June 2007 had a possible technical fault. As a precaution this panel was recalled by Marinatron.

During the period March to June 2007, Merbatty had installed this potentially faulty control panel into 100 boats. Marinatron supplied Merbatty with 100 replacement control panels (free of charge) in August 2007. Of the 100 boats fitted with this faulty component, 80 boats have been completed and delivered to customers. The other 20 boats, which are still under construction, have had the possibly faulty control panel removed and have been refitted with Marinatron's replacement control panel. Alain Mina, Merbatty's Technical Director - Systems and IT, is reluctant to send engineers to refit this control panel on boats already delivered to customers as he considers the risk of a fault to be negligible. He also does not want to inconvenience customers with the refit. Alain Mina does not consider that this operational problem should be referred to the Board.

Marinatron has asked Merbatty to return all of the faulty control panels to it for testing. Alain Mina's assistant, Joe Pickard, is very concerned that Merbatty has not yet changed these control panels. Joe Pickard has informed Tobias Houllier about his concerns.

Appointment of a consultant

At the Merbatty Board meeting held at the end of August 2007 it was agreed that a consultant would be appointed to advise the Board on the issues facing Merbatty.

2 November 2007 unseen

Requirement

You are the consultant appointed by the Merbatty Board. Prepare a report that prioritises, analyses and evaluates the issues facing Merbatty, and makes appropriate recommendations.

Adverse weather conditions resulting in reduced stock market confidence

As a result of increasingly unusual weather and harsh sea conditions linked to global warming, there have been a growing number of boats lost at sea. In fact, 30 boats sunk last year. After the required investigations, none of the boat models were found to have any design faults. In October 2007, following a severe storm, a further 4 boats, including a Merbatty-built boat, were lost at sea. These boat losses attracted much adverse press speculation.

The stock market has reacted to the current loss in confidence and all companies in this sector have seen a fall in share prices by around 7%. Merbatty's share price at the end of June 2007 was €3.65 but since the end of October 2007 the shares have been trading at around €3.40. Most manufacturers worldwide have seen a reduction in advance orders. As a result of the downturn in sales, some competitors have reacted by reducing their selling prices in order to stimulate sales.

Updated navigation software

As a result of this recent adverse publicity, Marinatron (Merbatty's supplier of on-board systems) has updated its latest satellite navigation software to include an enhanced early warning weather system. Marinatron has identified a strong demand for this enhanced early warning feature. The new navigation software system costs €70,000 per system, whereas the previous navigation software system was only €10,000. Marinatron is advising all boat manufacturers that they should install this latest navigation software system to all newly manufactured boats.

Marinatron has requested boat manufacturers to inform all of their previous customers of the availability of this new enhanced navigation software system, so that customers can decide for themselves whether they want to have it installed at an additional cost. Alain Mina, Technical Director - Systems and IT, does not believe that this new navigation software system is worth the extra cost and has made a decision not to procure this new system for boats currently in production. He also considers that the extra cost that Merbatty would incur, could not be passed onto customers, as the customers have already signed contracts for their boats. Additionally, Alain Mina has advised the Board that, in his opinion, this new navigation software system is not necessary and that if Merbatty's existing customers were to be asked if they wanted a new system, they may feel disappointed with the existing IT systems installed.

The Merbatty Board agreed not to inform existing customers of the updated navigation software system.

Merbatty's boat building facilities

Merbatty's new boat building facility in Surania opened, as planned, in September 2007 and Merbatty has selected this facility to construct all boats for customers based in the Middle East as well as to specialise in the construction of all large boats for customers worldwide. The Suranian boat building facility has already commenced work on a number of large boats.

As a result of strong competition in the USA, Merbatty has seen its boat sales from the USA fall significantly from the planned levels in 2007 and beyond. The original five-year plan (shown in **Appendix 5** to the pre-seen material) predicted that by 2011 24% of total sales revenue would be from customers based in the USA. However, it is now predicted that sales revenue from USA customers will be far lower.

Bernie Ritzol, Merbatty's Global Market Development Director, has prepared a proposal to the Merbatty Board to close the USA boat building facility during 2009 and to develop an additional boat building facility in Asia (originally planned for 2011), as much of Merbatty's recent growth has been in the Asia and Australasia regions. This proposal highlights that a boat building facility in Asia would result in a significantly lower cost base, due to lower staff costs. The differential between the two locations is forecast to be increased post-tax profits of €10 million per year.

If this proposal were to be agreed by Merbatty's board, then additional loan finance would be required in order to finance the required capital expenditure, as the USA boat facility would need to remain operational until the proposed new facility opened in Asia. The USA boat building facility could then be closed and the land sold to repay debt.

An alternative strategic proposal is to expand Merbatty's boat building facilities in Europe. A large plot of river-side land next to Merbatty's European boat building facility has been put up for sale which would allow Merbatty to extend its facilities, which would replace the need to expand to Asia. If Merbatty were to expand its operations in its home country then this site would be invaluable.

Tobias Houllier, the Operations Director, considers that Merbatty's expertise should be retained in Europe and he has prepared a proposal to acquire this European land for future strategic purposes. Tobias Houllier has highlighted that if Merbatty did not acquire it on this occasion, then it is unlikely that it would be able to get such a prime river frontage site in the locality again.

The land (only) is forecast to cost €40 million including legal and surveying costs. This cost excludes the construction of the boat building facility itself. A decision as to whether Merbatty should acquire this European land, or not, needs to be made by the middle of December 2007. This is to ensure that it is not acquired by another buyer.

Effect on Merbatty's profitability due to currency fluctuations

Merbatty has its cost base in Euros, US Dollars and the Middle East currency of Dinars. However, Merbatty is a European company and its profits are accounted and reported in Euros. Its revenues are generated in only Euros or US Dollars. Merbatty is a European company, listed on a European stock exchange, and its group profits are reported in Euros.

The majority of its costs are currently denominated in Euros, as all of the engines it procures for all boat models are from MNE, which is European based. However, over 60% of its sales revenues have historically been contracted for in US Dollars, as customers in the USA, Middle East and other areas prefer to pay in US Dollars rather than Euros. The company has a policy of hedging all currency transactions at the point of signing a sales contract so that the value of future sales receipts is known for certainty in Euros, its base currency. Merbatty is also able to net its payments and receipts in US Dollars including its agency fees and staff costs. Therefore transaction exposure is minimised as much as possible.

Due to the current exchange rate between Euros and US dollars, Merbatty has identified that over 90% of its customers in the last six months have chosen to contract for new boats in US dollars. If the trend in sales denominated in US dollars were to continue, which has allowed customers to purchase their boats at a lower price, then this would have an adverse effect on Merbatty's profits. The adverse effect is forecast to be around €6 million on post-tax profitability in 2008, unless action is taken by Merbatty.

Andreas Acosta, the Finance Director, has asked Stefan Gil, Sales Director, what actions could be taken to secure more sales in Euros or alternatively whether Merbatty should have its price list denominated only in Euros.

Higher operating costs than planned

Andreas Acosta has prepared an updated plan for the period 2007 to 2012. The updated plans are due to be discussed at a Board meeting in early December 2007. They show lower levels of profitability than the agreed five-year plan (shown in **Appendix 5** to the pre-seen material). However, the latest full year forecast for 2007, shows post-tax profits of €45 million, as planned, due to slightly higher sales earlier in the year, offset by higher operating costs.

The updated plan shows that post-tax profits could be €12 million lower than planned, at €39 million for 2008, rather than the original approved planned post-tax profit of €51 million. The post-tax forecast profit for 2008 of €39 million includes the forecast adverse effect of currency changes of €6 million post-tax, as detailed above and also the lower forecast sales in the USA (as detailed above). However, it does not include the impact of Stefan Gil's resignation (see later) and also does not include the impact of the proposed new sales agency in the USA (see later). Future years' post-tax profits are also forecast to be lower than planned.

Proposals to reduce operating costs

Henri Gaston, Merbatty's Chief Executive, has stated that actions need to be taken in order for the agreed profitability in the five-year plan to be delivered.

Henri Gaston has suggested that one possible area for cost reduction is to change the supplier of the engines for Merbatty's boats. The cost of engines represents the single largest bought in component in the boat building process. The cost of engines from Merbatty's sole engine supplier, MNE, amounted to €38 million in 2006. MNE increased its prices in May 2007. The price rise was slightly higher than Merbatty had incorporated in its plans. Another engine manufacturer, ENG (which is based in the USA) could supply Merbatty with engines for around half of its boat models at a lower cost, with no necessary redesigning of the engine space in the boat. Merbatty has considered using ENG in the past. Lukas Dian, Merbatty's Technical Director – Design, states that these alternative engines would not generate the same power, and could have an adverse effect on Merbatty's high reputation. It is estimated that if Merbatty were to select engines from ENG for half of its boat models, this could result in post-tax savings of around €4 million in 2008.

Henri Gaston has asked his fellow Directors to re-examine areas where additional revenues could be generated or reduced costs could be identified. He considers that it may be possible to increase the selling price on Merbatty's top priced boat, which is the model P3000, which currently retails at €4·7 million each, excluding revenues from additional features. The latest plan is that the number of boat sales of this model in 2008 will be 50% higher than the number sold in 2006.

Henri Gaston has asked whether Merbatty could reduce the specifications for some new boats by using cheaper, lower technology equipment. Henri Gaston has also asked whether Merbatty could reduce the expenditure on the development of new boat models, which is forecast to be around €8 million post-tax each year.

Henri Gaston has suggested that Jesper Blanc, Marketing Director, should immediately terminate both of the sponsorship contracts, which could save Merbatty a total of €6·5 million post-tax each year (the sponsorship contracts costs Merbatty €5 million each before tax).

Merbatty's Sales Director resigns

In early November 2007, Stefan Gil announced his resignation and stated that he was moving to CCL, a rival boat building company based in Europe. His contract of employment with Merbatty did not prevent him from taking up this position. It was agreed that it would be in Merbatty's best interests if he did not remain with the company during his three month notice period. He therefore left Merbatty on 9 November 2007. Stefan Gil still owns 5·4 million shares (3·0%) in Merbatty. At the November 2007 Board meeting it was agreed that Stefan Gil's deputy was too inexperienced to be promoted to Sales Director and in the meantime, Jesper Blanc has been asked to take on the Sales Director's responsibilities in addition to his role as Marketing Director.

Merbatty's sales agents in the USA

The majority of Merbatty's sales to end customers are made through agents. The commission cost of operating an agency service is 4% of sales revenue. In early October 2007, one of Merbatty's USA sales agents, LABS, (which sold only Merbatty boats) gave three months' notice of the termination of its agency for Merbatty. With effect from January 2008, LABS will sell boats for a major competitor. In the previous five years LABS sold approximately 60% of Merbatty's boats in the USA market.

In November 2007, after Stefan Gil's resignation, Jesper Blanc approached another experienced boat sales agency, SFBS, and invited it to switch from selling boats built by one of Merbatty's competitors. SFBS has a very good reputation. SFBS has officially responded to confirm that it would agree to exclusively sell Merbatty boats, but only if Merbatty were to agree to a higher agency fee of 8%. However, Andreas Acosta is concerned that other Merbatty agents around the world will learn of SFBS's proposed agency arrangements.

Take-over bid by CCL

One of Merbatty's boat building competitors is CCL. CCL is a listed company with sales revenue at around the same level as Merbatty, although its net profit margin is lower. CCL's share price has not grown as its investors had expected and the Board of CCL is under pressure to deliver higher earnings per share (EPS). CCL's Business Planning Director has been monitoring Merbatty's impressive growth in sales, and its recent listing. He has convinced the CCL Board that if it were to acquire Merbatty, it would help to improve CCL's EPS. CCL is the same company that has recently recruited Stefan Gil, Merbatty's ex Sales Director.

On 16 November 2007, CCL announced its intention to offer the equivalent of €4.20 per share, in a share for share exchange offer. CCL stated that it would require a majority shareholding if the acquisition is to proceed. Prior to the announcement of CCL's take-over bid, Merbatty's shares had been trading at around €3.40. After the take-over bid was announced

Merbatty's share price rose, due to speculation, and on 19 November 2007 was €3.74. Both companies had a P/E ratio around the market average of 15 before the bid was announced. At the scheduled Merbatty Board meeting on Monday 19 November 2007 the take-over bid by CCL was discussed. Together with its corporate advisers, Merbatty made a press statement advising shareholders to reject the bid. Alberto Blanc was quoted as saying 'Merbatty is confident that its long term growth prospects would be higher if Merbatty were to remain independent'.

Merbatty's main external investor, JKL, stated that it needed to be convinced as to whether it should accept, or reject, CCL's bid. Jesper Blanc considers that the CCL bid could be an opportunity for him to give up his responsibilities to Merbatty. He has spoken to his father, Alberto Blanc, the Chairman, about his plans to sell his shares. Alberto Blanc is very disappointed at his son's plans to sell his shares, as he had always wanted Jesper Blanc to be the Chairman of Merbatty one day. Alberto Blanc has promised that Merbatty will pay Jesper Blanc a loyalty bonus of €3 million during 2008 if Jesper Blanc agrees not to sell his shares to CCL.

Computer test program results showing possible faults

Merbatty has very recently upgraded its computer test program for a number of its larger boat designs. The test program was purchased from a leading software company, which developed this specialised software. It has proved to be very reliable in identifying small faults in boats under construction.

During October 2007 the test program indicated a number of errors and potential faults on four large boats. However, Alain Mina, Merbatty's Technical Director for Systems and IT, has told the test team to ignore these error reports, as he considers that they are likely to be computer systems errors, and not real faults with the boats. The customers for these boats are very influential individuals and Alain Mina is keen not to delay delivery of the boats to them.

Appointment of a consultant

At the Merbatty Board meeting held on 19 November 2007 it was agreed that a consultant would be appointed to advise the Board on the issues facing Merbatty.

16

Merbatty: answer

Introduction

This is the suggested answer to the **September 2007** unseen and requirement, written by BPP Learning Media. Your report will be different to this and may analyse different issues. This is as it should be, there is no one correct answer.

We have also included a suggested marking scheme developed by BPP Learning Media from the Post Exam Guides and Script Reviews following the exam.

1 Report

To: Board of Directors of Merbatty Boats

From: A Consultant

Date: 4th September 2007

Contents

1. Introduction
2. Terms of reference
3. Identification and prioritisation of issues
4. Discussion of issues
5. Ethical issues to be addressed by the board of Merbatty
6. Recommendations
7. Conclusion

Appendices

1. SWOT analysis of Merbatty
2. Porter's Generic Strategies
3. Stakeholder analysis
4. NPV of boat charter proposal

1. Introduction

Merbatty has a 33-year record of success in the luxury boat building industry against larger competitors such as Sunseeker, Ferretti and Princess in Europe and Riviera from Australia.

The capital it raised from its flotation last year put it in a good position to benefit from the growth in established markets which, according to *Showboats International Magazine*, enjoyed volume growth of 28% in 2005.

Significant growth will also be available in the emerging economies of China, India and the Middle East, all of which have held International boat shows in the past year and both Dubai and China have ambitious plans for marina development.

Merbatty needs to achieve its forecast profit targets but the costs of correcting hull problems and from the delays at Surania put this in jeopardy and may require the board to reconsider some of its plans in the short term.

2. Terms of Reference

As an independent consultant I have been asked to provide a report analysing and evaluating these issues and to offer appropriate recommendations the Board of Merbatty

3. Identification and Prioritisation of Issues

The issues below have been prioritised based on the potential impact each could have on the return to investors in Merbatty. A full SWOT analysis is presented in Appendix 1.

3.1 Resolving hull problems in the USA – priority number one

The fault in the hull coating has definitely affected 10 boats and Merbatty may incur repair costs of up to €11 million. Further boats may develop cracks later. The water leakage will harm Merbatty's reputation and the costs of repair will affect its profits.

This is given priority number one because it is essential that production using the technology cease immediately to avoid incurring any further repair costs.

3.2 Ensuring opening of Suranian facility – priority number two

According to the five-year plan the Suranian facility is responsible for producing up to 180 boats a year from September 2007. The Board cannot afford any further delays to opening beyond the end of January 2008 because this will mean it will fail to hit its profit and output targets for 2008.

This is given second priority because of the scale of investment at stake and the impact on shareholder attitude of missing targets. The power of shareholders as key players is illustrated by the stakeholder analysis in Appendix 3.

3.3 Taking and dealing with outstanding orders for Surania – priority number three

This five-month delay has jeopardised the delivery of 13 boats and cut 2007 profits by €9 million. Merbatty's agents continue to take orders and accept deposits for boats that Merbatty presently has no means of supplying. This places Merbatty in a position of disappointing clients and turning away valuable orders in one of the markets it regards as essential to achieving its growth plans. Its reputation with customers and agents in the area may be harmed and its forecast sales jeopardised.

This is given priority number three because a decision needs to be made immediately if the 13 boats are to be ready by the end of the year and whether additional orders can be accepted at this time.

3.4 Navigation control panels – priority number four

Eighty customers of Merbatty have boats with significant and potentially life-threatening faults in their navigation systems. The ethical aspects of this problem will be dealt with separately in Section 5 of this report.

The commercial aspect to this problem is the risk that a failure in these panels could inconvenience and even jeopardise Merbatty's demanding clients by stranding them at sea, sending them to the wrong place, or even running them aground. The financial and reputation risks are therefore significant.

This has been given fourth priority because, though less material than the issues assigned priorities 2 and 3, action does need to be taken quickly to mitigate these risks.

3.5 Proposal to enter boat charter market – priority number five

This proposal is forecast to provide 20.6% of Merbatty's 2008 profit (€10.5/€51 million) rising to 22.4% by 2011 (€17.9/€80 million). It is a significant contributor. However, building the initial 10 boats can only be done at the expense of using the capacity to ease the shortfall of capacity at Surania and will not deliver any revenue in 2007.

This has been given fifth priority because it needs to be considered as an alternative to allocating the capacity to provide the 13 boats promised from Surania and a decision is not needed until later, October.

3.6 Other issues facing Merbatty

3.6.1 Shortage of skilled employees

The five-year plan requires adequate labour resources or the boats cannot be made and the plan, and its financial targets, cannot be achieved. Poorly trained labour may also reduce the quality and reliability of supply from Merbatty. The fact that apprentices are leaving is of particular concern. This has been given a lower priority because there is no immediate operational problem to resolve and because a decision cannot be taken until further detailed proposals are drawn up.

3.6.2 Increasing sales to Australia

The additional earnings from this proposal are significant. But the forecasts of 150 boats per year on which it is based differ so much from the 70 boats per year in the five-year plan as to bring into question how feasible it is. It also represents a departure from Merbatty's established business model by abandoning agents and also by having boats available for sale.

3.6.3 Stock discrepancy

This is of importance because it reflects a lack of control over assets. This has been given low priority because the sums involved are less material than for the five prioritised issues above.

Ethical issues facing the Board will be discussed in a separate section. They include:

- Replacement of faulty navigation panels
- Alain Mina's withholding of information from the Board
- Bribes to Merbatty staff to get boats built quicker
- Dealing with cracks in hulls of customer's boats

4. Discussion of Issues

4.1 Resolving hull problems in the USA – priority number one

This problem is restricted to the USA facility and was used only on larger boats. It has affected 14 customers, six who now cannot use their boats safely, four whose boats have failed sea trials and four who have paid deposits and whose boats are under construction.

It is not clear whether the technology is inherently defective, has been used wrongly by Merbatty staff, or whether the chemicals used may have been faulty.

Continuing to make boats using the new spraying process means that the costs of re-work will rise as more bad boats are made. Management should consider suspending the use of the spray technology until the source of the problem can be isolated and corrected.

Customers who have placed orders for boats from the USA will face either a delay in delivery whilst the source of the problem is identified and the process made suitable, or a boat without the special coating. Advising them of the situation and offering them a cancellation, a boat without the sprayed reinforcement, or a delay would be unfortunate from a PR point of view but desirable from a customer-service perspective.

If boats are to be produced without the coating management will need to establish that the untreated hull is still seaworthy.

It is not possible to start work on repairing or replacing the boats until it can be decided whether the cracks can be repaired cost-effectively. If it seems likely that rebuilding is called for then this will need to be taken into account in capacity planning.

The 2007 profits will be adversely affected by potential cancellations of existing orders for boats and any penalty payments. The sales agents will certainly press for their commissions on any orders that Merbatty cancels due to production problems.

These costs, and the likely financial consequences to Merbatty from the need to re-work boats and from paying penalties, should be provisioned in the 2007 accounts too. This may affect the ability of Merbatty to deliver the €84 million profit forecast for 2007.

Some of the financial impact may be offset if the suppliers of the process, or of the materials used, can be made liable to pay compensation. This will depend on Merbatty showing a failure by suppliers.

Appendix 2 shows that Merbatty follows a competitive strategy of differentiation focus. Consequently producing boats with cracked or patched-up hulls is likely to undermine this positioning.

4.2 Ensuring opening of Suranian facility – priority number two

Merbatty has already invested €120 million in building the Suranian facility. There are now cost overruns of €20 million to add to this. These are committed (and sunk) costs and cannot be avoided.

Orders are presently being taken for boats from Surania which, if the facility is further delayed, will lead to further penalty fees or additional costs of manufacture. But declining orders will harm Merbatty's entry into this important new market which, according to Appendix 2 of the Pre-seen material, is to be a major growth market for the firm.

Further delays to commissioning must be avoided. The output and financial contribution from Surania are vital to achievement of the 2008 targets in the five-year plan.

Ensuring that Surania is able to start production in January will involve closer control over project management. The initial problems at the US facility were resolved by implanting a better team led by Bernie Ritzol and the Board could consider doing the same again.

The Board will wish to monitor the commissioning of Surania closely in the coming months.

4.3 Taking and dealing with outstanding orders for Surania – priority number three

Due to the problems with gaining a safety certificate for the Suranian facility the company has problems servicing orders for up to 30 boats to this important emerging market. Failure to meet this demand will reduce recorded profits by €9 million in 2007 as well as forcing a provision for €2 million penalties, ie. reduce recorded profits by €11 million in total. This would take operating profit down from the planned €45 million to €34 million (25% fall) with adverse consequences for investors and the share price.

Presently the facility is forecast to be certified and ready to commence production at the end of January 2008. Given the problems to date this should not be taken for granted. To ensure production in Surania does commence from late January may require additional scrutiny by the board and regular reporting on the progress of the facility.

Diverting production to Europe will cost €4 million in 2007, reducing the profits on the boats from the forecast €9 million to €5 million. If the board approves the proposal by Bernie Ritzol to enter the boat charter market, it would delay commencement of this business beyond summer 2008. This could potentially sacrifice the €10.5 million of post-tax profit from the charter business in 2008.

The board can decide to cancel the orders and reduce recorded profits by the full €11 million.

The board can decide to switch production to Europe at a cost of €4 million but also forego the initial launch of the charter business.

Given the importance placed by investors on Merbatty hitting its 2007 profit and output targets the course of action chosen should ensure that these are reached as far as possible.

In addition to financial considerations there is also the strategic consideration that the new agents in Surania will find it hard to want to sell Merbatty boats if Merbatty rejects the first five months worth of orders. This will reduce the ability of Merbatty to grow as planned in the Middle East.

4.4 Navigation control panels – priority number four

The Board has not yet been informed that a serious navigation fault potentially affects 80 of the boats it has supplied. This information has been withheld from the Board by Alain Mina.

Although perhaps negligible the fault does impose a considerable risk because Merbatty's clients would not hesitate to sue Merbatty for any loss or inconvenience they suffer as a consequence of malfunction. The manufacturer has advised Merbatty of the fault and offered to provide replacements. If a customer does suffer then Merbatty will be held liable.

Poor navigation is also potentially life-threatening.

Alain Mina's approach to the problem is to ignore it.

Another approach would be to notify clients of the problem, and offering to arrange for replacement of the units using the ones supplied by Marinatron. If clients regard this as too much of an inconvenience then at least Merbatty will have discharged its legal liability.

It is noted that Mariantron has provided free replacement panels but that it has not made any provision to cover the costs of Merbatty engineers travelling and changing the panels on customers' boats.

4.5 Proposal to enter boat charter market – priority number five

Appendix 4 shows a financial analysis of Bernie Ritzol's proposal to enter the boat chartering market. It demonstrates that, on the basis of the figures he has provided, the proposal will deliver a net present value of €27.61 million over the five years, on the assumption that the boats are sold at the end of 2012.

The NPV may be higher than indicated in Appendix 4. The calculation assumes that all the costs of building the boats are incurred in 2007, whereas it seems likely that some will be paid in 2008 and hence would increase the NPV of the proposal.

This is an unfamiliar business for Merbatty and the market is very competitive. There are a number of risks that should be borne in mind.

Commercial risks are that Merbatty may make losses on its business. A recent Plimsoll report revealed that over half the UK boat leasing businesses are letting their boats at a loss. This reflects the competitive nature of the market. Reputation risks may also be incurred if chartered boats are not available or satisfactory. Given the problems of 'boatjacking' and accidents there may also be asset risk because these boats will belong to Merbatty but their security and safety in operation will depend on the quality of crew used and how the boat is operated by the client.

In addition to the positive return on investment there are strategic considerations that favour Merbatty's entry into the charter market.

The forecast provided by Bernie Ritzol are for an initial commitment to 10 boats. There is the potential for an extension to the fleet if these are successful.

The customers who lease boats may later buy boats from Merbatty. This principle is already recognised by car makers who sell their vehicles to hire firms and driving schools at deep discounts in order to introduce their cars to drivers and gain market awareness. They also operate contract leasing arrangements for their cars.

A further benefit would be that the fleet would give Merbatty access to a stock of display models of its boats and also to boats which could be loaned to customers in the event of late orders or faults, such as from the present hull problems.

However, it must be recognised that a commitment to implement Bernie Ritzol's proposal would entail the cancellation of many of the orders that have been disrupted by the delay in commissioning the Suranian facility.

4.6 Other issues

[Tutorial note: BPP Learning Media recommends that exam time should not be spent discussing these lower priority issues until you have completely finished writing your discussion and recommendations for the priority issues and the ethical issues.]

4.6.1 Shortage of skilled employees

The five-year plan requires significant increases in output, which in turn requires additional manpower to carry out. The five-year plan also features a reduction in staff turnover from 20% in 2006 to 12% from 2009.

The loss of skilled employees and apprentices to other employers jeopardises Merbatty's ability to satisfy both sets of targets in its five-year plan.

Appropriate training affects:

- The ability of Merbatty to attract and retain sufficient staff to reach its production targets in coming years
- The quality of its products and reputation of its brand
- Its ability to apply new innovations (it is possible that the problems with hull spraying may have origins in poor training)

4.6.2 Increasing sales to Australia

This proposal is attractive on the basis of the post-tax NPV of €30 million but seems based on unrealistic forecasts of sales which exceed the sales in the five-year plan. There is little in Jesper's background, track record or the research he has conducted to give management confidence in this forecast.

4.6.3 Stock discrepancy

The amounts involved here are not significant in themselves but it does reflect a lack of security over the assets of the company. Conducting random checks and dismissing a member of staff for being in possession of a drill, possibly temporarily borrowed for a job at home, seems excessive and may also have led to some staff being dissatisfied with Merbatty.

Most firms would have a policy on staff use of company assets. They might also operate systems that required tools to be logged in and out of a central store or that required staff to be responsible for the custody of tools and their loss.

5. Ethical issues to be addressed by the Board of Merbatty

5.1 Replacement of navigation control panels

There is a potential risk that non-replacement of these panels in the 80 affected boats could lead to collision, damage and loss of life of our customers and their crew.

The board of Merbatty has an ethical obligation to take steps to avoid this.

For this reason, as well as for the commercial considerations outlined in 4.4 above, it is recommended that Merbatty notifies all 80 boat owners of the fault and offers to replace the panels.

The behaviour of Alain Mina has also been unethical. As a Director of Merbatty he has an obligation to report significant matters to the board. Joe Pickard considered the potential fault on 80 boats to be of sufficient importance to whistleblow so it is not really open to Alain Mina to claim he didn't realise.

It is recommended that Alain Mina be censured by the Board for not reporting or dealing with this matter. It is also recommended that Joe Pickard be thanked for drawing this to the Board's attention and that he be protected from any retribution by Alain Mina.

5.2 Bribery of Merbatty staff

The receipt of bribes by staff and agents to give priority to particular orders is unethical for two reasons. Firstly, it is unfair to customers who might otherwise expect orders to be dealt with on a first-come-first-served basis. To have their orders put back because of secret payments is not transparent and, no doubt, involves Merbatty staff in the telling of lies when giving reasons. Secondly, it is an abuse of position by agents and Merbatty staff to take money privately as a consequence of their role in the firm.

Allowing a culture of performance for inducements to grow up will be corrosive.

It is recommended that a policy be drawn up to make clear that taking inducements will lead to disciplinary measures and that customers or agents who have been found to have offered such inducements may have their orders cancelled, postponed without return of the inducement or their deposits.

It is recommended that no action be taken in respect of the two contracts undertaken. In the absence of a policy any sanctions would seem arbitrary and, given that the boats have been started, it would be expensive and disruptive to stop them. The agents and staff should however be interviewed by management and its disapproval of their actions expressed in strong terms.

5.3 Cracks in the US made boats

The ethical issues here are the duty of care to customers to ensure their boats are seaworthy and also the issue of telling them the truth about the situation.

The cracks have made some boats ship water which makes them unsafe. The owners need to be told this to avoid them endangering themselves and their crew. The remaining 18 boats have passed inspection but cracks could appear later. The owners of these boats should be informed of the findings and for the signs of cracks to look for. They should also be offered periodic inspections.

The causes of the cracks are unknown, and no remedy has been found. Merbatty must avoid giving the impression that the problem has been contained because this would be a lie and could lead to endangerment of crew and owners.

Merbatty should be prepared to offer a rebuild of the boat to customers if no repair can be found. If the boats are reparable a compensation payment should be offered to owners to cover inconvenience and also the probable fall in value of their investment.

6. Recommendations

6.1 Resolving hull problems in the USA – priority number one

Management should instruct the USA boatyard to cease using the spray coat process to avoid further re-work costs.

Urgent research should be commissioned into the origins of the problem and into ways to fix the affected boats. This should be done in conjunction with the suppliers of the process and materials to ascertain where legal responsibility rests. Using independent engineers may be advisable.

If the problem cannot be rectified quickly the agents should be instructed to advise customers for new boats that there may be a delay and to offer them the options to cancel their order, to have a boat without the coating, or to wait for Merbatty to rectify the problem and accept late delivery of their boat. Compensation payments should be offered.

Customers of all 18 unaffected boats should be offered periodic checks to ensure no cracks emerge in the years to come.

Customers who have defective boats that will need to be recalled should if possible be offered the loan of replacement boats, either from Merbatty's display models or by leasing in Merbatty boats from leasing companies.

If possible financial recompense should be sought from the suppliers of the process or from suppliers of defective materials.

The provisions of IAS 37 do not seem to apply here. The maximum provision for costs of rectification of €11 million should not need to be placed as a provision in the 2007 accounts as at the present time there is not a clear indication that this will be required. Given the unanticipated costs from the problems in Surania this may help profits remain on target for the year.

Management should be prepared to issue a statement to the media about the problem and to reassure them that it has been dealt with properly.

6.2 Ensuring opening of Suranian facility – priority number two

It is recommended that a project team, reporting to Bernie Ritzol, be sent to Surania to report on the situation at the facility and the likelihood that it will receive the necessary licenses and begin production at the end of January 2008.

The Board should receive weekly reports from Bernie Ritzol on progress at the facility. This will help ensure that resources are allocated and that, if necessary, contingency plans drawn up to deal with further late-running.

Once it is commissioned the reasons for the late-running of this project should be identified and recorded in a Post Implementation Review. This will help management learn about the project management weaknesses and so avoid them in future development of facilities, such as the proposed Asian facility in 2010/2011.

6.3 Taking and dealing with outstanding orders for Surania – priority number three

It is essential that the production of the boats on order be carried out in the European facility. Capacity should be earmarked immediately and materials ordered. This is essential to reduce the loss of 2007 profit. Also, it enables Merbatty to reach its production target and so satisfy investors.

It is recommended that agents continue to accept orders for further boats. The Suranian facility should be ready by the end of January or, failing this, capacity reserved at European boatyards. To refuse to take orders, or to announce problems at the Suranian facility, would damage the launch of Merbatty in the Middle East and could contribute to it missing the profit and output targets in the five-year plan.

Because it is likely that rumours of the Suranian problem will filter through to clients and agents a circular should be sent to them informing them of the decision to build the boats in Europe for the time being.

6.4 Navigation control panels – priority number four

It is recommended that the owners of all 80 boats be contacted, by letter with follow up call if no response is received, and informed of the fault, its origins, and likely effects and risks. The letter should offer replacement of the panel and invite owners to identify times and locations. This will retain customer goodwill and mitigate Merbatty's legal liability in the event of owners suffering a malfunction of the navigation system.

It is recommended that Marinatron be approached for additional compensation for this incident to include payment for the time of Merbatty engineers in travelling to marinas to change the panels.

6.5 Proposal to enter boat charter market – priority number five

It is recommended that the proposal be delayed until the present problems in Surania are resolved. This is because the capacity needed to make the initial charter boats, which will only impact on 2008 profits, is needed for meeting outstanding orders to protect achievement of 2007 targets.

The same capacity should be held as a contingency to cover future orders in case of further problems at the Suranian facility.

It is recommended that the charter venture go ahead once capacity is available to build the initial 10 boats. This is because it provides an additional revenue stream for Merbatty and provides a ready way to introduce potential owners to Merbatty boats. This may help reduce the downside risk of the venture.

The initial uptake of charter boats should be monitored before further boats are built. In the event of poor returns the boats could be used for display and demonstration models or sold. This reduces the risk of the proposal.

6.6 Other issues

[Tutorial note: BPP Learning Media recommends that exam time should not be spent discussing these lower priority issues until you have completely finished writing your discussion and recommendations for the priority issues and the ethical issues.]

6.6.1 Shortage of skilled employees

Merbatty should develop a programme of skills development and training for its staff.

It is recommended that this be developed by Marie Lopp in conjunction with the boat building industry and that it leads to a recognised award. This will help staff motivation.

Skills development will not, on its own, help staff retention unless pay and working conditions are also suitable.

It is recommended that exit interviews be conducted with staff to ascertain the reasons, such as pay or company policy, and that these too be addressed.

6.6.2 Increasing sales to Australia

This proposal should be rejected at the present time. This is because the forecasts are unrealistic and poorly grounded. In addition the capacity needed to build the 15 demonstrator boats would reduce profits in 2008.

The Board may wish to question whether the four months spent in Australia by Jesper Blanc has resulted in a valuable proposal for the business that rewards the costs of sending him there.

6.6.3 Stock discrepancy

Merbatty should draw up and distribute a policy forbidding the private use of company assets and making clear that they are not to leave the facility.

The policy of searching staff on exit should only be applied where there is other evidence of theft as it is an intrusive policy. Here the recovery of a €300 power drill has been achieved at the loss of a long-standing employee and potentially significant ill-will.

Making staff responsible for their own tools and the provision of lockable toolboxes should be investigated.

7. Conclusions

Merbatty is a successful company and can continue as such on an independent basis. Following the recommendations of this report should help assure that it reaches its 2007 and 2008 profit and output targets.

Appendix 1: SWOT analysis

Strengths	Weaknesses
• Established global brand giving access to premium market segments • Cash positive and profitable business	• Faulty hull coating process in US • Late commissioning of the Suranian facility • Lack of clear policies on acceptance of inducements • Poor control over tools • Increasing staff turnover • High proportion of sales made in lower margin products • High dependence on Aqua Designs and other key suppliers
Opportunities	**Threats**
• Development of boat charter business • Potential market in Australia • Global economic development creating further rich elites wishing to buy prestige products like boats • Lower costs of production available in emerging Asian economies	• Harm to owners and their crews from faulty navigation equipment and cracked hulls • Loss of market and goodwill in Middle East due to supply problems in Surania • Shortage of skilled boatbuilders in the industry • Lower cost producers from Asia • Other prestige products (private jets, luxury homes, helicopters)

Appendix 2: Porter's generic strategies

Porter argues that competitive advantage, and hence a level of long-run return on investment that is superior to the industry average, can be attained only by utilising one of the following generic strategies:

Cost Leadership – mass volume, standardised, pre-built boats

Differentiation – mass volume of high quality or high velocity boats (or some other differentiating factor)

Differentiation Focus – exclusive, high quality, bespoke, tailored boats for a wealthy and discerning market segment

Cost Focus – low cost, small volume boats for a particular type of customer

Merbatty is presently a differentiated producer and, by moving towards the making of bigger boats for richer clients, may move towards a differentiation-focus position.

Appendix 3: Mendelow's Matrix

Key players	Keep informed
• The executive Board of Directors • Key (repeat) customers • Key suppliers • JKL	• Employees • Non Executive Directors
Keep satisfied	**Minimal effort**
• Bank • Government agencies (tax, compliance etc.)	• Environmental Pressure Groups • Competitors (due to customer loyalty and differentiation)

Appendix 4: NPV of boat charter proposal

	2007 €m	2008 €m	2009 €m	2010 €m	2011 €m	2012 €m
Net cash inflow		10.5	13.9	16.9	17.9	26.6
Residual value of boats						7.5
Building costs	(32.0)					
Discount factor	1.000	0.877	0.769	0.675	0.592	0.519
Present value	(32.0)	9.21	10.69	11.41	10.60	17.70

NPV = €59.61m − €32.0m

= €27.61m

2 Suggested marking scheme

Note: This would be marked differently under the new assessment matrix which applies from September 2008. (See Chapter 2)

Criteria	Issues to be discussed	Marks	Total marks available for criterion
Technical	SWOT/PEST/Ansoff/Porter's 5 forces/Porter's generic strategies/ Mendelow/Suitability, Acceptability, Feasibility/BCG/Balanced Scorecard/Life cycle analysis/Marketing knowledge	1 each	Max = 5
	1 mark for EACH technique demonstrated (ie 0 marks for 'name dropping')		
Application	SWOT – to get full 3 marks must include risks from faulty hulls and navigation systems and reputation risk from late-running of Surania as threats; poor spray process and late Surania as weaknesses, and charter business as an opportunity	1–3	Max = 15
	Other technical knowledge applied to case material in a meaningful relevant way – on merit	1–3 each	
	Calculations:		
	NPV of boat charter proposal	3–4	
	Relevant costs of shifting Middle East boats to Europe	1–2	
	Impact on 2007 profit of cancellations to Middle East boats	1	
	Total available marks for calculations	7	
Diversity	Display of sound business awareness and relevant real life examples	1–5 on merit	Max = 5
Focus	**Issues to be identified:**		
	Need to cease production using faulty spraying process	1	
	Need to fix faulty boats	1	
	Need to replace navigation panels	1	
	Need to ensure Suranian facility completed quickly	1	Max = 5
	Need to reschedule middle east orders	1	
	Proposal to enter charter market	1	
	Jesper's Australian proposal	1	
	Resolving shortages of skilled employees	1	
	Total marks available (but max = 5)	8	
Prioritisation	8–10 marks if 5 issues prioritised and rationale for ranking good AND top priorities of ceasing spray process, complete Surania, rescheduling orders	Full 10	
	FULL 10 marks if all of the above PLUS replacement of panels		
	OR		
	6–8 marks if top 2 priorities are in top 5 but ranking rationale is weak	6–8	Max = 10
	OR		
	4 marks maximum (marginal fail) if EITHER ceasing use of spraying or ensuring Surania opens are not in top 5 priorities, irrespective of quality of rationale for ranking of other priorities	Up to 4	

Criteria	Issues to be discussed	Marks	Total marks available for criterion
Judgement	6 key commercial issues in this case of which 5 required analysis		
	Marks on merit based on depth of analysis and commercially realistic comments		
	1. Resolving hull cracking problem. To include comments on need to cease production using process, need to find reasons for problem, need to find remedies, and financial impact of provisioning who rebuild cost in 2007 accounts	2–5	
	2. Ensuring opening of Suranian facility. To include scepticism that Jan target will be reached, the potential lost reputation if future orders turned away, reputation risk with investors if targets not hit in 2008	2–5	
	3. Dealing with outstanding Middle East orders. Recognition that Merbatty must make boats to avoid profit and output targets being missed and reputation in new Middle East markets irrevocably harmed	2–5	Max = 20
	4. Replacement of navigation control panels. Recognition of commercial risks from legal action and risk to reputation if accident or loss occurs (as distinct from ethical issues)	2–5	
	5. Staff shortages and training. Recognition that problem affects only medium and long-term targets unless major morale problem leading to walk-outs. Explanation of cost of poor training, eg. quality, flexibility, innovation, process improvements etc	2–5	
	6. Boat charter market. Discussion of benefits: additional income stream, shows off boats, entice customers. Discussion of drawbacks: not core business, asset risk, competitive market, uses up capacity and capital	2–5	
	Total marks available (but max = 20)	30	
Integration	Judge script holistically and whether recommendations follow on logically from analysis of the issues and includes data in appendices	1–4 if weak 6–10 if script is good	10
Logic	General presentation and EFFECTIVE business communication	1–5	
	Recommendations:		
	(Marks on merit. Max 1 mark if only an unjustified recommendation is given)		Max = 20
	Hulls: stop process, investigate causes, investigate remedies	1–4 but (2 if whole 11m accepted as a cost)	
	Surania: Crisis team needed, contingency plans, Board scrutiny of progress	1–3	
	Outstanding orders: need for immediate transfer to Europe. Continue taking orders. PR management. Delay take up if charter opportunity	1–3	

Criteria	Issues to be discussed	Marks	Total marks available for criterion
	Navigation control panels: write to boat owners to warn, arrange replacement, PR management, obtain further expenses from Marinatron	1–3	
	Boat charter: take up in long run but delay till Surnania in production	1–3	
	Other relevant issues (on merit)	1–3	
	Total marks available (but max = 20)	27	
Ethics	Ethical issues in case include:	1–5 each including advice	
	Replacement of navigation panels to safeguard lives at sea		
	Behaviour of Alain Mina		
	Bribes to Merbatty staff to prioritise orders		Max = 10
	Fixing cracks in US boats safely		
	1–5 marks (on merit) for each ethical issue including detailed advice on each ethical issue		
	Max 4 marks overall if several ethical issues discussed but no meaningful or sensible advice given	Max = 4 if no advice	
Total			100

Flyqual
March and May 2007

17

Flyqual: pre-seen data

Introduction

This chapter includes the 'pre-seen' data for Flyqual, examined in March and May 2007.

.

P10 – Test of Professional Competence in Management Accounting

Monday 6 March 2007

PRE-SEEN MATERIAL, PROVIDED IN ADVANCE FOR PREPARATION AND STUDY FOR THE EXAMINATION TO BE HELD ON MONDAY 6 MARCH
INSTRUCTIONS FOR POTENTIAL CANDIDATES
This booklet contains the Pre-seen case material for the March 2006 examination. It will provide you with the contextual information that will help you prepare yourself for the examination on Monday 6 March.
The TOPCIMA Assessment Matrix, which your script will be marked against, is available as a separate document which will also be e-mailed to you.
You may not take this copy of the Pre-seen material into the examination hall. A fresh copy will be provided for you in the examination hall.
Unseen material will be provided for the examination: this will comprise further context and the examination question.
The examination will last for three hours. You will be allowed 20 minutes reading time **before the examination begins** during which you should read the question paper and, if you wish, make annotations on the question paper. However, you will **not** be allowed, **under any circumstances**, to begin using your computer to produce your answer, or to use your calculator during the reading time.
You will be required to answer ONE question which may contain more than one element.

Contents of this booklet:	Page
Pre-seen material – Flyqual Airlines	2
Pre-seen Appendix A	11

BPP
LEARNING MEDIA

Flyqual Airlines

Introduction

1 Flyqual Airlines (FQA) is a member of N, an aviation alliance which includes another seven airlines based in different regions of the world. The purpose of the alliance is to extend a large range of travel opportunities to passengers of each constituent airline and FQA is now able to provide travel to over 500 destinations throughout the world by using alliance partners' routes. The benefits include more choices of flights to suit the passengers' travel requirements, easier transfers between member airlines and access to their passenger lounges, priority check-in at airport terminals and enhancement of frequent flyer programmes. Greater frequency of flights is provided by the various codeshare agreements which FQA has entered into with various airlines which operate both within and outside the N alliance. A codeshare agreement is where flights to a particular destination are operated by an airline which accepts passengers who have purchased tickets from other airlines.

2 As its name implies, FQA prides itself on providing a first rate passenger service and enjoys a strong reputation for quality service to passengers. As a consequence, FQA does not need to apply a low pricing policy for airline travel in response to sensitivity of market demand and is able to charge premium prices. Established just after the Second World War, FQA itself now flies to over 100 destinations worldwide from its home base in Asia and employs over 20,000 people around the world as aircrew, cabin attendants, maintenance staff, airport check-in operatives and ground staff.

3 Two large listed companies together hold the majority of the shares of FQA and the company is listed on its home stock exchange. These two companies are not themselves engaged in the airline industry although one of them does have subsidiaries whose business is in the export of goods.

4 FQA holds a 45% shareholding in a smaller airline. This smaller airline is not a member of the N alliance and engages mainly in short-haul scheduled and cargo flights around the Asia-Pacific region. FQA does undertake some short-haul schedules in the Asia-Pacific region but its principal business is in long-haul intercontinental flights to the USA and Europe.

Future demand for passenger air travel

5 Some airlines offer services at both the high quality and the basic "with no extras", so called "low-priced" or "no frills" end of the market. FQA has chosen to offer services at the high quality end of the market only.

6 The largest consumer markets over the next two decades are likely to be China and India. This is expected to result in large growth in air travel to and from, and within these countries. This is likely to be generated by increasing wealth within the economies of these two countries in particular and continued inward investment from other parts of the world.

7 It is normal for increased air travel in emerging economies to begin with increases in domestic demand followed by international demand as income levels rise and greater inward investment takes place. Major centres of population and business tend to generate strong development of air traffic. It is estimated that 80% of air traffic between Europe and Asia is carried between only 17 major cities.

8 It is estimated that by the mid 2020's three-quarters of the entire world fleet of very large aircraft will be used on flights from the largest airports in the world and 60% of these airports are situated in the Asia-Pacific region.

Future demand for air cargo

9 Demand for international cargo services is also expected to increase in areas of high population and industrial growth.

10 Demand for air cargo is influenced by the nature of the goods being transported, for example the need to transport perishable foods quickly. However, high value goods which are demanded in very quick time, such as high technology equipment have also grown and represent about 75% of the financial value of exports from Asia but only 40% of exports in terms of weight. This has resulted in significant growth in demand for air cargo. For example, about 25% of high technology equipment by value was transported by air from China to Europe in the mid 1990's. A decade later, this had risen to 60%.

Aircraft replacement within the industry

11 Traditionally, replacement of aircraft has been a result of economic cycles and developments of

aircraft technology. Fuel prices have also had a major influence on aircraft replacement. Aircraft retirements on a large scale began to take place in 2002 following a slow-down in global demand. Many airlines replace passenger aircraft before the end of their economic life in order to take advantage of new technology. Market conditions, legislation on noise and exhaust emissions and strengthening competition have resulted in an increasing demand by airlines for more fuel efficient and quieter aircraft. Some forecasts state that by the mid 2020's only about 15% of the fleet which currently exists will still be operated by airlines across the world.

FQA's fleet of aircraft

12 The aircraft which FQA operate are all manufactured by either F (based in the USA) or C (based in Europe). The fleet of 170 aircraft is as follows:

13

	Leased	Owned	Seating capacity per aircraft
F 858	27	36	500
F 888	9	22	270
C 440	14	30	320
C 450	10	22	450

14 Of the 27 leased F 858 aircraft, seven are employed entirely for carrying cargo. The F 888 can be converted to fly long-haul, although it is normally used on short-haul routes. For conversion to long-haul, the F 888 would reduce the passenger capacity by 100 seats. The C 440 is used exclusively on short-haul routes. There are a number of aircraft whose leases are due to expire over the next two years.

Replacement of some of the fleet

15 A major dilemma faced by FQA, as well as other airlines, is which aircraft should it now procure in order to replace the ageing aircraft in its fleet. FQA could acquire newer models of the same type of aircraft which it currently has in service or obtain replacements from the next generation of aircraft which are being developed. In considering this matter, the directors of FQA need to take into account the way the airline industry is moving and the increasing trend for larger aircraft carrying more passengers and having a greater range capability. F and C are the leading manufacturers of passenger aircraft and are bitter rivals. Both F and C have produced prototypes of the next generation of passenger aircraft. The F 898 has a smaller capacity in terms of passengers carried than the C 491 but, in general terms, has greater flexibility. This is due to the F 898 being capable of reaching more destinations than its C rival as it is smaller and makes less demand on airports in terms of the infrastructure that is required to accommodate it. On the other hand, the C 491 can carry 600 passengers which is double the number which the F 898 can seat. Both aircraft have a similar range.

16 The C 491 will operate on a "hub" system whereby the aircraft will land at a central location in each country or region which then permits passengers to transfer to other flights to reach their final destinations. However, the C 491 is a major double-decked aircraft which requires considerable investment in airport infrastructure to operate. In addition to the requirement for longer runways for take off and landing, the C 491 will not be able to use the existing airport gates for embarkation and disembarkation from the aircraft because it is too far off the ground. On the other hand, the F 898 may take off and land on the conventional length of runway which will accommodate the current aircraft in FQA's fleet. As it is a single-decked aircraft it will also be able to use the gates which are currently available in airports.

17 The Board of FQA must decide whether it should:

- invest in the C 491 and be able to transport more passengers in a single flight but which may result in a degree of inconvenience to passengers as they will need to transfer to other flights for onward travel; or

- obtain the F 898 with the smaller passenger capacity, which has the same range as the C 491, but is able to land at more destinations.

18 The directors of FQA must consider the economies of scale associated with the larger passenger aircraft and the consequent loss of flexibility. In addition, with regard to the F 898, FQA needs to take account of the increased costs of paying more in landing charges for operating at a larger number of final destinations. This is a major item of cost bearing in mind that some countries offer landing slots to airlines on a bid system. Some landing slots at major airports in the world, which are located in

popular destinations, are extremely expensive.

19   Other issues which need to be considered by FQA include:

- expected levels of passenger demand over the period of the life of whichever aircraft it procures;
- the impact of competition over that period within the airline industry;
- the cost of manpower;
- re-training and operational costs such as fuel.

20   A further consideration is how other competitor airlines are likely to respond to the dilemma, as they all face the same issue of replacement of their fleets at some time or another. If the trend of the world's airlines favours one aircraft over the other, then FQA does not want to be committed to obtaining the aircraft which are less favoured by other airlines. This may cause spare parts to be less available and at a higher cost. However, FQA is itself an influencer given its market position and other airlines are likely to take account of the decision made by the FQA Board in making their own choices.

FQA Board members

21   *Chairman:*
Appointed Company Secretary in 1990, then a director in 1994 after relinquishing Company Secretary role. Appointed Chief Executive in 1998 and Chairman in 2005. Lawyer by profession and was a barrister specialising in aviation law until becoming Company Secretary in 1990. Holds 3 million shares in FQA.

22   *Chief Executive:*
Joined group in 1975 and has been a director since 1995. Holds 5 million shares in FQA.

23   **Chief Operating Officer:**
Was a pilot until 1993 and has worked with FQA in operational matters since then. Was sponsored by FQA to take a post graduate degree in Operational Management at an "Ivy League" University in the USA in 1993/4.

24   *Finance Director:*
Joined the group in 1998 and is a qualified CIMA accountant. Previously she held posts in the airline industry in Europe where she had good contacts in respect of obtaining investment capital. While working for a European airline, she successfully established a subsidiary low-priced airline but returned to her roots in the Far East for domestic reasons.

25   *Engineering Director:*
Previously employed by the International Civil Aviation Organisation and joined the group in 1992. He is an Aeronautical Engineer by profession. Holds 3 million shares in FQA.

26   *Director of Sales and Marketing:*
Held a variety of posts with FQA since 1988 and is a member of a recognised professional body in marketing having been senior sales manager for a rival airline until her appointment to FQA.

27   *Director of HRM:*
Appointed in 1996 from the board of a multi national conglomerate and is a member of a recognised professional body in the field of personnel management.

28   *Director of Corporate Development:*
Joined FQA as a management trainee in 1982 and is responsible for corporate planning. Holds 5 million shares in FQA. He has held a number of senior management roles in FQA and worked his way up the organisation culminating in being appointed to the Board in 2003.

29   *Director of Service Delivery:*
Has dual role as manager of Corporate Communication and also responsible for Information management. Her academic background is that she holds a PhD in software development and joined FQA in 1999.

30   *Director of Quality Management:*
Joined the group in 1984 and has no formal qualifications. Currently has responsibility for quality assurance and catering contracts. Holds 2 million shares in FQA.

31   All executive directors of FQA have share options.

LEARNING MEDIA

32   There are also 12 non-executive directors on the FQA Board.

New terminal

33   One area of which the Board is particularly proud is FQA's reputation for being one of the most punctual and safest airlines in the world. This in turn has given rise to national pride and the government has provided financial support in terms of grants and loans particularly in regard to a new terminal development at the airport in the capital city in FQA's home country. This airport is owned and operated by an airport authority which is independent of FQA.

34   In 2008, the airport in the capital city of FQA's home country plans to open a new passenger terminal which would be dedicated for the use of the airline. This will permit rationalisation of staff resources to take place, enabling FQA's ground passenger service staffing levels to be reduced. However, no negotiations on the required staffing levels have yet been undertaken with the trade unions (which are organisations established to negotiate pay agreements and improvements in working conditions on behalf of their members). Airline staff, however, have heard rumours of the likely rationalisation and this has resulted in enquiries to the Board being made by the trade unions. There has been no official response by the Board to this, but it is taking seriously the threat of strike action resulting from rationalisation. The threat of strike action has been reported in daily newspapers. The newspapers have attributed their source of information to the trade unions.

Managerial style of FQA

35   FQA always prides itself on having staff who are dedicated to providing a high quality service. The Director of HRM regularly reviews FQA's human resource and remuneration policy taking account of legislation, industry practice and market conditions. The Board has been under increasing pressure to reduce costs. This has resulted in much more emphasis being placed by the Board on individual and company performance than previously in determining human resource and remuneration policy. This has caused considerable staff discomfort over the last two years.

36   FQA faced difficult employee relations issues through the summer period of the last financial year. It encountered demands for higher pay from ground staff, for improved working conditions and reduced working hours from both air crew (pilots and flight engineers) and cabin staff. These demands led to hard negotiations with the trade unions. All operational staff at FQA, including flight crew and cabin staff, are members of trade unions.

37   These negotiations resulted in some improvements in pay for the baggage handlers and reduced working hours for air crew and cabin staff. However, the demands made by the trade unions were not met in full. The agreement made between FQA and the trade unions was on condition that targets in productivity increases were achieved. This has resulted in some voluntary redundancies being made in order to meet the productivity targets and a general reduction in the cabin staff on the payroll. The strong tactics employed by the directors of FQA have resulted in many cabin staff feeling that they have been mistreated by the company. They also feel let down by their trade union representatives, which has led to poor morale among the staff.

38   In addition, FQA has faced many difficulties with suppliers, particularly its outsourced catering service at its home based airport in the capital city. The issue has been that the main catering service supplier (CG) has complained that the hard bargaining stance by FQA management has reduced its margin to such an extent that it is barely making any profit.

39   At the same time, the Director of Quality Management has made serious complaints regarding the reduced level of quality in the catering service itself following an increasing level of complaints from passengers over recent months. CG's management has responded by threatening to withdraw the service altogether unless FQA agrees to re-negotiate the price for the service which is supplied. In reply, FQA has stated that it will only renegotiate on price when the quality of the service has shown improvement over a sustained period and has threatened legal action for breach of contract if the service is withdrawn.

Pressure from shareholders

40 The Chairmen of the two largest shareholders of FQA have held discussions with FQA's Chairman and Chief Executive in an attempt to find ways to increase shareholder value. They have made it clear that they believe the running costs of the airline are too high and must be reduced to enable the airline to become a leaner and fitter organisation. This, they argue, will enable FQA to be better able to increase market share in the increasingly competitive airline industry by being able to pass on cost reductions to passengers.

41 The Chairman and Chief Executive of FQA, advised by the Board, have replied to the two Chairmen of the largest shareholders that any significant impact on lowering costs can only be achieved by reducing the staffing levels which will in turn impact negatively on quality. They also point out that there has been a wave of voluntary redundancies in order to satisfy the increased pay levels and improved working conditions. The Chairman and Chief Executive have warned that further reductions in the staffing levels in the existing operations will erode staff morale even more and may be counter productive in terms of achieving greater market share. At the same time as making this point, the Chairman has instructed the Director of HRM to give serious thought to how further staff reductions could be achieved.

Financial results from previous two years

42 Extracts from the financial results for the previous two financial years for FQA are presented at Appendix A.

Competition data

43 The following information provides a short statistical comparison between FQA and two competitors in the last financial year:

44

	FQA	Competitor 1	Competitor 2
Revenue (in $ million)	10,895	17,784	8,632
Profit attributable to shareholders ($ million)	371	546	286
Share price at year end ($)	9.0	6.0	4.5
Shares in issue at year end (million)	520	1,100	600
Long-term liabilities ($ million)	4,220	6,400	3,330
Fleet size (number of aircraft)	170	290	165
Kilometres flown (million)	560	920	480
Aircraft departures (thousand)	152	250	130
Passenger load factor (overall % of capacity used)	80	75	73
Passengers carried (million)	27	42	22
On time departures (within 15 minutes) %	93	76	75

Cost structures

45 The constant challenge faced by all airlines is the increasing cost of fuel. Airlines are able to counter increased fuel charges in a number of ways. These include being able to make surcharges to the customer on fuel cost increases and by seeking ways of increasing efficiency in the fuel consumption of their fleets.

46 The following table shows the proportions of FQA's total costs which are accounted for by particular expense types:

47

Expense type:	% of total Operating Costs in the financial year ended: 30 September 2006	% of total Operating Costs in the financial year ended: 30 September 2005
Staff and employment overheads	21	21
Fuel	30	29
Landing and parking	10	9
Other (including maintenance, engineering and equipment)	39	41

48 FQA managed to reduce its exposure to increased fuel costs by using hedging techniques in the year to 30 September 2006 which was a year when fuel prices increased significantly.

New aircraft

49 **F 898**

F expects to manufacture and sell over 1,800 of its F 898 aircraft by the mid-2020's in aiming to accommodate a market demand which it estimates will be for about 3,500 aircraft of this type and size. It expects the first delivery to a customer to be in 2008 with production and delivery at full capacity two years after that. Currently it has 200 firm orders from all over the world, with about one quarter of these from China. Its seating capacity varies depending on its configuration and customer requirements but it is designed to have 300 seats. It will fly at around 600 miles per hour, which is below the sound barrier.

50 The construction of the aircraft uses an advanced lightweight composite material and a greatly reduced amount of aluminium compared with older style aircraft. This provides a more robust airframe which is less prone to corrosion as well as significantly reducing the aircraft's weight. This means that it is about 18 tonnes lighter in weight than its nearest competitor aircraft of similar size and seating capacity.

51 F claims that its 898 aircraft is 20% more efficient in terms of fuel consumption and produces 20% fewer emissions than similar-sized existing aircraft. This is partly due to improved engine technology. The company claims this will have a significant impact in reducing emissions of carbon dioxide and nitrogen oxides thus keeping the air cleaner. In terms of noise pollution, F has designed the aircraft to be quieter on take off and landing than those currently in service. Therefore, F believes that its 898 aircraft will improve the lives of people living and working near airports and of its passengers. It is expected to achieve a 35% reduction in maintenance costs in comparison with similar sized aircraft.

52 With regard to customer facilities, F intends that the 898 aircraft will have a window size which is 40% larger than other aircraft. In addition, it provides more comfortable levels of humidity in the cabin, improved lighting, wider seats and aisles and larger luggage space above the passengers. This all contributes to making the 898 a more environmentally friendly and customer focused aircraft according to F. It is intended to fly between cities which are up to 16,000 km apart without passengers needing to make connecting flights. The F 898 provides passengers with access to in flight web-mail and the facility to use mobile telephones in the air.

53 **C 491**

C has stated that its C 491 aircraft is the first in the world to have a full upper and lower deck for passenger transport, with two aisles running in between the banks of seats. It has a range of 16,000 km which it can fly non-stop. C is implementing internationally accepted quality standards and aims to put this into practice in every aspect of its organisation. New technologies have been introduced enabling the C 491 aircraft to significantly reduce noise on take off, landing and in the air.

54 Improved technology has enabled the C 491 aircraft to achieve lower fuel consumption per seat making it more environmentally friendly than previous aircraft. The structure of the C 491 aircraft uses very hard wearing composite materials which are strongly resistant to fatigue. It uses lighter but durable materials and thus reduces its overall weight.

55 With regard to customer health and safety, in addition to improvements in cabin air supply and humidity, C has introduced a medical site on board the C 491 aircraft. The site is a seating configuration which can be varied into a table for patients and has storage for medical equipment such as a respirator, oxygen and electrocardiogram. The cabin crew will be trained in the use of the equipment.

56 The seating configuration can be modified to suit customer requirements and doors on the main deck and upper deck can be used simultaneously to allow embarkation and disembarkation of passengers. With two loading belts, the aircraft can more speedily achieve transfer of luggage onto and off the aircraft. The turnaround time taking account of refuelling, passenger disembarkation, cleaning, re-stocking and embarkation of the next group of passengers takes about 100 minutes which is considerably less than the time taken on current aircraft in FQA's fleet.

57 The C 491 will permit the ratio of cabin staff to passengers to be reduced on each aircraft compared with the F 898.

Forecast comparative costs and revenues generated by each aircraft

58 The following information gives the forecast comparative costs and revenues for one aircraft supplied by each manufacturer operating at FQA's normal capacity of 80% passenger load factor. The normal operating life of an aircraft is in excess of 20 years but the Board of FQA has decided to review the comparative information over a period of 10 years as technology is developing at such a rapid pace. It can be assumed that there is no re-sale value of the aircraft at the end of the 10 years. In producing this information, it has been assumed that either aircraft, once selected, will be available to come into service on 1 January 2008.

59 All revenues and costs can be assumed to be stated at 1 January 2008 price levels:

Cash inflows	Per aircraft C 491 $ million	Per aircraft F 898 $ million
Annual		
Income from passengers	115	70
Income from cargo	35	18
Income from other revenue generating services	4	2

The following inflation allowances are made for each income heading and apply to both aircraft. These apply from 1 January 2008:

- Income from passengers, and other services is expected to increase by an average compound rate of 5% per year.

- Income from cargo is expected to increase by an average compound rate of 10% per year.

60

Cash outflows	Per aircraft C 491 $ million	Per aircraft F 898 $ million
Annual		
Staff costs	12	9
Landing and parking costs	22	12
Fuel costs	30	26
Maintenance costs	12	4
Contribution to airport developments	16	0
Other costs	4	3
Capital cost of each aircraft	250	150

61 **Notes**

    (a)   Staff costs take full account of estimated employment taxes.

    (b)   Revenue generated by FQA from carriage of cargo in the financial year ended 30 September 2006 represented about 5% of total revenue. Both the C491 and F898 have much greater carrying space available enabling a higher share of revenue per aircraft to be earned by carriage of cargo. The revenue earned by other activities besides that from passengers and cargo in the financial year ended 30 September 2006 was 2·6% of total revenue.

    (c)   FQA will be required to make a contribution to the development of the airports around the world servicing the C 491. This is a charge which will apply to each C 491 aircraft using the airports in order to provide facilities for handling it.

    (d)   Annual inflation allowances applying to both aircraft for each outflow heading are:

- Staff, maintenance and other costs are expected to increase by 3%.
- Landing and parking costs are expected to increase by 5%.
- Fuel costs are expected to increase by 15%.
- Contribution to airport developments is expected to increase by 4%.

    (e)   Depreciation is charged on a straight line basis over 10 years. Taxation depreciation allowances can be assumed to be calculated over a 10 year period also on a straight line basis.

    (f)   Corporate taxation in FQA's home country is at the rate of 25% per annum payable one year in arrears and it is not envisaged that this rate will change over the working life of each aircraft.

(g) A finance lease with a rental cost of $45 million (gross) per annum for the C 491 and $30 million (gross) per annum for the F 898 can be obtained. The lease payments will be made annually over 10 years and can be assumed to start on 1 January 2008. Alternatively, FQA has the opportunity to purchase the aircraft using a term loan over 10 years at the annual fixed rate of interest of 8% pre-tax.

(h) The Finance Director considers a suitable risk adjusted money cost of capital rate to be 10% post tax.

APPENDIX A: EXTRACTS FROM THE ACCOUNTS OF FQA

BALANCE SHEET

	At 30 September 2006		At 30 September 2005	
	$m	$m	$m	$m
Non-current assets (net)		8,408		7,918
Intangible assets		246		224
Total non-current assets		8,654		8,142
Current assets		2,669		2,469
Total assets		11,323		10,611
Equity and reserves		3,948		3,759
Long-term liabilities				
Bank loans				
(repayable 2008)	1,000		1,000	
(repayable 2009)	1,000		1,000	
(repayable 2012)	720		420	
Other long-term liabilities				
(including leases)	1,500		1,450	
		4,220		3,870
Current liabilities		3,155		2,982
Total equity and liabilities		11,323		10,611

Note: Paid in share capital represents 520 million shares at $0·50 each at 30 September 2006.

INCOME STATEMENT

	Year ended 30 September 2006	Year ended 30 September 2005
	$m	$m
Revenue	10,895	10,190
Total operating costs	10,135	9,745
Operating profit	760	445
Financing costs	-265	-235
Tax expense	-124	-53
Profit for the period	371	157

STATEMENT OF CHANGES IN EQUITY

	Share capital	Share premium	Retained earnings	Total
	$m	$m	$m	$m
Balance at 30 September 2005	260	1,714	1,785	3,759
Profit for the period			371	371
Dividends paid			-182	-182
Balance at 30 September 2006	260	1,714	1,974	3,948

Note: It can be assumed that the accounts for the year ended 30 September 2006 are final and have been audited.

18

Flyqual: some help from BPP

Introduction

The topic list below identifies examples of the type of activity which will be available in the BPP Learning Media Toolkit for your paper.

Topic list
1 Summarise the data in a précis
2 Financial analysis
3 Strategic analysis
4 Assessing risk
5 SWOT analysis

1 Summarise the data in a précis

What Flyqual Airlines does and how it is structured.

Flyqual Airlines (FQA) is a premium-quality airline specialising in flying passengers between its home country in Asia and the USA and Europe. It offers flights to 100 destination airports and, through codeshare agreements, and its membership of the N Alliance, is able to provide through-ticketing to over 500 destinations worldwide.

FQA operates a fleet of 170 aircraft of varying types. Of these it owns 65% and leases the remaining 45%. A number of these aircraft leases fall due for renewal over the next two years.

FQA has a unitary structure with one board controlling all aspects of its operations and its 20,000 staff around the world. It owns 45% of another airline that specialises in short-haul flights around the Asian-Pacific region. It is not clear whether FQA's board take a role in the management of this subsidiary. The board has a Chairman, ten further executive directors and twelve non-executive directors. The majority of the executive directors have spent the past 15 years working for FQA and have limited experience outside of FQA's home country. The exceptions are the Finance Director, appointed eight years ago following senior airline roles in Europe, and the Director of Service Quality who joined seven years ago.

The majority of FQA's shares are held by two listed conglomerate companies. These have shown willingness to exert pressure on the board of FQA to cut costs and to boost FQA's financial performance.

Flyqual Airlines present financial and competitive performance

FQA has enjoyed a 71% increase in operating profit in the last year feeding through into a 136% increase in post-tax profits.

FQA is a medium-sized airline, being smaller than Competitor 1 but larger than Competitor 2 and at 12.68 has a higher price/earnings ratio than its competitors. This suggests that its management and strategy enjoy the support of its investors. FQA has a generous dividend policy, paying out 49% of its earnings as dividends in 2006.

Despite its improving profit performance, FQA is not gaining significant additional business. Sales revenues rose only 7% in 2006 which suggests either modest volume growth or extreme price competition.

Compared to other airlines FQA is considerably more punctual and operates at higher load factors, suggesting it is more able to sell its seats.

Key issues faced by Flyqual Airlines: its opportunities and threats

Main short-term issue facing FQA board is how to respond to pressure from investors to reduce costs without triggering a strike by FQA staff.

A second short-term issue is how to deal with the potential disruption from CG if it refuses to improve meals or seeks to breach contract.

The long-term issue for FQA is how to take advantage of the growth in potential business in its region as travel increases with the growth of India and China. This will affect the type of aircraft it selects to replace its fleet, starting in two years time.

Information or meetings forthcoming which may affect Flyqual Airline's future

The main information outstanding is the Director of HRM's report on how to reduce staff numbers. This will affect the Board's response to the pressure from shareholders to reduce staff numbers.

2 Financial analysis

2.1 Financial details

Line		2006	2005	Competitor 1	Competitor 2
1	Operating profit	$760m	$445m	–	–
2	Long term capital (Equity + Long-term liabilities)	$8,168	$7,629	–	–
3	Return on capital employed (ROCE) (Operating profit/Long- term capital)	9.3%	5.8%	–	–
4	Debt	$4,220m	$3,870m	$6,400	$3,300
5	Equity	$3948	$3759	–	–
6	Capital Gearing (Debt/Debt+ Equity)	51.7%	50.7%	–	–
7	Interest paid	$265m	$235m	–	–
8	Interest cover (Operating profit/Interest paid)	2.9 times	1.9 times	–	–
9	Dividend payout ratio	49.1%	–	–	–
10	Current ratio (Current assets/Current liabilities)	0.85	0.83	–	–
11	Share price	$9.0	–	$6.0	$4.5
12	Earnings per share (Profit for period/Number of shares in issue)	$0.71	$0.30 (assumes no change in issued shares between 2005 and 2006)	$0.49	$0.48
13	Price/Earnings Ratio (Share price/EPS)	12.6	–	12.2	9.4

2.2 Financial situation

2.2.1 Profitability

In general FQA's financial position appears **favourable**. The net margin on business has risen from 4.36% to 6.98% between 2005 and 2006 and, as a consequence, profits increased by 71%. FQA enjoys a P/E ratio above that of their competitors (line 13), reflecting good investor support.

This healthy rise in profits is far greater that the rise in sales revenue over the period (6.9%) and reflects the **high operational gearing** of the airline business, ie that most of the costs are fixed and as a consequence additional sales revenue is mainly contribution that feeds into the operating profit.

These **fixed costs** are principally maintenance, engineering and equipment (39%) and staffing (21%). These will be independent of passenger volumes, being driven instead by number of flights and number of flight hours. Fuel costs are to some extent variable with passenger volumes, providing under-booked aircraft have an opportunity to reduce the fuel they carry.

The company's policy of using full-time staff at airports increases fixed costs and will make profits more volatile.

A feature of FQA's costs is that they are to a large extent **uncontrollable**. Fuel prices are under the influence of the cartel of oil producing countries, the tax regime of the government and the competitive strategies of the oil companies. **Hedging** will reduce the peaks and troughs in these but not their overall level. FQA can only reduce fuel costs by reducing fuel usage.

Maintenance will be dictated by the policies of the regulatory authorities with only limited room for efficiency gains by FQA, and parking and landing depends on the bids being submitted for landing slots by rival airlines.

An indication of **operational gearing** is given by the ratio of profit changes to revenue changes (71/6.9) = 10.3 times. This means that a 1% change in revenue will cause a 10.3% change in profits. The improvement in revenues between 2005 and 2006 fed through as extra profits. In a cyclical and uncertain industry like airlines we must expect similar falls in revenue in bad years, with a significant adverse impact on operating profits.

High operational gearing increases the **risk of** a business in several ways.

Firstly, it will affect the operating cash flows of the business. A fall in profits will lead to a fall in free cash available to pay creditors and dividends.

Secondly, it affects the share price because it influences earnings per share, which in turn affects the **sentiment** of investors. The present P/E ratio of FQA is 12.6 (line 13). If profits fell back to 2005 levels of $157 from $371 this would represent a 58% fall in profit. To re-establish the P/E ratio, the share price would decline from $9.00 to $3.78. In practice airline stocks will not move in such a volatile way because investors are already aware of the potential volatility and discount the value of shares in good years (and inflate the values in bad years) in anticipation of the next bend in the road.

Such **volatility** is accentuated by **high capital gearing** where high interest payments impose a second drain on operating profits and so reduce distributable profits.

2.2.2 Financial structure and liquidity

The level of capital gearing is **high and rising** and stood at 51.7% in 2006 (line 6). The level of interest cover stands at 2.9 times which could appear sufficient but for the volatility of profits described above, a fact that can be seen in line 6 where the interest cover in 2005 was just 1.9 times.

It is **unlikely** that gearing or interest cover will improve in the foreseeable future. Indeed the firm borrowed a further $300,000 during the financial year ending September 2006.

On the one hand, the Board is considering buying new aircraft. This will impose additional fixed payments under leases and interest and debt if purchased outright using loans.

Also there are loans **falling due for repayment**. The high dividend policy of 49.1% means that the amount of funds retained in the business in 2006 was $189m. Given that $2,000m of debt is due for repayment in the next four years it is hard to see how FQA will afford to repay this. It represents 10.6 years of 2006 undistributed profits.

Selling obsolete aircraft may not raise significant funds due to their obsolescence in the face of the need for greater fuel economy, less noise and lower emissions. On present forecasts 85% of planes like those in FQA's present fleet will need to be scrapped over the coming, 15 to 20 years. It is hard to see purchasers paying high prices for them.

3 Strategic analysis

3.1 Stakeholder mapping

Mendelow's stakeholder mapping framework can be used to represent the stakeholders in FQA.

INTEREST

	Low	High
Low	**Minimal Effort** • Casual flyers	**Keep Informed** • Regular flyers • Key accounts • Plane makers • Foreign governments and airport operators
High	**Keep Satisfied** • Regulators (eg ICAO) • Home government • Trade unions • N alliance members	**Key Players** • Board members • Institutional shareholders

(The vertical axis is labelled POWER, running Low at the top to High at the bottom.)

In Mendelow's model **interest** refers to how closely the stakeholder follows the strategies and performance of the organisation. This will depend on what the strategy is. For example, a decision by FQA to operate noisy planes would not be of interest to the government of a country not served by FQA, whereas an attempt by FQA to lobby its home government to exclude planes operated by firms from that country would be of high interest.

Power refers to the ability of the stakeholder to be a blocker or a helper to the strategies and operations of FQA. This again will depend on what strategy or operation is under consideration.

The purpose of the analysis is to assist FQA's management to adopt appropriate approaches to each stakeholder group and also to avoid adopting strategies unacceptable to stakeholder groups possessing the power to thwart it.

Casual flyers are occasional airline passengers who are not willing to become clients of FQA. They may be booked on FQA flights by N alliance members or other operators. No special effort should be made to attract or satisfy these passengers beyond the standard service given to other passengers as it is unlikely to be returned by future bookings.

Regular flyers include business people and politicians. They will have experience of a variety of airlines and will make choices. It is important that FQA ensures these flyers are aware of the service FQA offers and it should attempt to improve communication with them through creation of loyalty groups enjoying targeted magazines and emails. As a regular client of FQA, this group would react badly to not being informed of offers or changes to operations. These clients are a source of repeat business and recommendations.

Key accounts will be major travel operators, corporate travel departments and cargo shippers. Like regular flyers they will compare airlines and will value receiving privileged offers and advance information in much the same way as storecard holders receive offers and advance notice of sales.

Plane makers need to have advance notice of FQA's intention to purchase so that they can allocate capacity. Failure to do so will result in FQA suffering late delivery or having to pay supplementary prices. Similarly, advanced notice of any 'spares' required, usually due to servicing, will ensure that 'spares' are held as stock items. Plane makers also rely on airlines to provide information of safety issues and problems arising from the use of the aircraft. This enables product improvement and safety announcements. By having this two-way relationship with plane makers, FQA may benefit from goodwill.

Foreign governments and airport operators should be informed in a timely way of FQA's requirements and intentions in order that FQA can be incorporated in their transport planning and airport development plans. Presently, if FQA is to adopt the C 491, these stakeholders will need to know so that they can start to build or to adapt the airports. Intention to bid for landing slots should also be communicated to ensure FQA receives documentation in good time.

Regulators should be kept satisfied to ensure that FQA keeps its operating licenses and is not grounded or excluded from some airports. This will be done by ensuring compliance with regulations and engagement with requests from regulators for assistance or information. Once they are satisfied these regulators will not focus on FQA but rather on less well-regulated rivals.

Home Government provides many benefits to FQA which give it power. These include subsidies, airport infrastructure and privileged exclusive use of the main airport. In return for this FQA must continue to provide a punctual and safe service of which the country can be proud.

Trade unions have power in so far as they can facilitate or oppose the staffing changes proposed by the Board. To keep them satisfied, FQA should ensure it consults with unions and that its changes are introduced in agreement, such that the union will sell the benefits to its members. This said, there is some doubt that the unions currently have the power to deliver to their members, and there is a belief amongst staff that the unions have let them down.

N alliance members should be kept satisfied in order that FQA may continue to receive the benefits it enjoys under the alliance. This may involve reaching agreement on issues such as appropriate cross payments for transferred passengers, maintenance of service standards for passengers, and non-competition on routes or prices. The latter would be illegal of course.

Board members. As the executives of the firm, directors will inevitably have power. They will have high interest due to the need for success to maintain their positions and to increase the value of their shares and share options. They will principally wish to increase the value of FQA's shares but each will seek to balance this with ensuring their departmental interests are served and that they retain and advance their careers.

Institutional investors. Holding the majority of shares means they can appoint and dismiss board members and pass or vote down resolutions. Moreover, selling shares would cause a sharp decline in the share price and so the threat by one to do this would enable them to coerce other shareholders into accommodating their wishes. These investors have made their interests clear, they wish to see an improvement in profits. FQA already has a generous dividend policy as a consequence of their power and it is to be anticipated that this will need to continue.

3.2 Position audit

An appropriate framework for assessing FQA would be the **strategic capabilities** model of John Kay. This framework states that superior competitive performance, by which is meant shareholder value, is the result of the possession and harnessing of up to four groups of distinctive capabilities (or competences).

The strengths and weaknesses of FQA can be identified by the extent to which it possesses or lacks these capabilities in contrast to its rivals.

3.2.1 Strategic architecture

This is the organisational make-up of the firm and is further subdivided into three categories:

(a)   **Internal architecture.** FQA has sited its main management in its home country and prefers to employ its own ground staff. There is a sensible allocation of responsibilities on its Board and it has a unitary structure, ie it is structured principally to manage one line of business: transcontinental passenger transport. The holding of shares in a short-haul operator is consistent with this because it is managed at arm's length.

This national focus is a **strength in its present business** and has allowed it to attain the status of the national airline. Similar airlines, such as Quantas or Sri Lanka Airlines, harness this effectively to present themselves as the first choice for domestic passengers and as 'county experts' to travellers from outside the country. However, this is usually presented as a greater choice of flights, a cultural welcome or in the form of travel advice and holiday packages.

There is limited evidence that FQA has fully harnessed this yet and this is potentially a weakness in the changing global airline market. Significant growth opportunities exist in China and India and, in the initial stages, these are likely to be for short-haul domestic flights within the countries rather than for long-haul transcontinental flights.

Competences of national culture will not be relevant, indeed they could have negative connotations as Japanese Airlines (JAL) found in China when there was a wave of anti-Japanese sentiment, and attacks on Japanese-owned businesses by 'patriotic rallies' protesting against Japanese atrocities against Chinese citizens in the 20th Century and triggered by the self-serving accounts of these in new Japanese schoolbooks. FQA would need to shift from its present **ethnocentric culture** to a **global culture** as airlines like BA have attempted, or to become **polycentric** by adopting different cultural approaches better suited to each country of operation.

FQA will need to consider abandoning its unitary structure and instead introduce some geographical and product divisions too. This will have implications for the national composition of its board and the backgrounds of its staff.

(b) **External architecture**. This refers to relations with suppliers and customers. Instances of competences in this area might include superior customer relations (eg CRM), preferential supply chains and collaboration with aircraft providers. None of these are mentioned in the Pre-seen information. Indeed in the case of the F 898, the airline has fallen behind its rivals in ordering the aircraft.

(c) **Network architecture**: this is its relationship with other parties. In the case of FQA this would include the N alliance, the government of its home country and the short-haul airline in which it holds a 45% interest.

These are **strengths** in its present line of business. The relationship with the government gives it preferential access to the airport in the capital city of its home country. The N alliance allows it to offer a much wider set of destinations, and gain passenger referrals, than would be possible on its own. However these benefits are equally available to all other alliance members and for that reason it is not a **distinctive** competence but rather a shared **core** competence.

Once again it is hard to see how these competences would be relevant if it extended its business outside its present business domain. Its national government cannot provide much help in emerging economies and the rush for additional routes is likely to strain the alliance as individual airlines form new alliances or seek to go-it-alone.

FQA's reliance on the N alliance may turn into a weakness. The alliance shows some signs of failing to meet its business goals. FQA already has codeshare arrangements with airlines outside the alliance and it has not seen fit to include its short-haul subsidiary in the alliance. There is a danger that retaining its position in the alliance may hold FQA back from developing further business in the emerging economies and may leave its existing operations vulnerable to a breakdown in the alliance.

3.2.2 Possession of strategic assets

These are **unique valuable assets** owned by FQA and not available to rivals, nor substitutable at similar cost. Most of FQAs assets, such as planes and landing slots, are market-traded. Therefore they are available to all rivals. The only unique asset that FQA has is exclusive access to its home airport and, potentially, the newly expanded airport.

3.2.3 Reputation

Reputation can confer **value to products**, for example a brand, or encourage new business partners. FQA has few clear reputational assets other than that of 'being one of the most punctual and safest airlines in the world'. This is presently used to gain concessions and support from its home government.

This strength could be harnessed. Passengers may be comforted by it and inclined to book. Cargo customers, particularly those engaged in shipping high value items such as high technology equipment, will value the safety aspects. Punctuality is important to alliance partners to ensure smooth passenger transfer and would also interest couriers with parcel delivery commitments to meet.

Reference was made above to the potential drawbacks if FQA has a strong national reputation.

3.2.4 Innovation

Firms can gain **strategic advantage through innovation** by either gaining a strategic foothold early in the life of an innovation (a so-called *prime mover advantage*) or by using innovation to change the dynamics of the industry to their advantage. Innovation can open up new revenue streams and/or reduce costs.

FQA has very little obvious track-record of innovation and could be regarded as operating essentially the same business model as it developed at its formation shortly after 1945. The innovations it is presently considering seem mainly to be a **response** to the innovations introduced by the aircraft manufacturers and, hence, will be similar to the innovations of rivals.

Other issues which should be noted as **weaknesses** are:

- FQA has only limited internal capital due to its high dividend policy. This will make it hard to afford new planes
- FQA's board has very limited external experience. This will hold it back in trying to develop new lines of business or to adjust to new competition
- FQA's fleet of aircraft will need substantial renewal as a consequence of cost and environmental factors
- FQA is vulnerable to any decline in the volume of traffic to and from its home country

3.3 Environmental analysis

Given the information in the Pre-seen material, the most appropriate framework is a PESTEL analysis.

3.3.1 Political factors

(a) The **policies of national governments on opening up their airways to competition**, and their attitudes to foreign-owned airlines, will be significant. If FQA's home government permits greater competition this could harm FQA: a **threat**. Conversely, a similar decision by a foreign government would provide **opportunities** to FQA.

(b) **Trade relations between countries will affect demand for air services**. Trade relations that encourage inward investment will increase business travel. Cargo will be affected by trade agreements too. For example the cited exports from China of high technology could be affected by a breakdown in relations between China and customer countries, or by a decision from the Chinese government to cease export of high technology to countries where it could be a strategic threat. Recent investigations by UK authorities into alleged bribes by a leading aerospace manufacturer were halted by its government when they feared it could have repercussions for trade relations with a wealthy middle-eastern country.

(c) **International political tensions** affect the travel industry as a threat. US and UK foreign policy can affect the attitude of some countries to their flag-carrying airline. Business investment and tourism avoid regions where conflict is feared.

(d) **International regulations affect subsidies and costs**. Presently the World Trade Organisation is seeking to eliminate subsidies from domestic governments for airlines and aerospace manufacturers. This is a threat to FQA because it benefits from such arrangements in its own country.

(e) **Terrorist activities and local conflicts**: Aircraft have long been targets for terrorist groups through hi-jacking and ransoming passengers, shooting down, detonating bombs and using as flying bombs to destroy targets. There have been suggestions that they may be used to expose passengers to nerve agents and deadly viruses too. Similarly, passengers have found themselves trapped in war zones as rival groups blockade airports.

3.3.2 Economic

(a) **State of the economy in countries served by FQA**: this will affect demand for air services. The emergence of India and China will have profound impacts on the distribution of wealth across the world and hence the patterns of air travel.

(b) **Exchange rates**: affects the value of revenues received by FQA where sales are made in foreign currency. Similarly affects the cost of purchases denominated in foreign currency of which aviation fuel is the most obvious example.

(c) **Taxation policy**: this affects the costs of the airline, such as the example of carbon taxes, or the costs of tickets and hence demand, such as departure taxes which have recently been hiked in the UK on the pretext of improving environmental protection.

3.3.3 Social

(a) **Attitudes to flying and concerns over security**: the fear of bombs on planes will reduce passenger numbers. The downing of aircraft on September 11th 2001 is a particular example of this.

(b) **Health concerns over flying**: this is a threat and has included issues such as respiratory illness from recirculated air in planes, deep vein thromboses from sharp variations in atmospheric pressure and cramped conditions and back injuries from poor posture.

(c) **Prevailing expectations of airline service**: premium airlines compete to provide augmented services such as choices of meals, better in-fight entertainment, more comfortable seating, transport to and from airports etc. These then become basic minimum expectations, the costs of which cannot be recovered from premium prices.

(d) **Purposes of travel**: the aging populations in North America and Western Europe provides the opportunity for greater leisure travel. Business travel has to some extent been reduced by the threat of teleconferencing.

3.3.4 Technological

Technology provides both opportunities and threats.

(a) **Improved aircraft and engine design**: this has the potential to reduce costs but also imposes the threat of accelerating the obsolescence of the airline's existing fleet.

(b) **External technologies such as e-commerce** threaten to change the business models of airlines. Bookings and ticket comparisons are enabled by the Internet, and this reduces profits. However international trading of products is facilitated and this increases cargo volumes.

3.3.5 Ecological

(a) **Threat of concern over carbon emissions** means that airlines must either replace their fleets or pay the costs of carbon offset. There may be an opportunity for airlines able to present themselves as 'carbon neutral'.

(b) **Concerns over noise and disruption caused by aircraft** are leading authorities to demand quieter aircraft, but also to limit airport capacities and eliminate night-time flights. This will impose costs but also may reduce the operational loading on aircraft if they are trapped at airports overnight.

3.3.6 Legal

(a) **Threats of anti-trust activity**. Airlines have been prosecuted successfully for collusive practices on pricing, and unfair competition. FQA could face litigation in any of its destination countries for fuel surcharges, membership of alliances etc.

(b) **Regulations on air safety, emissions, security etc**: these are a threat as they would increase costs.

3.4 Ansoff analysis

The Ansoff matrix assists in the identification of the product/market directions available to FQA.

PRODUCT

	Current	New
Current	**Market Penetration** • Increase capacity on existing routes • Purchase direct rival • Increase cargo • Reduce price or improve service to gain passengers	**Product Development** • Additional destinations to reduce cross booking • Accommodation booking Holidays
New	**Market Development** • Open hubs in additional countries • New routes • Low cost air service • Executive travel	**Diversification** *Related* • Provision of maintenance services to other airlines • Provision of ground services to other airlines • Helicopter services *Unrelated* • Non-airline related business

(MARKET is labelled on the vertical axis.)

4 Assessing risk

4.1 Financial risks

4.1.1 Interest rate risk

A change in the interest rate can affect the **cash flows** of the company where there are debts owed by the company at variable rates. Similarly any incomes related to interest rates, such as from short-term deposits or where passenger or freight volumes are affected by interest rates, will also be subject to risk.

This risk can be managed in a variety of ways:

(a)   Avoidance of floating rate debt by switching funding to equity or fixed rate debt or interest hedging.

(b)   Deliberate purchase of floating rate debt such that the fall in earnings from business operations as rates rise can be offset by the increase in returns from the investments

(c)   Development of lines of business where earnings are negatively co-variant to those of FQA with respect to interest rates. For example, aeroengine manufacture General Electric has a lending arm, GE Capital which, it seems likely, will enjoy increasing returns during interest rate rises at the same time as selling and servicing less engines as passenger volumes fall.

4.1.2 Foreign exchange risk

Foreign exchange risk occurs when exchange rates change and affect the cost of servicing debts denominated in foreign currency, the receipts from payments denominated in foreign currency and the changes in the volumes of business as the foreign currency costs of tickets changes.

Methods of managing this risk include:

(a) Denomination of debts and sales in domestic currency where possible.

(b) Exchange rate hedging.

(c) Development of streams of earnings and expenditures that are matched for each currency. For example if FQA needs to pay sterling for meals supplied on return journeys from London it should consider using the ticket revenues from sales in UK to pay this. If these are insufficient then a sterling denominated airline shop should be considered.

(d) Diversification of operations across several currency zones.

4.1.3 Credit risk

Credit risk is the disruption to revenue streams by delayed payments from receivables or from bad debts.

This risk can be managed by:

(a) Credit control procedures.
(b) Debt factoring.

4.2 Operational risks

4.2.1 Regulation risk

This refers to the **costs** of complying with changes to aviation **regulations**, fines for non-compliance and of disruption to operations if aircraft are grounded.

This risk can be managed by:

(a) **Creation of mechanisms for consultation and advance warning with regulators**. The experience and contacts of FQA's Engineering Director will be an important part of this.

(b) **Compliance with regulations**. FQA will need to have robust procedures for all operations that can be inspected and verified by regulators.

(c) **Transfer sensitive operations outside the business**. Outsourcing maintenance, staffing, catering etc. means that the expertise of the provider may reduce some of the risk but also that they will bear the costs of changes to regulation or fines for non-compliance. Loss of earnings due to disruption of these activities can be recovered by FQA through legal action.

4.2.2 Culture risk

This deals with the danger of commercial failure, reputation damage, or disruption to operations due to **mismanagement of cultural interfaces** in the business. Examples include the adverse effects of staffing or advertising decisions, poor product or service provision. At the highest level it can include the fall-out from national cultural clashes for the firms in those nations.

This risk can be managed by:

(a) **Taking appropriate advice on cultural issues**: Many consultancies will provide FQA with practical advice on doing business in particular countries to avoid damaging cultural sensibilities.

(b) **Business partnerships with local operators**: These will be more experienced in dealing with differences.

(c) **Diversity policy**: FQA could take deliberate action to ensure that the breadth of cultures that it deals with are represented within its staff at all levels. Staff could also be given culture awareness training such as BA did with cabin staff to make them aware of the varyiability of dietary conventions, body language, name conventions, forms of address etc that will be encountered by a global airline.

(d) **Organisational development**: FQA could take the decision to shift from a national to a global organisation by a transformational change involving restructuring, recruitment and changing the perspective of existing staff towards persons from other cultures.

(e)   **Board composition**: To avoid operational risks the Board should have representatives of main operational areas represented such that the operational implications of Board decisions receives proper considerations and that operational concerns receive a proper airing.

It is noticeable that several key operations at FQA have Board representation, ie a Chief Operating Officer, and Engineering Director, Sales, HRM and IT/IS (via Director of Service Delivery).

4.3 Hazard risks

4.3.1 Contracts

The **extended supply chain** of FQA makes it reliant on suppliers of fuel, aircraft parts, air traffic control etc. Particular contract risks in FQA's present situation are its employment contracts with staff, contracts with CG and potential contracts with the makers of new aircraft. Risks arise where a counterparty is unable or unwilling to fulfil their obligations under the contract, such as a threat to strike or CG's threat to withdraw its service, or where FQA wishes to vary the terms of the contract but cannot without penalties.

Management of this risk can be assisted by:

(a)   **Proper procedures for supplier selection**. For example it is of concern that FQA appears to have struck a deal with CG which means that CG is making losses. Ensuring that CG could remain viable should have been part of the risk assessment undertaken at the time of awarding the contract.

(b)   **Development of dedicated procurement and contracts function** within FQA. FQA does not have a Board position for this at present.

(c)   **Multisourcing** of inputs to avoid excessive reliance on one.

(d)   **Financial redress for non-performance** of contract such as penalty payments.

(e)   **Relationship building** with counterparties to develop trust and commitment. Regular meetings to air concerns and address grievances will assist and will also provide FQA with early warnings of potential risk from the contracts.

4.3.2 Natural events

For airlines this includes hurricanes, snow, rain and fog. These lead to cancellations and diversions of flights resulting in displaced passengers and aircraft with subsequent **costs** of relocation (buses, alternative flights, empty flights), compensation and lost revenue. Such events can also affect demand for air services, such as a lack of snow reducing demand for flights to skiing resorts or the tragedy of a Tsunami making tourists unwilling to visit island and low lying costal resorts. For example, in 2005 Sri Lanka Airways reported a $40m fall in revenue and fall in passenger load factors from 70% to 20% in the aftermath of the December 2004 Tsunami.

Management controls that can be used include:

(a)   **Contingency plans** for dealing with disruptions such as alternative schedules, stand by arrangements with other transport providers and airports.

(b)   **Advance warning** such as use of weather forecasts

(c)   **Contractual clauses** limiting FQA's liability for costs of losses due to natural events and *force majeure*.

(d)   **Risk assessment of airports** used to assess vulnerability to fog, flood etc.

4.3.3 Suppliers

These are risks arising from the collapse or poor performance of suppliers or aggressive action on their part such as levying of increased prices.

Many of the management controls for contract risk discussed above apply here too. Additional controls would include:

(a)   Engagement of suppliers in **long-term contracts**.

(b)   Creation of **parallel sourcing strategies** to ensure suppliers remain competitive and sourcing approaches (eg a sole reliance on agents or e-trading) are not an additional source of risk.

4.3.4 Environment

The issues here can be assessed under the PESTEL mnemonic.

Management controls include:

(a) **Development of relationship with key stakeholders** (eg governments, environmental groups, local warlords etc).

(b) **Improvement to physical security of operations**. It is noticeable that FQA has no Board position for security and risk management.

(c) **Improve information** available by environmental scanning and creation of knowledge management within FQA.

4.4 Strategic risks

4.4.1 Competition

This imposes the **commercial risk** of reduced profits through lower prices and volumes and increased costs of participation in the industry (service quality, promotion etc).

Management controls include:

(a) Competitor monitoring and analysis

(b) Development of competitive advantage such as brand or unique access or technology.

(c) Pre-emptive action such as developing 'flanker' businesses. Faced with challenges from low cost airlines many full-service airlines developed cheaper second brands (eg BA launched Go, British Midland launched bmi-baby. Ryanair moved in the opposite direction by seeking to acquire the Irish long-haul operator Air Lingus).

(d) Diversification of business to reduce expose to particular competitors.

(e) Negotiation of understandings with competitors (potentially unethical and illegal).

(f) Acquisition of competitors.

4.4.2 Customer changes

This includes loss of key customers, failure of key target customers, or sharp changes in customer demand patterns. An example is the successful publicity by economy airlines to name and shame corporations who refuse to use them and hence expend shareholders' money on flying staff with expensive full-service airlines.

Management controls include:

(a) Operation of a **flexible fleet** able to be adapted to serve a variety of customer types and destinations.

(b) Provision of a **portfolio** of ticket prices and service levels (eg BA offer First, Business, Club and World Traveller classes).

(c) Avoidance of **reliance** on one or a few main clients or destinations.

(d) **Good quality customer information** to detect changing tastes or defections to rivals.

4.4.3 Industry changes

This includes the arrival of new competition, merger of rivals and the failure of rivals. These change the **nature of competitive pressure**. For example, a merger may create greater economies of scale for the larger firm, a threat to FQA, but may also reduce capacity in the industry and so relieve price pressure, an opportunity for FQA.

Management controls include:

(a) **Environmental information** on potential industry changes.

(b) Ability to launch **pre-emptive action** such as appeals to regulatory authorities or to mount counterbids.

(c) **Leasing** some aircraft to enable reduction or changes in fleet composition.

4.4.4 Customer demand

This refers to **unanticipated fluctuations** in demand. These are inevitable for airlines as a consequence of the strategic choice to be an airline. Their profits and survival will depend on developing strategies to cope. For example, the damage done to BA when the UK countryside was effectively closed to tourists by an outbreak of foot and mouth disease in 2001, which it blamed for a 50% fall in its operating profits. This can be compared to BA's status, with Virgin Atlantic, as premier travel partners of the successful bid to host the 2012 Olympic Games in London. This will increase volumes by an amount that will depend on the prevailing political and economic climate in 2012.

Management controls include:

(a)   Use of **flexible staffing** (part-time, contract etc.) to cope with peaks and troughs in passenger volumes.

(b)   **Dynamic pricing** to raise or lower prices to shift demand towards unfilled seats.

(c)   **Flexible** service and maintenance schedules which allow planes to be pressed into service during peaks and rested during troughs.

(d)   **Variety** of plane sizes to enable low demand routes to have small planes and so re-deploy larger planes to busy routes.

(e)   **Multi-skilled staff** able to cope with changes of aircraft on their route (in particular pilots who must be able to switch flight decks) or being asked to work a different route and so be familiar with passenger demands and able to give information on customs, formalities etc.

4.5 Internally driven risks

These are ones that result from the **operations of management**. The Risk Management Standard makes clear that some of these risks are incurred as a response to particular external risks, such as the investment of funds in R&D to gain strategic advantage to reduce strategic risk. Other internal risks leave the firm exposed to external risk, such as poor liquidity and cash flow leaving a firm exposed to the financial risks from higher interest rates or banks withdrawing credit.

The internally driven risks that can be identified in FQA are discussed below.

(a)   **Liquidity and cash flow**: borrowing increased during the 2006 financial year. FQA has a liquidity ratio below 1. This means that any interruption to its business and cash flows could potentially leave it unable to pay its creditors. Moreover it has insufficient retained earnings to meet its present operating capital needs, hence the increased borrowing in 2006 despite a modest increase in business activity, and so will not be able to repay the loans falling due in 2008 and 2009. Any fall in liquidity may make FQA unable to maintain its dividend and hence jeopardise its share price.

(b)   **Employees and supply chain**: both internal risk drivers are present with the increased dissatisfaction of employees with the voluntary redundancies resulting from the new terminal and, apparently, the loss of control over them by the decline in influence of the Trades Unions.

(c)   **Public access** is an inherent risk for all airlines. Admitting passengers and relatives to airport buildings, airplanes etc also means admitting potential illnesses (such as the avian flu virus) or terrorists.

(d)   **Intellectual capital**: the customer and flight information held by FQA is of high commercial value, yet under the codeshare arrangement, is sometimes shared with potential rivals. The board should remember the scandal that engulfed BA when it was revealed that its seat reservation system, leased to other airlines for their use too, was being used to break into the passenger details held by Virgin Atlantic for the purposes of poaching customers – the so-called 'dirty tricks' campaign. The damage to BA's reputation and the commercial damage to Virgin Atlantic from this episode illustrates the risks inherent in high dependence of IT/IS. [*Student note*: Report to Board should avoid direct criticism of Board members. However a significant risk factor for FQA is the limited background of the Director of Service Delivery].

5 SWOT analysis

Strengths	Weaknesses
• Membership of the N alliance • Wide range of routes offered • Reputation for quality service • Supported by home government • Punctuality of departures • Control over operations via employing own staff • Well regarded by markets – relatively high P/E ratio v Competition • High relative load factors • Opinion leader in industry	• Lack of external experience among the board • Staff unrest • Supplier unrest • Cost inflexibility due to employment of own staff • Unionised workforce • Lack of internally generated capital • Exposed to risk of reliance on home economy
Opportunities	**Threats**
• Projected growth in airline passenger numbers in India/China/Asia generally • Projected growth in cargo market, driven by Asian exports of technology products • Replacement of fleet with more cost effective models • Expansion into the "no frills" market via subsidiary company • Merger with alliance partners • Opening of new terminal • Lower costs via extension of outsourcing of jobs	• Rising fuel prices • New legislation on noise/emissions/green taxes • Increasing competition from existing/new entrants to the market • Global terrorism targeting airlines • Pressure from major shareholders to reduce costs

5.1 Prioritise your SWOT

Choose the TWO **most significant** Strengths, Weaknesses, Opportunities and Threats. Justify your choices.

Strength Reputation as quality airline	Reputation gains passengers, alliance partners and access to new markets.
High load factors	In a high fixed cost industry like airlines this is essential to recover the fixed costs and to make profit. It reflects good route planning and marketing.
Weakness Staff unrest	Staff unrest could bring an immediate halt to operations for a protracted period with consequent losses and deterioration of customer goodwill.
Lack of Board experience	FQA faces significant opportunities and challenges which represent a discontinuity from the business that the Board know how to run. This reduces FQA's ability to adapt.
Opportunity Growth in alternative markets	The volume of additional business will be significant if FQA can position itself to take advantage of it.
More cost effective fleet	This could raise margins significantly.
Threat Pressure from investors	This could trigger either a strike or a sell-off or seizure of control by investors if not satisfied.
Green legislation	This will force FQA to replace fleet ahead of time or pay high costs for 'permits to pollute'. This may affect cash flow, balance sheet values and profits.

19

Flyqual: unseens and requirements

Introduction

This chapter contains the unseen material and requirements from the March and May 2007 exams.

We have produced a suggested answer to the March exam in Chapter 20.

March 2007 unseen

Requirement

You are the consultant appointed by the FQA Board.

Prepare a report that prioritises, analyses and evaluates the issues facing FQA, and makes appropriate recommendations.

Capital Investment Appraisal

Capital Investment Appraisal calculations for both the C 491 and the F 898 have been produced. Extracts from the calculations are shown at Appendix B. (Appendix A is shown in the pre-seen material.) The appraisals were based on the C 491 having 600 seats and the F 898 having 300 seats and the normal capacity of an 80% passenger load factor was assumed. That is to say that the passenger income values assume that on average 80% of the aircraft seats will be sold on each flight. Taxation depreciation allowances were calculated over a ten-year period on a straight line basis. The calculations are for **one** aircraft of each type.

A decision on aircraft replacement must be made by 30 June 2007. It has been decided that all replacement aircraft will be leased. The decision to lease has no effect on the risk adjusted money cost of capital rate applied by FQA, which is 10%. Therefore the decision to lease has no effect on the NPV calculation shown in Appendix B. The Finance Director is confident that the total cash commitment of additional leasing charges can be met from future cash flows.

After the calculation shown in Appendix B had been made, it became apparent that assumptions relating to insurance premiums payable by FQA were incorrect. Insurance premiums had previously been excluded by the management accounting team leader responsible for preparing the calculation. This was because he thought that they applied equally to all the aircraft in the FQA fleet. Therefore the team leader concluded they were a common cost and could be excluded.

However, research by a member of the team leader's staff revealed that there would be a differential charge for insuring the C 491 as compared with the F 898. This additional insurance premium would need to be covered by FQA irrespective of how the acquisition of the aircraft was financed. The annual additional differential insurance premium for each C 491 aircraft would be at the yearly rate of $10,000 for each seat in the 600 seat aircraft, rising by 5% compound per year. The premiums are payable in advance, meaning that the first payment would be made on 1 January 2008.

The member of staff brought this to the attention of the team leader. The team leader refused to change the calculations already submitted to the Finance Director because he said it was "insignificant" with regard to the overall decision and instructed the member of staff to ignore it. The member of the team leader's staff was unwilling to ignore it and raised the matter with the Finance Director.

Landing rights at the airport in the capital city of FQA's home country

In an attempt to encourage increased competition in the airline industry, the government has awarded landing rights at FQA's home airport (in the capital city) to one of FQA's competitor airlines. These rights relate to a long-haul route which is in direct competition with one which FQA already operates and which generates a large amount of passenger traffic. The government made sure that the airline which was awarded the landing rights provides a high quality service similar to that offered by FQA. The new service is due to begin on 1 July 2007. The Aviation Minister has indicated that this may be the first award of a series of landing rights which may or may not be awarded to FQA in the future.

Maintenance Issues

As a result of budget cuts at FQA, some procedures were not completed and this led to a number of aircraft not complying with safety checks. This, in turn, led to an adverse safety report following a series of incidents which called into question the maintenance procedures employed by FQA. The Engineering Director produced a report which stated that the safety procedures were being improperly applied by three technicians whom he dismissed. The Engineering Director went on to say in his report that the maintenance procedures were now perfectly safe.

The pilots' trades union sought re-assurance from the Chief Executive of FQA that the safety of aircraft was not being compromised. In order to provide that re-assurance the Chief Executive appointed an independent engineering consultant to carry out a review of the maintenance procedures employed by FQA. The report of the independent engineering consultant concluded that there were serious faults with the maintenance procedures and that the Engineering Director should have known about these. The independent engineering consultant's report went on to state that in his professional opinion, the budget for maintenance needs to be reviewed as it is inadequate to carry out the required maintenance procedures and it was down to sheer luck that no serious incidents had occurred.

The trade unions argued that engineering management rather than the three technicians were at fault and these staff, who had been dismissed, had been used by FQA management to cover up the failings at a more senior level.

Trade unions negotiations

The maintenance issues coupled with the earlier difficulties with staff, had further damaged relations between management and staff within FQA. Seizing the initiative, the trade unions, who act on behalf of FQA employees, including maintenance workers, entered into negotiations with FQA. This was in an attempt to improve the earlier agreement on pay for ground staff and working hours for the air crew and cabin staff. The trade unions did not rule out strike action at FQA. They threatened that the dispute might be extended to involve other people employed in the transport industry, which although illegal in the UK, is legal in FQA's home country.

Pressure on FQA was further increased when the Aviation Minister informed the Chairman of FQA that unless a general transport strike was avoided by FQA settling its internal disputes, there would be a withdrawal of government financial support for the airline.

Cost of strike action

The Board has received an evaluation from the Finance Director that the cost of strike action, in terms of lost revenue, if the whole airline were to be closed down is estimated at $30 million per day. (Variable costs of running FQA are estimated at about 40% of revenue). Added to this would be the cost incurred by the loss of goodwill. In addition, the Director of Sales and Marketing has explained that the potential cost of recovering lost business is likely to be substantial after a strike. She further expressed that she would strongly resist the Board's proposal to significantly reduce marketing expenditure in the event of strike action being taken by FQA's employees. The Finance Director had also calculated that the cost of settling the claims on the trade unions' terms would be about $220 million per year.

Emergency Board Meeting

The Chairman of FQA called an emergency meeting and the directors were inevitably concerned to ensure that FQA's flights schedule was maintained, but insisted that any renegotiation of pay and conditions of service must be coupled with further improvements in efficiency and increased productivity.

Catering services

There had also been disruption to the catering service due to the continued hard bargaining by FQA with its main outsourced catering supplier (CG) in its home country. In effect, the only way CG could continue to provide the service was to reduce its own staffing levels or renegotiate its employment contracts with its staff. A reduction in the staffing levels would mean that the catering service capacity would be reduced leading to a reduction in supplies to FQA. The approach CG adopted therefore was to attempt to re-negotiate contracts with its staff which resulted in strike action. This reduced supplies of catering to FQA which resulted in a suspension of its entire catering service on all short-haul routes. In its place, FQA provided passengers with a voucher which they could use to purchase food at the airport when they checked in.

TV and press interview

A television and press interview was given by the Director of Sales and Marketing. After the interview, the Director of Sales and Marketing made confidential comments that the trade unions had taken an unreasonable position and complained that they had been opportunist and were "blackmailing" FQA. She further went on to say that the staff employed by FQA enjoyed very satisfactory pay and conditions of service and that if any employee felt they could improve on these they should seek employment elsewhere because " there are plenty of unemployed people in the country who can replace them and would be happy to work for FQA".

These comments were given to the press by an FQA employee to whom the remarks were being made. He passed the comments to the press because he felt the attitude of the Director of Sales and Marketing was unreasonable. He did not know how to raise this matter internally within FQA. Subsequently the FQA employee, to whom the remarks were made, was dismissed, and this attracted negative press comment.

Meeting between Chairmen and the Chief Executive of FQA

A private meeting attended by both the Chairman and the Chief Executive of FQA and the Chairmen of the largest shareholding companies was held. Between them the two largest shareholding companies own 60% of FQA. At the meeting FQA's Chairman and Chief Executive re-affirmed their position of not giving in to unfair trade union pressure. The shareholders represented by the other Chairmen accepted this position but only in the short term. They felt a lengthy strike would be extremely damaging and instructed the FQA Board to restore a reasonable working relationship with the trade unions and insisted that the Director of Sales and Marketing should give no more press interviews. Further, they instructed the Chairman to dismiss her if the trade unions insisted that they would not negotiate with the company if she remained on the Board.

At the end of the meeting, one of the Chairmen of the two largest shareholding companies brought to the attention of the Chairman of FQA a matter relating to fuel purchases. It was apparent that despite holding down its fuel costs in the financial year ended 30th September 2006, FQA had since then purchased fuel at a price which was higher than that which would be charged by an alternative supplier. The Chairman of the shareholding company was aware of this as he is a member of the Board of the alternative fuel supplier. On investigation, he had been told confidentially that one of FQA's senior purchasing staff had received an inducement payment to obtain the fuel at the higher price from a specific supplier.

Reaction of the Chairman of C

C manufactures a major component of its own aircraft in FQA's home country. The Chairman and Board of C are becoming increasingly concerned that the dispute at FQA may begin to affect their own company's production. The national leaders of the trade unions had made it clear to the Chairman of C that they felt that he should try to bring some influence to bear on the FQA Board to settle the dispute quickly. The national trade union leaders did not rule out the possibility of industrial action taking place at C's manufacturing plants in FQA's home country if it continued to negotiate the sale of the C 491 to FQA while the industrial dispute was still taking place. They reminded the Chairman of C that this action would be legal in FQA's home country.

Staff Turnover

Staff turnover at FQA is increasing as cabin staff, in particular, are seeking alternative employment. Some of the FQA pilots sought employment with other airlines which were willing to accept them providing they had vacancies. FQA pilots are highly regarded among other airlines as their training programmes and procedures are considered to be world class.

Extraordinary General Meeting of shareholders

An Extraordinary General Meeting of shareholders was called. The meeting was attended by all 12 non-executive directors as well as the main Board members. After receiving major criticism at the meeting, the FQA Chairman and Chief Executive both resigned with immediate effect.

It was agreed by the non-executive directors that a consultant should be appointed immediately to review the issues facing FQA.

APPENDIX B

Extracts from the Capital Investment Appraisal calculations for each aircraft

All figures are at 31 December of each year.

	Years									
	1	2	3	4	5	6	7	8	9	10
	$m	$m	$m	$m	$m	$m	$m	$m	$m	$m
C 491 (per aircraft)										
	2008	2009	2010	2011	2012	2013	2014	2015	2016	2017
Total income	163·5	173·5	184·3	195·9	208·2	221·5	235·7	250·8	267·1	284·6
Total outflows (before tax)	103·1	110·9	119·7	129·4	140·3	152·6	166·2	181·6	199·0	218·5
Pre-tax cash flows	60·4	62·6	64·6	66·5	67·9	68·9	69·5	69·2	68·1	66·1

NPV of after tax cash flows: $97 million

F 898 (per aircraft)

	2008	2009	2010	2011	2012	2013	2014	2015	2016	2017
Total income	95·4	101·2	107·3	113·9	120·9	128·4	136·4	145·0	154·1	164·0
Total outflows (before tax)	59·0	64·6	70·9	78·0	86·2	95·3	105·7	117·5	131·0	146·2
Pre-tax cash flows	36·4	36·6	36·4	35·9	34·7	33·1	30·7	27·5	23·1	17·8

NPV of after tax cash flows: $26 million

COST OF CAPITAL FOR BOTH NPV CALCULATIONS = 10%

May 2007 unseen

Requirement

You are the consultant appointed by the FQA Board. Prepare a report that prioritises, analyses and evaluates the issues facing FQA, and makes appropriate recommendations.

Industrial Relations at FQA

Much to the relief of all stakeholders in the airline, and in particular its shareholders, the threatened industrial relations unrest has not materialised. Although there is now a better understanding between the trade unions and management at the airline, the relations could not be considered to be friendly. However, both sides seem to have recognised that it is in their own best interests to try to avoid confrontation. Accordingly, the Aviation Minister has lavished praise on the Chairman and Chief Executive of FQA and also on the trade union leaders and publicly congratulated them as shining examples of industrial co-operation.

Catering Dispute

The previous difficulties experienced with the main catering supplier CG have now been resolved with a new contract agreed. CG is proving that it can supply catering of an appropriate quality and is comfortable with the price it has recently negotiated with FQA.

Corporate Entertainment

A leading national newspaper has revealed that some directors on the FQA Board have engaged in activities which included providing lavish corporate entertainment and offering substantial price discounts to potential corporate customers. This includes employees of government departments both in FQA's home country and abroad. As yet, there has been no direct link made to any government ministers by the national newspaper but now other media channels have taken the story and are progressing with their own investigations. This has led to speculation that senior government ministers may have benefited by receiving FQA's corporate entertainment.

There is speculation among senior FQA staff that this issue might also be high on the agenda at a meeting between the Chairman of FQA and the Aviation Minister which will be held soon. In response to the allegations, the Chairman of FQA has challenged the national newspaper to provide proof. The national newspaper has reported that FQA's external auditors use the airline for most of their domestic and overseas flights and has asked whether the auditors receive discounts or benefits from the airline which are not available to other passengers.

Capital Investment Appraisal and Leasing Evaluation

The Finance Director has been provided with a Capital Investment Appraisal calculation for each aircraft and from this the C 491 had been demonstrated as more financially attractive than the F 898. The NPV for the two aircraft were calculated as follows:

C 491: $97 million per aircraft
F 898: $26 million per aircraft

(These NPV values are calculated from the data contained in the pre-seen material.)

Based on this information and other non financial factors, the Board took the decision to acquire the C 491 rather than the F 898 or replace the ageing aircraft with new ones of the same type.

The Board is aware that the delivery of newly designed aircraft is often subject to delay.

Its initial order will be for 20 aircraft to be brought into service, one per month from 1 January 2008. The intention is that as each new aircraft is brought into service, one F 858 or C450 will be retired. In August 2009, when the 20th C 491 is received, FQA will dispose of four F 858s. The effect on overall passenger capacity from the acquisition of the 20 C 491s and the disposal of the 24 aircraft in the current fleet is a net increase of 200 seats.

The Board is confident that the increase in overall capacity and the faster turnround will enable FQA to take advantage of possible increased demand in passenger numbers. The Chairman stated at a news conference called to announce the decision to acquire the C 491s, that

> "FQA has a proud tradition of offering high quality travel solutions to business and tourist customers alike. We believe that the C 491 will provide the high standards required to take advantage of increasing customer expectations for worldwide travel and we look forward to a long and successful relationship with C."

FQA's Finance Director is confident that FQA will, if required, be able to raise sufficient funds to purchase all the new aircraft outright. In addition, however, she has received the information shown at **Appendix B** (Appendix A is shown in the pre-seen material) which relates to leasing rather than buying the C 491. The cash commitment to FQA of the annual leasing charges over the next three years will be as follows:

	$m
Financial Year ending 30 September 2008	405
Financial Year ending 30 September 2009	900
Financial Year ending 30 September 2010	900

Following negotiations with an alternative leading leasing contract company (whose Managing Director is the brother of FQA's Chairman) it became clear that a more advantageous leasing agreement was available to FQA. Under the terms of the proposed agreement, the leasing charge would be $35 million per year for each C 491 aircraft over a ten-year period, rather than the $45 million per year (as stated in the pre-seen material) over 10 years. The other terms and conditions for each of the two alternative leasing agreements are identical.

Change in safety recommendations

The government has introduced a new safety recommendation for aircraft which will come into operation from 1 January 2008. This is in response to a freak accident which occurred elsewhere in Asia (not involving FQA). The recommendation relates to door mechanisms and applies to all new aircraft but not for those currently in service. The cost of the new recommendation is expected to be $1 million for each C 491 aircraft. The Chairman of FQA has written to the Aviation Minister expressing his concern at the new recommendation as the changes required are by no means certain to improve the ability of passengers to leave the aircraft quickly in the event of an emergency. Further, the changes required by the recommendation would not be effective across the world and therefore will only apply to airlines registered as companies within FQA's home country. This means that only airlines such as FQA will need to comply with the recommendation and those from other countries will not be required to do so which the Chairman of FQA considers would put his company at a severe disadvantage.

The Chairman of FQA is worried about possible delays in delivery which may be caused by this recommendation as the doors fitted to the aircraft will now be different from standard. The Managing Director of C has made it clear that any conversion costs will not be borne by C.

Staff Re-training

Although the need for training of cabin staff on the equipment in the C 491 is very limited and can be undertaken very quickly, that required for the flight crew is extensive. In order to undertake the flight crew training, FQA engaged a supplier to provide flight deck training equipment called a simulator. (The flight deck is where the pilots and flight engineer are positioned at the front of the aircraft.) The supplier has informed the Chief Operating Officer at FQA that there is expected to be a three month delay in the supply of the simulator. This will mean that the programme of training for flight deck staff will be severely disrupted and cause a delay of up to three months.

The Chief Operating Officer has been in contact with other suppliers of the simulators but as yet has not found one that can improve on delivery. However, as a contingency, he has instructed his staff to try and find a way of halving the amount of training time needed on the simulator as an interim measure until FQA is back on track with its original schedule of pilot training.

Increasing competition

In addition to the increasing levels of competition being felt by FQA from foreign airlines, there is the ever growing threat posed by the low-priced (sometimes called "no frills") airlines. Three such airlines have been established in FQA's home country. They mainly operate on short haul routes although one of them is now planning to establish a long-haul route to the USA. Although the fares of these low-priced airlines are variable, they retail their tickets at substantially lower prices than those of FQA's economy fares on the short-haul routes. Seats on the low-priced airlines are not guaranteed and they notoriously oversell their seating capacity. This means that often passengers are left stranded at airports waiting for the next available flight which may not be on the same day. As they are low-priced, their tickets provide only minimal compensation should this occur.

Not surprisingly, the standard of service offered by the low-priced airlines is basic with extras such as food and beverages in the cabin being on sale whereas these items are a standard part of FQA's service. The ratio of cabin staff to passengers of the low-priced airlines is set to provide the minimum levels of cover in accordance with safety legislation. The cabin staff will only carry out the most essential services to satisfy basic passenger comfort.

Nevertheless, the market share of the low-priced airlines is increasing as many passengers are willing to accept lower standards of service for a cheaper flight. Some corporate customers are sending staff on low-priced airlines, especially where it is not essential that the employee arrives at the destination on a particular day.

FQA's Director of Corporate Development together with the Director of Sales and Marketing are presenting a joint paper to the Board which proposes that FQA should now enter the low-priced market on short haul flights at a reduced ticket price. This will be in addition to their normal full-fare services.

Delay in opening of new terminal at the airport in the capital city in FQA's home country

The new airport terminal at FQA's home airport in the capital city, due to be opened on 1 January 2008, is intended for the exclusive use of FQA and will provide the total service requirements for all its flights. Work on the terminal has not gone as well as planned in respect of the new configuration necessary to accommodate the C 491. Infrastructure delays are likely to result in a six-month delay in the terminal becoming operational. However, temporary measures are in place to enable the C491 to be operated from the airport but at significant inconvenience to passengers and staff.

The delay in the new terminal building has attracted much criticism in the press. This is because the existing arrangements operated by FQA in its home airport in the capital city already leads to long queues. There is also under provision of facilities for passengers at the peak holiday period. The Board has accepted that this will continue until the new terminal is opened.

FQA's financial performance

The Chairman of one of the two largest shareholders of FQA is seeking to increase the value of his company (called JJJ) as quickly as possible. This is because JJJ is now subject to a hostile take-over bid. Consequently, the Chairman of JJJ is keen to see an improvement in FQA's short term profits. FQA's Chairman and Chief Executive are resisting attempts by the Chairman of JJJ to publish a higher profit forecast. The Chairman and Chief Executive of FQA recognise however that current year growth in profit attributable to shareholders will not be as great as that achieved in the 2005/06 financial year.

New business opportunities

(i) *Bid for a landing slot on a new route*

The Board is considering tendering for a landing slot on a new route to the USA which is available from January 2009. The process is for airlines to bid for the landing slot. The landing slot is likely to be awarded by the Aviation Authority in the USA to the highest bidder, subject to it meeting the Authority's minimum standards laid down for operating.

(ii) *Opportunity for a new freight contract*

An opportunity has arisen for FQA to tender for a new freight contract. This would necessitate the C 491 being used due to the bulky nature of the highly toxic goods being transported. It has become clear that no other major airline is prepared to transport the goods as they consider them to be a very hazardous cargo. This contract is to a country in Europe, but if the contract were taken it would require significant alteration to two C 491 aircraft in the fleet. This is because FQA would need to guarantee a daily service which cannot be achieved by only one aircraft. This contract is available for two years from 1 January 2009 at first although it may be extended after the two years. The Finance Director has calculated that the contract will provide a cash pay back in the third year of operation and will achieve significant levels of surplus cash flows after that, resulting in a positive NPV at the end of the third year.

APPENDIX B

Extracts from a comparison between Lease and Buy for one C 491

Present value of cash flows for the buy option (that is to purchase outright by borrowing funds at a pre-tax rate of 8%) is -$209 million; that is it will cost $209 million to buy one aircraft in NPV terms based on:

1. An interest rate of 8%;
2. An effective tax rate of 25%;
3. A capital cost of $250 million per aircraft with the capital sum being repaid at the end of 10 years;
4. No re-sale value at the end of the 10 year period.

The NPV of leasing the aircraft is -$268 million based on:

1. Leasing charges of $45 million per year;
2. The first lease payment being made 1 January 2008;
3. A 10 year lease period;
4. An effective tax rate of 25%.

March 2007 – Assessment Matrix for TOPCIMA – Flyqual Airlines

Criterion	Marks	Clear Pass	Pass	Marginal Pass	Marginal Fail	Fail	Clear Fail
Technical	5	Thorough display of relevant technical knowledge. **5**	Good display of relevant knowledge. **4**	Some display of relevant technical knowledge. **3**	Identification of some relevant knowledge, but lacking in depth. **2**	Little knowledge displayed, or some misconceptions. **1**	No evidence of knowledge displayed, or fundamental misconceptions. **0**
Application	10	Knowledge clearly applied in an analytical and practical manner. **9-10**	Knowledge applied to the context of the case. **6-8**	Identification of some relevant knowledge, but not well applied. **5**	Knowledge occasionally displayed without clear application. **3-4**	Little attempt to apply knowledge to the context. **1-2**	No application of knowledge displayed. **0**
Diversity	5	Most knowledge areas identified, covering a wide range of views. **5**	Some knowledge areas identified, covering a range of views. **4**	A few knowledge areas identified, expressing a fairly limited scope. **3**	Several important knowledge aspects omitted. **2**	Many important knowledge aspects omitted. **1**	Very few knowledge aspects considered. **0**
Focus	10	Clearly distinguishes between relevant and irrelevant information. **9-10**	Information used is mostly relevant. **6-8**	Some relevant information ignored, or some less relevant information used. **5**	Information used is sometimes irrelevant. **3-4**	Little ability to distinguish between relevant and irrelevant information. **1-2**	No ability to distinguish between relevant and irrelevant information. **0**
Prioritisation	10	Issues clearly prioritised in a logical order and based on a clear rationale. **9-10**	Issues prioritised with justification. **6-8**	Evidence of issues being listed in order of importance, but rationale unclear. **5**	Issues apparently in priority order, but without a logical justification or rationale. **3-4**	Little attempt at prioritisation or justification or rationale. **1-2**	No attempt at prioritisation or justification. **0**
Judgement	20	Clearly recognises alternative solutions. Judgement exercised professionally. **16-20**	Alternative solutions or options considered. Some judgement exercised. **11-15**	A slightly limited range of solutions considered. Judgement occasionally weak. **10**	A limited range of solutions considered. Judgement sometimes weak. **5-9**	Few alternative solutions considered. Judgement often weak. **1-4**	No alternative solutions considered. Judgement weak or absent. **0**
Integration	10	Diverse areas of knowledge and skills integrated effectively. **9-10**	Diverse areas of knowledge and skills integrated. **6-8**	Knowledge areas and skills occasionally not integrated. **5**	Knowledge areas and skills sometimes not integrated. **3-4**	Knowledge areas and skills often not integrated. **1-2**	Knowledge areas and skills not integrated. **0**
Logic	20	Communication effective, recommendations realistic, concise and logical. **16-20**	Communication mainly clear and logical. Recommendations occasionally weak. **11-15**	Communication occasionally unclear, and/or recommendations occasionally illogical. **10**	Communication sometimes weak. Some recommendations slightly unrealistic. **5-9**	Communication weak. Some unclear or illogical recommendations, or few recommendations. **1-4**	Very poor communication, and/or no recommendations offered. **0**
Ethics	10	Excellent evaluation of ethical aspects. Clear and appropriate advice offered. **9-10**	Good evaluation of ethical aspects. Some appropriate advice offered. **6-8**	Some evaluation of ethical aspects. Advice offered. **5**	Weak evaluation of ethical aspects. Little advice offered. **3-4**	Poor evaluation of ethical aspects. No advice offered. **1-2**	No evaluation of ethical aspects. Unethical, or no, advice offered. **0**
TOTAL	100						

© CIMA – January 2007

Exam focus point

The format of the assessment matrix has changed from September 2008. (See Chapter 2)

Flyqual: answer

20

Introduction

This is the suggested answer to the **March 2007** unseen and requirement, written by BPP Learning Media. Your report will be different to this and may analyse different issues. This is as it should be, there is no one correct answer.

1 Report

To: Board of Flyqual Airlines
From: Independent Consultant
Date: 6 March 2007
Topic: Report on Issues Facing Flyqual

Table of Contents

Appendices

1. Introduction

The airline industry is currently facing many challenges with losses since 2001 in excess of $42 billion and no prospect of improvement. This is due to issues such as the ongoing threat of terrorism and the increase in the industry's fuel bill, which over the last two years has doubled to over US $100bn.

Flyqual Airlines (FQA) must assess its business strategy in order to combat the threats facing the airline industry as a whole and to maximise potential opportunities it may have by being based in the Asia-Pacific Region. In Asia-Pacific almost 10 million transport jobs support US $688bn of economic activity. It is the backbone of tourism and FQA must integrate this with its strategy in order to increase profitability and shareholder value in the future.

2. Terms of reference

This independent consultancy report was commissioned to prioritise, analyse and evaluate the issues currently facing Flyqual Airlines (FQA) and to make appropriate recommendations on how these issues can be resolved and actioned.

3. Review and prioritisation of main issues facing the Board of Flyqual Airlines

3.1 Loss of public confidence due to imminent publicity about poor maintenance – priority number one

The comments from the trade unions suggest that they have seen the independent consultant's report. The Board cannot hope to keep this from the general public or its regulators, the ICAO.

There is a strong likelihood that FQA could be grounded by the authorities or, short of this, that the travelling public will avoid using FQA. The staff may refuse to fly.

This issue presents enormous financial and reputation risks for FQA and an urgent plan is needed to deal with the inevitable and imminent leaking of this report. It must be dealt with immediately.

3.2 Loss of Chair and CEO – priority number two

The recent EGM led to the resignation of FQA's two most senior managers. As a result the company is without effective direction.

A company without clear direction will founder. This is particularly the case with FQA due to the criticism the Board has received for its past stewardship.

This is priority number two because a new CEO and Chair must be in place to enable the Board to decide on the remaining issues identified in this report. However, the first issue is too urgent to await suitable appointments to be made.

3.3 Potential strike action by staff at FQA and amongst staff at suppliers – priority number three

Industrial relations have worsened to the point that a strike by FQA staff is imminent and may threaten sympathy strikes elsewhere.

A strike at FQA would cause immense financial loss and further damage FQA's reputation. Secondary strikes would harm FQA's relations with the government.

This is the third priority because despite being a clear and immediate danger, it must be dealt with at an appropriate level of authority, ie by the CEO and Chair. Therefore, their appointment takes precedence.

3.4 Loss of exclusive landing rights and the need to take advantage of opportunities in emerging economies – priority number four

The loss of exclusive landing rights at its home terminal will subject FQA to greater competitive pressure in its core routes and this will affect financial returns.

Investors have already been critical of FQA's management at the recent EGM, and failure by the Board to bring forward a new strategy to improve financial performance will lead to further pressure from shareholders, who may make the decision to sell-out to a rival.

This is the fourth priority because it is the first step in rebuilding FQA's position following the appointment of the new CEO and Chair and the resolution of potential strike action. Decisions on the type of planes to purchase will need to wait but must take into account the routes currently being developed by FQA.

3.5 Decision on purchases of new aircraft – priority number five

FQA must make its decision on replacements to its fleet by 30 June 2007. The previous financial analysis of the C 491 is compromised and must be updated before this can be done.

The purchase of new aircraft is a significant investment and the choice of aircraft will have implications for the types of routes that FQA can service over the next decade.

This is the fifth priority because the choice of aircraft must be contingent on the decision of what routes to develop in future.

3.6 Other issues

The Board should also be aware of the following issues:

- The lack of control over procurement of fuel means that FQA is paying too much for a major cost item and staff are able to receive bribes
- The poorly-judged comments made by the Director of Sales and Marketing
- The need to restore meals on short-haul flights
- The loss of valuable staff

Ethical issues facing the Board will be discussed in a separate section.

4. Discussion of the main issues facing the Board of Flyqual Airlines

4.1 Loss of public confidence due to imminent publicity about poor maintenance – priority number one

The report of the independent consultant states that 'there were serious faults with maintenance procedures' and that 'it was down to sheer luck that no serious incidents had occurred'.

This means that FQA's aircraft may be viewed as dangerous at the moment. Failure to act on this information immediately is morally indefensible and, in the event of an accident, would almost certainly render the board members individually liable for negligence and FQA liable for corporate manslaughter. In the case of UK independent rail network operator RailTrack, similar lax procedures were the pretext for the firm being pushed into bankruptcy and taken into public ownership by the state. In this case, however, charges such as corporate manslaughter were not brought by the state.

The source of the poor maintenance appears to be the budget-constrained culture within FQA, which ultimately caused the Engineering Director to cut costs and corners. The Board is reminded that FQA's safety record and its reputation for punctuality (also attributable in part to proper maintenance), are the source of revenues, passenger volumes and the political support that are denied other less reputable airlines.

This report will not remain confidential for long. The Board must decide whether to be proactive and face-up to failings of past management or reactive, by which time the damage to FQA's reputation will have taken place.

The resignations of the CEO and Chair provide an opportunity to announce a review of many aspects of FQA by effectively blaming past failings on the recently departed senior managers, justifiably or not.

4.2 Appoint interim Chair and CEO – priority number two

The Chair and CEO of a firm are the persons principally responsible for the governance of the business. The recently-resigned Chair and CEO had clearly lost the support of both shareholders and the Board.

FQA must rebuild an effective Board and strengthen its relationship with investors and wider stakeholders such as employees, suppliers and its national government. Although the CEO and Chair may not have been wholly responsible for the errors of the past, they have been closely associated with FQA's hard line on industrial relations. Therefore they can be treated as scapegoats by the Board and the incoming replacements presented as bringing a fresh approach.

The past practice of FQA has been to appoint Chair and CEO from long-standing management and Board members. This has seemingly led to a lack of fresh ideas on the Board.

The appointment of a Chair from outside FQA would be valuable in signalling fresh ideas and may also change the relations with stakeholders if a more experienced 'safe pair of hands' can be found.

Of the existing Board members, few have significant experience outside FQA. Moreover, FQA's business model, developed shortly after 1945, has come under threat from 'open skies' policies and budget airlines, whilst new opportunities in unfamiliar markets are opening up.

An exception to this is the Finance Director who has experience of developing new airlines and who has a track record of gaining support from investors.

The UK airline British Airways replaced resigned CEO Robert Ayling in 2000, after four years in the post, by external recruits from rival airlines, first Australian Rod Eddington and then Irishman Willie Walsh.

4.3 Avoid strike action by staff at FQA and amongst staff at suppliers – priority number three

Given the history of bad-feeling between unions and the management of FQA, a prolonged strike seems likely.

The figures provided have been summarised in Appendix 4 and show that if the strike continues for more than 12.22 days, persisting with the tough line taken by the outgoing Chair would be financially unfavourable compared with agreeing to the unions' present terms.

This calculation underestimates the adverse financial impact of taking a tough line on industrial relations and risking a strike.

Additional 'costs' would be the loss of revenue in the run-up to the strike as passengers decide to book with other airlines to avoid wildcat action by FQA staff. This may be illustrated by the announcement by BA in February 2007 that a proposed strike by its cabin staff led to revenue losses of £80m (so assuming an exchange rate of $1.4 = £1 this would be $57m) despite the strike being called off a few days before it was due to start.

A strike would lead to further but incalculable loss of business after it ended, in addition to the costs of flying empty planes without cabin crew to ensure they were in the right locations to resume services once the strike was over.

The balance of power and the interests of stakeholders should affect the decision on pay. Appendix 2 presents a stakeholder analysis of the groups interested in the pay claim. It can be seen that, with the exception of FQA management, the remaining groups all favour a settlement rather than strike action.

Failure to avoid the strike could escalate into a general strike at home, in which case the Board's relationship with its home government would be jeopardised, resulting in loss of subsidies and grants and further awards of landing rights to rival airlines. If a general strike were to take place, the government would put pressure on FQA to settle. This could result in the Board paying the whole of the union's claim but only after the financial damage from the strike.

Continuing to pay poorly means that FQA will continue to lose valuable staff which will the make service less reliable and will increase the costs of recruitment and training of replacement staff.

Giving in to union demands will be easier now that the abrasive style of the past can be blamed on the resigned Chair and CEO. However the Board must be careful to avoid being seen to cave in to union pressure in case this encourages more ambitious claims now or in the future. There should be full negotiations.

The Board should consider very carefully the implications of following the investors' instruction to dismiss the Director of Sales and Marketing for her comments if requested to do so by the Union. The ethical aspects will be discussed below. On a practical point it would set an unfortunate precedent to allow management to be hunted out of office by unions. An apology may be in order, but offering directors as sacrifices may be a step too far.

At present the pay claim for $220m represents 29% of 2006 operating profit ($220m/$760m) and a 10.3% pay rise, ie $220m/($10,135m x 21%). It will be difficult to meet this expense. In practice it may be possible to pay less than the union demands, or to phase the payments over several years.

Tying the rise to some productivity gains, or acceptance of more efficient working practices at the new terminal, would offset some of the cost.

4.4 Development of competitive strategy to deal with loss of exclusive landing rights and to take advantage of opportunities in emerging economies – priority number four

Most governments are under pressure from the international community to adopt an 'open skies' policy. In part this is due to pressure from the World Trade Organisation. In the UK the announcement yesterday [*on the day before the actual day of the March 2007 exam*] that BA is to lose some exclusive slots at London Heathrow to US airlines has led to significant falls in its share price.

Exclusive access to the terminal at its home capital city improves the financial performance of FQA. It may also be significant in maintaining FQA's respected position within N Alliance.

The fact that its government is prepared to admit competition for slots does not bode well for the future of FQA. It may suggest a cooling of relations with the government or perhaps indicates a change of policy by its government away from protectionism. It could lead to FQA losing other advantages in due course, or open up a bidding war for slots between rival airlines, which would increase its costs or reduce its capacity.

FQA may consider action against further losses of slots at its home airport by improving its relations with government. The loss of the Chair may have disrupted these relations but the appointment of a new Chair with appropriate political profile may enable improvements to these relations.

The loss of exclusive access to the home capital airport will affect future profits. The extent of this will depend on the nature of the rival operation that commences in July 2007, which appears to be a direct competitor. The Board will appreciate that as an industry with high fixed costs, relatively small reductions in passenger volumes will cause large falls in profits. As an example, the 6.9% increase in revenues between 2005 and 2006 caused a significant, 71%, rise in operating profits. Depending on the routes attacked, it seems likely that FQA will lose substantial volumes to the new rival.

The government has publicly announced its decision to award routes. A similar announcement by the UK authorities yesterday [*ie 5 March, the day before students sat this examination*] led to a 20% fall in the share price of BA, its domestic airline, which had hitherto enjoyed preferential landing rights. For FQA the announcement is unwelcome as it comes at the same time as the resignations of both the CEO and Chair, and rumours of an impending strike action. The Board must urgently restore investor confidence before there is a significant fall in share values.

The loss of exclusive access means FQA needs to consider reducing its reliance on its home 'hub' and consider exploring profitable new markets that do not depend on its home country to the same extent.

The Board is aware of the data forecasting significant transfers of business from the traditional economies of USA and Europe, towards the emerging economies of Asia. These represent opportunities for FQA but will also require changes in FQA's business practices.

FQA has developed as a 'national airline' with close connections to its home country. Developing a business to serve India and China could be seen as simply an extension of this. This is not the case for several reasons:

(a)   Forecasts suggest that in the early years the majority of business in these countries will be internal flights. Running internal flights in India and China will necessitate working with local partners since the Indian and Chinese authorities will not permit businesses which are wholly foreign-owned. FQA has limited experience of working with other airlines. The decision to hold shares in the Asian short-haul subsidiary rather than manage it suggests the Board may be uncomfortable with such joint ventures.

(b)   Initial business will include cargo and, in view of the initially low per capita incomes in these countries, passenger flights may be at lower pricing points than FQA's traditional business. FQA follows a competitive strategy of differentiation focus (Porter) by concentrating on premium passenger business and operating from its homeland hub. Accessing India and China may require a change towards a cost-leadership approach in the early years. Porter has suggested that this may leave firms 'stuck in the middle' and reduce long-term ROI.

(c)   Operating in China and India confronts FQA with additional risks. These are outlined in the PEST analysis in Appendix 3. Taking on these risks, and the potential for reduced profits in the short run whilst the operations develop, may not win the acceptance of FQA's institutional shareholders. As conglomerates, they may prefer the stable incomes suggested by the 49% dividend payout in 2006.

4.5 Decision on purchases of new aircraft – priority number five

A decision on replacement aircraft is needed by June 2007, presumably to enable orders to be placed to reserve aircraft.

Appendix 5 shows the revised NPV for the C 491 taking into account the additional insurance payments in respect of the C 491. It can be seen that the NPV of the C 491 falls from $97m to $59m.

On this basis the C 491 appears the more acceptable option. This is reinforced by the observation that from 2015 the annual lease payments on the F 898 exceed the pre-tax and lease cash flows from its operation.

The aircraft cost different capital amounts, $150m and $250m. This is reflected in the relative size of the lease payments, $30m versus $45m. Basing profitability indices on the capital values, the F 898 returns $0.17 per $1 ($26m/$150m) whilst the C 491 returns $0.24 per $1 ($59m/$250m). Again the C 491 seems more acceptable on economic grounds.

It is surprising to note the comment by the Financial Director that she is confident that future cash flows will meet the commitment of the additional leasing charges. Perhaps group cash flows would be sufficient to pay the lease charges on the F 898, but from 2015 the aircraft would be pulling profits down and draining cash flows. This too may make it an unacceptable option.

Johnson and Scholes provide three criteria for assessing strategic options like this; suitability, acceptability and feasibility. NPV calculations are a test of acceptability, ie that the return on investment in the asset is sufficient to compensate shareholders for the risk of the asset. Both aircraft are acceptable under this analysis.

Suitability concerns fit with FQA's present and future strategy. On some criteria the F 898 seems the more suitable aircraft for present routes. It prioritises the passenger experience which is consistent with FQA's differentiated market position. It is also seemingly better for the environment given its low fuel consumption and lower noise. These are becoming important issues in many US and European cities. The C 491 on the other hand seems to be a noisier aircraft and, in order to run cost effectively, needs to seat 600 passengers and with an increased ratio of passengers to staff, which suggests a lower quality of service.

Another benefit of the F 898 which would make it suitable is its flexibility. It can use conventional airports and so can be used throughout India and China.

However the F 898 has a maximum capacity of 300, which means it would not be suitable for replacing the majority of FQA's present fleet, the 32 C450s and the 56 F 858s because they have much larger seating capacities. Adopting the F 898 would necessitate either more departures, and therefore more planes and landing costs, or reduced volumes of passengers carried. The C 491 is more suitable as a straight replacement for volume.

The increased volumes of traffic forecast to and from Asia and the potential for increased competition to reduce prices, are factors in favour of the C 491. Present day aircraft are able to carry both premium and low fare passengers on the same aircraft. For example BA offers four classes of accommodation on many of its 747 flights; First Class, Club Class, Business Class and World Traveller. The passengers are treated differently in terms of seating, staff attention, quality of food, entertainment and check-in procedures. Configuring the C 491 to operate in the same way on FQA's present routes may enable the present premium business to be sustained, but may also provide a barrier to entry against other airlines that might seek to enter down-market of FQA.

Another factor in favour of the C 491 is that its principle justification lies in lower costs. The two main investors in FQA have requested staff reductions and, to increase their incomes, are seeking to gain more profits from existing operations. They are unlikely to support the reduced volumes associated with adoption of the F 898, but will be more likely to favour the greater efficiency of the C 491.

Feasibility concerns whether a strategic option can be performed (ie is 'do-able'). Both aircraft are affordable. The issues here revolve around the availability of suitable airports for the C 491 and the availability of the planes themselves.

The C 491 requires specially converted airports. It seems unlikely that any but the main hub airports will be converted. This means running the C 491 may be suitable for most of FQA's existing 100 destinations but not beyond these for the time being.

The other issue is whether the planes will be ready in time. Both the new Airbus 380 and the Boeing 787, similar to these planes, are running late due to problems with new alloys or project management difficulties. Several airlines are cancelling their orders and instead opting to buy upgraded versions of existing aircraft such as the Boeing 777 or the new 'fat boy' 737. The same fate may affect either the C 491 or the F 898. There is insufficient data given to assess whether one or other aircraft is more likely to be ready on time.

The Board may like to draw a distinction between the choice of planes to replace those used in current operations and planes for new operations. It may be possible to adopt the C 491 to insulate FQA from the price competition on present routes, but transfer existing planes to emerging economies or, perhaps, adopt the F 898 for these in due course.

4.6 Other issues

The following issues were outlined in Section 3 above:

- Poor procurement practices
- The poorly-judged comments made by the Director of Sales and Marketing
- The need to restore meals on short-haul flights
- The loss of valuable staff

Fuel accounts for 30% of FQA's operating costs. A single senior member of procurement has been able to authorise a contract in return for a bribe. The ethical context of this is dealt with in a separate section below. Here it is noted as signifying poor financial controls which may be the tip of the iceberg.

It has been mentioned already that it would be inadvisable to allow the Director of Sales and Marketing to be witch-hunted by the unions. It would set a bad precedent of allowing unions and investors to dictate management appointments. It would also deplete the Board at a crucial time.

The loss of valuable staff may be avoided by agreement to new pay terms and the setting of better systems for rewarding performance.

The meals on short-haul flights may be less important than for long-haul but they are part of a differentiated airline's service offering. Reliance on single contractors does bring the risk of default or failure. A policy of multi-sourcing would be better as would the negotiation of better contracts and service level agreements to deal with this sort of eventuality.

5. Ethical issues to be addressed by the Board of Flyqual Airlines

Ethical issues concern matters of conscience and of moral right and wrong. This report identifies several ethical issues surrounding the present situation of FQA. The Board will be aware that it must balance ethical action with commercial considerations and these have been outlined below and recommendations made.

5.1 Sacking of technicians.

The three technicians seem to have been sacked for the consequences arising from bad maintenance procedures.

This is unjust because as employees within a system, they were merely following the direction of management. The Consultant's report seems to point to a failing by the Engineering Director and his team.

It appears that the Engineering Director has been covering up and misleading the Board given that the findings of the independent consultant contradicts the assurances he has given to the Board.

The treatment of these technicians has added to union and staff mistrust of management and has further poisoned the industrial relations atmosphere.

The continuation of poor maintenance at FQA is a breach of the duty of care of management for its staff and passengers which would have significant ethical and commercial implications.

This report recommends that the technicians be re-instated but suspended pending a further report into maintenance procedures at FQA. The Engineering Director should also be suspended until the findings of this report can be assessed. If it is found that the Engineering Director has been in breach of his duties and has lied to the Board he should be invited to resign.

It is also recommended that FQA's procedures for dismissals be reviewed to ensure they provide mechanisms for unbiased hearing of evidence in cases like this to avoid summary dismissals in future.

5.2 Offering of bribe for fuel contracts.

If this allegation by the investor is true, it represents corruption by the member of purchasing staff. They are using their position to line their own pockets at the expense of shareholders. The fuel supplier has also acted unethically by offering such bribes to FQA staff.

The member of staff should be informed of the allegation and then suspended, pending an internal investigation.

If the investigation reveals that the allegation is correct, the Board might feel obliged to pass the matter over to the authorities to prosecute both the supplier and the employee for fraud. However, in doing this, the Board should be aware that such an action will reveal a lack of control within the company.

This report recommends that, in the event of the allegation being found true, the employee should be dismissed without compensation. The supplier should be requested to pay over a sum at least equal to the excess costs of fuel as an alternative to facing court action.

The Board needs to ensure that the corporate code makes it clear that accepting bribes is a dismissable offence.

5.3 Potential victimisation of the Director of Sales and Marketing.

The unguarded comments of the Director are regrettable but are also unsubstantiated, save for the word of an FQA employee. However, it is not reasonable for the Director to be made a scapegoat for the general union discontent, given that her remit is marketing and hence it is unlikely that the policies being objected to were created by her.

This report recommends that the Director of Sales and Marketing be interviewed by the Board about her alleged comments and, if made, that she be invited to publicly apologise for them.

The sacking of the member of staff who relayed the comments also has an ethical element. This member of staff may feel they were a whistleblower and that leaking a private conversation to the press was their moral duty. It is hard to see that leaking the comments served any moral purpose at all. However, it is a clear breach of a duty of obedience to management and looks like mischief-making.

It is recommended that the staff member does not get reappointed or compensated for this breach of confidentiality.

It is also recommended that a code be established for 'whistleblowing' that designates a non-executive director as the correct recipient for such issues. It should also make it clear that alerting the media, regulators or others to such issues without first seeking action through this mechanism, would constitute gross misconduct and be a dismissable offence.

5.4 Team leader's reluctance to recalculate NPV for C 491

Accountants have an ethical obligation to present information that has integrity and is objective. The insurance payments due in respect of the C 491 have a material impact on its attractiveness and the calculations could have misled the Board.

It is recommended that the Team Leader be presented with Appendix 5 and asked to explain his decision to withhold these facts. He should be formally reprimanded for knowingly failing to provide accurate information.

6. Recommendations

6.1 Report on poor maintenance procedures

An urgent action task force should be convened immediately under the auspices of the Engineering Director, but with participation of representatives of the ICAO to help restore its confidence and that of the public and staff.

The independent consultant should identify specific procedures that were found to be defective and the consequences of these (eg aircraft affected, systems on aircraft affected). This should be done within three days.

Affected planes should be inspected immediately and safety vouched, or remedial maintenance undertaken. If the risks are found to be of sufficient importance, taking into account likelihood and potential impact, then flights may need to be suspended.

The task force should start work immediately on a contingency plan for the event of 20%, 30% and 50% of the fleet being grounded. This should include identification of which flights will continue, how passengers may be transferred to alternative carriers, and compensation. This should remain strictly confidential as it may not be needed.

A public relations protocol needs to be agreed. It is vital that the trade unions be involved and that it be made clear to them that divulging the contents of the report will threaten the future of FQA and therefore the security of their members' jobs.

6.2 Loss of Chair and CEO

The Board should appoint an interim CEO and Chair as soon as possible.

Investor confidence has been battered and there are important decisions on staffing to be taken to avoid a strike. There are also decisions on new aircraft to be taken in June and competition commencing from July. The business and the Board need direction.

It is recommended that a committee of Non-Executive Directors be convened to oversee the appointment of interim CEO and Chair and to oversee the search for, and appointment of, permanent successors.

It is recommended that the present Finance Director be offered the role of interim CEO on the basis of her experience within and also outside FQA. If she accepts, the Board must identify a suitable member of the Finance team to take over the operational duties of the FD during the transition.

It is recommended that the new CEO be allowed one year in post to see through the present problems and then to resign and put herself forward for re-election at the next AGM.

It is recommended that a present Non-Executive Director assume the role of Acting Chair but that Executive Search organisations be briefed to locate candidates with the correct profile of acceptability to government and investors, such as the Chair of other firms or former senior politicians.

6.3 Potential Strike Action

The Board should use the departure of the CEO and Chair as an opportunity to open renewed and more constructive talks with the unions and FQA. This must be done with the intention of avoiding a strike in the immediate term and to negotiate affordable pay rises based upon improvements to efficiency going forward.

This is recommended because FQA cannot afford the costs of a prolonged strike nor the damage to relations that would come from an escalating strike.

The new Chair and CEO should set up a meeting with trade unions at the earliest opportunity. The offer of this meeting may forestall strike action or, if still called, would enable FQA to present the unions as unreasonable and so potentially stop the spread of the strike.

The Chair should also take the opportunity to signal a change of attitude by making warm comments about the importance and quality of FQA's staff. This would also put distance between the Board's negotiation stance and the attitudes attributed to the Director of Sales and Marketing.

Such warm words, or indeed an apology from the Director of Sales and Marketing, are symbolic gestures that will signal a climb-down by the Board. It would pacify unions, investors, government and the management of C.

An initial offer of 5% could be made as a negotiation ploy with more promised in the event of productivity improvements. This needs to be judged carefully in the light of the 'going rate' for the industry. Too low an offer would convince unions that management were not serious and may trigger a strike rather than avoid it.

6.4 Loss of landing slots and new opportunities

The Board needs to take steps to reduce costs of flights to and from its home airport and to launch promotional activity to spoil the launch of the rival from July 2007. They need to explore ways to enter the Indian and/or Chinese markets.

This is due to the reductions in profit on present routes resulting from increased competitive rivalry. Also the opportunities in emerging economies allow the Board to escape the intensifying rivalry in its present business.

A sub-committee of the Board should be formed charged with developing a strategy to spoil the launch of the rival. This strategy could include promotional activity emphasising FQA's quality and punctuality, improvements to cabin service and check-in, and announcements of new aircraft to show confidence to the home government and investors. Price reductions should be avoided in favour of other incentives such as enhanced menus, improved baggage allowances, free tickets for partners etc or gifts. These measures would enhance rather than detract from FQA's image.

High level contacts with the domestic government should be set up to encourage them not to award any further slots to rival airlines. The approach to be taken is to assure them of FQA's commitment to the domestic economy and its intention to help improve the terminals for use by the new generation of planes. A decision to buy the C 491 for these routes may help 'oil the wheels' as it will provide jobs to industry in the home country. Also the provision of forecasts showing the likely impact on FQA's viability if competition increases may help convince the government to restrict competition.

Entry into the Indian and Chinese markets must be undertaken in conjunction with local partners. It is recommended that a joint venture company be established for each country that would enable local partners to participate, but also keep the new operation distinct from the established FQA business in the minds of staff and travellers. This may be essential given the likelihood that it will operate in a different way.

It also seems likely that the present investors in FQA may not wish to invest in this new business. For that reason separate financing, perhaps using the investment capital expertise of the Finance Director (and interim CEO), may be advisable.

The Board should set up a project team to research the Indian and Chinese market and to identify suitable potential joint-venture partners. The FD/CEO should make preliminary enquiries amongst present shareholders and banks to assess funding sources.

6.5 Decision on new aircraft

It is recommended that the June orders be placed for the C 491 but that in the long run, a mix of the two aircraft be adopted to allow flexibility.

The new aircraft are required to replace aging aircraft on FQA's existing routes. Given the potential price pressure and need for lower costs this, and the higher NPV of the aircraft, mean that the C 491 will be better able to compete.

A second benefit of adopting the C 491 is that it will provide jobs in the home country and so improve government relations and potentially forestall further allocation of slots to rivals. Similar issues have been rumoured in the UK where BA has been pressured to adopt the A380 plane because it is European and because its wings are made in the UK.

It is recommended that FQA develops a range of service levels from First Class to Economy Class to ensure these larger planes are full and that they can compete against potential entrants at different price points.

This decision doesn't preclude the ordering of F 898s for use in the future, particularly for serving India and China. However, as stated above, this will need to be a joint venture and hence the decision on aircraft for these countries will be left to the management of the joint venture and not the Board of FQA.

It is recommended that discounts be obtained from C because, as a well-respected airline, FQA can help the C 491 become adopted as an industry standard and this will be of benefit to C.

7. Conclusions

The future of FQA depends on restoring management, avoiding a strike and coping with competition. The recommendations of this report indicate ways in which this can be done.

Appendix 1 – SWOT analysis

Strengths	Weaknesses
Reputation for safe and punctual service	No Chair or CEO in post
Preferential (but no-longer exclusive) access to home airport	Very poor industrial relations
Access to 500 destinations via membership of the N Alliance	Poor judgement of the Director of Sales and Marketing
	Poor financial controls leading to bad investment appraisal and the giving of bribes

Opportunities	Threats
Potential new markets in India and China	Loss of public confidence due to publicity surrounding poor maintenance
Improvements to efficiency from purchase of new aircraft	Strike action by FQA staff and other workers in home country
Able to put past behind them with investors and staff by blaming outgoing Chair and CEO for failings	Further pressure for changes to management by institutional shareholders
	Greater competition on routes due to loss of exclusive landing rights

Appendix 2 – Stakeholder analysis of pay claim

Key Players (High power and high interest)	Keep satisfied (High power and low interest)
Institutional investors – favour a settlement to avoid strike	C manufacturers – favour settlement to allow negotiations over sale of aircraft
Trade unions – able to cost $30m a day and favour a settlement	N Alliance – want to be able to rely on FQA for business but also to carry transferred passengers
The Board of FQA – wish to avoid expense of settlement but also costs of strike	Staff – are leaving due to poor pay and bad management style
FQA home government – favour settlement to avoid national strike	

Keep informed (High interest and low power)	Minimal effort
Other investors – concerned with profit impact of deal	Resigned executives – might prefer to avoid being blamed for present industrial relations problems
Passengers – want normal service	

Appendix 3 – PEST Analysis of extension to India and China

Political	Economic
Different legal regimes which may lead to restrictions on actions or fines for non-compliance Protectionist governments suspicious of foreign investment Potential for trade wars between China and USA which could drag in businesses like FQA that seek to deal with both	Rapid economic expansion although prone to recessions. For example the indications of recession in China in early March contributed to considerable declines in world equity markets Exchange rate volatility. Neither country yet has freely convertible currencies Difficulties in obtaining profits from operations in these countries due to exchange controls
Social	**Technological**
Different customs and languages in China and India will necessitate changes to staffing and operations of FQA World concerns over human rights records of China may lead to backlash against it and against firms suspected of profiting from it	Limited airport infrastructures in rural areas Poor availability of ground service in some areas

Appendix 4 – Evaluation of effect of strike action

Lost contribution per day due to strike action: $30m x 60% = $18m

Cost of settling pay claims $220m per year

Number of days lost until settling more cost effective than allowing strike $220m/$18m = 12.22 days

	$m
Lost revenue per day	30
Less variable costs	(12)
Impact per day	18
Cost of resolving strike	220
Days of strike	12
Current revenue	10,895
1% reduction in revenue from lost goodwill	109
1% reduction in op profit from lost goodwill	65
2% reduction in revenue from lost goodwill	218
2% reduction in op profit from lost goodwill	131
4% reduction in revenue from lost goodwill	436
4% reduction in op profit from lost goodwill	261

Appendix 5 – Financial comparison of C 491 with F 898

Revised NPV for C 491

	0	1	2	3	4	5	6	7	8	9	10
	$m	$m	$m	$m	$m	$m	$m	$m	$m	$m	$m
Extra Insurance (paid in advance)	(6.00)	(6.30)	(6.62)	(6.95)	(7.30)	(7.67)	(8.05)	(8.45)	(8.87)	(9.31)	
Tax saved from insurance cost		1.50	1.58	1.66	1.74	1.83	1.92	2.01	2.11	2.22	2.33
Net additional insurance cost	(6.00)	(4.80)	(5.04)	(5.29)	(5.56)	(5.84)	(6.13)	(6.44)	(6.76)	(7.09)	2.33
DF @ 10%	1.00	0.909	0.826	0.751	0.683	0.621	0.564	0.513	0.467	0.424	0.386
PV	(6.00)	(4.36)	(4.16)	(3.97)	(3.80)	(3.6£)	(3.46)	(3.30)	(3.16)	(3.01)	0.90

NPV of extra insurance = $37.95m call it $38m

NPV per original appraisal = $97m

Less NPV of insurance = ($38m)

Revised NPV = $59m

Kadgee
September and November 2006

Kadgee: pre-seen data

Introduction

This chapter includes the 'pre-seen' data for Kadgee, examined in September and November 2006.

CIMA

P10 – Test of Professional Competence in Management Accounting
Monday 4 September 2006

PRE-SEEN MATERIAL, PROVIDED IN ADVANCE FOR PREPARATION AND STUDY FOR THE EXAMINATION TO BE HELD ON MONDAY 6 MARCH
INSTRUCTIONS FOR POTENTIAL CANDIDATES
This booklet contains the pre-seen case material for the March 2006 examination. It will provide you with the contextual information that will help you prepare yourself for the examination on Monday 6 March.
The TOPCIMA Assessment Matrix, which your script will be marked against, is available as a separate document which will also be e-mailed to you.
You may not take this copy of the pre-seen material into the examination hall. A fresh copy will be provided for you in the examination hall.
Unseen material will be provided for the examination: this will comprise further context and the examination question.
The examination will last for three hours. You will be allowed 20 minutes reading time **before the examination begins** during which you should read the question paper and, if you wish, make annotations on the question paper. However, you will **not** be allowed, **under any circumstances**, to begin using your computer to produce your answer, or to use your calculator during the reading time.
You will be required to answer ONE question which may contain more than one element.

© The Chartered Institute of Management Accountants 2006

LEARNING MEDIA

Kadgee Clothing

Clothing manufacturing in Europe

1   Since the 1960s there has been a decline in the number of UK and European clothing manufacturers due to competition from cheaper, and sometimes higher quality, imported clothes. The clothing industry generally has become much more fashion conscious and price sensitive. This has led to a reduced number of companies that are still in business in Europe. Some companies have moved all or part of their manufacturing processes to other countries to achieve a cheaper operating base, and up until recently this has allowed them to continue to compete on price.

2   Many companies have had contracts to supply High Street retailers for over four decades and are highly dependant on retaining these key customers who wield immense buying power over the small manufacturers. A number of family owned manufacturing companies, that had been highly profitable once, have ceased trading, or are operating at very low margins, as a direct result of the High Street retailers being able to dictate terms of business and prices.

3   An additional factor that has put the main High Street retailers under more price pressure has been the appearance and market growth of new High Street retailers and their new brands, who have procured their goods mainly from overseas sources.

4   The result is that the few companies that are based in the UK and Europe which are left in the business of clothing manufacturing are having to look very hard at their strategic plans in order for them to manage to maintain their business over the next few years.

History of Kadgee Fashions (Kadgee)

5   Kadgee was formed in post-World War Two in a European country, and has remained as an unlisted company, although its shares are now held by others outside of the founding family. Kadgee quickly established itself as a high quality manufacturer of both mens and ladies clothes. It had no difficulty selling its products to retailers, as the demand for ready-to-wear clothing was very high during the 1950s and 1960s. Kadgee recruited several designers who based their designs on famous designer labels, but without causing any copyright breaches.

6   By the 1960s Kadgee had a turnover equivalent to €25 million, and had nine factories operating in two European countries. The founder of Kadgee, Bruno Burnak, wanted to expand the manufacturing base and introduce new machinery, but the then Sales Director had considered that the company should continue to establish a stronger customer base before Kadgee expanded and invested further. Each of Kadgee's factories then employed between 70 and 100 employees, who were mainly female employees, with many working part-time. Some of the employees had a range of specialised skills and were considered to be very experienced. Kadgee's Head Office was run by the then Managing Director, Anton Kramer.

7   During the late 1960s Kadgee suffered its first major fall in sales, and found that it had large stocks of men's clothes that had been manufactured without specific sales contracts. Kadgee managed to sell off some of the stocks, albeit at below cost price. However, the management decided that it should not manufacture clothes without a firm contract from a retailer in future. The company had been caught unaware and had believed that the previous high demand for its products would continue.

8   In the early 1970s the range and design of its mens clothing was changed several times, but it continued to make little profit. In 1973, Kadgee sold its mens clothing range and designs and some of its manufacturing equipment to a large listed company. Kadgee decided to concentrate on expanding its ranges of ladies clothing to meet the growing demands of its main customers (see below). The reduced range of clothing, following the termination of all manufacturing of men's clothing, necessitated closing three of its factories. This left Kadgee with six factories operational in 1973.

9   During the next few years, Kadgee consolidated its position and its profitability increased again. In the early 1980s its then Chief Designer persuaded the Managing Director to expand its clothing range to include a range of girls' clothes. This new limited range was launched in 1982 and was immediately sold out, as many of Kadgee's customers realised that there was a demand for well designed and well finished children's clothing. Kadgee has positioned itself at the upper price range of clothing, and has never tried to mass produced low cost clothing.

10 During the 1980s Kadgee continued to expand its ranges of ladies and girls' clothes, but retained the same manufacturing base of six factories. New equipment had been installed and the overall manufacturing capacity at the six factories had been increased by over 20% due to new sewing and packaging machinery. A further change that occurred was that many of Kadgee's customers were starting to dictate the styles and types of clothing required and Kadgee's designers had to manufacture to customers' specifications.

11 However, during the 1990s Kadgee suffered a number of setbacks. It also saw many of its competitors suffer losses and cease trading. Kadgee had been able to stay profitable only because of its particular customer base and because it sold high quality clothes that commanded a premium price. However, Kadgee saw its margins on many product lines reduced greatly and also it started to lose many of its smaller customers, who choose to import, at much lower prices, clothing produced in Asia.

12 Bruno Burnak, the founder and then Chairmen of Kadgee retired in 1997 and his son Andrin Burnak took over as Chairman. Furthermore, the Managing Director, Anton Kramer left in 1998, and Andrin Burnak undertook this role in addition.

Kadgee's shareholders

13 Kadgee has remained an unlisted company and at the end of 2005 its shares were held as follows:

	Shareholding (%)
Bruno Burnak	29
Andrin Burnak	29
Anton Kramer	1
Dieter Stutt	8
Frankie Bayane	2
Andre Schnaffer	10
Employee-held shares	12
	100

14 The company has 200,000 shares of €0·10 each in issue and has a total of 400,000 authorised shares.

15 The shares are not traded but the last time the shares were exchanged was in 1998, when Frankie Bayane purchased shares at €8·00 each.

Kadgee's customer base

16 Kadgee manufactures clothing for a number of European and international clothing retailers, including many well known High Street retailers. It manufactures clothing in the medium to higher price ranges and its customers require top quality designs and finishing to maintain their brand reputation. Kadgee has several contracts that were established over 40 years ago, although it has two contracts that have been secured within the last 10 years. Kadgee still manufactures ladies' and children's clothing for two retailers who had selected Kadgee in the 1980s, when the children's range had first been launched.

17 The majority of Kadgee's clothing is manufactured for its customers under the customers' own label, for example, clothing manufactured for one of its customers called Portrait is labelled as 'Portrait'.

18 In 2005, Kadgee's customer base, analysed by sales value, was as follows:

	2005 revenue € million	% of Kadgee's total sales %
Portrait	24·0	32·3
Forum	16·8	22·6
Diamond	13·5	18·1
Zeeb	5·1	6·9
JayJay	4·5	6·0
Other retailers of ladies' clothes	7·3	9·8
Haus (children's clothes only)	3·2	4·3
Total	74·4	100·0

19   Most of Kadgee's contracts are renewed at the start of each fashion season. Kadgee is currently negotiating for clothing sales for the summer season of 2007.

Human Resources

20   In the clothing manufacturing business one of the most crucial aspects to achieve customer satisfaction is quality. Kadgee has been very fortunate in having a skilled, very dedicated workforce who have always adapted to new machinery and procedures and have been instrumental in suggesting ways in which quality could be improved. This has sometimes involved a very minor change in the design of a garment and the designers now work much more closely with the operational staff to ensure that the garments can be assembled as quickly and efficiently as possible.

21   The employees include a number of very talented people, whose skills are highly valued by the management team at Kadgee. There are five very highly skilled sewing machine operatives whose parents previously worked for Kadgee and they have passed their skills on. The machinery that is used to sew garments is very sophisticated but it is always the skills of the machine operatives which can make the difference to a finished garment. Additionally, Kadgee has always completed certain finishing touches by hand and this quality is appreciated by its customers. Kadgee is dependent on the skills of its employees to continue to deliver the same high quality on which it has established its reputation.

Losses made by Kadgee

22   Kadgee has suffered from falling operating profit margins due to the pressure exerted by its customers over the last ten years. For the first time in Kadgee's history, it experienced losses for five years starting in 1998 through to, and including, 2002. During this time Kadgee increased its loans and its overdraft to finance operations.

23   In 2000, Kadgee refinanced with a ten year loan, which was used to repay existing debt, and also to invest in the IT solutions discussed below, as well as to purchase some new machinery. Kadgee also invested in its design centre (see below), which was completed in 2001.

24   During 2001, the company invested in new IT solutions enabling its customers to be able to track all orders from the garment cutting process right through to completion of garments and through to the delivery to customers' premises.

25   The IT solutions also enabled Kadgee to monitor its production processes including machine usage, wastage at various stages of production and speed of production through the various stages. This has enabled Kadgee's management to reduce areas that did not add value to the finished garment. The use of TQM throughout the business has also increased Kadgee's efficiency and enabled it to eliminate some other areas which did not add value to the finished garments.

26   While margins are still low, Kadgee has been operating profitably again since 2003, albeit at lower margins to those achieved in the past.

27   Kadgee's employees have also taken an active role in increasing the throughput of garments and speeding up the manufacturing process. In fact, many of the changes made were at the instigation of key employees, who understood the actual processes and were able to identify where there were bottlenecks which caused delays. The reasons for the delays were reduced, leading to a faster manufacturing process. This enabled Kadgee to increase its annual number of garments manufactured from 8.25 million in 1998 to 10·9 million in 2005.

28   The consequences of some of the changes meant that some employees were made redundant at Kadgee's factories, and these were often part time workers, who worked fewer than 16 hours per week. The Kadgee management team fully understood that many of its skilled employees are female and that they do not wish to work full-time. However, Kadgee now do not employ anyone for fewer than 24 hours per week, and over half of the employees in the factories now work full-time. Many of these employees chose to work full-time rather than face redundancy. When employees are made redundant, Kadgee is legally bound to pay redundancy payments, which are payments made to employees as compensation for future salary payments, which are paid at the point when the employee's contract of employment ceases.

29. Many other European clothing manufacturers have ceased trading and Kadgee's employees have concerns that they would not find any other employment within their specialised field in the local area. Therefore, they chose to stay with Kadgee, but are working longer hours than perhaps they wish to.

Loss of sales contract with Forum

30. Forum is one of Kadgee's key customers and in 2005 generated revenues of €16·8 million, which is almost 23% of Kadgee's total revenue. The operating profit achieved on sales to Forum, in 2005, was €0·3 million. The operating profit on sales to Forum has been severely eroded over the last few years, with some product lines barely generating a positive margin at all.

31. Forum has over 50 retail stores throughout Europe and Kadgee has manufactured clothes for Forum since the early 1950's. The latest contract negotiations looked promising despite an expected price cut. Dieter Stutt, the Sales Director, felt that a price cut of 4% could be agreed. He had forecast that some of this lost operating profit could be recouped with cost savings that could be made in packaging and reduced material costs.

32. However, in the middle of April 2006, Forum's Managing Director contacted Andrin Burnak directly to state that Forum would no longer be purchasing clothes from Kadgee from the end of May 2006. Andrin Burnak was astounded that one of Kadgee's oldest customers was giving a mere six weeks notice of the termination of the supply contract. Following various high level negotiations, Forum has since agreed to extend the current sales contract though to the end of August 2006. After this date Forum will no longer purchase any clothing from Kadgee.

33. The loss of the Forum contract was announced to Kadgee employees during May 2006, before it was announced in the national press. Employees were naturally concerned about their jobs. Staff morale is low and the quality of the clothing currently being produced is lower than normal.

34. It is expected that initially there will be 34 redundancies in September 2006, affecting three of Kadgee's factories as a result of the loss of this major customer. Further job cuts are likely later in 2006 at the three factories which have manufactured the range of clothing for Forum.

35. Andrin Burnak has requested Peter Coletta, the Factory Operations Director, to take action to ensure that Kadgee's quality does not fall. Dieter Stutt is very concerned that two other major customers of Kadgee may try to use the excuse of falling quality to reduce their purchase price for further clothing contracts, following the discovery of a number of faults from recent production.

Changes in the supply chain

36. Many of Kadgee's customers have needed to speed up the process of supplying clothing to their shops, so as to meet the demands of the market and to remain competitive. Kadgee has worked closely with its customers in order to achieve shorter lead times from design to delivery of finished products.

37. In 2001, Kadgee introduced a new design centre, centralised at its Head Office. The design centre uses computer aided design techniques, which has helped Kadgee's customers to appreciate the finished appearance of new designs. Andrin Burnak is confident that this has helped Kadgee to win new business and to retain its current customers.

38. It has also contributed to Kadgee's ability to speed up the process from design board to finished article. Kadgee has also benefited from working closer with its customers and this has resulted in additional orders, which Kadgee's customers' would otherwise have procured from overseas sources.

Growing competition from China

39. During the 1990s and into the 21st century China has had a massive impact on the textile industry. China's manufacturing base is forecast to grow further and this will have a negative impact on many companies operating at a higher cost base elsewhere.

40. Many European companies have spent millions of Euros establishing manufacturing bases outside their home countries in the last 15 years. Many have opened factories in countries which have much lower operating costs. These include countries such as Turkey, Sri Lanka and Pakistan, as well as Eastern European countries.

41 The companies which have set up operations in these low cost countries did so in an effort to cut costs by taking advantage of low overheads and lower labour rates, but still managed to maintain quality. However, even the companies that have moved some, or all, of their manufacturing bases and have taken steps to reduce their costs, now have to reconsider their cost base again. This is because of the very low cost of Chinese imports, which they are having difficulty competing against.

42 Following the relaxation of trade barriers, there has recently been a deluge of Chinese clothing imports into Europe, the UK and the USA.

43 The quality of Chinese manufactured clothing is improving rapidly and it is now globally recognised that the 'Made in China' label represents clothing of a higher quality than many European manufactured garments. Furthermore, the Chinese manufactured garments are being produced at a substantially lower manufacturing cost.

44 Kadgee has so far been operating in a market that has not been significantly affected by imported goods, as it produces medium to higher priced clothing, rather than cheaper ranges of clothes. However, many of Kadgee's customers are now looking to reduce their costs by either buying more imported clothes or by negotiating substantial price cuts from their existing suppliers. The purchasing power of European retailers being exerted on its suppliers is immense and Kadgee is under much pressure to deliver high quality goods at reduced operating profit margins from all of its customers.

Appendix 1

Kadgee personnel

Bruno Burnak – Founder and first Chairman

45 Bruno Burnak retired from Kadgee in 1997, aged 75, but has kept a close personal interest in the company that he founded in 1947 using family finances. His son Andrin Burnak is the current Chairman and Managing Director. The Burnak family is very entrepreneurial and Bruno Burnak's brother founded another company after the Second World War, which is also still trading profitably. Bruno Burnak has still retained his 29% shareholding in Kadgee.

Anton Kramer – First Managing Director

46 Anton Kramer retired from Kadgee in 1998, as he felt that he did not have the necessary skills to direct the company into the 21st century. However, he has retained his 10% shareholding in the company and has confidence that Andrin Burnak will manage to increase Kadgee's profitability to the levels previously attained.

Andrin Burnak – Current Chairman and Managing Director

47 Andrin Burnak, son of the founder Bruno Burnak had studied textiles and had worked in another European country for over 10 years for a large clothing manufacturer. He returned home in 1993 and joined the family company. He took over as Chairman and Managing Director when his father retired in 1997. Andrin Burnak was concerned that the clothing manufacturing industry was undergoing rapid changes, and he was confident that he could introduce the changes that would be required in order for Kadgee to remain successful.

Dieter Stutt – Sales Director

48 Dieter Stutt, now 39, had worked in sales for a number of clothing manufacturers before Andrin Burnak recruited him in 1999. He has had a challenging time since joining Kadgee, not only trying to secure new sales contracts and negotiate on prices, but has had to fight to retain Kadgee's current customers.

49 Dieter Stutt has established very good relationships with many of the key personnel in all of Kadgee's customers' companies. He has spent a lot of time personally dealing with several layers of management at all of Kadgee's customers, to ensure that Kadgee can deliver what they want when they require it. His excellent reputation has enabled Kadgee to be one step ahead of many of the customers' requests. In many instances Dieter Stutt would have already established what the customers wants, or fed back to his colleagues some comments on current deliveries. He has often found out about the demand level for a

particular product line, or the need for a wider range of colours or perhaps fabric changes, from a manager within a customers' company, before Kadgee even receives the manufacturing order. This has enabled Kadgee to be seen to be meeting many of its customers' requests promptly and efficiently, due to Dieter Stutt's established connections.

Frankie Bayane – Chief Designer

50 Frankie Bayane, aged 35, joined Kadgee in 1998 from a rival manufacturing company. She has a degree in textiles and design and she first worked for a top couture house in France for three years and gained much experience. When she joined Kadgee, the two areas that she considered would have an impact on sales would be to increase the 'speed to the market' from design board to finished product at the retailer and to use the latest computer design technology to create designs. She considered that Kadgee had been too slow in the past reacting to changes in trends and latest fashions, and that there was a need to have a greater number of designs and smaller production runs, thereby giving customers a wider range of products to order. Frankie Bayane has trained and recruited a small team of designers over the last eight years who have worked closely with Kadgee's customers.

Andre Schnaffer – Finance Director

51 Andre Schnaffer, aged 48, has held the role of Finance Director for the last four years when the previous Finance Director retired early due to ill health. He has worked for Kadgee for over 18 years and prior to that had worked for several companies in a range of finance roles, all related to the clothing business. He has a good working relationship with Andrin Burnak, who trusts Andre Schnaffer's cautious judgement.

52 Andre Schnaffer has managed to renegotiate bank loans and has extended credit arrangements with many of Kadgee's material suppliers and this has helped Kadgee to manage its cash flow during several difficult trading periods.

53 Andre Schnaffer is very concerned over the number of rival manufacturing companies which have ceased trading, and he is very worried about the increasing pressure to reduce margins, which are very low already.

Sam Skala – Marketing Director

54 Until 2003, all marketing was undertaken by the Sales Director, but Dieter Stutt identified that all of his time was taken up in negotiating and securing sales and the important role of marketing was being neglected. Dieter Stutt pushed hard to get the Marketing Director role established, at a time when Andrin Burnak wanted to reduce management costs.

55 Sam Skala had established his reputation when he worked for a High Street retailer of ladies' clothing, which had expanded rapidly in the nine years he had held the role of Marketing Manager. Previous to that, he had worked in marketing for an international sportswear company. When he joined Kadgee he had hoped that the high quality of Kadgee's products and its ability to bring the latest products to the market quickly would enable him to establish its brand into many more high street retail chains. To date he has not been very successful in identifying new customers, but he has undertaken extensive, and much needed market research to try to establish gaps in the market for clothing manufacture.

Peter Coletta – Factory Operations Director

56 Peter Coletta, aged 52, has worked for several clothing manufacturers and joined Kadgee in 2001 when he was made redundant from his last company when it ceased trading following a severe downturn in business. He is very aware of the need to maintain quality and to reduce costs, having worked for his previous employer for over 15 years and seen the company decline due to competitive pressures. He has brought with him a wealth of operational experience and is well respected by all of the factories' employees, as well as by fellow directors. He has been instrumental in introducing improved working conditions and the use of TQM quality circles is as popular now as when it was first introduced in Kadgee by Peter Coletta's predecessor in 1990. The use of TQM has enabled Kadgee to be forever searching for new innovative ways to improve both the speed and quality of its output.

Lars Veel – Human Resource Director

57   Lars Veel, now 52, joined Kadgee in 1994, but he has not acquired any shares in the company. He has helped Kadgee to achieve increased employee efficiency and has seen the company's manufacturing capacity (in terms of the number of garments manufactured) rise by over 32% in the last seven years, still utilising the same six factories. This increase in Kadgee's manufacturing capacity has been achieved by changed work patterns, reduced wastage, changed factory layouts and much greater motivation by almost all of Kadgee's employees.

58   Lars Veel is very concerned for the future of Kadgee's employees, and understands the strains that have been put on them by high speed output and the need to maintain Kadgee's excellent quality reputation. He has had two employees, who are hard workers and have been with the company for many years, off work in the past 2 years with stress related illnesses, brought on by the constant pressure that all employees feel that they are under to achieve, or exceed, agreed targets.

59   Lars Veel introduced an employee share scheme 10 years ago, and many employees have been given free shares. However, none of the shares have been traded or sold yet. He has also encouraged the active involvement of all employees in the use of TQM techniques to reduce internal failures.

Jan Berzin – IT Director

60   Jan Berzin, now 35, joined Kadgee from the consultancy company that he had worked in for over ten years. Kadgee had appointed this consultancy company for advice on a range of IT solutions in 2000 and Jan Berzin was the consultant in charge of the Kadgee IT project. Jan Berzin quickly identified that there were several areas in which the use of IT could help Kadgee to compete with other manufacturing companies. Before Jan Berzin joined Kadgee, the Finance Director, Andre Schnaffer was responsible for IT. Andre Schnaffer agreed that Kadgee needed to embrace the use of IT in a far more comprehensive way than had been done and invited Jan Berzin to join the company. This additional expertise at Board level has enabled Kadgee to identify in which areas of the business the limited IT development budget could be best spent.

Extract from Kadgee's accounts for 2005 – Chairman's Statement

61

The clothing industry in general has seen another difficult year and competition from all areas of the world has increased. However, against that backdrop, we are pleased to state that Kadgee has had another successful year and that we have managed to retain all of our customers and to increase the volume of sales.

62

Despite a very slow and difficult year's trading, I am pleased to report that Kadgee is still trading profitably, which is a significant achievement following the trading losses made only a few years ago.

63

I would like to record my thanks to all members of the Kadgee management team and to all of our loyal and hard working employees who have committed themselves to achieving these good results.

64

Trading in 2006 started well and orders placed for the Autumn season are slightly up on this time last year and I look forward to reporting a further growth in sales next year. We continue to work closely with all of our key customers, all of whom I am pleased to report are still showing their continued commitment to buying Kadgee's high quality ranges of clothes.

Andrin Burnak

Andrin Burnak

Chairman

31 March 2006

Kadgee's Balance Sheet, Income Statement and Statement of changes in equity

Note: All data in this Appendix is presented in international financial reporting format

Balance Sheet

	At 31 December			
	2005		2004	
	€'000	€'000	€'000	€'000
Non-current assets (net)		9,830		11,514
Current assets				
Inventory	8,220		6,334	
Trade receivables and rent prepayments	19,404		18,978	
Cash and short term investments	119		131	
		27,743		25,443
Total assets		37,573		36,957

Equity and liabilities

	At 31 December			
	2005		2004	
	€'000	€'000	€'000	€'000
Equity				
Paid in share capital	20		20	
Share premium reserve	450		450	
Retained profits	21,787		20,863	
		22,257		21,333
Non-current liabilities				
Loans: Bank loan at 8% interest per year (repayable in 2010)		4,500		4,500
Current liabilities				
Bank overdraft	1,520		940	
Trade payables and accruals	8,900		9,667	
Tax	396		517	
		10,816		11,124
Total equity and liabilities		37,573		36,957

Note: Paid in share capital represents 200,000 shares of €0·10 each at 31 December 2005

Income Statement

	Year ended 31 December	
	2005	2004
	€'000	€'000
Revenue	74,420	75,553
Total operating costs	72,580	73,320
Operating profit	1,840	2,233
Finance costs	520	509
Tax expense (effective tax rate is 24%)	396	517
Profit for the period	924	1,207

Statement of changes in equity

	Share capital €'000	Share premium €'000	Retained earnings €'000	Total €'000
Balance at 31 December 2004	20	450	20,863	21,333
Profit for the period	–	–	924	924
Dividends paid	–	–	–	–
Balance at 31 December 2005	20	450	21,787	22,257

Kadgee's Cash Flow Statement

		Year ended 31 December		
		2005		*2004*
	€'000	€'000	€'000	€'000
Net cash inflow from operations				
Operating profit		1,840		2,233
Add back depreciation	1,965		1,949	
(Increase)/Decrease in inventory	(1,886)		(535)	
(Increase)/Decrease in trade receivables	(426)		(1,526)	
Increase/(Decrease) in trade payables and accruals	(767)		(604)	
		(1,114)		(716)
Net cash flow from operations		726		1,517
Finance costs paid		(520)		(509)
Taxation paid		(517)		(390)
Purchase of tangible fixed assets		(281)		(350)
Dividends paid		–		–
Cash Inflow/(Outflow) before financing		(592)		268
Increase/(Decrease) in bank overdraft		580		(194)
Increase/(Decrease) in cash and short term investments		(12)		74

Kadgee: some help from BPP

Introduction

The topic list below identifies examples of the type of activity which will be available in the BPP Learning Media Toolkit for your paper.

Topic list
1 Summarise the data in a précis
2 Financial analysis
3 Strategic analysis
4 Assessing risk
5 SWOT analysis
6 Key strategic issues

1 Summarise the data in a précis

What Kadgee Clothing does and how its structured

Kadgee is a European contract manufacturer of clothing for women and girls. Traditionally it has traded at the upper middle of the market, where it could gain a premium price for its quality and design.

Kadgee manufactures its clothing and apparel specifically to client order at 5 factories in Europe. IT has, since 2000, operated an advanced design centre equipped with CAD technologies and staffed by a small team of designers.

Kadgee's staff includes skilled machinists and operatives who, through a TQM philosophy and quality circles, have contributed to quality improvements and cost reduction through improved productivity.

Kadgee is an unquoted private company. 58% of its shares are held by Bruno (retired) and Andrin Burnak (CEO), Father and son respectively. The remaining shares are spread widely with 12% held in an employee-scheme, 10% each held by Anton Kramer (retired) and Andre Schnaffer (Finance Director), 8% by Dieter Stutt (Sales Director) and 2% by Frankie Bayane (Chief Designer).

Kadgee's present financial and competitive performance

Kadgee is struggling to compete in a tightening market.

It has seven clients, all retailers although one of these, Forum, (€16.8m revenue, 22.6% of turnover, €0.3m profit despite offering a 4% price reduction) will cease buying after 31 August 2006. A failing of management has been its willingness to rely on long-standing customers for its business rather than to spread its risk by forming links with other retailers.

Profits returned in 2002 following four years of losses but have declined between 2004 and 2005. The company also has cash flow problems, principally due to inventory building, that has lead it to relying on an increased overdraft in 2005.

The European clothing industry is under intense competitive pressure from its clients, large stores who wish to force the prices of clothing down, and also from cheaper imported clothing from Turkey, the Indian sub-continent and, more recently, China.

Kadgee is presently renegotiating its contracts and these will affect its activity and earnings through till Spring 2007.

Kadgee is also suffering falling quality due to deteriorating staff morale following the loss of Forum and the posting of 34 redundancies.

Key issues faced by Kadgee: its opportunities and problems

In the short run Kadgee needs to adjust to its loss of Forum either by finding replacement contracts or by downsizing its operation.

In the long run it needs to find an effective way to deal with the pressure it is receiving from its buyers and from cheaper producers.

There seem to be few opportunities open to Kadgee if it remains in its present line of business. There are opportunities in budget clothing as supermarkets sell expanded ranges of clothing. There are also margin enhancement opportunities if it is able to source its product from cheaper manufacturers rather than manufacture internally.

Information on forthcoming meetings which may affect Kadgee's future

The main issue will be the outcome of the present round of contract negotiations. These will determine production volumes and revenues for 2006/7.

2 Financial analysis

2.1 Financial details

	2005	Change %	2004
Profitability			
Revenue €'000	74,420	−1.5	75,553
Operating costs €'000	72,580	−1.0	73,320
Operating profit €'000	1,840	−17.6	2,233

Operating profit margin $\dfrac{1,840}{74,420} = 2.5\%$ $\dfrac{2,233}{75,553} = 3\%$

Average price of garment €

$\dfrac{\text{Revenue}}{\text{Total garments made in year}}$ $\dfrac{74,420,000}{10,900,000} = 6.83$

Average cost of garment €

$\dfrac{\text{Total operating costs}}{\text{Total garments made in year}}$ $\dfrac{72,580,000}{10,900,000} = 6.66$

Return on capital employed

$\dfrac{\text{Operating profit}}{\text{Equity} + \text{Non-current liabilities}}$ $\dfrac{1,840}{22,257 + 4,500} = 6.9\%$ $\dfrac{2,233}{21,333 + 4,500} = 8.6\%$

Asset base			
Non-current assets €'000	9,830	−14.6%	11,514

Revenue/Non-current assets $\dfrac{74,420}{9,830} = 7.6$ $\dfrac{75,553}{11,514} = 6.6$

Working capital			
Inventory €'000	8,220	+29.8%	6,334

Inventory days

$\dfrac{\text{Inventory} \times 365}{\text{Total operating costs}}$ $\dfrac{8,220 \times 365}{74,420} = 41.3 \text{ days}$ $\dfrac{18,978 \times 365}{75,553} = 91.7 \text{ days}$

Trade receivables and prepayments €'000	19,404	+2.2%	18,978

Receivables collection period

$\dfrac{\text{Trade receivables and prepayments} \times 365}{\text{Revenue}}$ $\dfrac{19,404 \times 365}{74,420} = 95.2 \text{ days}$ $\dfrac{18,978 \times 365}{75,553} = 91.7 \text{ days}$

Trade payables and accruals €'000	8,900	−7.9%	9,667

$\dfrac{\text{Trade payables and accruals} \times 365}{\text{Total operating costs}}$ $\dfrac{8,900 \times 365}{72,580} = 44.8 \text{ days}$ $\dfrac{9,667 \times 365}{73,320} = 48.1 \text{ days}$

	2005	Change %	2004

Liquidity

Current ratio
$$\frac{27{,}743}{10{,}816} = 2.6 \qquad \frac{25{,}443}{11{,}124} = 2.3$$

Quick ratio
$$\frac{27{,}743 - 8{,}220}{10{,}816} = 1.8 \qquad \frac{25{,}443 - 6{,}334}{11{,}124} = 1.7$$

Bank overdraft €'000	1,520	+61.7%	940

Gearing

Debt ratio

$$\frac{\text{Current liabilities} + \text{Non-current liabilities}}{\text{Total assets}}$$

$$\frac{10{,}816 + 4{,}500}{37{,}573} = 40.8\% \qquad \frac{11{,}124 + 4{,}500}{36{,}957} = 42.3\%$$

Gearing ratio

$$\frac{\text{Non-current liabilities}}{\text{Equity} + \text{Non-current liabilities}}$$

$$\frac{4{,}500}{22{,}257 + 4{,}500} = 16.8\% \qquad \frac{4{,}500}{21{,}333 + 4{,}500} = 17.4\%$$

Finance cost cover

$$\frac{\text{Operating profit}}{\text{Finance costs}}$$

$$\frac{1{,}840}{520} = 3.5 \qquad \frac{2{,}233}{509} = 4.4$$

Valuations

Net assets

$$\frac{\text{Total assets} - \text{current liabilities} - \text{non-current liabilities}}{\text{Number of shares}} = \frac{37{,}573{,}000 - 10{,}816{,}000 - 4{,}500{,}000}{200{,}000}$$

$$= \text{€}111.29 \text{ per share}$$

Price-earnings ratio

$$\frac{\text{Profit for the period} \times \text{Price-earnings ratio}}{\text{Number of shares}}$$

Using a industry figure of 17 (the current average P/E ratio for personal goods quoted in the Financial Times) and multiplying by 2/3 as Kadgee is unquoted

$$\frac{924{,}000 \times 17 \times \tfrac{2}{3}}{200{,}000} = \text{€}52.36$$

Accounting rate of return

$$\frac{\text{Profit for the period} / \text{Required rate on capital employed}}{\text{Number of shares}}$$

After-tax cost of debt finance = 8(1 − 0.24) = 6.08%

However shareholders will expect a higher return, so use 9%

$$\frac{24{,}000 / 0.09}{200{,}000} = \text{€}51.33$$

2.2 Financial situation

2.2.1 Profitability

Although there would not appear to be much difference between revenues dropping by 1.5% and costs by 1%, this has resulted in a 17.6% drop in gross profit. This together with the 2.5% operating profit margin in 2005 indicates that Kadgee's situation is very tight. If revenues in 2005 had been 4% lower (the figure put forward **unsuccessfully** by Kadgee to retain the Forum contract), revenues would have been €71,443,000, and with costs of €72,580,000, this would have meant an operating loss of €1,137,000.

2.2.2 Asset base

Although the company appears to be generating revenue more efficiently from its non-current assets, this is because of a significant fall in the value of non-current assets (14.6%). At some point significant further investment (particularly in information technology) will be required, otherwise the revenues and profits that the assets can generate will fall.

2.2.3 Working capital

There are concerns with all of the main areas of working capital – inventory, receivables and payables.

(a) **Inventory.** A 30% increase in inventory is very worrying, particularly as Kadgee is manufacturing for specific customers and has been trying to improve production processes. Holding about 40 days' worth of inventory in a fashion-based industry is hazardous as seasons will change and fashions can alter quickly. It is most likely that there is some unsold inventory in the warehouse, or that inventory is being supplied to retailers to hold that will be paid for only in the event of sale.

(b) **Receivables.** The average period taken is over three months' credit, which certainly appears excessive. It may reflect poor management of receivables, or more likely an unwillingness to antagonise major customers. (It is just possible that both year-end receivable figures don't reflect average receivables if a major customer pays a significant balance just after the year-end).

(c) **Payables**. Despite Andre Schnaffer's attempts to extend credit periods with suppliers, the payables period has fallen between 2004 and 2005 and at 44.8 days is less than half the receivables collection period of 95.2 days. This indicates that suppliers may be putting pressure on Kadgee to pay within its credit period because of concerns over its liquidity. Even if Kadgee is receiving discounts for rapid payments, these are likely to be outweighed by increases in overdraft charges.

2.2.4 Liquidity

The current and quick ratios have increased over the year, and are at levels (2.6 and 1.8) which for many businesses would appear to be safe. However they must be seen in the context of the increase in bank overdraft and the (small) negative cash flow. The profits for the year have not resulted in increased liquidity, but instead have meant increased inventory and receivables. Kadgee has not been able to use its surpluses to reduce its payables; the reduction in payables has had to mean a corresponding increase in the bank overdraft.

2.2.5 Gearing

Although gearing and financial cost cover appear reasonable at present, finance cost cover will deteriorate if there is a fall in profits. Possible lenders might also be deterred from advancing funds by the negative cash flows in 2005.

2.3 Valuation of company

2.3.1 General considerations

When considering appropriate valuations of the company the following issues need to be considered.

(a) As Kadgee is an unquoted company it may be difficult to realise full value for a significant shareholding, as there is no public market for the shares.

(b) It is not possible to use two common valuation methods, the dividend valuation model (no recent dividends) and future cash flows (we cannot use 2005 cash flows as these were negative).

2.3.2 Net asset valuation method

Basing the valuation of Bruno Burnak's shareholdings on the value of net assets as shown in the accounts suggests a value of:

$200,000 \times 0.29 \times 111.29 = €6,454,820$

Unusually this is a higher value than suggested by the other methods.

The main problem with using the net assets basis is that the accounts value of assets does not indicate the future cash flows the assets might generate. In addition there is doubt as to how much asset value would be realised – it may not be possible to dispose of the machinery for net realisable value, and inventory may quickly lose its value as fashions change. The value of receivables ought to be more certain, unless a major customer(s) of Kadgee runs into financial difficulties.

2.3.3 Price-earnings ratio

Using an industry price-earnings figure and adjusting for the fact that Kadgee is unquoted suggests a valuation for the shareholding of:

$200,000 \times 0.29 \times 52.36 = €3,036,880$

However the industry average may hide wide variations (particularly in a volatile industry such as the clothing industry). The adjustment made for Kadgee being unquoted is arbitrary, and does not necessarily reflect the difficulty of finding a willing buyer.

2.3.4 Accounting rate of return

This method attempts to discount earnings at a required cost of capital. The suggested valuation is:

$200,000 \times 0.29 \times 51.33 = €2,977,140$

The problems with this method are that:

(a) It uses earnings rather than cash flows (cash flows are a better indicator of value as they are not distorted by accounting policies).

(b) It assumes that current earnings can be maintained in the future.

(c) The calculation is very dependent on the required return figure chosen; the figure may well be higher than 9%, implying a significantly lower valuation of shares.

3 Strategic analysis

3.1 Ranking of stakeholders

Low Interest/Low Power	High Interest/Low Power
Local community	Five Key machine operators
End user of the goods	'Other' customers
Anti-exploitation pressure groups	Haus
	Non-shareholding employees
	Andre Schnaffer
Low Interest/High Power	**High Interest/High Power**
Chinese competitors	Domestic competitors
Anton Kramer	Bank
Bruno Burnak	Portrait
Home government	Diamond
Chinese government	Seeb
	JayJay
	Shareholding Employees
	Frankie Bayane
	Dieter Stutt
	Andrin Burnak

The rationale used here is the **current** (potential) **impact** each stakeholder group could have on Kadgee now. The key players are therefore:

(a) **Domestic competitors**

All competitors have a high power over Kadgee given the intense competition for business within the industry. Domestic competitors, feeling the effect of distant Chinese competition, may take a higher direct interest in Kadgee for consolidation/defensive merger solutions.

(b) **Bank**

High exposure to loan repayments and no real opportunity for further equity finance means almost total reliance on the bank. The recent loss of Forum will have increased the bank's interest dramatically.

(c) **Key customers**

High reliance upon their business for survival plus buying power in the face of Chinese alternatives

(d) **Shareholding employees (as a group)**

12% shareholding plus potential for strike action (thus affecting customer orders). Morale is low, no return on these shares is likely and 'safety needs' are utterly undermined following the loss of Forum.

(e) **Frankie Bayane**

Only owns 2% of the shares (not enough to make her stay) and design (together with finishing) is the key distinctive competence within Kadgee.

(f) **Dieter Stutt**

Has all the key contacts to drive the business' cashflows. There is no evidence of Key Account Managers (KAMs) and this means all the knowledge is in one place: Dieter's head. This is a high risk to the business. He could easily be poached by a competitor or customer (with whom he is in regular contact).

(g) **Andrin Burnak**

As Chairman and MD his interest and power are clearly high. He is unlikely to abandon the family business and possibly not a key asset at present, but the 58% shareholding within the Burnak family makes his power irrefutably high.

3.2 Ms Model

Strengths (Competencies)	Weaknesses
Men • Design competency (Frankie Bayane) • Networks of industry connections (Dieter Stutt) • Andre Schnaffer (managed cashflow during difficult periods – Pre-seen p. 9) • Staff 'buy in' to TQMTable Text	 • Andrin Burnak (appointment via nepotism: no business acumen/skill) • Staff morale • Sam Skala (not successful in winning new customers – Pre-seen p. 9)
Money (see Section 2 for detail)	(see Section 2 for detail)
Machinery (including IT and MIS) • Customer integrated extranet • TQM/throughput MIS • Centralised CAD design	 • No upgrade/reinvestment since 2001 • Surplus capacity from Sept 2006
Materials • Reduced wastage • Sources high quality (less waste, better for TQM etc)	 • Past instances of huge inventory write offs (many years ago however) • Higher relative cost than competitors ? • High inventory levels/ratios
Marketing Some evidence of relationship marketing by Dieter Stutt	 • Key customers lost (Forum) • No new customers won • Previously not seen as strategic activity (until recently undertaken 'part-time' by Dieter Stutt)

3.3 PEST Analysis

Political/Legal	Economic
• Govt embargoes/restrictions on imports • H&S legislation • Minimum wage acts • Working Time directives • (anti)-protectionist policies – WTO/GATT • Fair trade policies/Fair trade competitors • Govt subsidies to domestic industries (eg EU) • Impact of EEA type agreements within Europe	• Exchange rates • Hedging opportunities • Disposable income levels (they are in the higher price sector) • Expansion of Euro – Eastern Europe • Potential global economic downturn (following potential USA economic downturn) • Rise in domestic base rate affecting Kadgee K_d • Chinese economy impact
Social	**Technology**
• Difficult to predict trends • Seasonal fluctuations • Immediate response time • Public perception of overseas manufacturing and a fall in quality (M&S clothes)	• Fully automated apparel manufacturing – the 'holy grail' of the clothing industry • CAD/CAM/CIM technology

3.4 Porter's Diamond

3.4.1 Based on current location in Europe

Factor Conditions	Demand Conditions
• European workforce (educated but expensive) • Established technological infrastructure	• Intense, high expectations on quality and price – should drive Kadgee into high performance • Buyer's market due to choice
Related & Supporting Industries	**Strategy, Structure & Rivalry**
• Cotton industry weakened in Europe over last century • Computerised machinery industry and IT support strong in Europe	• Labour intensive manufacturing no longer the cultural focus of Westernised European business culture • Domestic rivalry weakening (therefore threat to competitive advantage) due to strength of Eastern markets

3.4.2 Porter's Diamond – Based on Far East/China

Factor Conditions	Demand Conditions
• Vast workforce ripe for investment in training • Cheap and available land for relocation	Customers expect goods from 'China' – equates to quality (Pre-seen p. 7)
Related & Supporting Industries	**Strategy, Structure & Rivalry**
• Close proximity to Asian cotton markets • Cheap distribution solutions available	• Extensive manufacturing/cheap labour intensive business culture predominates • Bottom heavy organisational structures the norm • Intense rivalry will drive businesses on to excel in this market

3.5 Ansoff's matrix

Existing Products/Existing Markets	New Products/Existing Markets
• Withdraw from manufacturing to concentrate on design • Withdraw from everything and become a selling agent for European customers • Consolidate remaining customers via legal tie ins • Consolidate via merger with one or more similarly positioned organisation	• Shoes • Hats (sportswear caps?) • Household items – eg curtains • Lingerie • Bed linen • Workwear
Existing Products/New Markets	**Diversification**
• Global sales of clothing (via internet direct selling) • Sale of surplus stocks to charities • Industrial segment (dustsheets to painters & decorators etc) • Franchising • Own shops • Mail order	• Design consultancy • Uniforms (schools, military) • Tents • Bags • Alteration /repairs service • Wedding services (Pronuptia) • Luggage

3.6 Value chain analysis

Firm Infrastructure		New design centre			
Technology Development		New machinery in 2001 – CAD/CAM	Customer access to throughout of designs		
Human Resource Management	Recruitment of fuller time time staff (min 24 hours per week)	Skilled, innovative, dedicated workforce, adaptable to new machinery	Peter Coletta tasked with specific quality assurance project (p. 6)	Contracts renewed at start of each season	
Procurement	High value materials purchased (p.5)		High value packaging (p. 5)		
	Goods made to order	Small scale production of high quality clothing		Long term contracts with Key Customers Some evidence of Customer Relationships	
	Inbound	**Operations**	**Outbound**	**Marketing & Sales**	**Service**

3.6.1 Comments

To date Kadgee has been driven by a differentiation strategy, focussing on high quality on most key areas of the Value Chain (material inputs, HRM, Technology).

After-sales service is clearly lacking from this consistent model, however – a potential reason for the loss of the Forum contract. It appears that once the goods have been despatched there is minimal after sales service for each particular order.

However market forces represent the greatest threat to Kadgee's current Value Chain which has been successful in the past. Customers can now effectively achieve both differentiated quality and minimal cost at the same time by taking advantage of changing PEST factors and Diamond factors in the Far Eastern markets such as China. Page 7 of the preseen highlights this 'quality at low cost theme'.

One option would be to niche their business as a very high value manufacturer for specialist tailors and protect their value adding activities based on quality from low cost Chinese alternatives.

4 Assessing risk

An effective risk-based management approach relies on a system of **internal controls** to ensure that risks are continuously monitored and properly controlled. To ensure that such controls are in place Kadgee should undertake a **risk audit.**

The purpose of a risk audit is to identify and evaluate risks, and on the basis of this evaluation to put in place a robust and effective control system for the management of those risks.
The risk audit involves the following five steps:

Step 1   **Risk identification**

The pre-seen information catalogues a whole array of risks currently facing Kadgee. These are:

(a)   **Organisational risk**. Combining the roles of Chairman and Chief Executive in a principal shareholder amasses a considerable amount of power within one individual.

(b)   **Customer dependency risk**. 73% of all business activity derived from only three major customers with one of them, Forum, already stating their intention to move their business from Kadgee.

(c)   **Reputational risk**. Any failures relating to quality, supply, etc could damage this business, which has built up such a strong reputation and goodwill over many years.

(d)   **Human resources risk**. The dedicated, talented and skilful workforce are critical to Kadgee's ongoing success, therefore any tendency to unsettle them (eg job insecurity) must be avoided.

(e)   **Financial risk** relates to financial management issues, which in the case of Kadgee is concerned with eroding operational margins, cash flow pressures and high levels of gearing.

(f)   **Operational risk**, which relates to the activities carried out within the firm. In particular changes to the supply chain management process at Kadgee will place additional pressures on staff and systems to deliver high quality goods in short lead times.

(g)   **Technology risk**. Through the recent introduction of CAD the firm is going to become more reliant on such systems (and the staff who operate them) to deliver the required level of performance.

(h)   **Globalisation risk**. The growth of the manufacturing base in China will continue to put pressure on Kadgee's ability to trade competitively in its traditional markets.

(i)   **Environmental risk** is a general term relating to changes in the external environment over which Kadgee has little influence. In particular **political risk** arising in the arena of World Trade negotiations could create a greater sense of uncertainty.

Step 2   **Risk assessment**

(a)   **Organisational risk**. If Andrin Burnak has too much power and influence by virtue of position in the firm, then his views are likely to dominate the thinking on the Board, which in turn could limit the strategic prospects of Kadgee.

(b)   **Customer dependency risk.** Having 'all one's eggs in one basket' is not a sensible way to manage a business. The impact that the loss of one major customer would have on the scale of operations, and thereby the size of the workforce, is immense.

(c)   **Reputational risk** often arises as a result of other downside risks being realised. Other customers might view for example the loss of the sales contract with Forum as an indicator of declining fortunes in the firm and this could have further negative effects. Equally if quality reduces as a result of the loss of key staff then Kadgee's brand value will suffer as a consequence.

(d)   **Human resources risk**. The impact on a business that has relied so heavily on the diligence and skill of its workforce and then being forced to shed staff through redundancy should not be underestimated. The firm cannot simply open a box of new staff should business fortunes turn around and there becomes a need for higher levels of human resource.

(e)   **Financial risk**. Currently Kadgee does not appear to be excessively geared, however the cost of servicing debt has placed so much pressure on cash flows that last year the overall amount of cash available to the firm decreased. This situation is not sustainable in the long run, and must be remedied by improving the cash generating from operational activities (ie margins).

(f) **Operational risk.** Changes in the supply chain are not in themselves the problem, but the resultant need to deliver goods both faster and too the required level of quality (in order to remain competitive) places new pressures on the operational activities of the firm that need to be managed and organised differently.

(g) **Technology risk.** As soon as information systems become an imbedded feature in an organisation, they cannot be removed. The introduction of CAD will mean that Kadgee will have to continue to invest in, and upgrade, this system to ensure it remains relevant to serve the changing needs of the customers.

(h) **Globalisation risk.** The ability of Chinese clothing manufacturers to produce goods of equivalent quality but at a significantly lower cost base means that they will compete with Kadgee on price. Already Kadgee makes less than 2.5% operating profit at current pricing levels so it could not reduce its prices further without a significant reduction in its operating cost base.

(i) **Environmental risk** needs continual monitoring so that early indicators can be acted upon. If, for example the current round of WTO talks result in further liberalisation of trading rules with China, then Kadgee will be placed under even greater pressure to reduce its prices.

Step 3 Risk profiling and prioritising

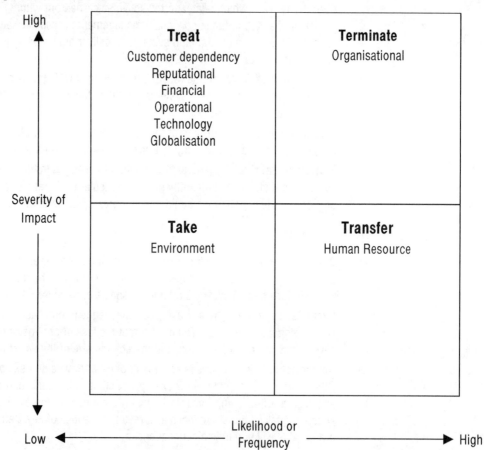

Obviously categorising risk in the matrix above is in part subjective and based on attitude to risk, so you may disagree in places. However it provides management with a starting point to prioritise and determine control actions required.

Treat: this is by far the most common action, or series of actions, as every risk in this category will require a different response. The control action aims to avoid the likelihood of the damaging aspects of the risk occurring.

Take: often means taking no further action either because any control action will have little or no influence on the nature of the risk (eg globalisation) or the costs involved in taking any control action far outweigh any likely benefits.

Terminate: this is the most drastic action where the firm should really consider withdrawing from this area of business or in the case of Kadgee, no longer accepting the legitimacy of the current organisational structure.

Transfer: it is becoming increasingly common is to transfer the risk to someone else. An option to Kadgee would be to outsource its human resources and buy in many non-core services to add flexibility.

Step 4 Risk quantification

In effect we are aiming to determine the damaging **financial impacts** of the various risks. Some are fairly easy to ascertain using basic mathematical techniques, others not so easy because of the largely qualitative and subjective nature of the risk assessment.

Using the risk matrix the firm could apply **probabilities** to the various risks along the x-axis. It is not acceptable to simply suggest high or low risk, as these are relative terms. By determining the probability of an outcome, using data derived from past performance or through benchmarking similar firms, and then realistically assessing the financial consequences of it occurring (eg increased cost, reduced market share, lower sales price), the result is the expected value of the risk.

Kadgee will then have an objective basis for determining a pecking order to deal with each risk.

Step 5 Portfolio risk management

When each individual risk identified has been quantified, they need to be re-assembled to derive the risk portfolio for Kadgee. It is quite likely that by viewing them in isolation, positive control actions for one could impact negatively on another.

Consequently the role of management is to view all of the risks collectively and determine a strategic approach, which will best manage the portfolio of risks for the firm within the risk tolerances acceptable to management.

5 SWOT analysis

Strengths	Weaknesses
• Still profitable	• No recognised brand of its own
• Expert operative staff who can make customised products	• Excessive reliance on small number of clients
• Design centre that enables it to speed up time to market to give clients latest fashions	• High cost relative to competition
	• Ineffective new business prospecting
• Good links to clients via Dieter Stutt	• Poor working capital management
	• Declining quality
Opportunities	**Threats**
• Margin improvement if product sourced from China	• Low cost imports
• Emergence of low cost but fashion conscious retail segment (eg TK Maxx)	• Loss of further key clients
	• Price pressure
• Supply chain integration to speed up design and replenishment	• Uncontrolled staff absence or losses

5.1 Prioritising your SWOT analysis

Key SWOT items	Justification
Strength	
1. Design strengths	These seemed to have turned the losses into profits after 2002. They are low cost to maintain and add value to the product. Essential even if manufacturing outsourced.
2. Expert machinists	Developing new lines of products needs high quality prototypes to show the stores buyers and also to iron out any production problems prior to sending off to manufacture.
3. Client links	These presently supply the income of Kadgee and will be needed in short run even if business is going to change.
Weakness	
1. Reliance on few key clients	The loss of one of these could threaten the short-run survival of Kadgee. Also they will use their position to drive down margins.
2. High cost manufacturing	In a market of falling margins this makes Kadgee unable to serve its clients profitably and threatens its survival in the medium term.
3. Poor client prospecting record	Any change of strategy or search for replacement clients will require considerable new client prospecting.
4. Declining quality	Falling quality will increase costs of poor quality (prevention, appraisal, internal failure and external failure) in the short run and so threaten cash flows and profits. It may lose clients mid-contract or cause penalty payments to be incurred. It may harm ability to tender for new business.
5. Poor working capital management	This makes the firm reliant on the bank and to pay higher interest costs. Presently no sign of bank withholding credit.
6. No brand	Limited importance given that its business doesn't presently use brands and there is no mention that rivals have brands or that competition is based around brand rather than cost.
Opportunity	
1. Margin improvement if product sourced from China	This could be available to Kadgee within 6 – 9 months and would shield Kadgee from some of the price pressures. Failure to find a way to reduce costs will threaten contract renewal and profits.
2. Supply chain integration to speed up design and replenishment	This could reduce inventories in the medium term and release up to €8m cash for repayment of overdraft and investment in business improvements. It is also essential if Kadgee is to meet the challenges of shirt life-cycle, high margin fashion markets. Rivals will certainly be offering this.
3. Emergence of low cost but fashion conscious retail segment (eg TK Maxx)	This is less of an opportunity because to service this segment would demand some fundamental changes to Kadgees business model.

Key SWOT items	Justification
Threat	
1. Loss of further key clients	Forum were able to give very short notice of cancellation so its seems contracts are short term. In the current negotiating climate this is a clear and present threat which, depending on client, could take away much of Kadgee's remaining revenue.
2. Price pressure	Keeping customers is critical but they must also be profitable. This price pressure, if 4% reductions are typical, will render Kadgee loss-making within months.
3. Low cost imports	This has become a threat recently due to the high quality of Chinese products. It will erode margins and volumes in Kadgee's market segment.
4. Uncontrolled staff absence or losses	From the Pre-seen Kadgee will be overstaffed after August 2006 so this is not a key issue providing the staff that leave are not high value machinists.

6 Key strategic issues

Your answer to this must be based on your prioritised SWOT otherwise your response lacks **Logic**.

Key Issue	Rationale
Retain present clients	Without this Kadgee may have no business by 1 September.
	Key clients essential to keep business operational while strategic changes can be made.
Improve working capital management	The bank cannot be relied upon to continue extending the overdraft to a firm in such a perilous market, unless it sees that these issues are being dealt with. Withdrawal of overdraft would mean Kadgee couldn't meet the next wages bill or buy material to manufacture clothing.
Deal with price pressure in the market before the firm becomes unsustainable	The competitive position has changed and will not revert back. Having secured its financial position in the short-run, Kadgee's management must develop a viable long-term strategy.
	Sometimes the key issues are very simple and clear. Don't feel tempted to bulk them out to get marks. The marks will be for spotting there are only a few and dealing with them.

23

Kadgee: unseens and requirements

Introduction

This chapter contains the unseen material and requirements from the September and November 2006 exams.

We have produced a suggested answer to the September 2006 exam in Chapter 24.

September 2006 unseen

Requirement

You are the consultant appointed by the Kadgee Board.

Prepare a report that prioritises, analyses and evaluates the issues facing Kadgee, and makes appropriate recommendations.

Meeting with Kadgee's bankers

Following the announcement of the loss of business from Forum, which was Kadgee's second largest customer, Kadgee's bankers, PGB, called a meeting in early July 2006. Both Andre Schnaffer and Andrin Burnak attended the meeting to reassure PGB that Kadgee had plenty of current orders and that business looked promising for the next 6 months. PGB has provided all of the loan finance to Kadgee which is due for repayment in 2010. Kadgee's existing loans of €4,500,000 are secured against the property owned by Kadgee. There is the capacity to borrow an additional €3,000,000 against Kadgee's assets.

PGB has also provided Kadgee with an overdraft facility. The overdraft is currently standing at €1,750,000 at the end of August 2006. This overdraft has increased from €1,520,000 at the end of December 2005. The agreed overdraft limit is €2,500,000. PGB stated that Kadgee will not be allowed to exceed the agreed limit, whatever the circumstances. PGB stated that if Kadgee were to exceed the limit, then the bank would call in the overdraft entirely.

PGB has requested Andre Schnaffer to supply a copy of Kadgee's cash flow forecast up to the end of 2006 together with a copy of Kadgee's latest financial plans, to reassure PGB. Andre Schnaffer agreed to these requests, and stated that they would be supplied after Kadgee had reviewed a number of strategic issues and possible contracts that it was currently considering.

Loss of another customer

In addition to the loss of one customer, Forum, another of Kadgee's customers, Zeeb, notified Kadgee in August 2006 that it would not be procuring any further clothing from Kadgee after its current contract for the 2006/07 winter season finishes. Sales to Zeeb amounted to 6·9% of Kadgee's sales revenue in 2005.

Some of Kadgee's other major customers are concerned about Kadgee's future ability to continue to manufacture and supply to them. Whilst Andrin Burnak has reassured all of Kadgee's remaining customers that Kadgee will continue to operate and manufacture to the same high standard that its reputation is based on, he considers that until a further large order is secured, Kadgee will see its profits substantially eroded. Andrin Burnak has communicated the loss of Zeeb to PGB (Kadgee's bankers) which has re-confirmed that the maximum overdraft that will be made available is €2,500,000.

Kadgee has six factories operational with a capacity to manufacture 10·9 million garments in 2005. The loss of both Forum and Zeeb results in an annual loss of around 3·3 million garments.

Forecast operating profit

The actual operating profit for 2005 was €1,840,000. Following Forum and Zeeb's decision not to place further orders with Kadgee, together with some deterioration in operating margins from other customers, Kadgee's latest forecast operating profit for 2006 is around €1,500,000. The forecast figures for 2006 include the 3 month trial for GREN (see below), but NOT the proposed one year contract with GREN.

The latest operating profit forecast for 2007, following the departure of both Forum and Zeeb, is €1,200,000. This does not include the proposed one-year contract with GREN.

August 2006 Kadgee Board meeting

At the Kadgee Board meeting held on 4 August 2006, the directors discussed how Kadgee could compete with the increasingly high quality output from China and the large volumes of imports into Europe.

The discussion included the following:

- Improve the quality or range of clothing, such as the proposed contract with GREN using recycled textiles, as outlined below;

- Move some, or all, of Kadgee's production to China. The Kadgee Board is agreed that the option of setting up in China on its own is not feasible, as it would face enormous obstacles which could delay production for several years. Therefore, a joint venture with a Chinese company should be considered. Alternatively, there is the possibility of subcontracting work to a Chinese manufacturer, as outlined below;

- Kadgee could aim to produce clothing for a selected market that is _not_ currently being targeted by Chinese manufacturers, such as the proposed WintaWarm range of clothing, as outlined below.

New contract won by Kadgee

In May 2006, Kadgee recruited a new designer who has established a reputation for designing ranges of clothes using recycled textiles. The recycled textiles are procured at a very low cost from an international charity. Each new manufactured garment is different and requires a higher input from skilled manpower, especially cutters. Following discussions, a contract for a three month trial period was signed in late June 2006 between Kadgee and a new customer, GREN for deliveries in July, August and September 2006.

GREN launched a limited range in one of its flagship shops at the end of August. GREN has over 120 shops in several European countries. The average sales price per garment to GREN for the trial was €18·00 for an agreed volume of 60,000 garments for the three month trial period.

The trial has been a media success for GREN, and the garments using recycled materials were sold out in days. GREN is planning to expand the range and volume of clothes in this new recycled range and has offered Kadgee a 12 month contract, to commence after the three month trial period, ending in September 2007. However, the proposed one year contract will be at a lower sales price per garment, of €16·20. GREN believes that Kadgee should be able to achieve economies of scale and reduced manpower time spent due to the learning curve effect, as the contracted volume in the proposed one year contract is for 1 million garments.

The marginal cost per garment for manufacturing clothes using recycled textiles is €15·60.

If Kadgee accepts the GREN contract for the next year it would utilize over 9% of Kadgee's manufacturing capacity of 10·9 million garments. The proposed manufacture of 1 million garments using recycled textiles will be undertaken at two of its factories only. These two factories have spare capacity following the loss of the Forum and Zeeb contracts.

GREN has requested Kadgee to advise its intention to agree to the proposed one year contract by the end of September 2006, before the trial finishes. GREN has also used other companies for the trial, but has offered the one year contract to Kadgee only.

The Kadgee management team is very pleased with the success of the trial of recycled materials and the proposed one year contract to the end of September 2007. However, the reduced sales price, and therefore the reduced margin, is a great concern to Andre Schaffner, the Finance Director. Andre Schnaffer also has concerns about GREN's ability to meet Kadgee's usual payment terms. Whilst some payment delays are expected, at present Kadgee has not received any payments at all for any of the supplies to GREN for the 3 month trial. The first deliveries that were invoiced during July are now over 60 days old and have still not been paid. GREN has a poor reputation in dealings with its suppliers, including regular late payment of around 4 months after delivery.

Andre Schnaffer has forecast that the proposed one year contract will necessitate working capital financing of €1 million. The finance costs of the increase in working capital would be 13% per year, based on Kadgee's current overdraft rate. The cost of financing the working capital is _not_ included in the above forecast cost figures.

Andrin Burnak was very pleased for Kadgee to be at the forefront of this new fashion trend. Additionally, Kadgee was receiving much positive PR associated with the high profile launch of the new recycled textiles.

Proposal to move some manufacturing to China

At the Board meeting in August 2006, there were some detailed discussions on the possibility of moving some of Kadgee's manufacturing to China. This could enable Kadgee to operate more profitably and would allow the company to be more confident in its ability to retain its existing customer base and also to allow it to compete much more effectively in order to win new business.

Andrin Burnak stated that Kadgee had been approached by a Chinese manufacturing company called LIN. It has proposed a joint venture with Kadgee. It proposes that Kadgee should concentrate on what it does best, which is designing and distributing to the European market. It proposes that Kadgee should continue to work with its current customers and agree designs, which could then be electronically transferred to a factory in China to manufacture. Kadgee would then continue to supply existing customers, but with clothes manufactured in China. This would necessitate closure of all six of Kadgee's European factories. The proposal is for the joint venture to be LIN 60% and Kadgee 40% for investment and all financial aspects of the proposed joint venture. The proposed joint venture with LIN would require the construction of a large purpose built factory with a manufacturing capacity of over 20 million garments per year. If Kadgee chose to invest in the joint venture, the investment cost is forecast to be €22·5 million, of which Kadgee's share at 40% would be €9 million.

However, both Sam Skala and Peter Coletta are very concerned whether the proposed joint venture could work well for the longer term and are worried about the security of Kadgee's intellectual property.

Andrin Burnak has also been consulting for the last few months with a Chinese businessman, Won Dong, who he has personally known for 30 years through business and family connections. Won Dong is based in China but travels extensively. Won Dong has advised Andrin Burnak of two different Chinese companies to which he considers Kadgee should subcontract work to, as an alternative to the proposed joint venture with LIN, which he knows little about. However, if Kadgee were to subcontract manufacturing work to either of the companies in China that Won Dong has suggested, it would necessitate closing most, or all, of its European factories.

Proposed new product line

Kadgee has, to date, only manufactured fashion clothing and has not made any outerwear such as jackets and coats. Following extensive market research by Sam Skala, he has identified that there is a substantial gap in the number of high quality coats manufactured for the North American market, including Canada.

Kadgee has purchased, on a trial basis, a small quantity of a new lightweight synthetic fabric called "WintaWarm" that is both warm and waterproof. The company manufacturing this new material is Ruzic, which is based in Europe. The new material is thin but hard wearing and has had favourable press coverage, following its launch in December 2005. All purchases of the material will be paid for in Euros.

Capital expenditure of €8 million will be required for the new product line.

Sales would be invoiced in US Dollars or Canadian Dollars. The NPV's in the table below _include_ the forecast capital expenditure of €8 million. This proposal requires Kadgee Board approval in order to meet a launch date of January 2007.

NPVs for WintaWarm proposal	Probability	Number of garments manufactured per year	NPV's of post-tax cash flows for WintaWarm proposal assessed over 5 years € million
High sales	10%	0·6 million	6·1
Medium sales	50%	0·5 million	3·6
Low sales	40%	0·4 million	0·9

However, Andre Schnaffer is concerned whether Kadgee can raise €8 million in loan finance to purchase the required new machinery. If the machinery is hired or leased instead of being purchased, the present value of the hire or leasing costs, post-tax, is forecast to be €10 million for the 5 year period over which the project is being assessed.

Legal case against Kadgee

Kadgee is facing a major legal case for allegedly copying designs by a major fashion designer, SM. Several of Kadgee's designs from its latest range bear a remarkable similarity to SM's designs, but Kadgee's designs were drawn up before the famous designer's clothes were launched. Kadgee has so far refused to back down and the publicity has boosted sales of Kadgee's designs to many of its customers.

Sam Skala has stated that all publicity is good publicity, and that Kadgee should not give into the pressure from SM, as the Kadgee management team is confident that it had not copied the designs. He stated that Kadgee should be flattered that it is being taken to court by such a famous fashion house. However, Kadgee's legal advisors are worried that if it is unsuccessful in the legal case, the damages could lead to major financial problems and that the costs of the case and legal damages, if Kadgee is unsuccessful, could exceed €3 million. If the case is settled out of court, Kadgee would have legal costs of €0·2 million and Kadgee would have to withdraw the designs.

The net effect on the operating profit of withdrawing these designs is forecast to be a reduction of €0·3 million in total for the lifetime of the designs. However, if Kadgee decides to defend the case, if it went to court, the chances of success are 50%.

Fire at one of Kadgee's factories

At the very end of August 2006, a fire broke out during the night at one of Kadgee's factories located in the town of Dem. The fire has destroyed the entire inventory of finished goods held there awaiting transportation to customers, as well as a large amount of work-in-progress and raw materials. The factory was one of Kadgee's larger factories, which manufactured 2·4 million garments each year.

In addition to the total loss of all inventories, there was several days loss of data from the computer systems at that factory. In accordance with usual routines, the IT systems had been backed up each night, but the back up files had not been stored in a fire-proof cabinet or off site, as required by Kadgee's IT instructions. Therefore, the factory manager has not been able to ascertain what deliveries have been made to customers over the preceding four days before the fire. Many of Kadgee's customers are still chasing Kadgee for deliveries in the confusion following the fire less than a week ago. Kadgee's management has been busy transferring orders to its other factories, and some orders may have been repeated. Also, as delivery data had not been transferred to the finance department, there was some confusion over what should, or should not, be invoiced, Several of Kadgee's customers have complained that they have been invoiced twice for goods that they never received.

The fire had also spread to neighbouring domestic houses and caused much damage. There has been much adverse press coverage of the fire and the damage caused. Local residents are seeking compensation from Kadgee for losses not covered by their own insurance policies. Kadgee is fully insured for the fire at its premises and there were no suspicious circumstances. The expected insurance payment, due in November 2006, will be for around €7·0 million. However, the forecast cost of rebuilding a similar factory with the same capacity, using the latest machinery, is €10·0 million.

The employees at the factory burnt down in the town of Dem are unwilling to relocate to any of Kadgee's other factories. The nearest of Kadgee's other five factories is over 200 kilometres away. The factory that burnt down employs 84 employees, all of whom have been put on half pay for 1 month. If the site is permanently closed, redundancy payments of €1·1 million as well as other closure costs of €0·3 million will be incurred.

Accidents at several Kadgee factories

Peter Coletta is under pressure from his fellow Board members to take action following a series of minor accidents during July and August at all six factories. Maintenance has been reduced and machine breakdown is common.

As a result of reduced maintenance and also due to much of the machinery reaching, or exceeding, the end of its useful life, there has been an increasing number of machine breakdowns. Most employees are under pressure to meet their daily targets of number of garments worked on, and choose to attend to the machine breakdowns themselves. They have had little direct training on machine maintenance. At one of the factories, when one of the main cutting machines broke down, many employees were unable to meet their daily targets and they lost a proportion of their wages that related to volumes produced. Therefore employees are keen to take action when machinery breaks down. In most cases the repairs are simple and straightforward and the machine is up and running again very quickly. However, there are a growing number of minor accidents that are happening on an almost daily basis and the employees are frustrated that management is ignoring these incidents.

The general feeling in the factories is that a major accident will occur before the management team either replaces the faulty and aged machinery, or improves the level of maintenance. The forecast costs of replacing _just_ the machinery that has the worst breakdown records is €3·0 million or alternatively the increased maintenance costs to attempt to prevent many of the breakdowns is forecast to be €0·8 million per year.

Other Human Resource issues

Kadgee's employees are very concerned for their future employment, having seen many other clothing manufacturers in the same towns in which they work cease trading. Kadgee's manufacturing capacity has increased due to efficiencies in recent years. However, there is increasing unrest amongst employees that all of their efforts are not appreciated. There are a few employees that are trying to demand a better pay rate for their skills, but to date have been unsuccessful. The standard of quality is starting to fall. Furthermore, Kadgee employs a high proportion of skilled female employees and many are unhappy and have complained that they are paid a lower pay rate than their male colleagues who are doing the same work. However, Peter Coletta has explained to Lars Veel, the HR Director, that this is due to the extra responsibilities that many of the male employees undertake.

Appointment of a consultant

At the Kadgee Board meeting held on 1 September 2006, it was agreed that a consultant would be appointed to advise the Board on the issues facing Kadgee.

November 2006 unseen

Requirement

You are the consultant appointed by the Kadgee Board.

Prepare a report that prioritises, analyses and evaluates the issues facing Kadgee, and makes appropriate recommendations.

New Managing Director joins Kadgee

Following the loss of the contract with Forum in May 2006, the Kadgee Board agreed that some serious changes were required for it to remain competitive and for it to retain its existing contracts. Andrin Burnak fully appreciated that he did not possess the skills required for Kadgee to compete in the challenging world markets now facing the company.

Andrin Burnak recruited Birgit Zeim as the new Managing Director, with the full backing of the Kadgee Board. She had established her reputation when she managed to turn around another fashion manufacturer. She was reluctant to join Kadgee at first, and it proved necessary to offer an attractive package including share options. Birgit Zeim joined Kadgee in July 2006 on a salary of €400,000 per year, making her the company's highest paid director. She also has share options to purchase 100,000 shares in Kadgee, within the next 5 years at a price of €3.00.

Birgit Zeim has not yet invested any of her personal finance in Kadgee. She would only wish to exercise her share options to purchase 100,000 shares at a total cost of €300,000 if Kadgee were to become significantly more profitable. By joining Kadgee, she has her professional reputation at risk if she is unsuccessful. She is confident that the company could become a leading global force in the manufacture of high quality clothing with a far greater level of sales and far higher profitability levels than currently being achieved.

Changes announced by the new Managing Director

Within a month of joining Kadgee and meeting all of the management team and visiting each of Kadgee's six factories, Birgit Zeim prepared a proposal for the Kadgee Board which met in early August 2006. Birgit Zeim stated to the Board that Kadgee could only survive in the long-term and become more successful financially if it were to undergo a _transformational change_.

In order to allow the Kadgee Board time to agree on what direction it should aim for, Birgit Zeim has introduced some short term measures to cut costs. The Board discussed and reluctantly agreed to each of the proposals. The following changes were announced in August 2006:

- An immediate wage cut of 5% for all operational staff working within Kadgee's factories

- Changes to the contracts of employment for operational staff working within the factories, which include a reduction of paid leave and other entitlements

- Immediate closure of one factory with compulsory redundancies of 54 employees

- Closer scrutiny of sick leave, which Birgit Zeim considers to be very high. She has stated that she would not hesitate to terminate the employment contract of any employee who she considers to be exploiting the company's generosity. Two employees with high sickness records have been dismissed as a result of this policy.

Birgit Zeim is fully aware that employee morale is already low, and that these measures would have a detrimental effect. To counter this, she wants all employees to have a share of up to 20% of the total profits achieved each year. However, the profit related pay would only be paid if all departments achieved agreed targets. She plans to introduce a range of financial and non-financial performance related targets during 2007.

Kadgee's bankers

The proceeds from the sale of the land at the factory that was closed in August 2006 are expected to cover the redundancy costs of the 54 employees and other closure costs. However, following the closure and imminent sale of this site, Kadgee's bankers, PGB, have stated that they would now only allow a maximum of any further loans of €2,000,000 due to Kadgee's reduced asset base. Kadgee's existing loan from PGB of €4,500,000 is secured on Kadgee's assets.

Additionally, Kadgee's current overdraft, standing at €1,604,000 at the end of October 2006, must not exceed the agreed overdraft limit of €2,500,000. PGB has informed Andre Schnaffer that if Kadgee were to exceed this limit, then the bank would call in the overdraft entirely.

November 2006 Kadgee Board meeting

At the November 2006 Kadgee Board meeting Birgit Zeim announced that the company simply could not carry on as at present as it is very vulnerable to losing further orders from its regular customers.

Birgit Zeim stated that she is looking at various ways in which Kadgee can undergo a *transformational change*, which would start within the next six months and that some of the changes will not be easy for the management or the employees to accept. The possibilities that she explained to the Board in November 2006 were as follows:

- Manufacturing in China on its own by setting up a large factory to manufacture clothing for the European and other markets

- Manufacturing in China in a joint venture with a Chinese manufacturer

- Moving all or part of Kadgee's manufacturing base to elsewhere in Asia

- Further investment in IT solutions to sell its clothing to a much wider market than it currently does.

Proposal to manufacture in China

Birgit Zeim stated to the Kadgee Board that no international manufacturer can afford to ignore China and that the company needs to have a strategy to deal with China.

Birgit Zeim reported that already almost 25% of the clothing sold in the EU has "Made in China" labels and that this growth is continuing to accelerate. She continued by reporting that to date Kadgee has not lost much of its business because it has managed to maintain a high quality output which has achieved premium prices aimed at the top end of the price range for women's and children's clothing. However, she insisted that the high quality of clothing produced in China made competition from that source highly likely in the very near future.

Birgit Zeim further stated that Kadgee cannot attempt to manufacture in China without the full support of the Kadgee Board and that it should _not_ be considered as an additional manufacturing factory as well as Kadgee's European factories. She stated that an investment in China would necessitate some of Kadgee's senior management to be based in China to manage the investment and that all of its European factories should close. However, many members of the Kadgee Board were not convinced on the proposed relocation of its manufacturing base to China.

Proposal to set up in China on its own

Andrin Burnak wants Kadgee to remain independent and is not enthusiastic about the possibility of a Joint Venture (see below). However, he recognises that the possibility of Kadgee expanding into China on its own needs to be explored very carefully.

Proposal to set up in China in a Joint Venture

Birgit Zeim proposes that Kadgee should enter into a Joint Venture with a Chinese manufacturer, so enabling it to reach a much larger global market and also to achieve cost reduction on a scale that would not be possible in Europe. Birgit Zeim has been in contact with several Chinese manufacturing companies for over a year, even before she agreed to join Kadgee, and she has selected Xina as a proposed joint venture partner.

Xina has been manufacturing low cost clothing for the last three years and now wants to enter the higher quality clothing market and is keen to work with a European company. If Kadgee does not choose Xina, then Xina has made it clear that it will select another company to work with.

The joint venture proposal is to establish a manufacturing base that would replace four of the five European factories that Kadgee currently has operational. Kadgee would retain one small European factory. The manufacturing and distribution centre in China would be a 60 /40 joint venture, with Xina having a 60% stake. If the joint venture is agreed then it would be established as a separate legal company.

The forecast total investment is the equivalent of €20 million, of which Kadgee's share of the investment would be €8 million. This will include a state of the art design centre, manufacturing facilities capable of producing up to 20 million garments annually, as well as warehousing and distribution facilities. The manufacturing capacity of this proposed new factory is almost twice that of Kadgee's current capacity.

The proposal is to invest in early 2007, if this proposal was chosen, and for the factory in China to be operational later in 2007. The table below shows the cash inflows for Kadgee's 40% share of the post-tax cash inflows only and the figures are shown in Euros using forecast exchange rates. Kadgee's share of the capital expenditure of €8 million is _not_ included in these cash inflows.

Kadgee's share of the forecast post-tax cash inflows	Probability	2007 € million	2008 € million	2009 € million	2010 € million	2011 € million
High	70%	2	8	10	12	14
Low	30%	1	5	6	7	8

As the project carries a higher risk than an investment in Europe, Andre Schnaffer recommends that a suitable risk adjusted discount rate is 14% post-tax and considers that this investment should be appraised over a five year period.

Kadgee's post-tax cash inflows between 2007 and 2011 shown in the table above could be overstated by as much as 15% across the entire 5 year forecast if the Chinese currency changes _further_ against the Euro than assumed in the above forecast.

Birgit Zeim also commented that additional payments (not included above) may need to be made to ensure that the joint venture is approved. She also stated that there is the potential problem of employees of the joint venture, or Xina itself, establishing "shadow" operations to compete directly with the proposed joint venture.

Investment in a new factory elsewhere in Asia (not China)

A further alternative strategy is to move some, or all, of Kadgee's manufacturing to a location elsewhere in Asia, but not into China.

The two alternative locations in Asia (not China) would have a similar manufacturing capacity as Kadgee had at all six European factories, of around 11 million garments per year. The proposed NPVs (post-tax) of two alternative proposals, evaluated over the next 5 years, each of which includes an investment cost of €7 million, and discounted at a suitable risk adjusted discount rate, are forecast as follows:

NPV's (post-tax) of 2 alternative locations elsewhere in Asia (including capital expenditure)	High sales (70% probability) € million	Low sales (30% probability) € million
NPV of Location 1	9·3	4·8
NPV of Location 2	9·9	3·4

Proposal to close Kadgee's European factories

If Kadgee did invest in China or undertake the strategy to move to an operating base elsewhere in Asia, it would involve closing some or all of the five European factories currently operating. The factory that was recently closed had a low resale value, but this is expected to cover the redundancy costs and closure costs associated with closing that site.

Of the five factories that are operational, which are all owned by Kadgee, only two of the sites have land that has a resale value, for possible residential use. The land at these two sites was valued in Kadgee's Balance Sheet at the end of 2005 at €6 million, but it has been recently revalued, for possible sale, at €12 million in total. The other three factories are located in run down industrial sites and have no resale value.

It is expected that the closure costs of all five factories to return the sites to a clean and safe condition is a total of €1·5 million. However, Kadgee is not legally obliged to clean up each of the sites. Andre Schnaffer has forecast that site closure costs could be reduced to a minimum of €0·3 million if the three factory sites that would not be sold, are simply closed and left derelict.

It is forecast that redundancy costs could be around €3·0 million, minimum. If Kadgee were to pay redundancy to many of the part-time workers, who are not legally obliged to receive redundancy payments, but many of whom have been employed for many years by Kadgee, the cost could increase to €4·0 million.

Investment in IT

This option could enable Kadgee to remain in Europe, or could be undertaken alongside any of the proposed relocations of Kadgee's manufacturing base.

Birgit Zeim has been persuaded by Jan Berzin of the importance of investing in IT in order to win new business. The proposal is to enhance Kadgee's existing IT systems to provide a secure "extra-net" system, which would be totally interactive, allowing existing, as well as new customers, to browse through all of the available designs that Kadgee is offering to manufacture and would facilitate ordering online. The system would also allow customers to personalise their orders as they would be able to choose the colours, the materials and the designs they wanted. In this way Jan Berzin is confident that much new business could be secured. He is also confident that a price premium could be charged for clothes that are "custom made" to customers' requirements, therefore enhancing the margins that could be achieved.

The proposal is forecast to cost €0·5 million for IT hardware and software plus additional IT staff costs of €0·2 million per year. The marketing budget would also need to be increased by €0·6 million per year for the first two years, resulting in a total additional spend of €0·8 million per year for two years, in addition to the IT investment costs of €0·5 million.

Sam Skala and Jan Berzin have already almost secured its first customer, BBZ, if the system is agreed to be implemented. BBZ is a medium sized retailer in Europe and has not previously bought any clothing from Kadgee. It is forecast that the operating profit (pre-tax) from BBZ's first order could be worth €0·2 million in the first year and a second order for the next year could generate in total an operating profit of €0·4 million. However, until the system is operational, BBZ does not wish to place any orders with Kadgee. It wants to remain free to procure from other manufacturers globally who do have an interactive ordering system.

Other issues affecting Kadgee's operational performance at present

Quality of production

As could be expected the employees' morale is low and the quality of the output has fallen. Despite all of his best efforts, Peter Coletta is unable to improve the general feeling of discontent and fear that Kadgee will close the remaining five European factories before long. With the ongoing concerns over possible future closures, a few key employees have recently left Kadgee, and Peter Coletta is concerned over the quality of the current output, and possible loss of further orders.

Machine breakdowns

In order to achieve agreed budget cuts, Peter Coletta has reduced training and much of the routine preventative maintenance has stopped. Engineers are only called in to attend to machinery when it breaks down, which it often does, when employees are unable to fix it themselves. When a packaging machine recently broke down, two employees were badly injured when they attempted to fix the problem themselves. The two injured employees had worked full time for Kadgee for three years but had received little training on the machines and they did not understand the health and safety issues surrounding machine repairs despite requests for additional training. They were trying to be conscientious in keeping production flowing, but instead caused a major delay in production due to this accident. It is considered that a major investment programme in new machines would be required to overcome these problems and Birgit Zeim is very reluctant to invest more in Europe.

Dismissal of Rita Scree

Another factor that has caused much concern amongst employees at the factories was the dismissal of Rita Scree in September 2006 by Peter Coletta for a poor attendance record. She had worked for Kadgee for over 35 years. She is a skilled sewing machine operative who had been hard-working and loyal to the company. Her current poor attendance record is entirely due to a family member being critically ill. Her fellow employees feel that she has been badly treated and have asked for her to be re-instated and to be given paid special leave.

Birgit Zeim has stated to fellow directors that she would _not_ allow the re-instatement of Rita Scree and has refused to discuss this matter further. She has instructed Lars Veel, the HR Director, to ensure that Rita Scree is not re-appointed as she considers this to be a point of principle. Birgit Zeim has informed her fellow directors that she needs their confidence in her ability to turn Kadgee around and that she would consider resigning from Kadgee if she is not supported by fellow Board members on this Human Resource matter.

The employees across three of the five factories have approached Peter Coletta and asked for him to re-appoint Rita Scree. They are threatening strike action if Rita Scree is not re-appointed.

Appointment of a consultant

At the Kadgee Board meeting held in November 2006, the strategic issues shown above were discussed and it was agreed that a consultant would be appointed to advise the Board on the issues facing Kadgee.

November 2006 – Assessment Matrix for TOPCIMA - Kadgee

Criterion	Marks	Clear Pass	Pass	Marginal Pass	Marginal Fail	Fail	Clear Fail
Technical	5	Thorough display of relevant technical knowledge. **5**	Good display of relevant knowledge. **4**	Some display of relevant technical knowledge. **3**	Identification of some relevant knowledge, but lacking in depth. **2**	Little knowledge displayed, or some misconceptions. **1**	No evidence of knowledge displayed, or fundamental misconceptions. **0**
Application	10	Knowledge clearly applied in an analytical and practical manner. **9-10**	Knowledge applied to the context of the case. **6-8**	Identification of some relevant knowledge, but not well applied. **5**	Knowledge occasionally displayed without clear application. **3-4**	Little attempt to apply knowledge to the context. **1-2**	No application of knowledge displayed. **0**
Diversity	5	Most knowledge areas identified, covering a wide range of views. **5**	Some knowledge areas identified, covering a range of views. **4**	A few knowledge areas identified, expressing a fairly limited scope. **3**	Several important knowledge aspects omitted. **2**	Many important knowledge aspects omitted. **1**	Very few knowledge aspects considered. **0**
Focus	10	Clearly distinguishes between relevant and irrelevant information. **9-10**	Information used is mostly relevant. **6-8**	Some relevant information ignored, or some less relevant information used. **5**	Information used is sometimes irrelevant. **3-4**	Little ability to distinguish between relevant and irrelevant information. **1-2**	No ability to distinguish between relevant and irrelevant information. **0**
Prioritisation	10	Issues clearly prioritised in a logical order and based on a clear rationale. **9-10**	Issues prioritised with justification. **6-8**	Evidence of issues being listed in order of importance, but rationale unclear. **5**	Issues apparently in priority order, but without a logical justification or rationale. **3-4**	Little attempt at prioritisation or justification or rationale. **1-2**	No attempt at prioritisation or justification. **0**
Judgement	20	Clearly recognises alternative solutions. Judgement exercised professionally. **16-20**	Alternative solutions or options considered. Some judgement exercised. **11-15**	A slightly limited range of solutions considered. Judgement occasionally weak. **10**	A limited range of solutions considered. Judgement sometimes weak. **5-9**	Few alternative solutions considered. Judgement often weak. **1-4**	No alternative solutions considered. Judgement weak or absent. **0**
Integration	10	Diverse areas of knowledge and skills integrated effectively. **9-10**	Diverse areas of knowledge and skills integrated. **6-8**	Knowledge areas and skills occasionally not integrated. **5**	Knowledge areas and skills sometimes not integrated. **3-4**	Knowledge areas and skills often not integrated. **1-2**	Knowledge areas and skills not integrated. **0**
Logic	20	Communication effective, recommendations realistic, concise and logical. **16-20**	Communication mainly clear and logical. Recommendations occasionally weak. **11-15**	Communication occasionally unclear, and/or recommendations occasionally illogical. **10**	Communication sometimes weak. Some recommendations slightly unrealistic. **5-9**	Communication weak. Some unclear or illogical recommendations, or few recommendations. **1-4**	Very poor communication, and/or no recommendations offered. **0**
Ethics	10	Excellent evaluation of ethical aspects. Clear and appropriate advice offered. **9-10**	Good evaluation of ethical aspects. Some appropriate advice offered. **6-8**	Some evaluation of ethical aspects. Advice offered. **5**	Weak evaluation of ethical aspects. Little advice offered. **3-4**	Poor evaluation of ethical aspects. No advice offered. **1-2**	No evaluation of ethical aspects. Unethical, or no, advice offered. **0**
TOTAL	**100**						

© CIMA – July 2006

Exam focus point

The format of the assessment matrix has changed from September 2008. (see Chapter 2)

Kadgee: answer

Introduction

This is the suggested answer to the **September 2006** unseen and requirement, written by BPP Learning Media. Your report will be different to this and may analyse different issues. This is as it should be, there is no one correct answer.

We have also included a suggested marking scheme developed by BPP Learning Media from the Post Exam Guides and Script Reviews following the exam.

1 Report

To: Board of Directors, Kadgee
From: A Consultant
Date: XX/YY/ZZ

Contents

1. Introduction
2. Terms of Reference
3. Review and prioritisation of issues facing Kadgee
4. Discussion of main issues facing Kadgee
5. Ethical issues to be addressed by the Kadgee board
6. Recommendations on immediate and longer term issues
7. Conclusions

Appendices

1. SWOT analysis of Kadgee
2. PEST analysis of move to China
3. Capacity requirements for Kadgee
4. Cash flow forecast to December 2006
5. WintaWarma coats

1. Introduction

Kadgee is a European apparel manufacturer facing intensifying competition brought about by retailers demanding lower prices to match those available from manufacturers from Asia.

Many of Kadgee's competitors in Europe have ceased trading as a consequence whilst others have transferred manufacturing from Western Europe in favour of cheaper locations abroad.

The profit outlook for Kadgee is poor following the loss of two customers and this has led to pressure from Kadgee's bankers, PGB, for a clear indication of Kadgee's strategic direction and also has stated that the firm's overdraft facility of capped at €2,500,000. The fire at the DEM factory provides a one-off windfall inflow of around €7m which should be invested for the future of the firm.

The Board is aware of three significant investment opportunities open to it: the GREN contract, the Chinese joint venture, or the WintaWarma coats proposal. It only has sufficient funds for one of these. There may be others such as merging with a competitor or outsourcing production to other countries which may come to light in the future.

The Board of Kadgee needs to make strategic decisions to safeguard its future. It is against this backdrop that the present report is written.

2. Terms of Reference

This independent consultancy report was commissioned to prioritise, analyse and evaluate the issues facing Kadgee, and to make appropriate recommendations on how these issues can be resolved.

3. Review and prioritisation of issues facing Kadgee

Appendix 1 contains a detailed SWOT analysis of Kadgee. Of the threats to the business the most significant is the continuing price pressure from cheaper imported apparel. This is likely to intensify as products are increasingly sourced from China.

The strategic position of Kadgee is described in Appendix 2 using Porter's 3 generic strategies model. This shows that falling profits are a consequence of Kadgee having become 'stuck in the middle'.

The key issues facing Kadgee at present are the need to stay within the lending ceiling laid down by its bankers whilst restructuring the company to safeguard its long term future against the threats around it.

The issues below are prioritised in terms of their impact on these two needs, commencing with the impact of the fire, its cash flows in the immediate term and how to secure its strategic future. Other issues are discussed later.

Factory fire – the number one priority

The fire last week at the Dem factory has destroyed significant inventories of stock and work in progress. The destruction of systems also means that delivery and invoicing is disrupted.

It is essential that customers receive the stock they expect to avoid further losses of clients.

This also has significant impacts on cash flows over the coming month due to the need to spend cash in replacing stock promised to clients and also the need to ensure cash is received from debtors.

The loss of capacity and the insurance settlement presents the Board with the opportunity to invest in the long term future of Kadgee. This flexibility has been denied the Board since its creation under Andrin Burnak since 1998. The money must be used wisely as it is a one-off opportunity.

This has been given first priority because, on the one hand, replacing lost orders needs immediate attention, and secondly the decision on what to do with the cash from the insurance is the most significant strategic decision facing the Board.

Cash flow management – the number two priority

Appendix 3 presents a cash flow statement demonstrating that in October, i.e. next month, Kadgee will breach the ceiling on overdraft imposed by the bank, principally due to the costs of closing the Dem factory. Its impact, if not resolved, is the potential liquidation of Kadgee.

The Board need to find ways of improving short-term cash flow and persuading the bank to advance further credit in the short run. The preparation of a one year business plan will be essential to this.

This issue is given number two priority because of its urgency, one month, is less than the urgency of replacing lost orders and also because it will be affected by decisions on the Dem factory.

Moving manufacturing to China – the number three priority

This is the most strategically significant decision facing the Board once the short term cash issues are resolved. It represents an opportunity for Kadgee to break out of the cycle of falling margins due its enduring of a high cost base in a market where prices are being forced down by cheaper imported product.

It has been given third priority because resolution of the fire and cash issues must be resolved immediately whereas there will need to be a greater period of investigation and reflection before committing to transfer production to China. However its long-term significance puts it ahead of the one-year contract with GREN below

New contract with GREN – the number four priority

The GREN contract represents one opportunity to replace some of the business lost due to the loss of Forum and Zeeb. However it needs to be concluded in the next 3 to 4 weeks and therefore the Board needs to consider the acceptability of GREN's offer before entering further negotiations.

The ongoing GREN contract agreement and adherence to credit terms is an essential prerequisite to negotiations.

To assist short term cash flow it is necessary that the €720,000 (€18 x 40,000) owed by GREN for production in July and August be paid as soon as possible and that the remaining €360,000 for September be paid promptly.

Accidents at factories – the number five priority

Accidents are already impacting on the ability of Kadgee to meet production deadlines and, in the event of major accident and injury, could lead to factories being closed by the authorities and substantial fines.

Remedying the faults also represents significant costs and cash outflows which mean that they impact on the primary problem of cash flow management.

This issue has been given fifth priority because of its impact on the risks of Kadgee and because of its financial impact on cashflows.

Other issues to be addressed by the Kadgee Board

The issues of the WintaWarm product line and the legal case are lower priority because they have lower potential financial impact and do not affect the strategy of the firm to the same extent.

The Human resource issues, notably the apparent sexual discrimination in payments, will be dealt with in a separate section on ethics below. The ethics section will also discuss the duties of the Board to local residents affected by the fire at the Dem factory and its duties to the staff being made redundant by the factory's closure.

4. Discussion of main issues facing Kadgee

4.1 Factory fire – the number one priority

Appendix 3 demonstrates that re-building the Dem factory is not required to meet foreseeable production requirements and therefore is not necessary. It is recommended that the plant remain closed and that staff be made redundant. The cash flow implications of this have been accommodated in the forecast in Appendix 4.

The urgent significance of the fire stems from the need to replace lost production and to satisfy outstanding orders, at least four days of which seem to have been lost in the accompanying systems failure.

To avoid loss of goodwill with clients it is vital that their orders are met.

The cash flow of the company is also affected by the loss of a record of invoices issued and the 4 days of deliveries that have been made.

Given that Dem manufactured 2.4 million garments a year and uncertainty over despatches affects only 4 days deliveries it can be estimated that orders for 36,923 garments are affected (2,400,000/260 days x 4 – assumes 5 day working week and 52 week year).

The maximum cost of producing all these garments again would be €245,907 (36,923 @ €6.66 each – calculated as 2005 operating costs divided by 2005 output i.e. €72.58m/10.9m). The actual cash costs would be much less due to these costs containing factory overheads and admin costs that would not increase as a consequence of the extra production.

The fire has also revealed a lack of proper controls over data in Kadgee. It is essential that firms like Kadgee have proper disaster recovery plans for IT/IS covering not just accounting data but also safeguarding the work of the Design Centre and the Supply Chain Management System.

Turning to the insurance claim for €7m. The cash flow forecast in Appendix 4 demonstrates that receipt of this money help avoid breaching the overdraft limit set by the bank.

More importantly it provides a windfall of cash that can be used to restructure Kadgee. The claim should be expedited to ensure it is paid in full and on time.

4.2 Cash flow management – the number two priority

Assuming that the Dem factory is closed and redundancy payments are made in October that Kadgee will breach the €2,500,000 limit set by PGB before the end of October 2006. Appendix 4 below demonstrates the forecast cash deficit for October is €3,236,666.

The deficit is forecast to disappear following the insurance payment in November 2006.

It has not been possible to produce a full cash flow forecast for Kadgee as the information provided does not include details of payments of wages, utilities, fabric etc, nor a schedule of expected receipts from clients. Therefore it has been assumed that the present overdraft of €1,750,000 will be sufficient to provide the working capital needed to sustain these clients.

One significant omission from the forecast is the extra funds that will be necessary to replace the stock lost in the fire and delays to payments resulting from the confusion over invoices. Given that the factory produced 22% (2.4/10.9) of garments in 2005 a rough calculation could assume it held 22% of inventories which will cost a further €1,808,400 (22% x €8,220,000) to replace during September.

Some of this additional cost may not be a relevant cost, i.e. actual cash being spent, because much of the replacement stock may be produced using the capacity at other factories released by the loss of Forum and, depending on when outstanding orders to them are completed, Zeeb.

However the need to buy fabric and to employ some workers on extra shifts will deepen the overdraft position.

In summary, the Board needs to resolve the October cash position as a matter of urgency.

The refusal by the bank to increase the overdraft in the wake of the loss of Zeeb should not be interpreted as a total refusal to extend further credit. Presenting a bank with a request for funds without a clear plan to pay it back is an invitation for refusal.

The October breaching is caused by the redundancy payments being made to the Dem staff. However the same event means Kadgee will be receiving €7m in November. It seems very likely that the bank would agree to increase the maximum overdraft temporarily against the surety of this money coming in later.

If this agreement is not forthcoming the Board could consider delaying the redundancy payments until November by maintaining staff on half pay through October.

Negotiations with the bank in future should be accompanied by plans to reassure them on the ability of Kadgee to improve its financial position in the future. In reality the bank is presently prepared to be owed up to €7m by Kadgee which suggests that it recognises that it either supports Kadgee and helps it trade through or risk having to take possession of its assets which may not repay the debt.

For the purposes of the present report the ceiling has been assumed to be fixed but the Board should recognise that it may be possible to increase it within the context of a properly presented budget and recovery plan.

4.3 Moving manufacturing to China – the number three priority

Shifting production to China would be a significant strategic move for Kadgee, not least because it would probably entail necessitate the eventual closure of all European operations. For example Kadgee has orders for 7.6m garments and investing in the proposed JV would entitle it to 40% of the capacity of the new factory, ie to 8m garments. It is hard to see that Kadgee would need its existing factories and it is very hard to see that they could remain competitive with production taking place in Europe.

The experience of European apparel makers has been that sourcing from Asia is essential to survival. The impact of global trade has been enhanced by the entry into the World Trade Organisation (WTO) of China and the ending of the EU's protective Multi-Fibre Agreement (MFA). This makes enhanced competition from China inevitable. Moreover this enhanced competition will force firms in other producing countries,

Vietnam, Thailand, Sri Lanka, Bangladesh, Burma etc., to cut prices too. This will squeeze most European manufacturers out.

Reductions in costs by moving production to lower cost economies may be essential to the survival of Kadgee.

Such a move would necessitate the Board gambling all of Kadgee's free capital on this one-off strategic move.

The joint venture would require €9m. This could only be afforded by Kadgee by using the insurance settlement of €7m plus taking on additional loans of up to €3m secured against the firm's remaining free assets.

Some of the funds would of course be used to pay the redundancy costs resulting from the closure of European operations in the remaining 5 factories. Using the estimate above of 25.5 full-time workers per 1m garments, and recognising that the fire at Dem has reduced capacity to 8.4m garments (10.9-2.5), this means making 214 additional workers redundant. At €13,095 per worker (see above) this suggests a total redundancy costs of €2,802,330.

Investing funds in this project could therefore preclude the GREN and the WintaWarm proposals because Kadgee would lack the capital for anything other than the JV.

Appendix 2 provides a full PEST analysis of the risks of shifting production to China.

There are however significant benefits to be had from entering the Joint Ventures to develop production operations in China:

- **Reduced costs** and therefore improved operating margins
- **Limited capital investment** and therefore limited risk in the event of commercial failure or loss of assets
- **Opportunity to gain from the expertise** of LIN in the management of staff in China and in taking advantage of local contacts
- **Ability to reduce prices** significantly and still remain profitable. For example the 4% price cuts offered to Forum by Dieter Stutt would be affordable if China could hold out potential for 20% cost reduction
- **Potential huge market in China**. Kadgee may discover new clients in China, or perhaps its existing clients will open stores there as European shops like Tesco have already done. By having a cost base in China country Kadgee could compete for these contracts. An additional advantage of this would be to create a real hedge on any currency fluctuations, i.e. that the costs of the Chinese operation could be financed from income earned from sales in the country.

Some of the dangers of the proposed JV are:

- **Commercial risk:** Kadgee has never commissioned a new factory in a new country before. If quality cannot be assured, or costs run out of control, then it will lose the value of its investment.
- **Counterparty risk**: LIN is an unknown quantity yet the success of the JV depends on its financial stability and also its experience in garment making.
- **Country risk**: investing in assets in China means that Kadgee will be affected by any changes in Chinese regulations affecting the industry or foreign-held investments. Similarly any profits made in China may be difficult to repatriate to shareholders in Europe due to the potential application of withholding taxes (premium tax rates on distributed profits) or exchange controls. A salutary lesson here is the recent experience of Shell in Russia, where it appears that the threatened withdrawal of environmental permits from its oil development operation in Sakhalin is being used to blackmail Shell into giving a greater control of the operation to the Russian state-owned energy firm Gazprom.
- **Foreign currency risk**. The costs of production will be paid for in Chinese currency, the Yuan (or sometimes 'Renmimbi' or 'Kuai') whilst the product will be sold to Kadgee's clients in European currency, e.g. Euros. China operates a fixed exchange rate system, backed up by restrictions on Yuan leaving the country. It seems to deliberately keep its currency low. It seems inevitable that political pressure, including from WTO for an end to its restrictions on movement of capital, will force the rate up as it was in July 2005 A rise in the Yuan will carry two risks. Firstly it will increase the Euro cost of paying invoices and so reduce profit margins below forecast and increase cash outflows. Secondly, a permanent rise in the Yuan will make Chinese product less competitive compared to other Asian countries and so put Kadgee at a competitive disadvantage.
- **Risk to intellectual property**. China has a reputation for producing cheap imitations of 'designer' products due to very poor laws protecting intellectual property. This means that Kadgee or its clients cannot use Chinese law to stop Chinese factories making copy products carrying apparently original labels (e.g. Portrait). Where these are sold in Europe legal action could be taken against importers or vendors but this is very expensive to pursue. Clients may be discouraged by this possibility, although it is true that Kadgee doesn't produce the 'designer label' products which are the main targets of piracy. The Board should seek to ensure intellectual property is subject to the laws of a European country.
- **Communication difficulties**: China is 8 hours ahead of Greenwich Mean Time. This means that a 10.00 call, or production change, from Europe will be received at 18.00 in Bejing. In other words the office hours of Kadgee in Europe may not overlap with office hours in China. Of course on or other party will be prepared to work extra hours but a production problem in China at 12.00 will involve a Kadgee manager being woken at 4.00. Also languages will not be the same. Europe has

many languages as does China. Most dialogue will be in English but this opens the possibility of miscommunication.

- **Time to market will be slower**. The European trend to 'fast fashion' requires regular drops of new product and quick replenishment of successful ranges. The shipping time from China adds 60 days to Kadgee's usual time to market. Most suppliers using China as a production base do so for generic items (white shirts, lingerie, football kit etc.) and not for fashion items. Kadgee has to some extent moved towards fast fashion since the Design Centre opened in 2001.

Extending its supply chains to China will involve further costs for Kadgee such as setting up a Virtual Private Network (VPN) with the JV by leasing high capacity communication lines from a service provider, and setting up IT/IS systems to allow Kadgee's SCM systems to operate.

There will also be increased working capital needs due to the length of time it takes to get garments from China to clients in Europe. Typically 8 to 12 weeks is quoted for shipping garments from China to Europe. This represents a significant increase in Kadgee's working capital cycle.

Subcontracting production to China is potentially worthy of consideration and therefore further investigation.

The benefits of such arrangements, over the JV, may be:

- **Cost flexibility**. Presently Kadgee carries all the fixed factory costs and depends on the contribution from its sales to pay these. If sales revenues fall, as they did between 2004 and 2005, then an increasing proportion of the revenue will be spent on these fixed costs and so leave less and less as profit or cash. By outsourcing the fixed costs are the problem of the supplier such that if Kadgee has falling orders it can escape fixed costs and so shield some of its profits.
- **Reduced need for capital**. A contract manufacturing arrangement would require only investment in working capital, systems development and redundancy costs.
- **No problems of profit repatriation** from a subsidiary company.

4.4 New contract with GREN – the number four priority

The GREN contract represents one of the few opportunities for the Board to recover business following the loss of the Forum and Zeeb contracts. The Board has one month to accept the contract.

Appendix 3 shows that the contract can be fulfilled within the capacity constraints at Kadgee's remaining 5 factories and would provide valuable additional work while production in China is set up and rolled-out. It would help keep the workforce together in case of problems with outsourcing or manufacturing in China.

The contract has a potential contribution of €600,000 during 2006/7 (i.e. 1 million garments at a contribution of €16.20 - €15.60 each). This would be helpful in defraying some of the fixed costs of the business and raise profits from its foreast €1,200,000 to €1,800,000 (50%).

There are additional potential strategic benefits to Kadgee of entering into the GREN contract:

- Recycled materials are a potential growth market for clothing in an age in which customers are starting to ask questions about the ethical consequences of their purchases. For example the CEO of UK retailer Marks and Spencer has stated that surveys show that 33% of customers would not purchase a garment if they believed its manufacture had undesirable ethical aspects. Kadgee could seek to differentiate itself (Porter) through developing supply chains and assurance systems to support the manufacture of clothing from recycled fibres. These could enable Kadgee to benefit from slightly better prices in the long run, perhaps above the €16.20 being offered by GREN.
- The present competitive strategy of Kadgee could be described, using Porter's 3 generic strategy model as 'stuck in the middle'. It may be possible to achieve 'focus differentiation' by starting to specialise in clothes made from recycled materials.
- The contract could potentially be rendered more profitable if the Board decides to move production to Asia, say to China under the arrangements discussed above. This said China has little history of recycling. In Europe concern over landfill and pollution has led to the enactment of legislation requiring firms to be responsible for the recovery of materials used in their products. Therefore there is a good supply of recycled materials available. This is not so common in China and so the

Board would need to be sure that shipping such materials to China would not eliminate the cost advantage from making the product there.

- The GREN trial has been an outstanding success and therefore the volumes may rise above the 1 million initial contract. Providing it is profitable this provides the opportunity for growth.
- The Board will be aware of the need to retain the support of PGB, the company's bankers. Securing the GREN contract can be used as good news to counteract the bad news of recent announcements of lost business.
- Similarly some shareholders, notably Anton Kramer and perhaps Bruno Burnak, have retained their support for the company through difficult times despite no dividend. Anton's continuing support seems to be conditional on the effectiveness of Andrin Burnak. Recovering from losses after 1998-2002 will have heartened shareholders but the losses of Forum and Zeeb (nearly 30% of sales) will have shaken this support. Winning a new client, one of only 3 in the last 10 years, can be presented to shareholders as a 'turning of the corner' and so buy the Board additional time to secure the company's future.

However, given the long credit periods taken by GREN, it would absorb much of the funds released from the insurance claim.The marginal costs alone to support the GREN contract run at €1,300,000 per month which, assuming GREN pays 4 months after receipt, would necessitate a peak of €5,200,000 of working capital to support it which, if the contract were to continue, would cost €416,000 pa in interest charges (€5,200,000 @ 8%) effectively eliminating nearly two thirds of the profit and putting Kadgee very close to the limits of its capital borrowing.

A condition of contract in any case should be that invoices are paid more promptly than 4 months after delivery. If this is not acceptable to GREN then the contract may not be worthwhile in the long run.

Before entering negotiations with GREN the Board should satisfy itself on the credit worthiness of GREN. It could ask for payment of outstanding invoices as a signal of goodwill from GREN.

4.5 Accidents at factories – the number five priority

On the data given Kadgee cannot afford to replace machinery.

The acceptance of the Chinese JV or the GREN contract, as has been shown, will potentially use up all additional borrowing capacity and will extend the overdraft to close to its ceiling.

The continuation of Kadgee as European-based manufacturer is unlikely given that most rivals have been forced to develop production bases in Asia to compete. Investing in new capacity in Europe might be a waste of money if, as seems inevitable, Kadgee will close its European factories in the coming year.

However continuation of the present situation of breakdowns and minor accidents is not acceptable for the following reasons:

- **Increased costs of poor quality**: machine down-time, increased scrap and defective product impose costs on the company.
- **Potential risk of a serious accident**. This could halt production during an investigation by the authorities and would carry significant reputation risk for Kadgee as a 'dangerous and careless employer' with also potential punitive damages being awarded in the future.
- **Closure by Health and Safety officers**: if a serious accident did occur, or member of staff 'blew the whistle', there might be an investigation by the government Heath and Safety authorities. This could result in the factory being declared unsafe and its closure ordered. Given that, as Appendix 3 shows, Kadgee may soon be working at full capacity, this would be disastrous because it would mean missed orders and client goodwill or costly overtime working at remaining factories.
- **Morale effects of ignoring staff**. Kadgee operates TQM and has benefited significantly from staffs' willingness to contribute ideas. The Board must be seen to respond to these if such goodwill is to continue. There are already worrisome reports of falling morale following redundancies and the effects of this on product quality.
- **Missing of targets set by clients**. Delays in production mean missing delivery targets. Clients may extract penalty payments for this as well as bring it into consideration when deciding whether to renew contracts.

- **Ethical implications**. As a responsible employer Kadgee should not allow even minor accident to occur if they could be avoided.

Many of the costs alluded to above have not been estimated yet. The Board should ensure this is done as a matter of urgency because avoiding these, and avoiding paying the cash flows associated with them, may help recover the expenditure.

Conducing minor preventative maintenance over the coming months would cost €66,666 a month (€800,000/12) and would be affordable.

4.6 WintaWarm Coats

This proposal requires €8m investment. This would preclude the other options, the Chinese JV and the GREN contract.

Appendix 5 shows that this investment would yield an Expected Net Present Value of €2.77 after the investment.

If the assets were leased at a cost of €10m over the 5 years this would have cash flow advantages because Kadgee would not need to finance all the investment up-front. However it would reduce the NPV to €0.77m.

The leasing option is affordable but unattractive for the following reasons:

- **It carries significant risk**. For example a sensitivity analysis reveals that a 7.7% adverse change in project NPV would render it against the shareholders interest (€0.77/€10). This could come about as a result of foreign exchange rate changes between European currencies and US or Canadian dollars.

- **It has a low rate of profit**. The project makes a 7.7% return on the lease which is below the 8% that Kadgee presently pays on debt.

- **The forecasts have wide degrees of dispersion**. There is a 90% chance that NPV will be €4.5 or less, but only a 10% probability it will be greater at €6.1. This higher value is an outlier which is skewing the assessment of ENPV above.

- **Uncertainty**. The data provided gives probabilities, yet it is clear that this is a new market using a new product. Therefore these are subjective probabilities, educated guesses at best, and cannot be relied on. If they are more that 7.7% optimistic on assumptions such as sales volumes, prices, production costs or capital costs the project is not worthwhile.

- **Ignores working capital**. These coats will be made for stock and payment will depend on their sale to stores and the time stores take to pay. This is likely to represent a significant cash drain that has not been allowed for.

- **Not Kadgee's traditional business model**. The history of Kadgee shows that investment in stocks of products without firm orders has caused problems before.

4.7 Legal case against Kadgee

Pursuing a case with a 50% chance of losing at a cost of €3m has an expected cost of €1.5m (0.5 x €3m). Presumably some of this will be paid out of the €0.3 it will earn from continuing with the designs assuming the court case takes longer to settle than the lifecycle of the designs. A net cost, undiscounted, of €1.2m.

The undiscounted costs of settling now would be €0.2m of legal costs and €0.3m of lost earnings from having to destroy the stock and stop using the designs. A total cost, undiscounted, of €0.5m

Clearly a cost of €0.5m is better than a cost of €1.2m. The Board should settle on financial grounds alone.

This settlement has been included in the cash flow forecast at Appendix 3 and may be affordable.

Lawyers' assessments of success and award are unreliable as it is the courts that will decide. They are unpredictable. Apparel manufacturer French Connection United Kingdom discovered this when the courts refused to give it copyright protection for its initials on the grounds that it was an anagram of an expletive and so unworthy of protection.

The use of a probability in the calculation above is potentially misleading because it is not €1.5m that Kadgee will pay. It will be nothing or it will be €3m. An award of €3m against Kadgee, which would be the outcome of a successful case, would seriously threaten its cash flow and so the likelihood the bank will stop the overdraft. There is no up-side to a successful verdict for Kadgee as the most it can hope to recover are its legal costs and these with publicity surrounding it. It incurs the reputation risk of the stigma of being a 'copyright thief', albeit one with a good lawyer.

The only risk from an early settlement is that other designers, even SM, will be tempted to claim the same thing for other designs in the hope of being paid off.

5 Ethical issues to be addressed by the Kadgee board

The main ethical issues are:

- human resource issues, notably the apparent sexual discrimination in payments
- the duties of the Board to local residents affected by the fire at the Dem factory
- duties to the staff being made redundant by the factory's closure.

Ethics concerns the moral correctness of actions and decisions. This report does not presume to lecture the Board on right moral thinking. Ultimately these are matters of personal conscience. It merely seeks to point out where ethical issues arise.

The Board of Kadgee has some moral duties to its staff that go beyond the legal provisions of the employment contract. For example the turnaround in the company's performance since 1998 has been in a large part due to the efforts of its staff and the suggestions they have made. These have been unpaid as far as we can see.

The vulnerability of the staff to job cuts is clear. They have specific skills which are not demanded in the local labour market. Loss of jobs at Kadgee would consign them to lower standards of living and perhaps inability to meet their current financial commitments.

For these reasons there does seem to be a moral argument both for paying staff more in recognition of their contribution and for trying to avoid redundancies and, at the very least, keeping staff informed of what is happening. The fact that staff have been absent with stress also raises ethical issues about the pressure management is exerting on staff.

However it is obvious that, given its financial position, Kadgee can hardly afford to make significant pay awards or to avoid making staff at Dem and elsewhere redundant. If the Board were to pay more and also to protect jobs they would endanger the whole firm and therefore the jobs of all the staff within it, as well as within suppliers and the local communities depending on it.

In the present situation the Board may be forced to adopt the utilitarian ethical position based on taking actions that secure the greatest good for the greatest number. In other words, to forgo paying more to a few and protecting some jobs in order to continue employing the majority. Also if Kadgee doesn't 'bite the bullet' and start producing at lower cost overseas it will lose contracts and so be forced to make people redundant anyway.

A possible way forward is to minimise redundancies and also to give all staff the opportunity to apply for redundancy so that job losses would fall on those most able to bear it. This is the policy recently announced by the Ford Motor Company as its financial difficulties have forced it to forfeit its previous commitments to lifetime employment.

Sexual discrimination in payments is a serious legal and ethical issue. Equal opportunities legislation in most European countries makes it an offence to discriminate between genders in payment, as well as appointments, terms of work and termination. Successful cases by staff can result in punitive damages being awarded against employers. Past management practices of Kadgee also raise questions. The pressure exerted on part-time staff to increase hours from 16 to 24 could be deemed 'indirect sexual discrimination' because, in practice, part-time workers are more likely to be women and so it could be argued that this policy bears disproportionately on women by offering them the choice of no job or 24 hours.

The ethical dimension arises from women's right to equal and proper consideration regardless of their gender. To do otherwise is unjust and unfair, both essential principles of ethics.

The defence offered by Lars Veel, that different payments and for different responsibilities, could be legally valid. Discrimination in pay arises where woman are paid less than men for work of equal value. However this merely invites the accusation that women have not been given the opportunity to take these 'more responsible' jobs and so a different form of sexual discrimination will be alleged.

The Board needs to base payments on job roles through formal job evaluation. Moreover an equal opportunities policy is needed to avoid discrimination in appointments. A staff appraisal (or performance appraisal) process will also give a basis for payments and, if needed, selection for fair dismissal.

It is recommended that Lars Veel commence the development of these. Inviting participation from workplace nominees may assist in defusing the discontent that is surfacing without the need to expend cash immediately on payments and promotions.

6. Recommendations

6.1 Factory fire – the number one priority

The factory should not be re-built. The staff should be made redundant as soon as possible to avoid unnecessary payments of wages.

Urgent steps should be taken to avoid disruption to clients resulting from non-delivery of anticipated stocks:

- Members of Kadgee management should immediately canvas clients by telephone or visit to ascertain which orders remain outstanding and to pass them to Peter Coletta for prioritisation. It seems likely, given the integrated and powerful nature of Supply Chain Management systems in the apparel industry, that clients own systems will have a very clear mirror image record of what has been shipped and received and also what monies are owed.
- Where there is doubt, and client stocks are low, the order should be remade. Although it is important that costs are not incurred duplicating production that has already been despatched it seems that here the costs are not likely to be material compared to the risks of losing a client.
- Management should also circularise clients explaining the problem and requesting details of outstanding invoices. The Board must accept that some loss of revenues is inevitable here and that it will be necessary to accept the clients' word on outstanding invoices except where documentary evidence exists to the contrary.

The latter measure will also help to secure cash flows from clients and so to help Kadgee stay within the cash limits set by PGB.

Given that the fire has caused a breakdown in systems security an urgent investigation should be conducted by Jan Berzin into the adequacy of existing policies and procedures and recommendations made to the Board.

The insurance claim should be expedited to release the funds needed for the future of Kadgee. The following aspects of the claim need investigation:

- The settlement doesn't take account of the third party loss claims from residents. The policy should be scrutinised for such 'public liability' clauses and indemnification sought from the insurers. This issue will be returned to in the ethics section of this report.
- The settlement should include an allowance for loss of earnings due to the loss of the factory and the need to make up lost orders. Kadgee does not have an accurate assessment of these consequential loses, and therefore the proposed settlement seems to be based on the value of the factory assets destroyed. A supplementary claim should be submitted for these additional amounts.

6.2 Cash flow management – the number two priority

It has been shown that Kadgee will breach its overdraft limit in October and, possibly, in September due to the costs of replacing the inventory lost from Dem.

It is recommended that a meeting be set up with the bank to explain the impact of the redundancy payments on the overdraft but also to explain the likely insurance settlement. It is the judgement of the present writer that this will convince the bank to lift the overdraft limit temporarily.

If the bank is not prepared to do so the following actions are recommended.

- Credit control would be one source of cash. Inspection of the accounts for 2004 and 2005 reveals that receivables have increased from 91.7 days (18,978/75,553 x365) to 95.2 days (19,404/74,420 x 365) between 2004 and 2005. Given the €230,000 rise reported in the overdraft during 2006, it seems likely that there may have been a further extension to the credit given. Using 2005 figures as an example, insisting on a 90 day credit period could reduce receivables to €18,344, 118 and so release €1,059,882 of working capital. Unfortunately this will be hard to enforce due to the high bargaining power of High Street retailers.

- In the case of the money owed by GREN there may be some scope for getting prompt payment. Some of the invoices are already 60 days old and GREN seems to have a poor reputation for creditworthiness. Stock is due for delivery to GREN during the coming month and it seems reasonable and prudent to insist on payment of at least the July invoice as a condition of delivery and to apply a 30 day credit policy to the rest. This would raise up to €720,000 by the end of October.

- Before the fire at Dem Kadgee held substantial inventory, €8,220,000 at the end of 2005 compared to €6,334,000 on reduced turnover. This is not necessary. It may be possible to liquidate some of the remaining inventory by factory sales ('Famous name brands at factory gate prices') to raise immediate cash and to improve inventory management to reduce funding needs going forward. It is not possible to forecast the inflows from this from the data available.

- A final source of extra cash could come from extending credit taken from suppliers. In 2005 Kadgee took 44.8 days credit from suppliers (8,900,000/72,580 x 365). This should be compared to the credit taken the previous year, 48.1 days, and to the credit being given to clients, calculated above as 95.2 days. Increasing credit taken from 44.8 days to 60 days from the beginning of September would provide about €3m additional working capital (8,900,000 x 60/44.8 – 8,900,000).

Offering one-off discounts to clients for early payment of outstanding invoices is another way to improve cash flows. However in this situation it should be avoided. This is because we have been informed that major clients are expressing concern that Kadgee may not be able to continue trading. Offering substantial discounts now will deepen client's worries and may cause them to place contracts elsewhere rather than to be exposed to a failure by Kadgee.

6.3 Moving manufacturing to China – the number three priority

Some shifting of production to China is inevitable and should be planned for.

Further details are needed on the proposed joint venture.

The Board should seek clarity on the following issues in its negotiations with LIN:

- Further financial commitment: the initial capital investment of €9 million may be affordable but what will be the basis of further investment by Kadgee in fixed and working capital?;
- How will profits and losses be shared?;
- Control: how will production resources be allocated between the demands of Kadgee and the demands of LIN? How will the strategic development of the JV be determined?;
- Security and confidentiality: how will client's designs be safeguarded from piracy?
- Mediation: in the event of disputes between Kadgee and LIN how will these be resolved and under which laws will the JV contract be actionable?

It will take at least a year to agree the JV and to commission a new factory and start production.

Mr. Wan Dong is not the only source of such JV and production contracts. China is not the only potential supplier. It is recommended that investigations be widened to consider manufacturers in other parts of Asia and that a decision be taken by early 2007

It is recommended that a Chinese agent be approached to establish contract manufacturing arrangements for the short run to gain experience in working with Chinese manufacturers.

6.4 New contract with GREN – the number four priority

This contract should be accepted for one year subject to satisfactory credit references for GREN.

The Board should seek to establish better payment terms than GREN's present 4 months.

The Board should assess whether is possible and viable to produce this contract in China, as contract manufacturing initially. Particular attention should be given to the availability of recycled fabric and also to the length of time to market.

6.5 Accidents at factories – the number five priority

A risk assessment should be undertaken and minimum remedial maintenance should be undertaken, prioritised to those factories where the risks are greatest.

Remedial maintenance should commence immediately at those plants where risks are greatest.

Staff should be informed that this assessment is taking place. It may help to improve morale in the short run. In the long run the findings of the assessment can be presented as the reasons for the selective closing of factories as production is shifted to another country.

6.6 WintaWarm Coats

This proposal should be rejected on the grounds it does not fit with the present business model of Kadgee.

6.7 Legal case against Kadgee

The claim should be settled by prompt offer of payment of legal costs and withdrawal of the offending items from sale.

If this payment could be delayed until November, perhaps on technicalities in the drafting of the legal settlement, it would help the firm's cash flow.

To avoid other designers cashing in, or loss of face for Kadgee, the payment should be made subject to a confidentiality agreement barring disclosure of amount and which also debars SM from alleging breaches of copyright against Kadgee in respect of other past.

7 Conclusions

The future of Kadgee hands in the balance. The propoals here for cash flow will help the firm survive. Using its windfall funds to conduct an orderly transfer of manufacturing to China or other low cost location represents the best chance of commercial success in the long run.

Appendix 1 – SWOT analysis of Kadgee

Strengths	Weaknesses
Good Design Centre CAD systems and designers Contacts with retail buyers Reputation for quality Profitable	High cost manufacturing base Falling margins and profits Limited funds available from bank Excessive reliance on traditional customers Poor maintenance of machinery leading to breakdowns and poor safety Poor systems backups leading to loss of financial records Poor staff morale and policies on treatment of female staff

Opportunities	Threats
GREN contract Joint venture with lower cost supplier Potential cost reductions and improved flexibility from outsourcing Rationalisation of capacity following DEM fire WintaWarm production	Low cost competition from Chinese-based manufacturers Bank calling in overdraft of borrowing becomes excessive Further client losses Winding up by debtors in even of overdraft limits being exceeded Accidents or other lost production due to poor maintenance in factories Loss of clients and earnings due to impact of fire at Dem

Appendix 2 – PEST Analysis of move to China

Political/legal	Economic
Cheap production due to no minimum wage regulations and more relaxed laws on employment protection and health and safety Potential for sharp changes in policy due to totalitarian government Potential for instability as increased metropolitan wealth leads to calls for democracy (eg like South Korea) Possible trade wars with USA Insistence on part local ownership Corruption at national and local levels	Undervalued currency making exported clothes cheap Rapid economic growth leading to emerging apparel market in China Potential for punitive taxation on foreign firms in the future

Social	Technological
Much lower living standards in China Different languages and culture from Europe will make management difficult Potential rejection of Chinese products in Europe due to concern over working conditions	Poor infrastructure (power losses, telecommunications etc.) may make production unreliable

Appendix 3 – Capacity requirements for Kadgee

	Garments 000's
Current capacity (2005)	10,900
Reduction (Forum & Zeeb)	3,300
Current utilised capacity	7,600
Dem factory shutdown	(2,400)
Remaining spare capacity	900
GREN contract capacity	(1,000)
Balance of capacity (assume can be spread among remaining 5 factories via productivity gains)	(100)

Conclusion: Accept GREN and do not rebuild DEM factory

Appendix 4 – cash flow forecast to December 2006

	Line	September	October	November	December
Cash b/f	1	(1,750,000)	(1,793,333)	(3,236,666)	4,080,001
Factory closure	2		(1,400,000)		
Insurance payout	3			7,000,000	
GREN July debtor	4			360,000	
GREN August debtor	5				360,000
Finance costs	6	(43,333)	(43,333)	(43,333)	(43,333)
		(1,793,333)	(3,236,666)	4,080,001	4,396,668
Overdraft limit		2,500,000	2,500,000	2,500,000	2,500,000
Breach		No	Yes	No	No

Notes

Line 1   September balance from unseen material.

Line 2   Employees have been paid for month of Sept so assume redundancies paid Oct.

Line 3   Assume no compensation payout in 2006 for loss of business and other consequential loss

Line 4   Assumed payment 4 months after invoice.

Line 5   Assumed payment 4 months after invoice.

Line 6   For convenience assumes current annual outflow of €520,000 spread evenly and no mitigation of interest from positive balances in November and December

Appendix 5 – WintaWarm Coats

Garments	Prob	NPV	NPV EV
0.6	0.1	6.1	0.61
0.5	0.5	3.6	1.8
0.4	0.4	0.9	0.36

Overall NPV EV = 2.77

This assumes capital outlay of 8 million.

2 Suggested marking scheme

Note: This would be marked differently under the new assessment matrix which applies from September 2008. (see Chapter 2)

Criteria	Issues to be discussed	Marks	Total Marks available for criterion
Technical	SWOT/PEST/Ansoff/Porter's 5 forces/Porter's generic strategies/Mendelow/Suitability, Acceptability, Feasibility/BCG/Balanced Scorecard/Life cycle analysis 1 mark for EACH technique demonstrated ie 0 marks for 'name dropping')	1 each	5 marks
Application	SWOT – to get full 3 marks must include China and increased competition as Threats	1–3	
	PEST – to get full 3 marks must be related to move to China	1–3	
	Other Technical Knowledge applied to case material in a meaningful relevant way – on merit	1–2	
	Calculations		
	Cash flow analysis	1–2	
	Capacity calculations following the fire	1	Max = 10
	Evaluation of GREN proposal (for full 2 marks must identify net margin as €470K, otherwise 1 mark for wrong answer)	1–2	
	Evaluation of WintaWarm proposal (for 2 marks must get NPV of €0.77 million, otherwise 1 mark for wrong answer)	1–2	
	Relevant ratios	1–2	
	Total available marks (but max = 10)	**17**	
Diversity	Display of sound business awareness and relevant real life examples	1–3 on merit	
	Relevant research on manufacturing specifically in China	1–3 on merit	Max = 5
Focus	**Issues to be discussed:**		
	Recognition of declining profitability of clothing manufacturers in Europe	1–2	
	Discussion on Kadgee's banker's concerns	1	
	Recognition of capacity issues	1	
	GREN 1 year contract proposal	1	
	WintaWarm proposal	1	

	China – general discussion on manufacturing
	    – Joint Venture proposal with LIN
	    – Sub contracting proposals
		1
		1
		1
			Max = 10

	Fire and customer relations	1	
	Staff issues	1	
	Other relevant issues (on merit)	1–2	
	Total marks available (but max = 10)	**13**	

Criteria	Issues to be discussed	Marks	Total Marks available for criterion
Prioritisation	Full 10 marks if 5 issues prioritised and rationale for ranking good and top priority of delivering customer orders after the fire included in top 3 priorities.		
	Customer order after the fire should be in top 3 priorities as Kadgee could lose further customers if they are not kept satisfied.	Full 10	
	OR		Max = 10
	6–9 marks if top priority of customer orders in top 3 priorities but ranking rationale is weak	6–9	
	OR		
	4 marks maximum (marginal fail) if customer orders after the fire is not in top 3 priorities, irrespective of quality of rationale for ranking of other priorities	Up to 4	
Judgement	7 key issues requiring analysis in this case:		Max = 20
	Marks on merit based on depth of analysis and commercially realistic comments		
	1. Delivery of customer order after the fire. To include comments on cash flow implications of delayed payments by customers, the need to deliver outstanding orders to customers ASAP and the damage to customer relations / loss of goodwill	1–4	
	2. Cash flow and Kadgee's bankers (PGB) To include comments on ways to manage the overdraft, that Kadgee's loans are secured against the European assets, other long-term financing issues and what to do with €7 million payment from insurers following the fire	1–4	
	3. GREN proposal To include potential for the future, that this would fill spare capacity (following loss of other customers), that the proposal is profitable or that there are cash flow considerations due to GREN's track record as a slow payer	1–4	
	4. WintaWarm proposal Marks to be awarded in Judgement only if analysis results in rejecting this proposal due to the risks involved and the possibility of a negative NPV.	0 if accepted or Up to 3	
	5. Move of manufacturing to China Discussion and analysis of LIN Joint Venture proposal or sub-contracting of manufacturing to Chinese manufacturers.	1–3	
	Up to an extra 3 marks if Intellectual Property (IPR) risks discussed and ways to protect Kadgee's IPR's	+ up to 3	
	6. Legal case by SM – marks ONLY available for conclusion that Kadgee should settle out of court 0 mks for conclusion that this case should go to court	0 or 2	

Criteria	Issues to be discussed	Marks	Total Marks available for criterion
	7. Alternative business strategies for Kadgee such as selling to a competitor or liquidating the business.	Up to 5 on merit	
	Total marks available (but max = 20)	28	
Integration	Judge script holistically and whether recommendations follow on logically from analysis of the issues and includes data in appendices	1–4 if weak 6–10 if script is good	10
Logic	General presentation and EFFECTIVE business communication	1–5	
	Recommendations:		
	(Marks on merit. Max 1 mark if only an unjustified recommendation is given)		
	Delivering customer orders after the fire Cask and banking situation China strategy GREN proposal WintaWarm proposal (1 mk only if rec is accept) Alternative strategies: sell company or liquidate Need to retain customers Need to win new customers Recommendation NOT to re-build in Europe (0 marks if re-building is recommended) Other recs (on merit)	1–2 1–2 1–4 1–2 1–2 1–2 1 1 2 1–4	Max = 20
	Total marks available (but max = 20)	27	
Ethics	**Ethical issues in case include:**		
	China – loss of IPR's		
	– redundancies of Kadgee employees in Europe	1–5 each including advice	
	– ethical aspects of employing staff in China on very low salaries / poor conditions		
	Compensation to neighbours after the fire	Max = 4 if no advice	
	Accidents and maintenance issues		Max = 10
	HR issues – training, motivation, morale, male an female pay rates and equal opportunities for promotion		
	GREN poor treatment of suppliers – late payments		
	1–5 marks (on merit) for each ethical issue including detailed advice on each ethical issue		
	Max 4 marks overall if several ethical issues discussed but no meaningful or sensible advice given		
Total			100

Review Form & Free Prize Draw – Paper P10 Test of Professional Competence In Management Accounting (TOPCIMA) (5/08)

All original review forms from the entire BPP range, completed with genuine comments, will be entered into one of two draws on 31 January 2009 and 31 July 2009. The names on the first four forms picked out on each occasion will be sent a cheque for £50.

Name: _____   **Address:** _____

_____

_____

How have you used this Text?
(Tick one box only)

☐ Home study (book only)

☐ On a course: college _____

☐ With 'correspondence' package

☐ Other _____

Why did you decide to purchase this Text? *(Tick one box only)*

☐ Have used BPP Texts in the past

☐ Recommendation by friend/colleague

☐ Recommendation by a lecturer at college

☐ Saw information on BPP website

☐ Saw advertising

☐ Other _____

During the past six months do you recall seeing/receiving any of the following?
(Tick as many boxes as are relevant)

☐ Our advertisement in *Financial Management*

☐ Our advertisement in *Pass*

☐ Our advertisement in *PQ*

☐ Our brochure with a letter through the post

☐ Our website www.bpp.com

Which (if any) aspects of our advertising do you find useful?
(Tick as many boxes as are relevant)

☐ Prices and publication dates of new editions

☐ Information on Text content

☐ Facility to order books off-the-page

☐ None of the above

Which BPP products have you used?

Text	☑	*Success CD*	☐	*Learn Online*	☐
Kit	☐	*i-Learn*	☐	*Home Study Package*	☐
Passcard	☐	*i-Pass*	☐	*Home Study PLUS*	☐

Your ratings, comments and suggestions would be appreciated on the following areas.

	Very useful	Useful	Not useful
Introductory section (Key study steps, personal study)	☐	☐	☐
Chapter introductions	☐	☐	☐
Key terms	☐	☐	☐
Quality of explanations	☐	☐	☐
Case studies and other examples	☐	☐	☐
Exam focus points	☐	☐	☐
Questions and answers in each chapter	☐	☐	☐
Fast forwards and chapter roundups	☐	☐	☐
Quick quizzes	☐	☐	☐
Question Bank	☐	☐	☐
Answer Bank	☐	☐	☐
OT Bank	☐	☐	☐
Index	☐	☐	☐

	Excellent	*Good*	*Adeqate*	*Poor*
Overall opinion of this Study Text	☐	☐	☐	☐

Do you intend to continue using BPP products?   *Yes* ☐   *No* ☐

On the reverse of this page are noted particular areas of the text about which we would welcome your feedback. The BPP author of this edition can be e-mailed at: julietgood@bpp.com

Please return this form to: Nick Weller, CIMA Publishing Manager, BPP Learning Media Ltd, FREEPOST, London, W12 8BR

Review Form & Free Prize Draw (continued)

TELL US WHAT YOU THINK

Please note any further comments and suggestions/errors below

Free Prize Draw Rules

1   Closing date for 31 January 2009 draw is 31 December 2008. Closing date for 31 July 2009 draw is 30 June 2009.

2   Restricted to entries with UK and Eire addresses only. BPP employees, their families and business associates are excluded.

3   No purchase necessary. Entry forms are available upon request from BPP Learning Media Ltd. No more than one entry per title, per person. Draw restricted to persons aged 16 and over.

4   Winners will be notified by post and receive their cheques not later than 6 weeks after the relevant draw date.

5   The decision of the promoter in all matters is final and binding. No correspondence will be entered into.